Black Empowerment

social work
in oppressed
communities

Black Empowerment

social work
in oppressed
communities

Barbara Bryant Solomon

columbia university press
new york

Library of Congress Cataloging in Publication Data

Solomon, Barbara, 1934–
  Black empowerment.

  Includes bibliographical references and index.
  1. Afro-Americans—Social work with.   I. Title.
HV3181.S64   362.8'4   76-26972
ISBN 0-231-04086-5

Clothbound editions of Columbia University Press books are
Smyth-sewn and printed on permanent and durable acid-free
paper.

Columbia University Press
New York   Guildford, Surrey
Copyright © 1976 Columbia University Press
Printed in the United States of America
10 9 8 7 6

to Donald, Hugo, Jerome,
Jeffrey, and Marcia
. . . my power sources
that never failed.

contents

Black Empowerment

social work
in oppressed
communities

introduction

This book has been written primarily for social workers in train-ing and in practice who are seeking more effective strategies for helping clients in black communities achieve personal and collective goals. However, it is recognized that social work does not have sole professional responsibility for problem-solv-ing with black clients. Psychology, psychiatry, nursing, educa-tion, and even religion have many points of intersection where common theories, objectives, and practice strategies are evin-ced. Therefore, the content included in this book may have pragmatic value for a variety of professional disciplines.

The position of the black faculty member in the white univer-sity is at the center of a vortex of distinct, vested and often stridently espoused interests. Kramer and Miller have identified three consequences of the action at the vortex for the faculty member: (1) role strain created by often conflicting loyalties to the black community and to the university; (2) involvement in the problems of conflict and coalition as experienced by dif-ferent subgroups of students; and (3) involvement in the nego-tiation of a potent black perspective which is compatible to a basically white system.[1] This perceptive analysis has been borne out by my own experiences over the past decade as fac-ulty member of the School of Social Work at the University of Southern California. During this period, the School has engaged in intense efforts to address the issue of racism as it has permeated the practice of the helping professions. The

sheer energy expended in workshops, institutes, confrontations, retreats, encounters and colloquia by faculty, students,
agency staff, community representatives, and various and
sundry significant others could easily have moved mountains.
Yet, all of the collective force has at times seemed barely capable of sustaining forward momentum as counterforces of skepticism, lack of interest, or just plain fatigue have threatened to
push the issue of racism and its implications for social work off
the list of priorities.

As part of the search for a mechanism whereby integration of
the potent, black perspective in the curriculum could be achieved, I taught for two years (1972–1974) an experimental course,
"Social Work Practice in Black Communities." It was experimental in the sense that it eschewed traditional educational
models in which an "expert" instructor imparts knowledge and
direction to a group of students; it was instead designed as action research involving students, field instructors, agency staff,
and others in an intensive search for the concepts and principles regarding problem-solving in black communities which
had apparently escaped us too often in the past.

After teaching the course the first year, it became painfully
clear that we were too far removed from the targets of concern
and from the center of the action. Therefore the following year,
the course was taught in a "grass roots" community agency in
the center of one of the most disadvantaged neighborhoods in
the black inner city of Los Angeles. The teen-agers, the young
adults, the old people who came to the Wesley Social Service
Center seeking help were invited to come to our class sessions
and they accepted the invitation. They came and they struggled
with us as peers in the effort to identify the source of their
problems, the goals they had set for themselves, and the ways
that the agency and its workers might be useful to them in
achieving these goals. It was an exciting adventure for all of us
who participated. Nevertheless, our excitement did not prevent
some members of the faculty as well as some social workers in
the community from raising questions regarding the scholarly

basis for the course, its objectives, and the possibility that it represented an unfortunate resegregation of blacks in an educational as well as in a professional sense.

Of course, the fact that an effort to study social work practice from a black perspective engendered controversy is not at all unusual. An article in the *Journal of Social Work Education* written by a black faculty member of the Temple University School of Social Service Administration recounts the difficulties involved in attempting to develop an elective course for black students on "The Role of the Black Social Worker." [2]

Although the course was specifically related to the identity crisis often experienced by the black student who enters a school of social work and perceives the professional education offered as distancing him from the black community, the perception encountered was that it was a case of reverse racism, since white students were excluded. This perception, however, fails to take into account that it is not at all unusual for certain students to be excluded from classes in the interest of educational goals; e.g., courses in schools of social work have excluded anyone not in a particular field placement, not specializing in a particular method of practice, or not pursuing some specific career goal. The difference is that in these instances, the courses were perceived as *for* these special categories of students, whereas a course to be developed for black students was somehow interpreted as discrimination *against* white students.

The course taught at the University of Southern California did not exclude white students; however, its objectives were not the same as the proposed Temple course. The USC course aimed to develop a theoretical framework for practice in black communities and, since that practice will be implemented by both black and white social workers, it seemed imperative that black and white social work students as well as black and white field instructors should be included in the educational process. It has been suggested elsewhere that "theory of black social work must of necessity emerge from a black process and be

reflective of the black experience." [3] I am not in total disagreement with that point of view; however, I believe that the equifi-
nality principle from systems theory is most relevant here—
namely, the principle that a system can reach some final desired state from different sets of initial conditions and along
diverse pathways.

The concern with insuring black direction of black processes—educational or service delivery—was a theme that also
emerged from the intense and sometimes heated deliberations
in the experimental course. It was also an issue in another controversial course dealing with racism and offered in the University of Pennsylvania School of Social Work.[4] The faculty
member responsible for the course writes of an incident that
threatened to terminate it completely. A black welfare recipient
had been invited to participate on a panel discussion of racism
and in her presentation had made remarks about "the Jew
teacher" and "the Jew social worker." Many of the Jewish students thought that her remarks were anti-Semitic and not only
expressed feelings of persecution but threatened to boycott the
course. The incident not only divided the faculty but generated
considerable criticism of the course in the community. The faculty member, however, suggested that "this is a lady in domestic service who sees her employer (a Jewish person) as an oppressor, who sees the school (a Jewish teacher) as an
oppressor, who sees the welfare worker (a Jewish social worker) as an oppressor." He then declared bluntly that since these
people all perceived of themselves as "helping her," the dis-
crepancy between the client's perceptions and theirs needed to
be reviewed if practice skills were to be improved. This was obviously not an adequate defense in the eyes of a practitioner,
who wrote a scathing letter to the editor of the journal in which
the article appeared, denouncing the faculty member for his reverse racism and support of anti-Semitism.

Ironically, the tensions that have been produced within
schools of social work have often been mirror-images of the
tensions in the total society. When the intergroup conflict has

been between black students and Jewish students, it has been particularly divisive; after all, Jewish participation in the civil rights movement and in the fight for human rights in general has been impressive. The rise of militant black self-interest which at times has threatened to incorporate overtones of anti-Semitism has elicited at least two types of Jewish response. The first is a restatement of commitment to the fight for equal rights for blacks and, even if met with instances of anti-Semitism from the black group, the instinct to help is not abandoned. The second is an expression of hurt and outrage at becoming the target of attack by the people in whom so much time, money, and energy had been spent: "So if that's the reward they can go to hell!" Our analysis of minority-group relations in the experimental course would suggest that the latter is far more "helpful" to the cause of black equality than the former. Certainly, the worst approach to helping would be to do it in ways that power remain in other than black hands—even when those hands are tender and caring.

The significance of powerlessness in the etiology of problems faced by individuals, families, and groups in black communities became a persistent theme in almost every issue raised in the course. It emerged in the consideration of the hard-working, low-earning parents with high aspirations for a teen-age son whose poor grades, truancy, gang membership, and contempt for authority were tearing them apart. It was manifested again by a senior citizen who spoke of her middle-aged daughter as a person who had succeeded in becoming a teacher but had not found a husband with credentials to match her own and had made at least one suicide attempt. In these and many other problem situations, the underlying and overweaning motif was unerringly the stamp of powerlessness to exercise the kind of interpersonal influence needed to achieve the cherished objective. In fact, this apparent preeminence of powerlessness in almost every problem situation encountered led us to question whether this was in fact a universal phenomenon aside from race, ethnicity, class, or religion. At first, it ap-

peared so. The mere fact that assistance from a helping professional is sought or required in order to solve a problem
suggests greater power in the hands of the helper. However,
when similar problems brought by blacks and non-blacks to
the agencies in which the students were placed were subjected
to critical analysis, it appeared that a qualitative difference was
present in the problem situations of black clients. Furthermore,
that qualitative difference was somehow related to limiting factors associated with the black experience in this society. It was
recognition of this fact that sent us in search of the specific
referents of the qualitative difference observed and which resulted in the conceptualization of empowerment as process
and goal in social work practice with black clients.

This book is about empowerment. Empowerment refers to a
process whereby persons who belong to a stigmatized social
category throughout their lives can be assisted to develop and
increase skills in the exercise of interpersonal influence and
the performance of valued social roles. Power is an interpersonal phenomenon; if it is not interpersonal it probably should
be defined as "strength." However, the two concepts—power
and strength—are so tightly interrelated that they are often
used interchangeably. In any event, the transformation of the
abstraction of power into an observable reality will be the dominant theme of the chapters that follow.

Part I presents basic considerations of power and powerlessness. It must be strongly emphasized that the conceptualization of empowerment contained in it represents some beginning ideas to be used in the construction of a theoretical
framework and does not represent a tightly detailed system of
concepts and principles. Instead, its sometimes loosely connected propositions are put forward in the spirit of experimentation and above all risk-taking. The open objective is to
provide a framework for research and testing of practice. Part II
comprises three chapters, each concerned with a specific set
of philosophical and scientific issues that provide the context
in which empowerment will have to be considered. This in-

cludes the definition of black communities and the dynamics of their relationship to the larger society. It also includes the historical operations of social work and the other helping professions in black communities and the extent to which the efforts of each have addressed the issues encompassed in the conceptualization of empowerment. Finally, this section reviews the impact of the scientific method and scientific explanation in the implementation of the helping professions, the negative perceptions in black communities of science and its intentions, and the importance of scientific method to the conceptualization of empowerment as process and as goal. Part III, in each of its five chapters, critically reviews a particular set of negative valuations or "images" which have led to increased powerlessness among individuals and groups in black communities. Part IV has as its primary focus the management of the helping process itself. Thus, "Engaging Black Client Systems," "Empowerment Strategies as Practice Skills," and "Designing Service Delivery Systems" bring greater specificity to the set of professional activities to be carried out in efforts to empower client systems. Finally, the Epilogue is my surrender to the temptation to predict at least one alternative future for black communities.

Books, particularly textbooks, are believed to be relatively useless in helping to develop sensitivities which can only come from experience. This criticism may have merit, although I have read a few books in my lifetime which have given me the most intense kind of emotional experience and opened up new and vital ways for me to experience the human condition. I cannot presume to expect that such an experience will happen to the readers of this book. However, I can keep faith with my own conviction about the primary value of experiential learning by including exercises at the end of each chapter which suggest opportunities for experiencing its content. These exercises, designed to generate experience, are sometimes in the form of vignettes for role-playing in class or for discussion with others; sometimes suggestions for more direct experiences in black as

well as white communities; and sometimes suggestions for empirical research which simultaneously provides a sensitizing
experience and much-needed data on adaptive mechanisms
and coping strategies that *work* for those who must live in an
often hostile social environment. If successfully implemented,
the experiential opportunities may be more important for learning about *practice* of helping professions in black communities
than the specific theoretical content included in the chapters.

part one

defining
empowerment

Perhaps the most common word association for "power" in our society is "glory." The connection of power and glory has religious connotations (". . . for thine is the kingdom and the power and the glory, Amen!). However, it is also attached to war, politics, and international oil cartels which may, in fact, be religions of a kind. At any rate, power begets glory and glory is synonymous with honor, fame, pride, and the adoration of heaven. These positive valuations made of those who hold power are exactly the opposite of the negative valuations made of the powerless—especially those who belong to minority racial or ethnic groups. The chapter which constitutes Part I of this book explores the concept of power as an abstraction with relevance for all oppressed people as well as the concept of powerlessness as it relates to people in black communities. Finally, it proposes empowerment as the kingpin goal and process in the implementation of social work practice in black communities.

chapter one

empowerment: in search of the elusive paradigm

There is a patina and frothiness to most of the images of city life drawn in the myth-making media. In musical comedies or sleuth tales, New York is not Harlem but the desirable blocks of Park Avenue and Fifth Avenue or perhaps Greenwich Village. Houston is not the muddy streets and mosquito-infested bayous along which black and Mexican-American poor have planted their shanty houses but penthouse suites where ladies and gentlemen of the "new" South sit on lily-white corporate boards and are prideful of the "integration" that has taken place in their city. Los Angeles is Wilshire Boulevard and the Greek theater but not Central Avenue or the Watts Towers. The reality of pain and survival generated in the day-to-day exigencies of the urban condition are relegated to sociological textbooks and "rap sessions" in indigenous self-help groups with names like Synanon, Bridge Back, or Ujimaa. Yet, the slender but strong thread of twentieth-century humanism in our society has refused to permit the collective social consciousness to rest without making the effort—however tentative, misguided or hypocritical—to seek remedies for the pain. The fact that the helping professions charged with the task of finding the remedies have had such minimal effect in resolving the intransigent personal and social problems encountered in black communities may be laid in large measure to deficiencies that reflect the deep-seated racist biases within society itself.

The theme of powerlessness among minority groups in the

United States is a constant ringing in the ear of the nation. Certainly it has been identified as a predominant consequence of the black experience. Powerlessness of black individuals, groups, and communities arises through a process whereby valued identities and roles on the one hand and valuable resources on the other are denied—all of which are prerequisite to the exercise of interpersonal influence and effective social functioning. Binstock and Ely have suggested that everyone is powerless in some way. Although in broad terms, black and Hispanic ghettos in urban inner cities are most likely to fit the criteria of powerlessness, numerous other groups may be also considered powerless to lesser or different degrees—"black sharecroppers and white 'rednecks' in the rural South; Skid Row derelicts; impoverished older persons in isolated downtown flats."[1] In short, anyone who is haunted by severe limitations of their self-determination and an inevitable sense of dependency. Despite the prevailing power deficiencies in the lives of people who present problems in social functioning, our theoretical frameworks for practice have dealt more extensively with those concepts which are central to problems of middle-class, Anglo populations—anxiety, repression, and self-realization—than with power which is more central to the problem constellations encountered in minority racial and ethnic populations. Social work practice in black communities is ultimately concerned with the creation of a coherent theoretical framework, richly heuristic in regard to specific principles of practice with black client systems. In search of that elusive paradigm, the concept of power is a light shining down hitherto dark corridors.

The major thesis of this book is that individuals and groups in black communities have been subjected to negative valuations from the larger society to such an extent that powerlessness in the group is pervasive and crippling. Negative valuation is admittedly a construct and as such can only be observed by way of some set of indicators. Indicators of negative valuation of black people in American society abound. Not only are they observable in the discriminatory practices of major social institutions but in the very language itself. Burgest has noted, for example, how language has been used to indicate negative valuation of blacks by (1) the attachment of negative or inferior connotations to the word "black" and applying them to "black" people; (2) "the attachment of positive or superior connotations to the word "white" and applying them to white people; and (3) the implication that black culture is inferior and white culture is superior.[2] Thus, a "black lie" is bad but a "white lie" isn't—at least not as bad. In like manner blacks are declared as culturally disadvantaged rather than culturally different. Negative valuations identify the collective as "low-down," insignificant, inferior, or any other of a variety of expressions that assault self-esteem. However, although administered at the individual level, these negative valuations are made strictly on the basis of the individual's membership in the stigmatized collective.

Despite the universality of negative valuations directed toward blacks, the experience of these negative valuations is not uniform throughout the group, so that there may be a multiplicity of individual responses to negative valuation based on the differential exposure. Furthermore, responses may be perceived as instrumental or noninstrumental, depending upon their effectiveness in protecting the self-concept and permitting effective social functioning. However, most people in black communities who come to social agencies for assistance have not escaped the more serious consequences of society's negative valuation of them as members of the stigmatized group. One of the more insidious of these consequences is an overriding sense of one's powerlessness to direct one's own life in a course leading to reasonable personal gratification.

The utilization of power as a pivotal concept in social work practice provides both rich opportunity and serious risk. The opportunity lies in the possibility of connecting the increasing knowledge about power operations in society to specific strategies for achieving change in the lives of traditionally power-

less people.[3] The risk, however, lies in the fact that this knowledge in its current state is so fragmented and contradictory
that contradictory practice strategies can be fostered. For example, bureaucracies are defined by the degree to which their
procedures and regulations, policies and role expectations are
"standardized." Since standardized procedures are designed
so that there is an absolutely consistent response to all who
make use of the procedure, it would appear at first blush to
provide a foolproof guarantee of nondiscrimination by definition. Thus, the power of bureaucracies with their standardized
procedures could be seen as power working in behalf of minority individuals to render inactive or ineffective the individual
biases or prejudices that may enter into decisions in nonstan-
dardized systems. We would therefore support *development* of
bureaucratic organizations as a means of reducing discrimination. However, this is misleading. The fact is that if "stan-
darization" is done along lines consistent with the values,
norms, life styles, etc., of the dominant group, then a form of
discrimination is evident. This has been defined as "institutional racism" or discrimination. We might on the basis of this
knowledge oppose the *creation* of bureaucratic organizations
that have standarized procedures. The horns of this dilemma
are sharp and provocative!

The bureaucratic example is not a random choice to describe
a dilemma. The fact is that social workers operate for the most
part in bureaucratic systems—probation departments, welfare
departments, social agencies, hospitals and clinics, health departments, etc. Lerner has described the bureaucracy as "the
modern version of authoritarianism . . . transforming service
delivery systems in ways that have profoundly adverse effects
on those who provide service, or those who receive it, and on
the nature of service itself." [4] Thus if power deficits are perceived as an overriding problem in black communities, one
may well wonder how involvement in an authoritarian system
could help—it appears to be the old question of the value of
water to a drowning man! In Pruger's opinion, however, social

workers can become "skilled bureaucrats." [5] The skilled bureaucrat is able to negotiate the constraints of the organizational environment in order to maintain maximum range for discretionary behavior to be enacted in the clients' behalf.

Despite the problem of making bureaucracies work *for* powerless people instead of *against* them to reduce their powerlessness even further, there is considerable evidence that power must be the key concept in social work with black and other minority clients. The paradoxes and contradictions must be confronted head on; e.g., the dual commitment to the maintenance of established social institutions and to the empowerment of powerless people. Confrontation may assist in the evaluation of an effective approach to social work with minority clients that will change the pervasive image of social workers as "dirty workers" wedded to a status quo.

Bertrand Russell has observed that the concept of power is fundamental in the social sciences in the same way that energy is fundamental to physics.[6] Yet the social sciences are not a single discipline but many, and there is disparate conceptualization of power depending upon whether one deals with it from a psychological, economic, political, sociological, or even philosophical perspective. One effort to pull together psychological and social perceptions of power was made by Kenneth Clark, who related feelings of powerlessness to lack of self-esteem. He suggests that self-esteem "is not determined by forces inherent within the organism but is dependent upon external supports and reinforcements, and controlled by the judgments of others who themselves are afflicted with the universal human anxiety of self-doubt." [7] A more in-depth analysis of the social dimension, i.e., external supports and reinforcements, would also inevitably uncover economic and political power operations which act to increase or decrease the individual's sense of self-esteem. Thus, blacks and other minorities are dependent upon the judgments of their fellows for sanction and latitude to exercise control over the major decisions which will affect their lives. However, in a racist society this makes them

vulnerable to those whose self-doubts send them on a relent-
less search for the symbolic scapegoat on which to project
feelings of weakness and inferiority. In essence, they are subject to externally imposed powerlessness. Therefore, an analysis of the dynamics of power and powerlessness may provide
insights into the possibilities for effecting an inequitable and
oppressive power distribution in social systems.

POWER AND POWERLESSNESS
Power is most often studied as a macrosystem concept, useful
in understanding détente, apartheid, or urban revolts but limited in providing insights into the chronic unemployment of Joe
Johnson, his wife's nervous breakdown, his children's un-
derachievement, or the inexorable deterioration of the neighborhood he lives in. However, Ullman suggests that power may
be the key concept linking microsystem and macrosystem processes.[8] In fact, people generally described as mentally ill may
be perceived as persons deprived of adequate social solutions
to the problem of individual growth and development. Furthermore, community-level disruptive behavior also stems from a
power deficit as a result of the lack of adequate social solutions to the problem of community growth and development.

  As pointed out above, it is not by chance but by design that
the "adequate social solutions" are least likely to exist for minority racial group members and their communities. This "institutional racism" implies that the negative valuation of minority
individuals and communities has resulted in their experience of
systematic disadvantage from the policies, procedures, value
sets, and normative behaviors in our major social institutions.
Thus, a definition of powerlessness emerges. Powerlessness is
defined here as the inability to manage emotions, skills, knowledge, and/or material resources in a way that effective performance of valued social roles will lead to personal gratification.
The power deficiency so often seen among minority individuals
and communities stems from a complex and dynamic interrela-

tionship between the person and his relatively hostile social environment. Therefore, it is important to consider the relationship between power, powerlessness, and the processes of human growth and development in order to clarify the nature of the possible consequences for black individuals and communities.

There is an assumption that each individual in the society will proceed through a certain sequence of events which constitute a benevolent circle. First, the individual experiences a complex series of events monitored by the family or surrogate family which involve the self, significant others, and the environment. These experiences result in the acquisition of personal resources such as positive self-concept, cognitive skills, health, and physical competence. These personal resources lead to the development of certain interpersonal and technical skills such as sensitivity to the feelings and needs of others, organizational skills, and leadership ability. The personal resources as well as the interpersonal and technical skills can then be used to perform effectively in valued social roles such as parent, employee, or community leader.

The negative valuation of minority racial groups and the discrimination against them that is generated by negative valuation can impinge upon the individual at any step in the complex developmental process outlined above. It may act indirectly or directly to decrease the individual's power to deal effectively with problems that arise in the course of his life.

Indirect power blocks are those that are incorporated into the developmental experiences of the individual as mediated by significant others. These indirect power blocks may operate at three levels. At the primary level, negative valuations or stigmas attached to racial identification become incorporated into family processes and prevent optimum development of personal resources as described above; i.e. positive self concepts, cognitive skills, etc. At the secondary level, power blocks occur when personal resources that have been limited by primary blocks in turn act to limit the development of interpersonal and technical skills. At the tertiary level, power blocks occur when limited personal resources and interpersonal and technical skills reduce effectiveness in performing valued social roles.

Direct power blocks can also be experienced by the minority group individual at three levels. These are power blocks based on negative valuation that have not been incorporated into the developmental experiences of the individual but are applied directly by some agent of society's major social institutions. At the primary level, this may occur when inadequate health services in a community lead to poor health conditions for specific individuals as well as for the community as a whole. Thus, there is a direct block to the development of good health—a valued personal resource. At the secondary level, blacks as individuals may be denied an opportunity to develop interpersonal or technical skills through limitations placed on educational opportunities, continuing education, or staff development opportunities within organizations. The individual has the personal resources required to develop these interpersonal or technical skills but is not permitted to do so. At the tertiary level, either the valued social roles themselves are denied or some material resource important to effective performance of the role—e.g., adequate income for performance of the parental role or adequate funding for a social program serving the black community—are withheld.

Assessment of the effects of power blocks on the etiology of problems and capacity for solving them require knowledge of the nature and dynamics of "growing up black." Direct power blocks experienced when social institutions limit or refuse access to social resources are more likely to be open and observable to worker and client system. However, direct power blocks are far more difficult to resolve than many indirect power blocks precisely because they are relatively impervious to change within the individual client or client system and can be resolved only by dealing directly with the power sources. It is also made more difficult by the fact that the helping professions have developed a number of potentially effective ways of bringing about individual change but have been relatively ineffective in producing changes in social institutions.

Given the centrality of negative valuation and powerlessness in the lives of black clients, empowerment may be seen as an important goal and process for social work with these clients. Empowerment is defined here as a process whereby the social worker engages in a set of activities with the client or client system that aim to reduce the powerlessness that has been created by negative valuations based on membership in a stigmatized group. It involves identification of the power blocks that contribute to the problem as well as the development and implementation of specific strategies aimed at either the reduction of the effects from indirect power blocks or the reduction of the operations of direct power blocks.

In the group instance, from the moment of its inception, there is a more or less explicit process that powerlessness may also affect. Whereas the powerlessness of an individual has been defined as his inability to obtain and use resources to achieve his personal goals, powerlessness in groups and communities may be defined as the inability to use resources to achieve collective goals. Groups in black communities are often prevented from completing some task or achieving some goal due to power deficiencies as a consequence of black identity. Again, power deficiencies may be direct or indirect. It is indirect if it is related to underdeveloped personal resources and interpersonal skills of group members, again because of their experience of discrimination in the larger society. Power blocks are direct if the group is prevented from obtaining specific resources needed to complete its task; e.g., funding, political sanction, etc., by some representative of the larger society.

At the community level, there is a process whereby the growth and development of the community results in the presence within it of various community resources such as schools, parks, civic clubs, advisory groups to various social and civic agencies. The better the resources that have been developed, the more successful the community will be in developing effective responses to problems it encounters; e.g., crime, unemployment, housing problems, etc. In the case of black communities there is greater likelihood that the initial growth and development as a community will contain destructive elements inimical to maximum community development due to stigmatization from the larger society. This constitutes the indirect power blockage which stifles the development of community identity and cohesion. However, the community may also experience the direct power blocks that derive from systematic discrimination of the community by the larger society; e.g., "redlining" real estate practices, miserable public services, low priority for major development, etc., which again represents blocks to the acquisition of important social resources required for further development of the system.

The relationship between powerlessness and negative valuation is a complex one, primarily due to the indirect ways that this negative valuation may operate in an individual's life situation. For example, when powerlessness is a consequence of the idiosyncratic way that a family or family surrogate has mediated the individual's life experiences, it may be difficult to connect the resulting problems to the negative valuations which may have acted to produce the family idiosyncrasies. For example, Rollo May describes in some detail his therapeutic work with Mercedes, whom he described as "black and impotent." [9] Mercedes grew up in a black community, was forced at the age of eleven into prostitution by a stepfather, supposedly without her mother's knowledge. At the time she entered therapy with May, her marriage to a white man was failing because of her frigidity, depression, and repeated miscarriages which appeared to be brought on by emotional stress. The negative valuations which she had incorporated through family processes may or may not have been reinforced by direct messages from the external environment; however, her emotional state at the time of entry into therapy was one of extreme helplessness, feelings of unworthiness, and apathy. More importantly, the strategy used by May of confronting and counteracting the negative impact of family processes rather than dealing with any negative valuations from the larger society apparently had therapeutic benefit for Mercedes, who was able to gain considerable sense of her own significance and autonomy from the experience.

There are some individuals or groups whose exposure to negative valuations have been so intense that they accept these valuations as "right" or at least inevitable and therefore make no effort to exert power at all. These are the individuals or groups who may not recognize a "problem" and who are often the targets of outreach efforts. The powerlessness that they exhibit can be considered power absence rather than power failure. It is interesting that the thrust of minority racial groups for greater power has raised the consciousness of other groups that traditionally have been negatively valuated—the handicapped, women, homosexuals, etc.—and they too have begun to push for reduction of their powerlessness.

Some negative valuations do not result in powerlessness because strong family relationships or strong, cohesive group relationships provide a cushion or protective barrier against the negative valuations from the larger society. Despite these negative valuations, some blacks, for example, are able to obtain and utilize a broad range of personal, interpersonal, and technical resources to achieve goals effectively. Not all blacks are powerless! This fact places into focus the goal of empowerment, which is not to reinforce the stereotyping of a total group on the basis of characteristics of only some of its members, but to perceive clearly the risks encountered by the group and utilize this perception in the various stages of the problem-solving process.

It should be clear from the foregoing that the concept of empowerment may be an appropriate goal for social intervention in any community or with any individual or group, provided there is the present and pervasive condition of systematic, institutionalized discrimination. It deals with a particular kind of block to problem-solving: that imposed by the external society by virtue of a stigmatized collective identity. Empowerment is culture-specific since it assumes the experience of belonging to a socially stigmatized category; this differential experience of the group leads to differential attitude sets and response sets which may in turn require modification of those goals of intervention or those techniques of intervention which have been based on the dominant society's norms. Thus, the history and unique set of experiences of the group are at least as important as the history of the individual, and the interrelatedness of the two histories influence the nature of intervention. Therefore the concept of empowerment can be built into existing theoretical frameworks for practice to enhance their implementation rather than as a substitute for these existing models.

When considered as a process, empowerment refers to the development of an effective support system for those who have been *blocked* from achieving individual or collective goals because of the severity or complexity of the discrimination they have suffered. Discrimination can be extremely severe when applied in both community systems and family systems during the individual's early growth and development. At the same time, it may be extremely complex when derived from a variety of interlocking sources—the stigmas of living in a slum neighborhood, parents so devastated by the impoverishment of their own lives that they cannot provide emotional gratification to a child, sporadic and irrational brutalization from police and other social control agents, insensitivity of the educational system, etc.

MODELS OF PRACTICE
If the decadé of the sixties was characterized by the rhetoric of powerless people demanding equal treatment in the sociopolitical institutions, then the seventies will perhaps be remembered as the decade in which the dimensions of equality were at last determined and the processes for achieving it were actually hammered out. In the helping professions, this has meant

translating the ideal of nonracist theory or the demand for black-community relevant models of practice into concrete referents which can be absorbed into the curriculum of professional education. It has also meant a sometimes painful awareness that some of the most richly satisfying concepts in our rhetoric—"Black Power," "community control,"—require far more operational definition than currently exists if they are to be used to illustrate our models of practice.

Chien has described models as scientific devices that aid in exploring certain segments of data universe and in "testing certain propositions." [10] Synonyms include such concepts as pattern, recipe, analog, etc. Models are particularly open to criticism and controversy since they hardly ever come close enough to an approximation of reality to avoid exceptions, inconsistencies, or gaps. Furthermore, the practice of social work—as well as other helping professions—is a complex multidimensional set of activities, so that we have generated a wide variety of practice models each of which emphasizes a different aspect of the activity set. For example, one model may be concerned primarily with portraying the functions of practice: e.g., treatment, environmental modification, advocacy, planning, etc., while largely ignoring the stages through which change takes place. Another will display consummate interest in the sequence of the helping process without equal consideration given to the nature of the problems with which the process is most likely to be effective. Most frequently a model will be based on a particular method of approaching change, e.g., casework, social treatment, community organization, social group work, group. Some of the methods emphases can extend beyond the field of social work per se to encompass methods developed in other fields: e.g., group psychotherapy, psychodynamically oriented psychotherapy, client-centered counseling, behavior modification, or reality therapy.

Models of practice are often creatively combined by the practitioner so that there is a more comprehensive set of directions for every intervention at every stage of the helping process. Yet despite the internal flexibility within the social work profession which permits, sanctions, and even encourages experimentation of practitioners with a variety of practice models, there has been relative failure in identifying practice models that have a particular relevance, or success rate when implemented with black client systems. Several factors are possibly contributing to this weak spot in the armamentarium of the profession. There is the value system of the profession that tends to emphasize common humanity, that recognizes both the uniqueness of clients and the common needs they share with all other human beings. This would appear to be enough to insure that every client will receive individualized attention and that our practice models specifically do not suggest *any* disadvantage to minority clients in general or black clients in particular. On the other hand, our models of practice tend to emphasize commonalities rather than uniqueness; i.e., *all* individuals develop defense mechanisms to deal with intolerable anxiety; or *all* individuals respond positively to unconditional positive regard; or *all* individuals will experience transference phenomena in the relationship with a therapist; or *all* individuals will tend to perform those behaviors more frequently if those behaviors are rewarded. Yet, these universal statements are at a level of abstraction that have drained out the unique manner in which some individuals may interpret unconditional positive regard or what constitutes a reward or how transference is differentially experienced when the therapist and client are of different racial background.

Recent efforts have been made to identify common elements in models of practice. Argyris has looked at intervention at the level of the organization to propose a general theory and method of intervention that is not specific to a particular organizational form or process.[11] Bloom has pointed out that models of scientific problem-solving utilized in the helping professions wears many guises (e.g., task-centered casework, client-centered encounter groups, behavior modification, etc.).[12] However, each is characterized by seven sequential steps from beginning to end: (1) orientation to problem-solving; (2) problem definition and formulation; (3) generation of alternatives regarding probable causes; (4) decision making; (5) implementation; (6) verification; and (7) termination. This general model of practice in the helping professions can be utilized to identify the relationship of empowerment to the strategies of practice.

As pointed out by Binstock and Ely, powerlessness may be an issue to some extent with all clients who come to help settings, and all problem-solving strategies need to take into account the degree to which powerlessness is derived from the experience of systematic negative valuation based on membership in a stigmatized racial or ethnic group.[13] The consequences of this experience are varying degrees of alienation from, and mistrust of, societal institutions, lowered self-esteem, fatalism—all of them obstacles to a successful helping encounter.

In the first stages of the general model of practice posed by Bloom—orientation to problem-solving and problem definition and formulation—modifications are required in its implementation with minority clients in order to deal with their noninstrumental responses to the negative valuations made by the larger society. Thus, empowerment activities in these stages should be directed toward overcoming these specific responses in order to engage the client system in the problem-solving process. Succeeding stages in that process also relate to the location and removal of obstacles and the identification and reinforcement of supports to effective problem-solving. In the case of minority clients, the obstacles are often of a special nature relating to the negative images of black incorporated into self-systems, reverberating through family systems, and institutionalized in the discriminatory practices of major social institutions. Thus empowerment activities must be designed to insure that the problem-solving process itself serves to counteract the negative valuations.

It is difficult to identify a particular social work function or practice strategy as an empowerment activity, since outcome often depends upon how it is implemented by the practitioner and how it is interpreted by the client. For example, advocacy by a practitioner on behalf of the client who belongs to the majority group may be perceived by that client as only what is "due" him as client, as citizen, or as human being. Thus, the practitioner is fulfilling an obligation to serve the client. On the other hand, for the minority group member who has had intense exposure to negative valuations from the larger society and for whom the "system" has rarely even appeared to be cooperative, advocacy may be perceived only as "doing something for me because they either don't want me to do it myself or believe that I am incompetent to do anything myself anyway." Thus the practitioner must demonstrate an understanding of the dynamics of powerlessness and its consequences in order to develop expertise in utilization of practice skills in the service of empowerment. These activities can generally have one or more of the following goals:

(1) Helping the client perceive himself as causal agent in achieving a solution to his problem or problems.

(2) Helping the client to perceive the practitioner as having knowledge and skills which he (the client) can use.

(3) Helping the client to perceive the practitioner as peer-collaborator or partner in the problem-solving effort.

(4) Helping the client to perceive the "power structure" as multipolar, demonstrating varying degrees of commitment to the status quo and therefore open to influence.

Thus, the overall goal is that of helping client systems that have been subjected to systematic and pervasive negative valuations to perceive themselves as causal forces capable of exerting influence in a world of other people and capable of bringing about some desired effect. It should be made clear that this does not deny the power and the significance of external forces in the creation of their problems or problem situations; however, it does place an overarching emphasis on the limitations of "giving up" and the latent potential in black individuals and black communities to deal more effectively and more creatively with oppression and the oppressors. This emphasis on individuals as causal forces does not imply that they *are* the cause of their problems or that their problems can be solved by merely effecting change in self; on the contrary, it focuses away from the medical model of finding a cause, a germ, a disease entity to be cured and accepts the complexities of multiple contributory factors in any problem situation. (Thus, the conceptualization of the individual as a causal force emphasizes the forces effecting change or solving problems rather than the inimical forces which created the problem.)

Perhaps most importantly from the standpoint of social work practice, the emphasis on the individual in the minority community as a causal force in effecting change in his problem situation, or on the minority community as a causal force in solving community-wide problems, permits the social worker to consider practice as a matter of "combining forces" rather than giving aid and assistance. Again the distinction may be subtle but it is unquestionably important in the pursuit of empowerment. The combination of forces in the individual or in the community with forces present in the professional intervention system is in the tradition of corporate mergers, political coalitions, military alliances, and similar strategies common to our political and economic structure. Thus, it avoids the negative connotation of aid or assistance which is more in the tradition of welfare systems; or our relationships with (the) more underdeveloped nations.

Finally, it is apparent that the failure or success of empowerment activities must be influenced eventually by the service delivery system itself as obstacle course or opportunity system. The frustration felt by most social work practitioners in attempting to deal with the powerlessness of minority clients has been the intransigencies in the organization of which they are a part. Thus consideration must be given to the structure and process of service delivery systems that have the greatest potential for facilitating empowerment of minority clients.

SUMMARY
This chapter has introduced the concept of empowerment as
process and goal in social work practice. Power is a concept
which is present in almost any discussion of human relationships—whether from a psychological, sociological, economic, political, or philosophical point of view. Thus, it can be
an integrative concept in the effort to obtain an understanding
of the various forces which serve to determine relationships in
a social system. It can also be utilized as a basis for problem-
solving when it is conceived as the necessary element required
to obtain adequate solutions to social and psychological problems. Powerlessness, therefore, has been defined as the inability to obtain and utilize resources to achieve individual or collective goals. More specifically, it refers to the inability to
manage emotions, knowledge, skills, or material resources in a
way that makes possible effective performance of valued social
roles so as to receive personal gratification. The powerlessness
that we are concerned about in this book is powerlessness as a
consequence of negative valuations of minority collectives and
of individuals based on their membership in the collective.

Negative valuation can be experienced directly or indirectly
by the individual. It can also affect the social functioning of
groups and total communities as well as of individuals. The
relationship between negative valuation and powerlessness is
complex. When powerlessness is a consequence of the idiosyncratic way that a family or family surrogate has mediated
the individual's life experience, it may be difficult to connect
the resulting problems to the negative valuations expressed in
the family idiosyncrasies. There are some individuals and
groups who believe their negative valuation is right or inevitable. Since they rarely even try to exert power over their life
situation, these persons may be perceived as demonstrating
power absence rather than power failure. Finally, some negative
valuations do not end in powerlessness because of the protective cushion provided by strong family and primary group
relationships.

Models of practice in the helping professions have been developed to deal with powerlessness as it is expressed generally by almost all client systems. Yet, for the black client—or client who is a member of a minority racial or ethnic group—there are some special characteristics of their response to negative valuation which require consideration in the problem-solving process. This can be described as the need for specific techniques or strategies of empowerment. Empowerment is defined as a process whereby the social worker or other helping professional engages in a set of activities with the client aimed at reducing the powerlessness stemming from the experience of discrimination because the client belongs to a stigmatized collective. These activities are specifically aimed at counteracting such negative valuations. The success or failure of empowerment is directly related to the degree to which the service delivery system itself is an obstacle course or an opportunity system.

experiential exercises

These exercises aim to provide an experience of feeling and/or observing powerlessness in a situation in order to gain greater understanding of the plight of people who have been rendered chronically powerless.

1.
Devote a class session to the simulation game, "Star Power," a commercially produced simulation game that can be used effectively in the classroom situation (Copyright 1969 by Western Behavioral Sciences Institute, La Jolla, California). "Star Power" is a game in which, a society of haves and have-nots is

built through the distribution of wealth in the form of chips. It permits participants to experience the importance of the social system in determining individual behavior. In "Star Power," a situation is deliberately created that is competitive with few winners and highly unbalanced with regard to the distribution of power. The consequence—as in our society itself—is almost invariably the production of aggressive, authoritarian behavior.

2.

Attend one or more of the following: (i) a city council meeting at which petitions from residents of a black community will be heard; (ii) committee or commission hearings at the federal, state, or local level which are dealing with issues of importance to black and other minority communities, e.g., civil rights legislation such as fair employment practices, opening housing, bussing to achieve school integration. Discuss the following:

(a) Who are the spokesmen for the black community?

(b) What is the nature of the "power" or influence that spokesmen attempt to use in order to bring about a favorable decision?

(c) What kind of response do the spokesmen elicit?

(d) What is your evaluation of the effectiveness of this strategy (petitioning a city council, appearing before a governmental commission, etc.) in achieving collective goals in black communities?

part two

philosophical and scientific foundations of empowerment

In the previous chapter, some abstractions were introduced which relate to powerlessness as it affects people in minority racial or ethnic groups—power blocks, power shortage, empowerment. However, there are some assumptions that require exploration before these abstractions can be accepted with confidence in the implementation of social work practice with black client systems.

An assumption is being made that black communities do exist as differentiated social systems. However, this assumption has not been accepted without question. For example, there is the question of whether the conceptualization of black communities facilitates problem-solving efforts or instead reinforces stereotypes and negative valuation. Do efforts to define and intervene in black communities merely distract from the more important focus on the individual? In chapter 2, the various dimensions of these and other issues are explored.

There is also the assumption that social work and the other helping professions have made a commitment to provide services to all clients equally, regardless of race, color, or creed. However, the depths of racism in society are of such magnitude that the authenticity of this commitment has been challenged— by black professional social workers as well as by black clients. The issue may then be, to what extent are these professions part of the problem or part of the solution? Chapter 3 traces the evolution of the contemporary helping professions including their traditional responses to black client systems.

Finally, it has been assumed that given a commitment to help, there are potentially effective models of practice which can be utilized in helping people in black communities solve their social and psychological problems. However, this assumption must also be questioned in view of mounting skepticism and active criticism leveled against social work, psychology, and psychiatry in regard to their practice theory. Therefore, in chapter 4, the scientific base for practice of these professions is explored, including its function as another source of negative valuation of people in black communities.

chapter two

black communities: myth or reality?

The amazing complexity of human societies has intrigued scholars for centuries. There is an accumulation of evidence that communal structures and processes have persisted from the African genesis of mankind to the post-industrial present. The solutions to the enigmas contained in the rise and fall of human communities have proved as challenging as the most intricate nest of Chinese puzzle boxes. The rise of nationalism in the seventeenth and eighteenth centuries increased the complexities as the earth was carved up into nation-states comprising within their boundaries networks of communities bound together by common history and relatively homogeneous culture. These communities, particularly in the larger nations, again have comprised a variety of social aggregates—families, voluntary associations, organizations all interrelated by mutual interests such as religion or ethnicity.

Definitions of community found in the social science literature are remarkably diverse. In some instances, the only apparent conceptual glue holding a group of people into a social unit is that of physical proximity. In other instances the definition involves several constructs only vaguely defined, such as "sense of shared fate" or "cultural homogeneity." In many descriptions of human communities, there is no real attempt to define the term; it is as if by virtue of membership in the human race we are expected to have instinctual knowledge of this aspect of human experience.

Most of the massive social programs of the 1960s—the "War on Poverty" or the "Great Society" programs—had as stated objectives the strengthening of communities that were, for the most part black. Strengthening included the notion of the transfer of power in regard to decision-making on community salient issues from the traditional power holders to community residents themselves. In fact, the identification of who is and who is not a member of the community became one of the most divisive issues in these conflict-ridden community programs.

The position taken in this chapter is that neither the strategies aimed at changing the power distribution as it affected predominantly black communities nor the strategies aimed at helping individuals in those communities to function more successfully in the larger social system achieved these goals to any appreciable extent. The lack of success in the former instance was due primarily to a misunderstanding of the dynamics of the relationship between black communities and the larger society both on the part black community residents and others who wanted to assist them in achieving collective goals. For example, "integration" and "separatism" were often posed as alternative means to the goal of improved status of black individuals, groups and communities. However, both these alternatives were bankrupt, given the structural and functional realities of contemporary American society. On the other hand, lack of success at the individual level was due at least in some measure to ignorance of the help givers regarding cultural patterns developed in response to and reinforced by forces within the community.

The remainder of this chapter will describe the structure of black-white relationships in the society, identify the distinctive characteristics of black culture, and explore the relative fit between the defining characteristics of communities in general and those characteristics as observed in black communities. Both the helping professional for whom the community is context of the change process and the helping professional for whom the community is target of the change process should find insights in the diverse conceptualizations of black-white relationships and perceptions of black community characteristics which can be useful in constructing more effective intervention strategies.

BLACK-WHITE RELATIONSHIPS IN THE UNITED STATES

It is perhaps presumptuous to assume that relationships between blacks and whites in the United States can be rationally described, since there are so many examples of the irrational and illogical which have characterized black-white relationships past and present. Booker T. Washington pointed out that at the time white southerners were most vitriolic in their insistence on "separation of the races," there was no attempt made to keep the white man from placing his grocery store, his dry goods store or other enterprise right in the heart of the Negro district.[1] At the same time that discrimination against blacks was justified on questionable theories of biological inferiority, there was no questioning the notion that nine-tenths white genes were insufficient to compensate for the one-tenth "inferior" black genes in an individual; at the same time that the American credo of individualism was given great social value, laws were enacted which permitted value judgments to be made not on individual achievements or merit but solely on the basis of group identity. Yet, despite the irrational stream that flows through the history of race relations in the United States, sociologists have attempted to find a rational model which can explain what appears to be unexplainable behavior. Four major models will be discussed here—assimilation, amalgamation, cultural pluralism, internal colonialism; and a fifth model which appears to be more useful as a component of the theoretical base for practice in helping professions will be proposed.

Assimilation is essentially a process whereby minority groups become more and more like the majority group; i.e., it is a theory emphasizing conformity to majority cultural norms. Gordon differentiates, however, between cultural assimilation and structural assimilation.[2] Cultural assimilation occurs when the minority group changes its cultural patterns to those of the core culture, the majority group. Structural assimilation occurs when there is large-scale entrance into clubs, institutions, and primary groups of the majority culture. Gordon suggests that in the case of black Americans, middle- and upper-class blacks have achieved cultural assimilation but not structural assimilation. Black intellectuals have attacked this model as essentially ethnocentric, as if the desirable goal for the society is the conformity of all its subgroups to majority cultural norms. Dobriner's counterattack emphasizes the relationship between core culture and class values:

> Some black militants argue that Negroes should not slavishly copy white middle-class patterns but should demand the equality of black values along with white. Such a position is sociologically impossible and represents a confusion of class with ethnic-racial variables. . . . It is not a matter of the Negro community losing its black pride as the militants charge, but of assimilating into middle-class culture *so as literally to integrate into the mainstream of American society* . . . 10% of the population.[3]

Dobriner's proposition that cultural assimilation is the road to equality ignores some haunting questions. The first is to what extent can true cultural assimilation occur without structural assimilation? There is evidence that, first of all, Dobriner's identification of middle-class values as "family stability, normative responsibility, cleanliness, personal discipline, scholarship, trimmed lawns and painted houses," could also be found to a large extent among lower-class blacks who, however, often lack the social supports to help them to implement these values. Furthermore, in adapting to racial isolation and the struggle to survive, differential emphases may be placed on these values. Finally, middle-class blacks who remain structurally isolated from the core culture may cling to cultural contents reinforced by their continuing association with others who have shared in their experiences of ethnicity and isolation. It is these contents that are often overlooked by whites who have been programmed when observing middle-class blacks to see only those behaviors which support their perceptions regarding the primacy of class over race.

It is important here to consider the class-race controversy in some detail since it is often the basis of violent disagreement among blacks and whites. Greer has given perhaps the most cogent argument for the importance to see class oppression as more virulent in American society than racial oppression. He fears that racism has been used as a cloak to obscure the basic facts of immobility in the American economic system. He states:

> . . . ethnic-centered analyses serve to perpetuate the illusion of classlessness and the legend of equal opportunity and mobility. It is a pernicious syndrome. In large measure these myths account for the rationalization of poverty in this country through the promise that everbody who is willing and able can eventually make it. In other words, a secular state of grace is instituted that legitimates the existing pyramid of power, encourages competitive and oppressive relationships along the various ethnic horizontals on the pyramid, and diverts attention from the parallel oppression and exploitation of the larger class system.[4]

In this sense, then, Greer is an assimilationist who perceives ethnic division as diversionary in the pursuit of true social justice. This would require an assimilation of ethnic interests into class interests and, hopefully, the recognition of class conflict as the essential problem of society to be resolved.

Amalgamation essentially refers to a process whereby the interaction of a majority cultural group with minority cultures produces a culture which includes aspects of each but is different from any. The black author Albert Murray has perhaps stated this view as graphically as any social scientist:

> The culture of the nation over which the White Anglo-Saxon power elite exercise such exclusive political, economic and social control is not white by any measurement ever devised. American culture, even in its most rigidly segregated precincts, is patently and irrevocably composite. It is regardless of all the hysterical protestations of those who would have it otherwise, incontestably mulatto. Indeed for all their traditional antagonisms and obvious differences, the so-called black and so-called white people of the United States resemble nobody else in the world so much as they resemble each other. And what is more, even their most extreme and violent polarities represent nothing so much as the natural history of pluralism in an open society.[5]

Murray appears to be saying that the "natural history" of pluralism is amalgamation punctuated by outbursts from pockets of resistance. Ironically, Murray is attesting to the validity of the melting-pot concept which so many black intellectuals have rejected. The difference appears to be that he gives recognition to the fact that melting can occur without an essential acceptance of its value or reality, particularly by the majority group, and without equality as a consequence. Given these characteristics, it might well be said that the criticisms of the "melting pot" have not been so much denial of cross-cultural influences resulting in changes in all component cultures but rather in regard to the mistaken notion that this melting process has been complete with the obliteration of group distinctions.

Cultural pluralism refers to the coexistence of groups retaining their essential identities with whatever melting that occurs being ineffective in changing these identities. Thus over time, both majority and minority groups retain their differences. This has been a popular conceptualization for many minority group activists and scholars who have, perhaps goaded by the intransigence of the Anglo majority, decided that assimilation is not a desirable goal and to seek it is to deny what is positive in one's own group. Greer has pointed out that all three of these processes—assimilation, amalgamation, and cultural pluralism—refer to a process of Americanization which, "judged on the basis of its own avowed criterion—namely equal opportunity—must be declared a charade." [6] Novak has rendered even sharper indictment of what has become the now national ideology, i.e., ethnic pluralism rather than the melting pot:

> No one has yet contrived an image, let alone a political system, for living in a genuinely pluralistic way. The difficulties are obvious. How can each cultural minority be true to itself without infringing on the rights of others? How can each person belong to a given ethnic group to the extent that he or she chooses, and be free as well to move into other groups? [7]

Greer expands the criticism:

> The problem is that neither ethnic identity nor ethnic solidarity has meant understanding and tolerance of other groups in this country. It has not meant a peaceful, pluralist, international policy . . . further, the primacy of ethnicity has generally meant an identity of defense against and exclusion of other groups, and there is little in American family patterns—whatever the group—that seems to be based on the kind of consensual relations that could gavor individual growth and autonomy. [8]

What appears to be mixed again here are the concepts of cultural and structural integration of ethnic groups in this country. In a pluralist society, there may be distinct cultural groups but with or without political and social equality. White South Africans may argue that apartheid is the ultimate protection for the maintenance of cultural pluralism in that country but sees no contradiction in the fact that the political control and norms governing social stratification are squarely in the hands of the white minority. The emphasis on political relationships rather than cultural has led some social scientists to identify these as the most significant relationships in minority-majority interaction.

Internal colonialism is a concept developed during the hectic decade of the 1960s when "the movement" was struggling for an ideology to power its protest. Stokely Carmichael and Charles Hamilton first described in detail the notion of black people in the United States as colonized subjects in relation to the white society.[9] Harold Cruse had coined the term "domestic colonialism" to differentiate it from cases where subject peoples were colonized by external powers.[10] Blauner preferred internal colonialism to refer to those instances in which (1) colonization begins with involuntary entry of colonizers (conquest) or colonized (slavery); (2) colonizing power deliberately constrains or changes indigenous cultural forms; (3) the lives of the subject group are controlled by the colonizers; (4) there is separation in labor status between colonizers and colonized; and (5) racial or cultural superiority is used by the colonizers to justify exploitation, control, and oppression of the colonized.[11] The validity of this model when applied to black communities can be seen in the Haryou Report on the situation in Harlem:

> The community can best be described in terms of the analogy of a powerless colony. Its political leadership is divided, and all but one or two of its political leaders are shortsighted and dependent upon the larger political power structure. Its social agencies are financially precarious and dependent upon sources of support outside the community. Its churches are isolated or dependent. Its economy is dominated by small businesses which are largely owned by absentee owners, and its tenements and other real property are also owned by absentee landlords. Under a system of centralization, Harlem's schools are controlled by forces outside the community. Programs and policies are supervised and determined by individuals who do not live in the community.[12]

Whereas there has been much more attention given to describing the nature and consequences of internal colonialism, there has been much less written in the way of concrete hypotheses regarding how "liberation" of the colonized black communities would occur. Carmichael and Hamilton suggest that "Black Power" is the answer.[13] This concept rests on a fundamental premise that "before a group can enter the open society, it must first close ranks." Thus, it is necessary for blacks in the United States to "unite, to recognize their heritage, to build a sense of community . . . to define their own goals, to lead their own organizations and to support those organization." A black community operating under this philosophical orientation might, for example, require merchants doing business in their community to reinvest forty to fifty percent of net profit into the indigenous community in the form of providing additional jobs for black people, supporting certain types of community-based agencies, or scholarship funds for students. The power to enforce such sanction would be the power of the boycott. Blauner has indicated, however, that such unity of political action would be difficult since racism has fractionated the black population. Thus, some violence is inevitable in the decolonization process since in the absence of power available from unity, the greatest power available to blacks is power to disrupt. Whites can avoid this by supporting rather than fighting community liberation movements and substituting technical assistance when sought by black communities for the current direct control and exploitation of these communities.[14]

Tabb has viewed the options open to the colonized peoples of black America as similar to those of any developing nation; i.e., determining how much "foreign" influence is desirable. It is doubtful that isolation has any more viability in the case of national subsystems than it has had in regard to international subsystems. At the same time that there is pressure from the oppressed for change (termed "liberation"), there is a strategy already developed by the oppressors to deal with the pressure. To quote Tabb:

> Black people could run the schools, the libraries and the local parks, but to get money that would have to go outside the

ghetto. Once black leaders are chosen and start dealing with those who hold real power, they will find that in order to get concessions they must first get rid of the militants who are "causing trouble and alienating whites." This type of political pressure will probably be combined with efforts to create a middle class among blacks: homeowners and capitalists. Such a group would serve as a bulwark against those who would tear at the fabric of our society . . . In addition to the carrot of ownership for an enlarged middle class, manpower training for a growing working class, and welfare for the rest, there is still tactical police force and other counterinsurgency forces.[15]

Robert Allen in his *Black Awakening in Capitalist America* would use a multifaceted approach to deal with the strategy Tabb outlines above:

With respect to encounters with White America, a black (political) party should not rely on exclusively legal campaigns, nor should it restrict itself to all-out street warfare. Instead it must devise a strategy of calculated confrontation, using a mixture of tactics to fit a variety of contingencies. The object of this strategy should be to abolish, by any means possible, the real control of white society over the black community and to exact needed reforms. Tactical innovation should be the order of the day and anything workable goes—depending on specific conditions and the relation of forces—from legal struggle to electoral politics, to direct action campaigns, to force. In short what is required is a coordinated, multifaceted, multilevel struggle which will enable black America to defeat corporate imperialism and free itself from the shackles of domestic neocolonialism.[16]

What is clear from this review of theories which seek to explain the relationship in the United States between whites and blacks is that: (1) It is difficult to identify a single linear process applicable to all minority groups from entry of a minority group into American society until some point of stabilization in its relationship to the core cultural and political systems. (2) The black-white relationships have demonstrated that racism is an

intervening variable which sharply molds the direction of cultural change by severely limiting structural integration of the
black and white. What in fact might be said is that all four of
these conceptualizations are valid at some point in time in
black-white relationships. Thus, the colonial model is accurate,
but the psychological context is quite different when the oppressor is the nation rather than an outside power and one to
which there has been extensive socialization process developing loyalty and faith. It is analogous to the difference in trying
to deal with injustices perpetrated against one by a relative in
contrast to a nonrelative. In the former case there are some
psychological constraints on suitable tactics as well as varying
levels of guilt created by the conflict. Despite the fact that most
blacks would vow no real love for "whitey," we are caught up
in the socialization process which is constantly associating our
gratifications with white sources: movies, TV shows, football
games, etc. Thus, we need a conceptualization which permits
us to view the black community and its relationship to the rest
of society in such a way as to account simultaneously for social
regularities and contradictions; for social structure but also
psychological feelings in regard to that structure. Assimilation
obviously has not worked in the black case; amalgamation has
to some extent, but it has had little effect in changing basic
social relationships; cultural pluralism also may be a structural
reality but has not changed power relationships in the system.

THE OPEN ETHNOSYSTEM
There is definite value to be gained from eschewing the simple,
linear cause-effect models of human behavior and shifting to
the open-system model as an analytic framework. Sutherland
has indicated wherein this value lies:

> . . . the tendency to try to take social systems apart, or to
> partition human behavior into isolated compartments, is
> scientistic. For, except for the very rare entity which will meet

the criteria for the essential mechanism, behavioral properties of any real significance are generally dependent upon a context for their viability. From the systems perspective, this means that the search for the whole cannot end simply with an inventory of parts analyzed in effective isolation or with partitioned expressions of their interrelationships . . . the complex system tends to become a *temporal gestalt,* carrying on interchange with other temporal gestalts within a field which, itself, must be defined and treated as a gestalt rather than a mechanism.[17]

The conceptualizations of the structure and process of black-white relations depend upon a context for their viability. Black individuals, white individuals, black communities, white communities, American society are all open systems, "entities whose viability depends on a continuous interchange with successively more encompassing systems." This continuous transaction of open systems which is characteristic of human societies demands that explanations of behavior emanate from two important perspectives: (1) a holistic perspective from which any set of behaviors is studied as part of a whole; i.e., the social system that embraces an entire network of relationships in addition to those of immediate concern; and (2) an interdisciplinary perspective which permits the utilization of the fundamental work of psychologists and physiologists on the single individual as well as the traditional sociological, political, economic and anthropological formulations of humans in collectivities. Thus, the trouble with the assimilationists, amalgamationists, or culturally plural views of black-white relationships is that they are essentially sociological in concept and ignore some critical economic, political, and psychological realities. On the other hand, the trouble with the internal colonialist conceptualization is that it is essentially political, again ignoring some important economic, social, and psychological realities. It is necessary then to seek a model which permits a more multicausal, holistically derived explanation of black-white relationships in the United States.

The concept of American society as an open ethnosystem is

relevant here. An ethnosystem can be defined as a system comprising smaller groups or collectivities of individuals whose ethnicity serves to define them and their relationship to the whole—either by self-determination or by determination of others in the system. More specifically then, an ethnosystem is defined as (1) a collectivity of interdependent ethnic groups, (2) each in turn defined by some unique historical and/or cultural ties, and (3) bound together by a single political system.

Thus, this definition emphasizes the interdependent, interrelatedness of ethnic collectivities in the United States— generally the Anglo, black, Chicano, Asian-American, Jewish, Puerto-Rican, Indian, or native American. This is further complicated, however, by the fact that the Anglos—largest of the groups—may under certain conditions splinter into Irish-American, Polish-American, Italian-American, etc. This latter phenomenon appears to be a consequence of what Schrag in *The Decline of the Wasp* has called the "cultural prison break of the 1960s." [18] The important thing is that, from a conceptual standpoint, the characterization of the United States as an ethnosystem—a collectivity of ethnic groups, each controlling unequal proportions of the system's resources—makes it possible to view all groups as peers. The system *belongs* to all groups it comprises. Therefore, the other ethnic groups in this country are not beggars at the door of the resource-rich Anglo masters but are more like angry peers determined to have their fair share of the family cake which the bullying biggest brother has hoarded for himself.

"Ethno" is a common prefix which has been borrowed here from anthropology and which deals with the description of the differences and similarities that exist between human groups. Therefore, it is the study of the variations in man's behavior as a member of human society. The variations of major concern are generally language, material resources, and social organization. The concept of social system, which has been used here so far without definition, refers to a more or less stable pattern of relationships among component parts which form a whole with characteristics not manifest in the separate parts. Combining the two concepts, we create "ethnosystem," which must by definition then comprise groups which vary in modes of communication, in degree of control over material resources, and in the structure of their internal relationships or social organization. Moreover, these groups must be in a more or less stable pattern of relationships which have characteristics transcending any single group's field of interaction; e.g., the ethnosystem's political, educational, or economic subsystems. The notion that the ethnosystem has a "life of its own" transcending any single group within it and different from the mere sum of behaviors in its component parts, is a cardinal idea in the development of both theoretical approaches and practice strategies that appear in this book and therefore should not be forgotten.

Perhaps, however, the most pervasive characteristic of the ethnosystem as mentioned earlier, is the centrality of both race and ethnicity in almost every aspect of human interaction within it. Let us take as example a white, Anglo family receiving Aid to Families with Dependent Children—the aid category which most people think of when public assistance or welfare is mentioned. It is headed by a disabled father who has no one else to help him support his eight children. The family is in a state of desperation this month because unexpected school expenses have depleted their monthly allowance and there are still six days to go before the next welfare check. This family belongs to the largest ethnic group in the ethnosystem, but the inadequate societal response to its problem is undoubtedly influenced by racist attitudes in the general public who support the welfare system only begrudgingly because of reluctance to support programs which serve large numbers of blacks. Wilson has expressed the opinion that not only is public hostility to welfare related to the popular stereotype that it is a social institution for blacks but the growing neglect of urban public schools is related to their becoming also increasingly black.[19] Thus, when viewed at the microlevel—the manner in which whites will behave in regard to other whites—it is impossible to predict. Whites may treat other whites well or badly *depending on the context.* However, if we know the context, e.g., the welfare system, we may be able to predict quite well based on our knowledge of the transcendence of racism over concern for individual differences or individual needs in that system. This is an example of a phenomenon defined by systems theorists as "macrodeterminacy."

> This is a situation which occurs when a system may be treated as deterministic at the higher levels (or at the level of the whole itself) but where the lower order components of the system may not admit to determinacy, this may mean that the system itself is capable of prediction . . . even though we cannot treat the parts or lower-order components as deterministic.[20]

A deterministic system is one where, for any given set of starting-state conditions, there is one and only one event which may be assigned a significant probability of occurrence. This is in contrast to a stochastic system where, for any given set of starting-state conditions, a number of events must be assigned significant probabilities of occurrence. Furthermore, stochastic systems differ by degree. It is mildly stochastic if it will exhibit a range of qualitatively similar responses; severely stochastic if it will exhibit a range of qualitatively different responses and indeterministic if the range of responses is entirely unpredictable.

We may consider black communities as total systems with groups and individuals as subsystems. The community-level system may be deterministic in regard to its response to certain issues or stimuli, whereas its subsystems are not. For example, if subjected to an overt act of prejudice or discrimination, the community's response might be almost entirely predictable—e.g., a wave of active forms of protest such as press conferences called by community leaders (whose identity would also be predictable), protest marches, editorials in the black press, etc. On the other hand, if one of the community's sub-systems—a group or individual—is similarly subjected to an overt act of prejudice or discrimination, the response may be predictable only within a range of qualitatively different responses. Therefore, we cannot treat the lower-order components of the black community system as deterministic at all in this regard.

A related idea is that generalizations also may have some value in regard to collectives but not in regard to the individual. For example, generalizations may identify a central tendency in a group in regard to some attitude, response, or behavior pattern but the variation may also be relatively wide. This identifies the danger in approaching individuals in the ethnosystem as a stereotype of the collective. The practitioner guilty of stereotyping has not appreciated the complexity of the process whereby generalizations are used as "sensitizing" inputs which must be tested against the information provided by the individual before its applicability can be determined.

THE TRANSMISSION OF CULTURE
The conceptualization of American society as an open ethnosystem does not really resolve the controversy over whether or not blacks in the United States are *culturally* distinctive from other racial or ethnic groups. In fact, it sharpens the arguments on both sides of the issue as it becomes exceedingly clear that the question is whether or not blacks should be perceived as having a unique culture when they are constantly in transaction with the other groups in the ethnosystem and cannot help being brought under cultural influences from these external systems. At the same time, however, it can also be pointed out that the very nature of open systems insures that this will happen; however, it does not mean that any subsystem or component of a whole is subject to the same influences with exactly the same consequence for developing cultural patterns. Even more importantly, there are some experiences in every subcul-

ture which are unique to it and therefore insure that no system will be able to duplicate exactly that of another.

Myrdal, in his *American Dilemma,* influenced an entire generation of liberal sociologists with his view of blacks in the United States as an exaggerated American whose values are pathological elaborations of general American values.[21] However, long before Myrdal, practitioners in social agencies had agonized over the issue of cultural distinctiveness of blacks in the United States. In the 1923 volume of *The Family,* the social work journal which later became the prestigious *Social Casework,* Corinne Sherman wrote a five-part article on "Racial Factors in Desertion," covering the experiences of the New York Charity Organization Society with Italian, Polish, Irish, American, and Negro families.[22] Miss Sherman described Negroes as a "race that has done little of itself at home (Africa) but that has already made a distinguished success in adapting itself to the needs of others in a strange land."

The thrust of the article was to enhance recognition of the extent to which the behaviors of blacks which bring them to the attention of social agencies, e.g., desertion of families by black males, may be what their "forebears have done for countless generations." She points out that in the history of the black slave trade and later experience in the United States "the influence of their owners somewhat raised the standards of the easygoing savage but hardly sufficient to effect great permanent improvement." Thus, understanding the African tribal system with its matrifocal family relationships, its acceptance of women making living arrangements with other men in the tribe when their husbands were away for long periods of time, etc., would help the social worker to understand Negro men who desert their families, refuse to live at home and support the household but nevertheless keep a "sort of supervisory interest and make friendly visits to their wives at regular intervals." In a subsequent issue of *The Family,* a faculty member of the Atlanta School of Social Work (the first professional school of social work in a black institution) wrote a scathing critique of

Sherman's article. She pointed out Sherman's naïveté in the descriptions of African tribal customs and declared that "social weaknesses" of Negroes could be attributed to nothing more than the failure of white people to treat them "decently and fairly."

In the half century since Sherman's article appeared, the controversy over the persistence of Africanisms in black life in the United States has continued. Further, it appears that at any given time, an examination of those in black communities who support the idea that African culture is a powerful determinant of behavior will serve as an indicator of the shifts in the perceptions of the relevance of African interests to black political perspective in the United States. At the center of the controversy, however, is the question of the extent to which racial or ethnic groups who come to live in the United States can retain aspects of the original culture in view of pressures toward conformity to middle-class, Anglo-American patterns of communication, belief, values, and social behavior. Upon closer scrutiny, this question breaks down into two rather than a single question. The first is to what extent have Africanisms persisted in black communities? The next is to what extent do they constitute all or part of a distinctive Afro-American culture?

Assimilationists have viewed the persistence of Africanisms as a temporary phenomenon, so that each succeeding generation moves closer to conformity with Anglo culture. Hansen suggests, however, that empirical studies of third-generation families in the United States reveal that there is an inevitable and identifiable tendency to seek ties again with the cultural traditions of immigrant ancestors. In the case of blacks in this country, the immigrant paradigm and its end-point of cultural assimilation is obviously inappropriate although the tendency has been to treat their situation as if it corresponded to that of other ethnic minorities who have entered the United States. In fact, however, the social science literature contains three distinct notions of cultural transmission among black people in this country. The first is akin to the view espoused by Sherman and perhaps its first scholarly and thoughtful presentation by Herskovitz in *The Myth of the Negro Past.*[23] The view essentially is that strong African influences have survived into the American present and provide for the uniqueness of the black cultural experience. It is in fact then a cultural pluralist point of view. A number of contemporary black social scientists and historians have also supported this view.[24]

The second notion is of black American culture as essentially *American* whether negatively American or positively American and little that relates to the African experience of blacks remains.[25] This view can be encompassed by advocates of radical social change who perceive the American social system as essentially oppressive and therefore failing to permit black Americans to enjoy the cultural desiderata held in common with all other Americans, as well as by advocates of "go slow" change strategies, who perceive evidence of increasing assimilation of blacks into mainstream American life and increasing acceptance of the contributions which they have made to mainstream culture.

A third view is that black American culture is unique but with persistence of original African roots as a small part and impact of American experience as a large part in determining the cultural distinctiveness.[26] Blauner has described this view exceptionally well as he points out:

> . . . the black cultural experience is more like an alternating than a direct current. The movement toward ethnicity and distinctive consciousness has been paralleled by one toward becoming more "American" in action and identity. Sometimes these conflicting vectors characterize different time periods; sometimes they reflect different segments of the large and diversified black minority; sometimes both contradictory cultural tendencies have been present simultaneously and within the psychological and social orientations of a single individual. Underlying these phenomena are the many and varied historical and social conditions that have produced Afro-

American culture. Black culture cannot be understood in terms of the model that is reasonably satisfactory for rural, European ethnic groups.[27]

The enduring force of the controversy over whether or not black Americans and white Americans have the same or different cultural orientations may well be related to the confused definitions—and multiplicity of definitions—we have in the literature to define concepts of culture, race, and ethnicity. In addition, there is little clarity in most arguments in the literature as to how the interrelationships of these concepts are being perceived.

Ashley Montagu wrote a scholarly treatise in 1942 (*Man's Most Deadly Myth*) in which he indicated that race is an undesirable term and suggested that "ethnic group" be substituted for "race" whenever possible.[28] However, although race as used by the general public is full of distortions and ambiguities, for the purposes of a general description of three identifiable subgroups in the human population—Asian, Caucasian, and Negroid—into which most (but not all) persons can be categorized, the term has some usefulness. This is particularly true since race refers exclusively to *physical* characteristics which distinguish the three subgroups, and since these characteristics have been demonstrated to be weak or even nonfunctional as determinants of behavior, the influence of race in interpersonal relationships is almost entirely a function of social attitudes. Thus, demonstration of the attitude, almost endemic in American society, that there is a connection between racial, i.e., physical characteristics and social behavior and that, in this regard, some races are inherently superior to others reveals essentially what is meant by the term racism.

Ethnicity, on the other hand, does not refer to physical characteristics but to cultural relatedness. Culture has been defined as a body of rules which demarcate the ways in which individuals in a population should communicate with each other, think about themselves and their environment, and behave toward one another and objects in their environment. These rules—often imposed originally by external forces—serve to limit the range of variation in the group in regard to patterns of communication, belief, value, and social behavior. Obviously, racially similar groups, e.g., Koreans and Japanese or black Americans and black Brazilians, may be ethnically quite different. Black Americans, furthermore, are both a racial *and* an ethnic group. In a racist society, race tends not only to transcend ethnicity in the responses elicited from others in the social system, it tends even to shape the cultural content that defines the group's ethnicity. It is this complex interrelationship of social characteristics that has so confused the liberal establishment (to which so many white helping professionals belong) who perceive racial equality and cultural distinctiveness as conflicting social goals.

In the next section, those forces which tend both to define black communities and to identify the rules which limit variation in the group will be discussed. Thus, territoriality, personal intimacy, and social cohesion are shown to differentiate black communities from others in the ethnosystem as well as to insure greater cultural similarities than cultural differences among the members. This implicitly confines our discussion of specific cultural characteristics to the total system level, which as indicated earlier is to some extent deterministic. It thereby avoids stereotyping individuals whose behavior can only be predicted probabilistically—even when controlling for culture.

DEFINING CHARACTERISTICS
To most whites, black community means a Harlem or Watts, a Hough or Fillmore district or other areas in cities across the country where slum conditions prevail, the crime rate is high, and almost no whites reside. Despite the fact that most blacks in the United States live in predominantly black areas of our urban complexes, the territorial boundaries of black communities are difficult to specify. If we accept the fact that most

blacks cannot escape identity as members of a black community—even if he would desperately like to—then the term
must be inclusive enough to transcend strictly geographical
boundaries. On the other hand, when we need to consider
questions relating to community control over its institutions we
must be able to define geographically the area which contains
those institutions.

Rose has defined black communities in an urban area to be
made up of three types of neighborhoods: those neighborhoods in which 75 percent or more of the residents are
black, usually constituting the ghetto core; neighborhoods with
50 percent to 74 percent black residents representing usually
ghetto fringe neighborhoods; and neighborhoods in which
blacks, although in the minority, are in large enough numbers
to precipitate "white flight" and consequently future dominance of blacks.[29] Of course, it is clear that the mere fact that
the territory is being occupied by blacks usually defines it as
less desirable for white occupancy. It also means that in areas
currently being occupied by whites there will be resistance to
the entry of blacks due to the inevitable loss of status the
neighborhood suffers as a consequence. This racist principle
in this country is mirrored in the social science terminology for
black entry and subsequent dominance in a geographic area as
black "invasion" and "succession."

There has been considerable criticism of territory as a basis
for defining community. Thus Rose's utilization of the census
tract as the basic unit of classifying neighborhoods for inclusion in the overall concept of black community would be perceived as a statistical artifact rather than a real social unit.
There is no reason to believe in most instances that because a
person resides in the same census tract with others that there
is some sense of common interests and shared fate. However,
in the case of blacks this criticism may be inaccurate. In this
sense, the community is defined not only by the fact that they
live in physical proximity to each other but by the fact of their
being black, which in a sense has decreed a special rela-

tionship to others in the ethnosystem and increased the likelihood they will live in physical proximity to each other.

Greer has suggested that the community be perceived as a
field of social interaction rather than as a particular geographical entity.[30] Within a given field, major functions are carried out
by social organizations. It is only, in fact, when ethnically related individuals live voluntarily in an area in which their group
predominates that a true ethnic community exists. The "voluntarily" almost precludes the definition of black communities as
"true communities" since forces beyond their control often
dictate the limited residential options available. However, because of this, there is no way of knowing whether in many
cases, particularly in gilded ghettos, whether blacks would
choose to live in or close to other blacks or whether all would
seek predominantly white neighborhoods.

Despite the primacy of race in establishing the concepts of
black communities, historically, the territorial nature of these
communities has been evident. In the years preceding and following World War I, large segregated Negro communities were
created within many American cities:

> "Niggertowns," "Buzzard Alleys," "Nigger Rows," "Black
> Bottoms," "Smoketowns," "Bronzevilles," and "Chinch
> Rows" developed elsewhere, North and South. . . . The Dis-
> trict of Columbia was noted for its supposedly decadent
> Negro alleys: "Tin Can Alley," "Coon Alley," "Hog Alley,"
> "Moonshine Alley," and "Goat Alley." So closely have the
> terms "alleys" and "Negroes" been associated, a historian of
> Washington's Negro section wrote, that in the minds of the
> older citizens they are inseparable.[31]

The continuing concentration of blacks within urban spatial
configurations has continued almost unceasingly since that
time so that in 1970 there were more than 70 urban places in
the United States with more than 25,000 blacks. These have
been considered to constitute a national network of ghetto
centers which might well be the referent when one speaks of
urban black communities in the United States.

Suburbanization of blacks has occurred essentially in the same way that inner cities ghettos have been created; i.e., in the few select locations, clusters of predominantly black communities arise. During the 1960s, the only urban centers with substantial suburban black ghettos emerging were New York, Newark, Miami, Chicago, St. Louis, and Washington. In a number of instances blacks constitute the majority population within the suburban ring communities. Since the process of redistribution of blacks to the suburban areas is little different from that which operates in inner city areas—black entry, white flight, and ultimately black dominance—these might be referred to as suburban satellite neighborhoods to the core urban neighborhoods.[32]

Downs has proposed several possible strategies which might be used to change the nature of the black ghetto situation in our urban centers.[33] The first would entail the concentration of blacks in specific territorial space, the development of locally based supportive institutions—social, economic, and political—and pumping resources into the area to produce positive change. This is essentially the strategy encompassed in the model cities concept. The concept of "new towns in town" also would represent this strategy. A second strategy would involve the concentration of blacks in the central city core but with the encouragement of the return of whites to create an "integrated core" with appropriate resources to develop the kind of housing and services which would attract whites and blacks to the area. There has been little real evidence that this strategy appeals to the power structure except for a few attempts to scatter low-income housing so that it is placed along with other housing. A third strategy would involve dispersal of the inner-city blacks into suburban areas in new black communities supported by input of resources to spur development and enrichment. This is little different, however, from enrichment of inner-city ghetto areas, since this strategy usually represents merely the spillover beyond the inner city. When it does occur some distance away from inner city it generally affords an alternative environmental option for blacks, although it can rarely be implemented without resistance from whites already residing in areas to which blacks are to be dispersed. A final strategy is to try to develop new concentrations of blacks in existing white suburban areas to create an integrated community supported by whatever inputs are needed to make it an attractive situation for blacks and whites alike.

Despite the theoretical feasibility of all these strategies, none has been implemented with any degree of intensity so as to seriously change the direction of the kind of growth of black communities that has existed for nearly a century. Years of research indicates that residential integration is fought more intensely than any other form of integration, including school. Suttles refers to "the defended neighborhood" and suggests that fears which surround possible negative influences in childhood contacts seem to generate the phenomenon of such neighborhoods.[34] There is an attempt to enclose children in a smaller territorial context where there is a closed informational system which discourages mere impression management since "they have to keep their stories straight." Thus, by allowing for close proximity among those involved in socialization of the child, such as parents, teachers, storekeepers, youth officers, the parents of peers, etc., the defended neighborhood acts as "a container which helps keep together an informational network surrounding each child."

The physical proximity of peoples in some geographical location is not enough to define community. A degree of personal intimacy must also be present among the residents of the physical space. This aspect of community has generally been ignored by social scientists whose image of community has been colored by those characteristics amenable to quantitative analysis, e.g., income level, crime rate, or incidence of hospital admissions. Personal intimacy, however, is indicated through the existence of such relationships as friendship and marriage and such feelings as confidence, loyalty, and interpersonal trust. Much of the literature indicates that black communities are in fact seriously deficient in such feelings of intimacy, made evident in the lack of cooperative spirit, unity of purpose, or even stability and gratification in the basic social relationships of marriage and family life.

Despite the pointers to difficulties in black communities in regard to the development of personal intimacy, there are some countervailing forces which perhaps reduce the significance of the negative indicators. For example, there is an extremely small proportion of marriages in America among major racial groups in the United States. Only about 7 percent of marriages reported in the 1970 census were across racial lines. Of all such marriages, approximately one-fifth are black-white marriages. Kahn reports, on the 1970 census, there were 23,566 white husbands with black wives and 41,223 black husbands with white wives. An even more fascinating statistic considering the history of race relations in the United States is that half of these couples were living in the South; furthermore, although outside the South, three of five mixed marriages involved a black husband and a white wife, in the South the reverse held true, i.e., two-thirds of the mixed marriages involved a white husband and black wife.[35] Most importantly, however, the fact remains that 93 percent of marriages in the United States do *not* cross racial lines. Clearly then, marriage—the most ultimate of interpersonal relationships—involves for the most part "blacks only" in black communities.

Friendship bonds show almost the same ethnic exclusivity as does marriage. Lauman, in a sample drawn from a metropolitan area in which nearly one in five are black, found that among 3,000 friends reported, only two were black.[36] This might well indicate the reason why there is so little access of blacks or whites to the communities of the other. Even in integrated situations, the process whereby friendship usually develops among neighbors and co-workers is distorted and rarely successful: Murray writes:

> The minute a Negro moves into any integrated situation in the United States he becomes blacker than ever before. Ever so

friendly white suburbanites almost insist that their black neighbors identify themselves as part of black suffering every-where. White integrationists are far more likely to condemn and reject their clean-cut, professionally competent black neighbors for not being black enough than to congratulate them or simply accept them for not being problems. "Man," said one middle-aged black resident of Westchester County, a man who had spent his whole life working for better Negro education, job opportunities and civil rights, "you go to one of those parties and fail to show the proper enthusiasm for Malcolm, Rap and Cleaver and then some ofay millionaire and his wife will call you an Uncle Tom to your face. But damn man, the minute you sound off you realize that they have tricked you into scat dancing for them; because they are all crowding around, like watching you masturbate, like they are ready to clap their hands and yell, "Go man go, get hot man." But Goddamit, you know what they really want you to be? A blind man with a guitar! [37]

The insularity of intimate social relationships in black communities has proved a strength, as pointed out by Hill.[38] In families with no children under eighteen at home, black families are more likely than white families to take in young relatives. In husband-wife families, relatives under eighteen were taken in over four times as often by black families than white families. In families headed by black women, 41 percent took in relatives under eighteen as compared to only 7 percent of white women who were heads of households. It was among older women, however, that the greatest difference of all was observed—48 percent of black families headed by elderly women had relatives under eighteen living with them as compared to 10 percent of white elderly women who are also heads of households. This tremendous tendency to incorporate children into other than nuclear families is an expression of the power of kinship bonds in black communities which have served to mitigate the pernicious effects of the lack of child welfare services in these communities. This phenomenon, which could only be a consequence of intimate feelings in black communities, has helped therefore to document the existence of such feeling and therefore of community itself.

In the low-income neighborhoods which constitute the ghetto core, there is a special poignancy in the matter of personal intimacy and its significance. There is in fact clear recognition that the best of all possible worlds, people care about others, are helpful and can be depended on. On the other hand, the pressure to survive has meant that few can live up to this ideal and therefore you cannot trust anyone to do anything when it is not in their best interest to do so. This mistrust of others is not supposed to be generalized to one's relatives, friends, and neighbors. Yet as Rainwater has pointed out in this study of relationships in Pruitt-Igoe, in close relationships there are greater risks of exploitation; relatives are a greater danger than friends, and friends greater than neighbors or acquaintances, because the closer the person, the less likely you are to be on guard, even though you should know better.[39] What is often overlooked, however, is that trust is relative, and whereas it may appear that there is little hope that one's husband or brother-in-law or next-door neighbor can be depended on in a crisis there is certainly every indication that there is *even less* conviction that persons outside the community, particularly in its major institutions such as welfare or health care, will be more dependable. Coleman has pointed out that the presence of such interpersonal trust would "create an enormous asset . . . through the creation of community institutions that would provide a variety of services and aids that could partially compensate for the absence of individual economic resources."[40]

Territoriality and personal intimacy do not alone constitute community in the sense that has significance for helping practitioners. Families, for example, or peer groups could meet those criteria without constituting a community. Social cohesion is a necessary aspect of the structure and function of communities. The emphasis here is on interdependence of social roles performed by individuals. To the extent that major social roles are interdependent and occur within the boundaries of the black community, there can be a high level of social cohesion. In this instance, the requirement is that the major sources of gratifications will come through participation in community social organizations. The essence of social cohesion is present when family, friendship groups, occupational groups, religious organizations, and basic service systems (food, clothing, banking, insurance, mortuary, etc.) are all community-based and tied together in a relationship which is mutually reinforcing. Thus there is overlapping of members but, more importantly, there are normative behaviors which are enforced on a community-wide basis. In almost any community as defined by territorial characteristics, there are three kinds of relationships held by individuals: (1) neighbors who confine most of their activities to within the boundaries of the neighborhood but who do not participate to any extent in its major organizations; (2) community actors who are the primary forces in the operation of the social organizations of the community; and (3) isolates who are involved in neither the formal nor informal social units of the area.[41] Where there is high community cohesion there is congruence among neighbors and community actors and few isolates at all. On the other hand, when there is low social cohesion, there are many isolates, whereas neighbors and community actors are rarely congruent.

In a community which has high social cohesion there is a feeling of shared fate; i.e., that conditions or events that affect other community members will also affect one's self. This kind of feeling is most likely to occur in ethnic communities when there is a common history which provides positive images and is a source of high aspirations. One of the dramatic confrontations of the sixties was between black community groups and the public schools in this country which had ignored black culture and black history and in many instances denied black children access to that history, particularly in the urban North. The segregated schools of the South at least made it possible for its black teachers to transmit some of this history and culture to its children.

A socially cohesive community is also one in which there is a stratification system based on community-specific criteria

which is different from that of the larger society. This has been
a controversial issue in regard to black communities. Lieberson
reviewed a number of studies in which blacks and whites were
compared in regard to the status they ascribed to individuals in
a wide range of occupations. Despite application of extremely
sensitive statistical techniques, he was unable to find any significant differences between blacks and whites:

> The assertion that there is a community-wide prestige hierar-
> chy of occupations within the Negro community based on
> Negro experiences in occupations, just does not square with
> the facts. Instead, Negroes appear to be evaluating occupa-
> tions in the same world as everyone else evaluates them and
> to be employing essentially the same information and the
> same combination of criteria as everyone else. . . . The fail-
> ure of the Negro subculture to reflect the very different expe-
> rience of its members in this central aspect of living—earning
> a livelihood—can only be taken to indicate that we do not
> know enough about how subcultures work to employ them in
> explaining anything.[42]

Lieberson's rather embittered statement regarding the
weakness of the concept of subculture in predicting behavior
shows lack of consideration for the systems concept of macrodeterminacy. The whole (in this case, subculture) may at some
point be deterministic despite the fact that one of its component parts (occupational experience) is apparently not deterministic in ascribing occupational prestige.

Billingsley has offered an estimation of the social class structure in black communities based on some limited studies and
comprehensive census data on the education, income, and occupation of Negroes.[43] Thus, in the urban areas where 75 percent of black families live, approximately 10 percent would be
considered upper class, 40 percent middle class, and 50 percent lower class. However, the indices of social class are distinct from those used in the white community; for example,
upper-class blacks comprise families of physicians, educated
ministers of large congregations, and businessmen who would

be middle class on the basis of criteria used by whites. According to Billingsley, "it is difficult for any college graduate with any degree of visibility in the community to escape the attribution of status much higher than he could command in the white community." [44] Thus, Lieberson's study may, in fact, have indicated that perceptions of the relative prestige of occupations is no different when black and white communities are compared; however, this has not begun to get at the complex definition of social status. A black doctor may be rated higher in prestige than a black high school principal in the abstract, but when it comes to their participation in social organizations and the deference given them by lower-class persons, the *functional* social status may be indistinguishable.

There have been few attempts to develop culturally specific theoretical perspectives on social stratification in black communities and these are required before data can be collected which will contribute to theory-building. It is clear that, as Billingsley points out, "It [social class] is completely inadequate and inappropriate for describing behavior or values or preferences or styles of life or child rearing patterns in the Negro community." [45] The new theoretical perspectives needed will have to take into account some discernible regularities in the assignment of status in black communities. For example, status is often awarded on an individual basis as well as on the basis of family. For example, a single extended family may include individuals who are at every level in the class structure from upper class (e.g., a lawyer or wealthy businessman) to middle class (a postal employee) to working poor (a domestic worker) and finally to nonworking poor (an elderly welfare recipient). In addition, the new perspective must also include some measure of security. Thus, jobs that have high-sounding titles such as management specialist, project coordinator, or program analyst signifying substantial salaries but under the auspices of governmental agencies whose funding is often short-termed and quixotic would have a low security index. On the other hand, civil service jobs at lower salaries but likely to be dissolved only in case of a major depression would have a high security index. Finally, the significance of variables other than employment in the assignment of status should be measured; e.g., level of involvement in social or community organizations, involvement in organizations *outside* the black community as compared to internal organizational involvement, length of time in the community, etc.

In a socially cohesive community, there is also generally a community-specific system of communication through press, radio, and other media. Clark contends that in black communities, the press has reduced its power through its "rampant sensationalism which by its repetitiveness dulls the need to respond." He goes on to say:

> The Negro newspaper is a symbol of pseudocathartic power; it neither satisfies the deeper psychological needs of its readers nor does it assume responsibility for sustained fundamental change . . . many upper class Negroes take pride in announcing that they do not read the black press and they rely on the metropolitan or the white press which is basically unsatisfactory too since it underscores his own feelings of self-doubt by its own past tendency to ignore the Negro community.[46]

Yet, the significance of the press in the life of a community is profound. As one speaker at a convention of the Congress of African Peoples declared, "There is no community without communications." Yet, the black communities in America are faced with the anomaly of black-oriented media that are either supported very little by the masses or, if supported, are for the most part controlled by whites. For example, there are from 200 to 250 black newspapers in over 100 cities. Yet, their circulation is small and declining. In 1969, four of the major black publications—the New York *Amsterdam News,* the Pittsburgh *Courier,* the Chicago *Defender,* and the Norfolk *Journal* had a combined circulation of 194,078. Newspapers serving black communities are black-owned but they have been accused of being heavily influenced by white advertising which, though minimal, is in fact crucial. Therefore, the newspapers tend to be conservative and specialize in reporting violent crimes and social events rather than support causes which are unpopular in the white community. The problems of the black press have been exacerbated by the white press, which has lured away some of the best journalistic talent in an effort to demonstrate a token integration of the staff. Despite this "brain drain," only 1.9 percent of the staff of white newspapers is black.[47]

The situation is no better and sometimes far worse in the other communications media. Of the more than 7,000 radio stations licensed in this country, and about 360 which are programmed or oriented to the black community only nineteen are black-owned. Furthermore, of the black-oriented stations, nineteen are owned by white men who have become millionaires in what has been considered the exploitation of black listeners.[48] This point of view has been scathingly expressed by Imamu Amiri Baraka (LeRoi Jones).

> The environment of the so-called soul station is the new plantation. The 75% "soul music" 20% commercials program format of these stations is actually almost 95% (of that 95%) addicting to slavery as it is, and at its crudest. Spirit and products that enslave, that glorify slavery. And the remaining space given over to "news," which is actually just predigested "ripoff" (they're called that in the trade) slips from racist news services, little tidbits of so-called "community service" in reality distorted . . . all very decent rilly . . . type garbage with undertone of This is Yow Community Station . . . beeping on before and after the tidbit, so it's actually an ad for cracker some'gin. Healthy programming relating to the development (and as defense) of the Black Nation is minuscule.[49]

Goodlett suggests that, based on population, blacks should own 770 radio stations and 88 TV stations. In 1974, the number of black-owned radio stations had increased to 33—still far below the expected number based on population. There were still no black-owned TV stations.[50] So, regardless of the specific nature of the media, the situation is almost identical. There are black-oriented newspapers, radio stations, and TV programs; however, they are for the most part white-owned and the content is perceived as means by which blacks are controlled, i.e., kept involved in meaningless although gratifying entertainment and away from communication which could contribute to individual and group "uplift" as well as entertain.

Although there is considerable evidence that black communities exist at least in an ideological and even geographical sense, there still may be question as to whether or not they meet criteria utilized by ethnographers whose concern is the definition and mapping of ethnic boundaries. Levine has indicated that there are rigid doctrinaire ways in which ethnographers in the past have defined ethnic communities but the rigidity and the orthodoxy have decreased. Levine has therefore indicated five structural characteristics of ethnic relationships which *no longer* deny validity to the concept of black community.[51]

The first characteristic is termed *territorial interpenetration,* which refers to "the situation in which ethnic communities are interspersed as multiple enclaves in a region, so that it is not possible to draw a single continuous boundary that separates them but in which they maintain an ethnic ideology." This would certainly describe many black communities in the United States.

Another phenomenon is *continuous variation in cultural and linguistic characteristics,* which means in effect no boundaries at all, so that it is difficult to discern variations among adjacent groups in such characteristics as language, religious patterns, or family patterns.

A third phenomenon is *noncongruent variation,* which means that several characteristics do not vary together so that if one were to draw ethnic boundaries on the basis of the outer limits of each characteristic, different ethnic divisions would be produced and each would appear to have little real significance.

Thus, if the boundaries of a defined black community were drawn first according to black residents in census tracts, then according to proportion of registered voters who are black, or again, according to proportion of blacks in public schools, there would be three different pictures of where the boundaries of the communities were drawn, none of which would make too much sense.

A fourth phenomenon is *disagreement among residents of a geographical area about ethnic community boundaries or labels.* Now it is accepted that such disagreement does not preclude the existence of the community. There is considerable disagreement in Los Angeles as to where the boundaries of Watts lie—insurance companies have decided to set differential and therefore higher rates for fire and theft insurance in an area far exceeding the outermost perimeters of the "Watts riots." Yet, no one denies that there *is* a black community designated "Watts."

Finally, *ethnic identities may shift in these communities as individuals or groups decide to change their ethnic affiliations on the basis of their perceptions of some strategic advantage to be gained.* Thus, there may be times when individuals indicate a preference for another group and yet this factor will not negate the existence of community. Sharply defined boundaries, relatively unchanging, do not constitute a universal characteristic of community.

SUMMARY
This chapter has provided background data from the social sciences—particularly sociology and anthropology—in an effort to determine whether community as a concept has pragmatic value for understanding and eventually changing the negative valuation of black people.

The structure of black-white relationships as a basis for understanding the creation of black communities was explored. Assimilation, amalgamation, cultural pluralism, and internal colonialism were described as four models of this structure which have been proposed at various times in the social science literature. Yet, there is strong evidence that assimilation has not worked in the case of blacks; amalgamation and cultural pluralism have occurred to some extent but neither has helped to change basic social relationships or the distribution of power. Internal colonialism appears to be a dead-end concept, ignoring some basic contradictions in the society regarding the validity of the model in its entirety and leading to a single strategic goal—revolution. Thus, the concept of ethnosystem is introduced as a more useful model of the structure of black-white relationships for use in the helping professions.

The issue of the distinctiveness of culture in black communities was discussed from three perspectives: the view that black culture has its roots deep in the African heritage; the view that it is essentially American, even exaggeratedly so; and the third view that it is in fact distinctive with some small persistence of original African roots and a larger component derived from the impact of the American experience on the collective. Culture is part of the definition of ethnicity; and in a racist society, race transcends culture as a determinant of behavior. For example, membership in a racial group that is negatively valued will blind a racist observer to the member's cultural similarities to himself as well as to the positive aspects of the cultural difference. Cultural distinctiveness would be considered antagonistic to racial equality only in a racist society.

The criteria used to define community were discussed, particularly in regard to the extent that these criteria are met in communities also defined as black. These characteristics include territorial boundaries, personal intimacy, and social cohesion. In regard to each of these characteristics, there is evidence that supports the notion that these criteria have been met in black communities.

Finally, the ethnographic criteria which tend to be more rigorous than sociological criteria in general were reviewed. Levine has suggested that ethnographic criteria formerly adhered

to have been dropped by many ethnographers so that characteristics which would have denied community definition to
some areas no longer do so; e.g., territorial interpenetration,
continuous variation in cultural and linguistic characteristics,
different boundaries depending upon the dimensions observed, disagreement among residents regarding boundaries
or labels, and shifting ethnic identities. Since all of these can
be considered more or less characteristic of black communities, this further supports the acceptance of black communities
as legitimate social units for analysis utilizing community-level
concepts. Furthermore, the particular structure and dynamics
of black communities appear to have high relevance for those
interested in solving problems characteristically encountered
in them.

experiential exercises

1.
Interview five residents of a predominantly black community
within an urban area in order to determine the *five* most important physical landmarks which *for them* symbolizes their urban
area; e.g. you may ask the question, "What five buildings or
street corners or locations represent this city to you? If you
were far away from here and wanted a picture of this city in
your mind, what physical landmarks would you remember?"
Now, interview five residents of a predominantly white community within the same urban area and repeat the question.

(a) To what extent are their responses similar or different?

(b) On the basis of the two sets of responses, to what extent
do their significant environments overlap?

2.

Select five black persons whom you would define as "middle class" and who live in a predominantly black neighborhood. Discuss with them their reasons for living in their neighborhood as well as the consequences they would anticipate if they were to move into a predominantly white neighborhood. Now select five white persons whom you would also define as "middle class" and who live in a predominantly white neighborhood. Discuss with them their reasons for living in their neighborhood as well as the consequences they would anticipate if they were to move to a predominantly black neighborhood.

(a) To what extent are their responses similar or different?

(b) On the basis of the two sets of responses how would you assess the likelihood of extensive residential desegregation in the near future?

3.

Select five black and five white individuals who attend your school, work in your organization, etc. Interview each regarding both the most recent party they attended and the most recent party they hosted in their home. In each instance determine (a) the number attending; (b) the proportion black vs. non-black; (3) the type of food, drink and activities engaged in; (d) the proportion attending who lived within a one-mile radius of where the party was held.

(a) To what extent were the parties of whites and blacks similar or different?

(b) On the basis of the responses, to what extent would you assess the level of interracial social contact in your community?

chapter three

the helping professions in black communities: the sociohistorical perspective

A directory of black social agencies and "grassroots" agencies in the Los Angeles area was compiled for the first time in 1972 by the Los Angeles chapter of the Association of Black Social Workers. The goal of the directory was "increasing the awareness of the organizations available to provide human services in the black population, expanding the options of social service workers in making adequate referrals for their clientele, and pointing out by absence the gaps in community resources in the black community." [1] Despite the fact that the directory did not include *all* agencies, those included and those omitted by intent provide a good indication not only of the range of service organizations and their auspices in that community but also the definition of a "community resource" as perceived by black social workers. It is also particularly important since the publications of the National Association of Black Social Workers attest to the considerable variance in the perceptions of black social workers and the perceptions of white social workers regarding the effectiveness and ultimate value of social work as practiced in black communities.

A total of 157 agencies were included in the directory of the Los Angeles ABSW. Six were agencies providing legal services, 26 provided educational services, 9 provided employment services, 25 were health agencies, 53 were community action agencies, 21 were social service agencies, 14 were recreation and cultural agencies, and three provided housing services.[2] Not included in this group were some traditional agencies providing services to the total Los Angeles community but which were not perceived as "community agencies"; e.g., the Los Angeles County Department of Public Social Services as well as some private agencies such as Family Service of Los Angeles, Salvation Army Family Social Service Center, the YWCA, and the Welfare Planning Council of United Way.

Although these agencies represent a sizable commitment of energies and funds directed toward characteristic problems encountered in black communities, relatively few (41 percent) were fully supported by local funding. Furthermore, the heavy dependence on federal funding for continued existence has meant that many of these resources are highly vulnerable and must operate on the basis of extremely short time projections.[3] The negative impact on the quality of services that can be provided under these conditions can only be speculated upon here, but the probability is that it is high. One of the agencies included was The Brotherhood Crusade, which is the counterpart of United Way and makes an intensive effort to obtain funds for agencies providing services in the Los Angeles black communities with community support but which do not meet the criteria for funding by United Way.

The directory, in some respects, can be considered the tip of the iceberg in regard to the total level of social programming in black communities in Los Angeles. For example, the Family Service Association of Los Angeles was not included; however, a nationwide survey of member agencies of the Family Service Association of America conducted in 1970 indicated that approximately one-fifth of all agency clients in metropolitan areas in which blacks are concentrated are black.[4] Also, the directory was primarily concerned with social agencies whereas churches and voluntary associations in black communities have historically been a source of help to those for whom the established help systems have been inaccessible or in some way perceived as undesirable.

It should be pointed out that most of the agencies included involved a variety of professional, paraprofessional, and volunteer staff. The professional disciplines included not only social work but psychology, psychiatry, vocational rehabilitation, educational specialists, nursing, and others. No one can argue that either the human effort or the material resources provided in these and other programs are commensurate with the deepseated problems encountered in black communities; however, more is not always better, and the injection of more programs, more professionals, more volunteers will not insure effective service without some basic commitment of the society to solve the problems and some demonstrated expertise available to be used in the problem-solving effort. The professions are supposedly society's mechanism whereby its commitment is expressed and expertise is made available for use by those who need it.

The remainder of this chapter will consider the historical development of those helping professions most deeply responsible for assisting individuals, groups, and communities in solving their problems of living. Of particular interest will be the extent to which these professions themselves have contributed to the negative valuation of blacks in the past; to what extent these negative valuations continue in the present; and the implications of the increased number of blacks joining the professional ranks for effecting changes in the orientation of the professions to the delivery of services in black communities.

SOCIAL WORK AND SOCIAL WELFARE

The social welfare field encompasses the broad spectrum of activities which aim to improve the human condition through implementation of policies in a wide variety of social institutions. The rise of a complex, urbanized society created the need for institutionalized measures of facilitating social adjustment and for intervention in areas of social dysfunction. Although efforts to enhance the relationship between man and his environment are within the sphere of many professions, the dominant profession within the social welfare field is social work. While professional social work may be regarded as a product of the twentieth century, its antecedents—charity, poor relief, philanthropy, social reform—appear early in American history. These early efforts to deal with the poor and infirm were infused with heavy doses of moralistic judgment and evangelism which served to separate help seekers into two categories: the worthy and the unworthy. Blacks—slave or free— were rarely deemed worthy.

Prior to the Civil War, it was expected that slaves would be cared for by the slave-owners. Those Negro slaves who were freed or who became fugitives often found conditions in society so difficult to endure that some voluntarily re-entered slavery. These conditions were exacerbated by the fact that economic opportunities for Negroes were restricted and they were excluded from welfare services in many areas. The only relief available for the Negro poor in most areas was that provided through taxes on the meager resources of free Negroes. Rabinowitz has reviewed the status of health and welfare services for Negroes in the South in the twenty-five years immediately following the Civil War and finds that during this period, in all but rare instances, Negroes were excluded from poorhouses, orphanages, hospitals, or state facilities such as insane asylums and institutions for the blind, deaf, and dumb.[5] By the turn of the century, a coalition of Northerners as represented by the Freedman's Bureau, the United States Army, and radical politicians along with concerned Southerners, was successful in initiating the development of segregated health and welfare service delivery system. Thus, the shift was made from exclusion to separate but unequal treatment.

It is generally agreed that social work as a profession received its initial impetus in the Charity Organization Society movement which came to the United States from England in the last quarter of the nineteenth century. The COS, through local bodies, aimed to organize the relief-giving resources of the community in order to meet the needs of those who were without means or those who possessed meager resources of their own. A history of the COS movement in the United States reveals that family rehabilitation services—a major thrust of the organization—were provided almost entirely to white families.[6] It was the general feeling among COS staff members that it was wiser to concentrate on the problems of poverty among the whites, leaving problems among the colored for the future. It was pointed out, however, that the COS in Memphis operated a Negro auxiliary known as the Colored Federated Charities, which had a Negro board of directors and operated with its own committees and workers. It also ran its own fund-raising drive which met approximately 25 percent of the operating costs of the Negro department's operations. This is only one instance of many self-help efforts of Negroes during this period, often ignored in the social welfare histories written by white scholars.

It may be questioned at this point whether the delivery of social welfare services was influenced by any theoretical frame of reference other than a purely moralistic one. Goldstein suggests that the notion of causality was pervasive in social work practice at its beginnings.[7] Thus, it was assumed that if adequate knowledge could be obtained about the individual, some form of action would logically follow. However, the action was simplistically determined: if a problem was caused by lack of employment, then work was needed; if the problem was illness or disability, then medical help was required. Thus professional activity was directed toward the collection of "facts" in order to establish a cause-cure relationship. This dependence on simplistic causal relationships to determine the nature of services needed placed blacks at a distinct disadvantage. In fact, the ascendancy of Social Darwinism in the sociology of the period and its message that some groups were genetically superior to others provided sufficient "cause" for practitioners to choose to provide services to those persons with greater social potential.

Social work as a profession changed dramatically in regard to its theoretical base for practice immediately following World War I. As a result of exposure to psychiatry and the new Freudian psychology in army neuropsychiatric hospitals during the war, social workers began to look more and more for psychological causes in the etiology of personal and social dysfunction. This new emphasis led to the diminished concern with social, situational, or interpersonal factors in problem-solving and greater concern with intrapsychic processes and the development of insight. Unfortunately for blacks, this new emphasis held little more promise of help with their problems than had the former one. In fact, the profession was experiencing a new clientele—the voluntary client from the more affluent middle class whose problems were not economic but expressed in the new terminology of the mental hygiene movement. The social worker who embraced the Freudian model was no longer a provider of concrete services but a catalytic agent who helped marshal the individual's intrapsychic processes to increase insight and thereby increase capacity for problem-solving. Again, blacks were rarely perceived as amenable to treatment since in most instances the problems of survival transcended all others and the social work profession was ill-equipped to handle so massive a need.

The Great Depression and the economic stress it visited upon the nation pushed many social workers out of the role of therapist and back into the business of dispensing relief. Poverty was suddenly within the experience of persons who had never before had to pinch pennies or worry about tomorrow's bread. Yet despite the prevalence of economic and social stress at all levels in the society, Negroes continued to be the most disadvantaged group. Although Negro organizations were occasionally successful in securing amelioration from the most flagrant discrimination, they were not able to force the Roosevelt administration to make sure than an equitable portion of government benefits would actually reach the masses of black farmers and workers. While Negro leaders appealed for equity and justice, their requests were seldom granted because almost invariably they conflicted with better-organized white interests. For example, Negro efforts to remove certain onerous sections of the National Labor Relations (Wagner) Act failed, so that the act not only did not outlaw racial discrimination by unions but legalized the "closed shop," which effectively supported the stranglehold lily-white organized labor held on the American labor market. Government officials candidly admitted that the claims of better-organized, more powerful white interests had rendered these appeals ineffectual. Almost the only New Deal programs which benefited large numbers of blacks were the federal work relief programs and the public assistance programs. Yet, the disparity between rhetoric and reality could not help but disgust many persons in the social welfare field who had any degree of social consciousness, because of the depth of the racism and the critical need for social reform.[8]

World War II seemed to solve, at least for a while, the deep economic ills of the nation, but it also increased the tempo of protest among blacks themselves as opportunity systems which had been opened up by the war brought a heightened awareness of relative deprivation. Myrdal, Kardiner and Ovesey, and other behavioral scientists made it clear that any Negro, regardless of the presenting problem he might bring to an agency, had heavy intrapsychic conflicts as a result of racist oppression.[9] The only way to deal with these products of oppression would be to remove the oppression. This inevitably led to an overriding pessimism about dealing with the emotional problems of black people. If you cannot remove the oppression, what can you do? The response most often made was, "Nothing." This attitude persisted—despite tremendous social change, including more complex, more differentiated, more positive responses to oppression than Myrdal or his adherents had ever imagined.

A dramatic example of the prevailing pessimism among social workers about dealing with other than concrete needs of black clients was demonstrated in an intensive case study of a family agency in southern California.[10] The black population served was not in the lower end of the socioeconomic scale, yet the agency was underused by this population. In fact, throughout the 1950s there was a decline in the level of utilization. Most importantly, case records revealed that psychological problems presented by black clients were often overlooked, referrals were made for public assistance with little attempt to deal with other emotional problems, and even a parent's comment that her son had "bitten a neighbor child's penis" was given little attention. In a sense then, black clients have been caught up in a Catch-22 situation; when the profession embraced psychological conflict as paramount in problem-solving activity, blacks were deemed poor candidates for therapy because of the concrete nature of their problems, their inability to articulate emotional content, or their unwillingness to "open" in a therapeutic encounter with a white therapist. On the other hand, when attempts were being made to balance professional activity with concern for social, economic, and political factors in the etiology of problems, the deep-seated racism in society was perceived as a social reality so intransigent that any attempt to deal with social or emotional problems of blacks was doomed to failure. At the same time that social work practitioners and educators were insisting on the need to deal with racism in the larger society, they showed little awareness of its presence in their own ranks; this led to an editorial in the March 1964 issue of Social Casework in which the failure of the profession to address the issue squarely was implied:

> The relative dearth of literature on the racial factor in case-
> work treatment . . . and the conspicuous absence of re-
> search on the subject suggest that repressive psychological
> mechanisms may be at work. Perhaps it is difficult for a pro-
> fession committed to humanistic tenets to engage in honest
> appraisal of possible disparities between its ideals and its ac-
> complishments."

Efforts toward the "honest appraisal" called for in this editorial were not long in forthcoming and more and more practitioners, educators, and community people identified the short-
comings of the social work profession in meeting its avowed
aims in regard to black clients and black communities. The
deluge of words sometimes obscured a common intonation; a
sharp accusatory tone which pointed to social work's professed commitment to alleviate the suffering of those who have
been battered by operations of "the system," while the system
itself was left unchanged and unchallenged. In the words of
one writer, "The basic challenge that the new thrust by black
people presents to social work, then, is to reconstitute its assumptions and modify its technology so as to be more realistic
about the dynamics of power and their relationship to the
needs of the black community." [11] More specifically, critics as-
sailed the tendency within the profession to define problem situations—whether involving crime, drug addiction, or neighborhood deterioration—in terms of psychosocial dysfunction of
individuals involved. Since the sources of many of these problems lie in the racist operations of major social institutions, the
demand was made that change strategies be directed at these
institutions and not at the victims. In fact, the traditional therapist types within the bureaucratic systems of public and private
agencies were declared to be "dirty-workers" assisting individuals in their adjustment to negative social conditions.

Under the pressure of this kind of criticism, the social work
profession has responded with some efforts to change; e.g.,
new content and new courses on racism and minority group

experiences; workshops, colloquia, and seminars for agency personnel to "sensitize" staff to minority life styles and value systems; and increased efforts to recruit black and other minority students into graduate schools of social work. A new kind of pressure was also being felt, however, from new professional disciplines which professed greater knowledge and skills relating to system change than that provided in social work education. These urban specialists are being trained in new university departments of urban planning, urban affairs, or urban development. Some schools of social work have countered with subspecializations of urban planning or social planning within their own programs. The theoretical framework rationalizing the activities of these new professionals has been constructed, for the most part, from systems theory elaborated with concepts from political science, law, organizational psychology, and even computer technology or systems engineering. In essence, the aim is to step out of traditional professional molds and to create a new model of a professional who is skilled in changing complex social systems in order to enhance the quality of life for the maximum number of urban residents. In order to develop the skills, this new kind of professional will be required to master a wide variety of conceptual systems and therefore must step out of the comforting limitations and illusory boundaries of traditional academic and professional disciplines. Yet, these urban specialists have already been criticized for what some call a mechanistic approach to problem solving, as they have placed heavy emphasis upon statistics, computerized information systems, and other techniques for quantifying the urban condition. At the same time, these professionals who are hired into the municipal, state, and federal planning agencies find themselves under the same constraints experienced by social workers in welfare, probation, or public school systems: the power to restructure society is at another level somewhere out of reach.

Another development in the social welfare field which is somewhat antithetical to the development of urban specialists is the development of the paraprofessional, indigenous worker, case aide, or social technician who does not have the professional "credential" but who has been given increasing responsibility in the delivery of services, particularly in minority communities. This movement has perhaps been provided with theoretical justification in the tradition of humanistic psychology. Whether labeled Rogerian, existentionalist, gestalt, etc., the central core of the psychology is a concern with relationship. The relationship is in fact the significant factor which permits one person to influence another to change. There is still the emphasis on the individual as the target of change efforts, but it is now suggested that traditional professionals may not always be the best agent of change; in fact, those persons who have experienced the same problem—the alcoholic, the ex-addict, the former mental patient, the ex-convict—should be able to extend aid effectively to those currently experiencing the problem. In like manner, a person who shares with another a particular social environment is more likely to be able to understand the significance and the impact of that environment in a problem situation than an outsider.

Goodman indicates that the inclusion of these nonprofessional workers in the delivery of health and welfare services has made it possible for blacks and other minority group members to utilize untapped talents in interpersonal helping.[12] There has been an increase in the use of persons from ethnic communities who are not trained professionals but whose life experiences and personal attributes qualify them to deliver a wide variety of services. However, this development also has been criticized by people who insist that these nonprofessionals have become the poor men's therapists; i.e., under the guise of more relevant service delivery, an inferior untrained brand of human service worker is being foisted onto poor and minority communities. Other criticisms relate to the major contribution the new careerists were supposed to make to the organizations in which they were incorporated; i.e., their utilization would improve the quality of service, as they would become bridges from the agency to clients in the community who would not ordinarily come for services. However, recent research indicates that the bridging concept is not a realistic expectation for paraprofessional workers who tend very quickly to identify with the agency, to aspire to higher positions, and to define their role in terms other than bridging the communication gap between agency and client.[13]

Social work has carved out a vast array of problem situations as targets for its armamentarium of skills. It operates in a variety of subsystems including health and medical care, law and justice, education, income maintenance, and family welfare. Its practitioners must relate to a host of other professional, quasi professional, and nonprofessional persons including physicians, lawyers, nurses, teachers, urban planners, occupational therapists, new careerists, and politicians. The fact that social work is practiced almost entirely within institutional structures—part and parcel of the system which blacks have defined as racist and oppressive—sharply defines the issues which swirl around in any dialogue pertaining to social work practice in black communities. It is one thing to recognize the liberating force that the black community's control of the institutions within it would constitute for its residents; it is quite another to give up the power and the security that one's professional status derives. The rationalization is that the liberal white or the "qualified" white is an asset to the black community and should be accepted. It is one thing to define the current public welfare system as punitive, unwieldy, and an abysmal failure; it is another to refuse to work in such a system because it violates one's professional ethics. The increased numbers of helping professionals who are themselves black and who are acutely aware of the lack of congruence between avowed professional ideology and actual professional practice has led to the creation of professional caucuses; e.g., the Association of Black Social Workers. The primary goal of ABSW and similar organizations is to translate into actuality the humanistic rhetoric that has characterized most of the pronouncements of the helping professions.

PSYCHIATRY AND PSYCHOLOGY

If racism is construed to include not only instances of overt prejudice and discrimination but also neglect and lack of concern, then racism in the history of the mental health movement in this country is undeniable. The conspicuous absence of even passing reference to blacks as patients in the psychiatric literature is only one example of this early form of benign neglect. It would appear that the psychiatrist or psychologist interested in human behavior would have been almost consumed with curiosity regarding the consequences of the "peculiar institution" of slavery on the individual and group psyche. Moreover, it should have been of great interest to determine the kind of strategies used by the slave to cope with the demands of a changed social reality once the formal structure of slavery had been dissolved. Unfortunately, what little evidence is available would lead to the conclusion that such interest among the early mental health professionals was absent or of little consequence.

Benjamin Rush, who has been called the father of the mental health movement in the United States, wrote an antislavery pamphlet in 1773 at the age of twenty-eight in which he took a position radical for his time, which was that the only difference between blacks and whites was the color of their skins.[14] However, Rush's rationale for this position was his belief that the black complexion was a legacy to blacks from a time in the early evolution of the human race when a great leprous-type disease swept across Africa. Thus the problems of interracial conflict and the devastating effects of this conflict on the psyche of both blacks and whites could best be solved by a medical "cure" for the aftereffects of the disease which would return the skin to its original white state and in so doing erase the primary cause of interracial hostility. Szasz has censured Rush for this blatant racist notion that "white" is the only healthy skin color and thereby justifying segregation for reasons of ill health rather than racial inferiority.[15] However, Rush's ideas must be evaluated within the historical context and his total philosophical stance. He was an articulate opponent of slavery, and considering the fact that his ideas about the origin of the skin color of blacks were expressed at a time when others were defining blacks as scarcely human, he should be accorded a modicum of respect for a humanism advanced for his time.

In 1840 an attempt was made to count the number of mentally disturbed persons in the United States as part of the national census of that year. Although a number of Northern communities were found to have no "colored" residents, for some strange reason the same towns were reported to have colored insane:

> In Maine, the town of Limerick is stated to have no colored persons but four colored lunatics. Scarboro had no colored people but six colored lunatics. In Massachusetts, Freetown, Leominster, Wilmington, Sterling, and Denvers are all stated to have no colored persons of any age or sex, yet each is stated to have two colored insane.[16]

Perhaps the most unfortunate consequence of these obviously distorted statistics was the basis it gave essentially racist politicians and other policymakers for declaring slavery to be a benign institution. Since these statistics showed a much higher incidence of insanity among Negroes in the North than in the South the conclusion was that slavery was actually a beneficent bulwark against the strains and responsibilities which all too often drove free blacks crazy. Only a little less serious was the conclusion of Boudin, author of a work on medical and geographical statistics, after he noted that the insanity rate of Negroes according to this 1840 census was 1 to 4,310 in Louisiana, 1 to 1,309 in Virginia, 1 to 257 in Pennsylvania, 1 to 44 in Massachusetts, and 1 to 14 in Maine, then it must be true that "cold vitiates the mental health of the Negro." [17]

Even the redoubtable Dorothea Dix (1802–1887), waving her banner of protest against inhuman conditions and treatment of the mentally ill, was taken in by the defective evidence as she proclaimed to the Senate in 1848, "those tracts of North America inhabited by Indians and the sections inhabited chiefly by the Negro race produce comparatively very few examples of insanity." [18] Again, the apparent infrequency of mental illness among blacks in the South where they were in some places in the majority, according to census data, might lead one to that conclusion. This rosy view of the mental health of blacks was due largely to a lack of awareness that, first of all, the slaves who were permitted to survive were in fact those that had "adjusted" to the often cruel demands of a slaveholding society. The numbers of those who could not adjust were at the same time perhaps kept low by virtue of maternal decision and/or slave-owner life-and-death prerogatives.

The myth of the institution of slavery as a benign institution persisted and was strengthened by the great increase in the number of Negro patients admitted to state mental hospitals after the Civil War. It appeared that, having been wrenched from a hard but dependable social system, the now free blacks were unable to cope with their freedom. O'Malley, writing in the *Journal of Insanity* in 1914, indicated that while the Negro population had increased 111 percent during the period from 1860 to 1910, the number of insane Negroes had increased 1,670 percent.[19] Although these statistics appear overwhelming at first glance it should be immediately stated that they are of little value since mentally ill Southern Negroes were not included in the official census of 1860.

In an address before the National Council of Charities in 1908, Dr. William Drewry of the VA State Hospital for the Insane in Petersburg, an institution exclusively for the care of Negro patients, attempted to set forth the reasons for the great increase in psychosis among the group.[20] Although he granted that there doubtless was some mental illness among the slave population before the Civil War, his main theme was that emancipation was largely the cause of the current problem. Drewry painted an idyllic picture of the Negro on the plantation—contented, well-fed and comfortably clothed, living an open-air life with wholesome employment and cared for by his master when ill—all measures preventive to mental breakdown. Emancipation, he thought, had left the blacks unprepared to care for themselves and they became victims of their own animal appetites; they had acquired habits of indolence and promiscuity, and the use of whiskey and cocaine and other drugs had contributed to their general deterioration.

Later, Dr. E. M. Green, clinical director of the Georgia State sanitarium at Milledgeville, published a paper on the same subject—the social and emotional functioning of blacks since emancipation. His analysis of the causes of the proportionately higher admission rate of Negroes to whites in that hospital since 1900 was based on a comparative study of a sizable group of patients.[21] However, more disturbed Negroes than whites had later been diagnosed as suffering from pellagra. This nutritional disease was widespread in the South and more Negroes than whites were afflicted, due to greater dietary deficiencies. Untreated pellagra results in severe emotional disturbance which can be labeled insanity. Previous studies had overlooked the extent of the relationship between physical and emotional conditions and as a result tended to give credence to the hypothesis that increased emotional disturbances among freed Negroes were a direct consequence of losing the supportive system of slavery. With Green's study, it appeared more likely that the increase was due to the totally unsupportive system subsequent to emancipation which provided almost no opportunity for healthy survival.

The question of the existence of racial disparity in admission rates to psychiatric hospitals remains and if anything is as prevalent as ever. In 1957, Wilson and Lantz published a paper on the subject which caused heated controversy.[22] They contended that there had been a tremendous increase in the non-white admission rate in the preceding forty years and attempted to interpret this increase in terms of "the uncertainties of the Negro race as they cross from one culture to another." The paper went on to state that "cultural changes which are forced on people against their will by fiat or by authority from outside or above, have been found by the experts of the United Nations to produce major disturbances of mental health." The authors invoked the solid erudition of Margaret Mead, who had warned that change must be made slowly and that in the recent past little had been done to protect the Negro or the white man as changes in their relationships have been brought about. According to their view, as lower-class black and white populations live under adverse economic and social conditions and are most vulnerable to the emotional stress precipitated by the push for racial integration, they are simply in no position to maintain, care for, and tolerate a disturbed individual. Such individuals are consequently institutionalized. Furthermore, since more blacks than whites are at the lower end of the socioeconomic scale, they are proportionately overrepresented in hospital admissions statistics.

Sixteen years after Wilson and Lantz presented and interpreted their data regarding differential hospital admission rates for blacks and whites, Kramer, Rosen, and Willis completed an in-depth analysis of the prevalence of mental disorders in the United States and utilization patterns of psychiatric facilities by race.[23] The trend in increased utilization of such facilities which had been noted by Wilson and Lantz was also noted in their analysis; in fact, if admission rates by race observed in 1969 prevail, it was estimated that between 1970 and 1985 there would be a 45 percent increase in non-white admissions so that they would closely approximate the non-white proportion in the general population. In contrast to the simplistic explanation for the increase given by Wilson and Lantz, these authors present alternative explanations; e.g., discriminatory practices may result in the admission of a disproportionate number of blacks as compared with whites to a mental institution; racist attitudes may affect the consistency with which clinicians apply diagnostic criteria in determining the presence or absence of mental disorder in cases of minority persons; whites may have easier access to more effective treatment methods so that prevalence rates can be lower for whites than for blacks. At the same time, there is clearly a need for intensive research to acquire the data needed to assess the extent of emotional dysfunction among blacks, to determine the role of genetic as well as social factors in the etiology of mental illness, to establish the manner in which racism affects the incidence of such dysfunction, and to establish base lines against which to measure change. It is pointed out that the major stumbling blocks to the implementation of such research is the lack of distinct and generally accepted diagnostic categories which can be applied uniformly and reliably to various population groups. This lack, however, is directly related to the problems of a coherent theoretical base for practice.

As was pointed out in the previous section, the end of the nineteenth century witnessed the incursion of Freudian psychoanalysis in the practice of psychiatry, psychology, and social work in the United States. It is interesting to note that Freud in his original writings did not advance ideas of racial superiority. However, when transplanted into the American context with its history of racism, Freud's followers were able to penetrate the wall of scientific objectivity with their own racist biases. The first volume of Psychoanalytic Review, published in the United States in 1913, contained an article by Lind, a physician at the Government Hospital for the insane in Washington, D.C., "The Dream as a Simple Wish-Fulfillment in the Negro." Lind reported a study which aimed to test Freud's theory that children's dreams are simpler than those of adults because their psychic activities are less complex. Lind studied a sample of one hundred blacks on the premise that blacks represented the childhood stages of human development and therefore their dreams should be simple wish-fulfillment without the distorting effects of psychic censorship; for example, a twenty-five-year-old laborer in jail recounted his dream that he was free, and to Lind this frank expression of wish-fulfillment was prima facie evidence of a primitive type of mind.

The conception of blacks as primordial, elemental, even subrational when compared to whites was of course racism at its worst. However, the irony of using dream interpretation to demonstrate it was unfortunate. In 1935 Stewart was first encountering the isolated jungle tribe of the Malay peninsula known as the Senoi. The average Senoi adult is involved in dream interpretation as a regular feature of education and daily social intercourse. Through the medium of dream interpretation, the Senoi child is involved early in a meaningful and constructive problem-solving process which becomes the deepest type of creative thought. According to Stewart:

> In the West, the thinking we do while asleep usually remains on a *muddled, childish or psychotic level* [emphasis added] because we do not respond to dreams as socially important and include dreaming in the educative process. This social neglect of that side of man's reflective thinking, when the creative process is most free, seems poor education.[24]

Lind's interpretations of black dreams give ample evidence of his noncreative, elementary approach to dream research. In fact, the highly rational character of the dreams reported by Lind's black respondents could well have been an indication that blacks had moved more closely in the direction of the Senoi objective, i.e., "when the dream life becomes less and less fantastic and irrational and more and more reflective thinking and problem solving . . ."

In any event, the intense preoccuptaion of psychiatry with Freudian analysis and with intrapsychic rather than interpersonal events did not exactly support increased services to blacks, not only because of the distorted derivations of psychoanalytic theory which stigmatize blacks as infantile but also because of the survival problems which precluded their participation in extented encounters and interminable forays into the past. On the other hand, the psychodynamic principles which have been incorporated even into the theoretical systems of Freud's severest critics represent a lasting contribution to the science of human behavior and are constantly being used to explain behavior of all Western peoples, including blacks. Erikson recalled Freud's consciousness of inner identity and related the psychoanalytically derived concept of identity to the issue of race relations.[25] Pinderhughes has discussed the similarities between the fundamental psychoanalytic concept of repression as a psychological phenomenon and the repression of racism as a social phenomenon.[26] Kovel, Dollard and Miller, and Comer have defined racism in psychoanalytic terms. Thus racism is described as "a low-level defense mechanism," "displaced aggression," or "rooted in infantile instinctual forces." [27]

It should be noted that there are strong reactions against psychoanalytic interpretations of behavior among blacks or of black-white relations. For example, Thomas and Sillen have protested the heavy emphasis placed on psychogenetic explanations of racism and a concomitant lack of attention given to its profound social dimensions.[28] Although psychological consequences may reinforce the social institutions of racism, significant changes will not occur unless the social institutions are attacked; i.e., the elimination of inequalities of civil rights, education, and job opportunity. Jones and Jones have warned of the dangers of applying Freudian concepts which evolved out of his Viennese experience to twentieth-century black communities in the United States.[29] An example is the Freudian concept of penis-envy; described as the woman's subconscious, and sometimes conscious, feeling that she has been castrated as an infant and thus deprived of the rights and privileges that are enjoyed by sexually complete fathers and brothers. This may have been a valid deduction in nineteenth-century Vienna, which was a patriarchal society where the father is the absolute authority and the lowliest brother takes precedence over all sisters. However, it is a mistake to transfer this notion to black low-income communities where the male role is much less enviable.

Given the limitations of psychoanalytic theory placed within the context of contemporary black experience in the United States, it is not surprising that there are few black patients who seek psychoanalysis and few black psychoanalysts. Hugh Butts, one of the few, has proposed that the ideal situation would be white patients treated by black psychiatrists and black patients treated by white psychiatrists. In this kind of "ethnotherapy," there is the best opportunity to uncover racist attitudes which can serve as catalysts to speed up the treatment process. Furthermore, he states:

> Since racist projections are so rampant in this country, I would submit that questions about racial attitudes ought to be raised and worked through directly by the knowledgeable therapist—even in those situations in which both therapist and patient are white and in which racial issues are not obvious elements of presenting psychopathology.[30]

Certainly, there will be vast differences in what content can be explored in the therapeutic encounter based upon the structure of the encounter. The long and to some interminable span of time required for psychoanalysis has meant that it is more likely to be utilized by educated, articulate, introspective and affluent individuals. However, the number of psychiatrists who are also analysts is a small proportion of all practicing psychiatrists. A large number of psychiatrists utilize approaches based on behaviorist psychology. The basic research on learning and conditioning upon which behavioral methods are based began with the work of Thorndike and Pavlov at the beginning of this century. In contrast to the highly subjective nature of goal-setting and the evaluation of change in psychodynamic therapy, behavioral approaches—which may be termed behavior modification, operant conditioning, desensitization—emphasize specific target behaviors which can be observed and measured. Therefore, "observation is favored over introspection, measurement over imprecise reckoning, firsthand empirical knowledge over speculation, theory, and single-organism research design over uncontrolled case studies or cross-sectional studies of aggregates of subjects." [31]

Behavioral approaches to problem-solving have steadily gained adherents in the past decade, particularly among clinical psychologists. However, its critics have argued that it opens up the possibility of authoritarian control over vulnerable populations; e.g., inmates of correctional institutions who tend to be disproportionately black. Bandura, one of the leading theoreticians of behavior therapy, discounts the validity of this criticism:

> There seems to be a feeling that these techniques can be used for authoritarian control without the knowledge of the subject. There is a common belief that by manipulating the consequences, behavior can be changed dramatically and deviously. There is a lot of evidence that change doesn't occur unless the subject understands what is being reinforced. . . . When the person whose behavior is being modified elects for the technique, I think the issue of control is a pseudoissue. [32]

Bandura does not deny that electric shock, prison abuses, psychosurgery, and "all other sorts of horrors" exist but staunchly disengages such activities from the traditional behavioral approaches to solving-problem behavior.

Hayes has delivered perhaps the most powerful statement of support for behaviorism as a theoretical framework for problem-solving in black communities. Hayes castigates the psychodynamic literature which attempts to explain psychological phenomena—including black behavior—by resorting to hypothetical mental structures, presumed needs, attitudes, and other products of a conceptualization process which is often biased. The alternative as perceived by Hayes is "Radical Black

Behaviorism." The basic principle of Radical Black Behaviorism is that behavior is determined by its consequences. Because consequences are observable, this emphasis is more objective and therefore more scientific than the emphasis on speculative causes:

> Clearly, black people have been the victims of explanations whose major focus was on cause rather than on consequence. Blacks have higher absenteeism rates in industry *because* they are lazy and unmotivated; blacks do not perform well on achievement tests *because* they are intellectually inferior. Seldom are the differences behavior related to different rates of performance between blacks and whites in work and academic settings. Radical Black Behaviorism rejects the specification of previous life events as causing behavior as unscientific and harmful to the well being of black people.[33]

Hayes, in his acceptance of consequences as the only regulator of behavior, expresses the radical environmentalism of Skinner, perhaps the greatest contemporary theoretician of behavior therapy. However, it can be argued that although human beings are controlled by contingencies, often these contingencies *are* of their own making. For example, a white landlord who rents to blacks and then decides to sell because "they didn't take care of the property" may have insured that consequence by his own negative attitude toward the tenants.

There is another theoretical orientation which has been embraced by growing numbers of psychiatrists and psychologists; it has been referred to as "the third force" in psychotherapy and comprises a variety of approaches under the rubric of humanistic psychology. Carl Rogers and his nondirected therapy, the Gestalt therapy of Fritz Perls, Bugental's existential therapy and the various encounter therapies can be placed in this category.[34] The psychologist Maslow has been a considerable influence in this movement with his definitions of needs which every individual has and which are ordered hierarchically.[35]

Maslow postulates that the first needs to be satisfied are the
self-preservation needs—food, sex, and shelter, followed by security. Then man fulfills his community needs or the need to
belong and to love. After these needs are fulfilled, man seeks
self-esteem and finally self-actualization. As the theory goes,
those individuals still struggling to meet survival needs will
have little psychic energy remaining to deal with the higher
needs, such as belonging or self-actualization. Yet, most psychotherapy is attempting to assist the individual to achieve
these higher needs by "freeing" the personality from rigid defensive patterns which have blocked this achievement. Thus,
the dependence on traditional psychotherapy as a problem-
solving strategy in black communities is deemed inappropriate
and even premature.

Like most theoretical formulations, the hierarchical structure
of needs is an abstract representation of reality and neither
complete nor sufficient to explain that reality. Furthermore, it is
perhaps reflecting most effectively the perspective held by
middle-class theoreticians who have been, if anything, observers rather than participants in the life experiences of minority persons. That perspective has led to the assumption that
low-income, minority persons are impoverished of anything but
the struggle to survive and bereft of the passion and drive to
love and belong, to gratify their aesthetic sense, to master their
environment so that they can wrest from it a positive self-concept and a sense of relationship to mankind rather than to pa-
rochial man. Yet, black history in the United States is replete
with case histories of individuals who, despite the constant
struggle to survive, were able to seek and find fulfillment for all
those needs. Thus, Maslow's hierarchy of needs must be considered an elitist notion born of limited perspective despite its
rich conceptual texture.

Psychologists and psychiatrists are more rare in black communities than social workers. Until the community mental
health movement gained impetus in the early sixties, only the
most irrational behavior requiring institutionalization was likely

to expose a black person to these mental health professionals. Since the majority of psychiatrists and psychologists are in private practive or private psychiatric facilities, this fact is not surprising, particularly when connected to the fact that there is a pattern of exclusion of blacks from health and related professions; blacks constitute about 2 percent of all physicians (1.8 of all psychiatrists), 2 percent of psychologists, 5.6 porcent of nurses, and 10.9 percent of all social workers. The figures are even more unbalanced when it is recognized that the majority of black professionals, other than physicians, are in public hospitals, clinics, and social agencies because of both the greater opportunities for blacks in public when compared to private employment and because of the small demand for private psychiatric or psychological services from residents of the black community.

OTHER PRACTITIONERS
So far, it is apparent that the many varieties of human service practitioners have had limited presence in black communities, which may account at least in part for their general ineffectiveness and scant appeal. Even the arguments over whether or not individuals or social institutions are the appropriate target for change efforts are essentially intellectual exercises indulged in by professionals but rarely by lay residents in black communities. In fact, despite oppressive social institutions—economic, political, or judicial—which impact their lives, many blacks, particularly low-income blacks, do not perceive the oppression as having a direct effect on them. Furthermore, they do seek help for personal problems such as marital problems, child-parent problems, or for symptoms of emotional distress far more than for collective concerns; i.e., police brutality, neighborhood deterioration, fraudulent credit operations, or juvenile gang activities. Research has shown that residents of black communities would seek help from some external source since they often experience a lack of sense of control

over their own destiny. More specifically, they are inclined to believe that external forces and agencies exclusively control the rewards they receive; i.e., reinforcement is not contingent upon effort and skill. If the solution to problems is perceived as emanating from external forces, then it is rational to make an attempt to connect with these forces.

The Minister as Counselor. The church as a force in the black community is almost legendary. The minister of a black church is a more powerful figure in community life than is his white counterpart. Whereas black church members, as in other ethnic groups, often seek help from the minister for nonspiritual problems, e.g., problems with aging parents, child-parent conflicts, or even conflicts between neighbors, the black minister is less likely to have had training in counseling techniques and more likely to consider the resolution of the problem in prayer than in specific actions of the individual. However, given the prevailing attitude in many low-income black communities that the individual is left to the hands of fate (chance, God, the devil, etc.), it is understandable that the minister, who is often perceived as having special access to heavenly blessings, is sought after for help with a wide range of problems.

Plumpp has proposed that the black church is the only institution in the Black community which can serve as an instrument of self-determination for blacks and can ultimately effect major change in the quality of their lives.[36] He states that it is only when blacks can combine technology with a strong belief that God is on their side that such social change can occur. Plumpp further suggests that basic education for black children should be church-related, with developmental psychologists performing a significant role in structuring and administering the educational system.[37] Taylor, in reference to this, has made the even bolder suggestion that perhaps some black psychiatrists should become ministers.[38] Thus, the technical know-how in regard to human behavior and clinical practice would be wedded to a role which has traditionally elicited trust, hope, and faith from community residents. This is not so outlandish when one reviews the results of research on psychotherapy as well as on so-called "miracle cures" which have led to startlingly similar conclusions: the significant variable in a healer's effectiveness—whether minister, psychiatrist, or magician—is the troubled individual's belief in his skill.

Not all blacks are religious, despite the major role religion has played in black life and black history. According to Hill, a sizable minority (seventeen percent) are ambivalent or hostile toward the church.[39] This is particularly apparent among young blacks who are discontent with the level of involvement of the church in the secular concerns of the community. In fact, recent studies indicate that the more deeply the individual in the black community is involved in religion, the less likely it is that he will also be involved in militant activities aimed at upsetting the system. It is this fact that has turned away young militants from religion, but it is also evidence of the tendency for religion and its leaders to perceive change—personal or social—as out of the hands of the individual and in the hands of God. Marx points out that persons who belong to the more fundamentalist sects such as the Holiness groups and the Jehovah's Witnesses are relatively uninvolved in movements aimed at changing secular institutions.[40] Indeed, the more nontraditional the religion, the more likely it is that faith healing—including the healing of both physical and mental complaints—will be an integral part of the religious orientation. While only a minority of blacks actually belong to the fundamentalist sects or cults, the proportion is higher than among whites.

For those who are nonreligious, there is a variety of astrologers, prophets, fortunetellers, or other advisers who advertise their services in the black community. For example, the Los Angeles *Sentinel,* a weekly newspaper serving the black community, averages about twenty ads each week in its classified section from these lay counselors who announce, "I give never-failing advice upon all matters of life, such as love, courtship, marriage, divorce, business transactions of all kinds. I never fail to unite the separated, cause speedy and happy marriages."

Briar and Miller have pointed out that faith healers, fortune-tellers, and other self-proclaimed miracle workers often share goals, objectives and even techniques with psychiatrists, psychologists, and social workers.[41] Furthermore, they are often as effective as professionals in "curing" ills. Most importantly, effectiveness appears to be related to their ability to convince persons who seek their help that they have the power to influence change. There is in fact no credible evidence that faith healers are more or less effective than professionals. In the absence of definitive research—which does not appear to be likely in the near future—it can only be said that in some instances an astrologer or faith healer has been able to help some people. However, their impact has been minimal, since obviously there are fewer people, even in black communities, who have any faith in their ability to solve problems of living. The failures of professionals, moreover, can be studied since these represent instances in which a scientific hypothesis is not supported; there is a methodology for seeking alternative explanations and developing new hypotheses which then get tested in actual practice. Thus, there is a built-in mechanism for *improving* practice. This does not at the same time deny a considerable artistic component in the helping process which opens up the likelihood that there will always be some super-stars whose effectiveness can only be duplicated by others with similar talents.

Despite the fact that there are already scores of professionals with overlapping functions in the delivery of human services, there is evidence that new kinds of help-givers may be just over the horizon. Ben-David has pointed out that although social scientists are rarely in charge of programs aimed at solving social problems, i.e., "social therapy," their work has become an integral part of such therapies.[42] Thus, social scientists should become "social clinicians" who not only conceptualize problems and devise solutions but take responsibility for creating programs aimed at putting these solutions to work. However, Ben-David does not deal with the fact that social problems are most often expressed as individual problems; there is no crime problem without criminals, there is no employment problems without people who cannot find jobs. The social therapist may soon find himself caught up in the age-old problem of individual versus collective "good," and the mingling of basic and applied science will present far fewer problems than the dual role of social and Individual therapist.

In the controversy over priorities—individual change or systems change—Targ has accused the supporters of systems change of not going far enough. Broad-based systems change—change that would influence such phenomena as alienation, racism, the centralization of political power, and an expansive foreign policy—requires more radical proposals than have currently been made. The proponents have not really developed visions of whole new societies or whole new conceptions of what constitutes viable human communities. He suggests that:

> . . . the building of a new social order can be aided by the utilization of structured and/or unstructured simulations. Simulations could provide participants with parameters analagous to contemporary communities with problems requiring some adjustment or systems change. Participants then would guide the social scientist through the simulation in new and fruitful directions. Also, simulation can be extended to include communal experiments with the researcher acting as participant observer. In essence, the simulation and living experiment involves actually living the new social order posited.[43]

Basic to Targ's own prescriptive model of a new social order would be the formation of communities on the basis of ethnic and/or life style homogeneity as well as decentralization of political and social control. Such utopian models, of course, are themselves considered as solutions to problems of human need and human conflict. Therefore, related strategies of change are discussed primarily in terms of techniques for bringing about the new order. They require an unprecedented coalition between scientist and activist, and the strategies for achieving this unlikely coalition are not described.

Given the current interplay of human service personnel who move in and out of black communities, any effort to understand the potential they represent for maximizing the potential of the community's residents requires that some assumptions be made about the nature of change in the ethnosystem:

1. The society will always show a gap between the optimum level of physical and social functioning for all its members and the actual level its members achieve.

2. In some instances, the functioning gap will be in terms of total social institutions and therefore expressed in systematic terms; e.g., problems in the economic system, the criminal justice system, or the educational system. In other instances, the functioning gap will be in terms of the individual and will therefore be expressed as personal or interpersonal problems, e.g., marital conflict, juvenile delinquency, or schizophrenia.

3. Society will always provide specialists in problem-solving defined by their special knowledge that enables them to help resolve problems of social functioning at individual or institutional levels.

4. Theoretical perspectives on which these practitioners base their activities will reflect the attitudes, priorities, and values of the total society.

5. In a society which is an ethnosystem, there are unique characteristics of the helping process as it occurs within ethnic subsystems and across the interface of the ethnic subsystem and the ethnosystem itself.

SUMMARY

This chapter has suggested that black communities have been the setting for a variety of social and psychological programming to meet inordinate needs created by inordinate stresses generated in the ethnosystem. Black social workers as represented by the National Association of Black Social Workers have been extremely critical of the kind of services delivered in these programs and of the professions responsible for service delivery. Of those agencies in the Los Angeles area designated by the local chapter of the Association of Black Social Workers as a "community resource" in 1972, the majority tended to be subject to the vagaries of federal funding for their existence. Furthermore, the involvement of large numbers of professionals, paraprofessionals, and volunteers may well be inadequate for the magnitude of the task, but it is difficult to measure, given the broader question of the commitment of the professions with major responsibility for delivering these services and to provide services equal to those of other communities.

The historical development of social work and social welfare, and psychiatry and psychology was traced with emphasis on the response of these professional disciplines to the needs of people in black communities. Racism has been observable in each of the disciplines, although in much less virulent form in present-day operations than at first. Contemporary issues relate more to the relevance of their services rather than to outright denial of services.

The professions have not been the only service-providers in black communities, as black ministers for the religious and fortunetellers for others have played a significant role for many people in their difficult life situations. At the same time that these "old" and traditional helpers are still competing with the professional helpers, new approaches such as "social clinicians" and simulation of community processes are being proposed. There would appear to be inevitable gaps in what people need and what they have. In these situations "helpers" will be required and the helping process will be influenced by the ethnic context.

experiential exercises

1. AN ORAL HISTORY EXERCISE

Interview a black community resident who is over seventy-five years old. Find out how the family coped with personal problems during his or her childhood, adolescence, and young adult years. Note any anecdotes involving help-seeking behavior. What does your respondent think of psychiatrists? psychologists? social workers? ministers as sources of help with family problems?

2. AN OBSERVATIONAL EXERCISE

Select two similar agencies—one in a black community and one in a white community; (e.g., family service agencies, community mental health centers, public assistance agencies, family planning agencies, employment offices, etc.). Sit in the agency's waiting room for two hours.

> (a) What are the similarities and differences in the clientele of the two agencies?
>
> (b) What type of communication occurs between staff and clients? clients and other clients?
>
> (c) Which would *you* prefer going to if you needed help? Why? (In this exercise, it is advantageous to sit and observe without indicating to staff why you are there unless you are specifically asked. If you are asked, you should indicate that you are a student observer and request permission to remain. You should note, however, any changes in staff behavior subsequent to finding out that you are an observer.)

3. A WHOLE-GROUP EXERCISE

Divide the group into interracial teams of two or three persons. Each team will visit a different predominantly black church and a predominantly white church on consecutive Sundays. The experiences are to be discussed in seminar format. The group members should describe their perceptions of the relationship of the minister to the congregation in each church visited; the opportunities provided for members to seek help with personal problems as indicated in communication inside or outside the services, and whether they personally would seek help from the ministers observed.

chapter four

the mystique of science-based practice

Empowerment as a goal of social work practice assumes that the knowledge and skills that the professional social worker places at the service of the client system will be useful in the problem-solving process. However, this may not be perceived by the client whose orientation is other than scientific. Consider the case of Mrs. Jackson.

The county hospital fills a vast depression where several freeways criss-cross before plunging into the city's heart. The buildings are a collection of low concrete boxes surrounding a towering central core. Inside one of the boxes, a giant IBM 3600 hums continuously as data are received, processed, and returned to the medical decision-makers at distant terminals. On the tenth floor of the tower, an elderly black woman watches apprehensively from her bed as a nurse's aide unpacks her large canvas bag. Myriad multicolored bottles, candles, bags of herbs and incense, and tattered books with occult symbols are among her belongings. "I don't think I am supposed to let you have a lot of this stuff here on the ward, Mrs. Jackson." Mrs. Jackson's bright black eyes flash as she raises up on an elbow. "Please, honey, I've got to have them things, 'cause they's been blessed. I ain't going under no knife 'less I have my blessin's close by!" The aide pushes bottles and bags to the back of the small bedside night stand. "You surely must be the most blessed lady in this hospital, Mrs. Jackson." Mrs. Jackson, relieved that her precious assortment will remain with her, leans back on her pillow. "Doctors are all right, honey, but you needs spiritual healing too. Prophet Bell done tole me that I'm goin to walk out o' here long as I heed his word, and I aims to do that."

Mrs. Jackson perceived no conflict between faith healing and medical science; they were different resources to be called upon when needed. The anthropologist Melville Herskovitz was intrigued for most of his lifetime with the transplanted "new world Negroes," particularly the syncretism they had achieved between Christian belief systems and those of their pagan ancestors. He was interested in the phenomenon he had observed among Cuban, Brazilian, and Haitian Negroes who professed to be Catholic but still retained membership in fetish cults.[1] In the ceremonies and ideologies of these cults, Catholic elements had been incorporated so that there were even specific identifications made between African gods and Catholic saints. However, the integration was essentially between pagan and Christian religions whereas the most powerful adversary of religious explanations for human behavior and human events has been the growth and confidence in scientific methods. Science has provided explanations for aspects of life formerly covered by religion, and science's "gurus" wield an ever-increasing power.

The professional practitioners' heavy commitment to a scientific base for practice may not be reflected in the expectations of the consumers of their services. There is even some evidence that the particular scientific frame of reference which serves to identify the professional social worker—psychodynamic, behavioral, humanistic—may be more significant to his colleagues than to his clients. It is not unlike the case of critics who praise or pan television shows, movies, or books on the basis of structure, technique, or esthetic form while audiences, blissfully unaware that such concepts exist, either like or dislike the product solely as determined by personal "turn-offs" or "turns-ons." Yet, it is not merely the personal attraction of the worker to client that will determine whether or not the worker will be perceived as an appropriate help source. It is also the client's perception of how his problems have come about and therefore where the "control" or solution lies.

Where control over the physical environment as well as over interpersonal behavior is believed to rest with some supernatural power, it is only logical to seek help from someone who stands in extraordinary relationship to the supernatural—priest or minister, medicine man or witch doctor. However, in Western technological societies, the power to explain, predict, and control natural as well as physical phenomena emanates from science. Professional specializations have evolved in these societies which are defined by the kinds of problems they solve through application of scientifically derived knowledge; these include engineers, physicians, agronomists, clinical, psychologists, social workers, and a host of others.

Contemporary American culture is interlaced with competing and often contradictory myths. Since it is an ethnosystem, where communities express different myths and where individuals function within their own communities as well as within the larger ethnosystem, it is constantly necessary to come to grips with the contradictions. Science may represent a superior myth at one point in time, religion may represent the more powerful myth at another time. Furthermore, each of these belief systems implies a different set of specialists capable of dealing with human problems. As Herskovitz discovered, blacks have been able for centuries to integrate effectively the different myths they have had to live with. The black experience with helping specialists in the United States has been complex due not only to variations in the degree to which blacks have adhered to alternative myths but also because of the extent to which others in the ethnosystem have made certain kinds of assistance available or accessible. In fact, the nature of societal response to personal and social dysfunction in black communities provides a dramatic account of competing philosophies and theoretical perspectives within the helping professions in particular and within the society in general.

The significance of scientific practice for empowerment of powerless people comes from the role that knowledge plays in the problem-solving process. Indeed, knowledge is power. Thus, when power is viewed as pluralistic—emanating from a variety of sources—knowledge is conceded to be one of those sources. An individual's "power" may be defined as "all the resources—opportunity, acts, objects, etc.—that can be exploited in his behalf." In that sense, then, the knowledge of the professional practitioner which can "be exploited in his behalf" represents a possible increase in his power if utilized. If the professional social worker is actually perceived by the client system as having this knowledge, the motivation to engage in a collaborative problem-solving process is greatly enhanced.

There is, however, considerable evidence that explanations of behavior derived from the behavioral science theory have not always increased our ability to control that behavior—either our own or someone else's. Problems in black communities have been explained variously by the high incidence of "matriarchial" or one-parent families, apathy, low IQ, social disorganization of the ghetto, etc., which would suggest that solutions to the problems lie within the individuals. On the other hand, blacks themselves have countered with other explanations, such as racist oppression of major social institutions which would direct change strategies to systems external to those communities. This search for *the* cause of problems rather than *contributing* causes rarely is made with adequate appreciation of the fact that causation in the social world, as opposed to the natural world, is more often multiple (i.e., several factors acting together to bring about a particular effect) and even plural (i.e., several factors in differing combinations will produce the same effect).

Concepts of causation are deeply impregnated into the philosophy and language of psychosocial intervention and the sciences that support it. However, the significance of a causal notion is often dependent upon the purpose of the explanatory statement of which it is a part. For example, the statement that the high juvenile delinquency rate in ghetto communities is primarily a consequence of family instability incorporates a causal notion which is tantamount to a prescription for action. However, the exact prescription will depend upon the purpose of the statement. If made to the administrator of a community social agency, it may signal the need to institute social programs aimed at improving family relationships; for an anthropologist doing cross-cultural studies of deviance, it may serve to define the differences between juvenile delinquency in the United States and other countries in regard to perceptions of etiology; to a conservative practitioner, it may be an important bit of information to include in his speech wherein he denounces massive community action programs as ineffective, inappropriate, and wasteful. The social researcher may see the need to differentiate several types of family instability in order to determine if the statement can be given better precision. In addition to the diversity of uses of the causal notion in the explanatory statement, other noncausal notions could be used to further expand the statement; e.g., "juvenile delinquency deals only with acts committed by persons under eighteen for whom parents still retain legal responsibility," or "family instability in the black ghetto is more evidence of the basic social and moral inferiority of the black man." Thus, in order to assess the power of scientific knowledge to function as a roadmap to effective intervention in the helping professions, it is necessary to clarify the relationship of scientific explanation to alternative explanations.

THE NATURE OF EXPLANATION
Nettler in his seminal work on the nature of explanation has confirmed that there are different kinds of explanations for different situations.[2] Four kinds of explanations of human behavior are described. The first is explanation by definition which attempts to translate one set of verbal symbols into more familiar or understandable ones. An example of this type of explanation occurs when concepts like scapegoating, internal colo-

nialism, or radical black behaviorism are clarified by using synonyms, giving examples, subsuming under a type or class, or by the identification of procedures whereby the concept may be observed. Criticisms of science are sometimes made when concepts have been explained by more than one definition and the research or theory in which the concept appears either does not clarify which definition is being used or ignores the difference. Concepts which would apply here include "race", "establishment," and "matriarchy."

A second kind of explanation is explanation by empathy-building which occurs when the response to a why question identifies to the interrogator amalgams of feelings, beliefs, identifies from his own life experiences which seem to provide "good reasons" for the behavior. For example, the explanation of why the administration in Washington is cutting back on social welfare programs that emphasizes the insensitivity of Republicans to human needs and the backlash against the demands of the poor and minorities for equal opportunity will be acceptable to a liberal Democrat but not to a conservative Republican, while the reverse will be true if the explanation is that the administration is responding to a mandate from the people to stop the "sponging" off the taxpayers being done by those "unwilling" to work. Some philosophers have advocated this kind of explanation as the best or only mode of thinking in the explanation of human behavior. There is a rich tradition in the social sciences in defense of this style of comprehension that runs from Vico through Comte to such moderns as Cooley, Znaniecki, Weber, MacIver and others.[3]

Ideological explanations rest on statements that are unproved, unprovable, or false. The theme common to this type explanation is "group supported patterning of beliefs of inadequate empirical referent where such beliefs are energizing in attack or defense of values, and comprehension." Ideology is disdainful of facts and does not hesitate to change the meaning of truth in satisfaction of its distinctive motives. These motives are directed more toward justice than knowledge; ideological explanations have significance when they are believed rather than as they are verified.

The black movement has been richly endowed in ideological explanations that have incorporated concepts of black pride, liberation, and nation-building, and have been related to coping strategies, and give promise and hope to persons whose lives have been riddled with failure and frustration. These are in fact little different from the ideological explanations of American "greatness" by promoting the power and glory inherent in its democratic government and hard-working people.

Scientific explanation is of course supposed to adhere to rules of evidence which maximize validity or, in other words, reduce the probability of error. Moreover, explaining man is not only difficult but may not provide the answer desired when a request for explanation is made. As Nettler points out, today's significant questions are moral questions, not the technical ones that science might satisfy and the answers of science may even threaten valued social conditions.[4] Thus, the antiscience forces in society as a whole and in black communities in particular are discernible, comprehensible, and bound to affect the practice of the human service professions. Before considering in some detail the manifestations of the antiscience thrust in the black movement, it should be illuminating to look also at roughly parallel social movements in which similar if not identical attitudes have emerged.

SCIENCE AND THE PSEUDO-POWERLESS

The counterculture is essentially an expressive cultural movement reacting to the main varieties of alienation, inner estrangement, aimless, and personal impotence. Roszak, in his writings, has defined for us its boundaries and major themes which radically diverge from values and assumptions that have been in the mainstream of our society at least since the scientific revolution of the seventeenth century.[5] Regardless of differences of opinion about exactly how many young people are involved, it is clear that no longer does a scientific world view thrust up out of the Graeco-Roman past have the firm grasp on the minds of large numbers of mostly young people. There is limited interest in the social engineering role in society with its emphasis on rational thinking, precision control, and scientific methodologies. The interest of the counterculturists is instead in a new form of relatedness-merging fragments of Oriental mysticism, anarchist social theory, left-wing ideologies, the psychologies of alienation and self-awareness, and a romantic world view. At the heart of Roszak's social criticism is the denial of the pursuit of scientific objectivity as the only valid means by which we can come to know our world. Furthermore, in his view, even the question, "How shall we know?" should be subordinated to another; namely, "How shall we live?" This effectively places science—the pursuit of knowledge—into a subordinate position in relation to ethics.

Despite the anti-establishment stance which characterizes both the black movement and the counterculture, there are some striking differences. As pointed out by Hedgepeth, blacks have been engaged in a vertical insurgency as they have set out to seize for themselves certain benefits and privileges enjoyed only by those in a superior position in established society.[6] On the other hand, the counterculturists are lateral insurgents who have simply gone off in another direction to develop values and institutions counter to those of established systems.

Whereas the social interventionists are looking to perfect a technology which will permit greater control over human events, the counterculturists decry science as the mastermind which feeds the twin devils of materialism and technology. The technological society is the creation of materialistic motives and its excesses have pushed society into an ecologically and spiritually wasteful pursuit of an ever higher standard of living which is somehow antithetical to a humanistic standard of living. This corpulent society is like a spoiled and overripe fruit which sickens rather than nourishes. Most blacks, on the other

hand, are not rejecting the basic values of this society but reject their exclusion from the opportunity systems whereby materialistic goods can be amassed. Science is, for the counterculturists, restricting, limiting, or an inadequate means to
"know" reality. For blacks, science is a tool of the oppressor
used oftener than not to justify that oppression. Counterculturists
speak of oppression also, but it is an oppression of constraint,
limiting options, and not of exclusion, persecution, or discrimination. Perhaps that is why in the denigration of the scientific
method, the counterculturists perceive science as pernicious,
destructive in its single-mindedness, and therefore either to be
avoided or to be ridiculed for its swollen, undeserved status.
The counterculturists, by definition, are not committed participants in the technocratic society. Moreover, they are at times
difficult to identify as different scholars have specifically included or excluded different groups. Adelman has viewed the
counterculture movement as a heterogeneous mix of both cultural and political components:

> Core counter *culture* envelops decidedly "apolitical" alterna-
> tive life styles. To borrow from Charles Reich, its Con I Divi-
> sion involves the New Agrarians, Hip Craftsman, "alternate
> media" people, the organic food table, geodesic domers, et
> cetera. The "Otherworldly Division" embraces cult of drugs,
> assorted mysticisms, Jesus freakisms—in effect, just about all
> the tent placards at the Whole Earth Fair and Festival of
> Peace held at Boulder, Colorado, in July 1970. Krishna Con-
> sciousness, Yoga exercises (big draw), Zen, Astrology, Buck
> Fuller's World Game, Chasidism, and various theorists assert-
> ing their own ascendant therapeutic models.
>   Core counterpolitics runs a genetic chain from anarchist
> revolutionary trashers and street theater people to a division
> that recognizes a social order, a division that thus includes
> New Left ideologues and heavy black revolutionaries.[7]

Not all have been certain that the counterculture anti-es-
tablishmentarian rhetoric is persuasive or serious or that its
members are any but a small minority of people in this
country—too small a minority to have any modifying influence

on the form and substance of our cultural life. Adelman uses phrases like "latent right-wing anarchism" or "politbullshit" or "alibi-mentality" as he slashes at the counterculture movement, and he refers to their supporters as "Bucky" Fuller, "Charlie" Reich, and "Teddy" Roszak.

Roszak includes, in his description of the counterculturists, "a strict minority of the young and a handful of their adult mentors" but insists that this minority is sizable enough to be a critical force in contemporary society. He excludes the militant *black* young, based on a conviction that their political concerns are narrowly defined in ethnic terms that is "as culturally old-fashioned as the nationalist mythopoesis of the nineteenth century." [8]

The most cogent criticism of the counterculture then is that it does not truly represent the majority of young people in America who, after all, will be more likely to sit in the positions of power in the years to come. The fact that these youth do not represent the majority of American youth has been documented. One example of this is a Michigan State University study of 4,220 thirteen- to seventeen-year-olds in the Midwest, conducted in 1972, which found that over two-thirds of their respondents agreed that "obedience and respect for authority should be the very first requirement of a good citizen." [9] Furthermore, nearly two-thirds agreed that "the Bible is God's word and what it says is true." While this appears to indicate that the majority of America's youth are likely to place religious belief over scientific validity and to accept the right of the establishment to exercise authority, it should be remembered that distrust of science and authoritarianism has traditionally been higher among working class farmers or factory workers than among the middle and upper-class, university educated elite. Yet it is the sons and daughters of this latter group who are now questioning both the authority of science and the political elites and often opting for astrology, witchcraft, or oriental philosophy and the emphasis on subjectivity and the unique human experience.

Despite the obvious differences between young black activists and their white counterculture peers, the point of their agreement is that science has failed in its attempts to deal "objectively" with human experience, since it has placed its own supposedly infallible methods above human values. However, the counterculturists have opted to retreat, having been surfeited with the material fruits of scientific enterprise and starved for the spiritual and humanistic values it ignores, and they can afford to turn their backs on what personal experience has demonstrated to be ungratifying. On the other hand, blacks have not been admitted to the plenty. An unconscionable proportion are included among the "hard-core" poor. Most have never experienced the securities inherent in abundance; for as Roszak has pointed out, the abundance sinks only so far down the status hierarchy and then stalls to fatten limitlessly. Thus, rather than retreat, young blacks are fighting tenaciously to utilize every weapon in technology's armamentarium to achieve parity. This involves engaging science, confronting its inadequacies, demanding a change, insisting that it spread its golden consequences out to reach the heretofore excluded black population.

Another group of pseudo-powerless are the so-called radical scientists. Killian has suggested that "a great body of scientists uncommitted, independent, and scrupulously objective, is the best insurance that there will be no abuses of the profound public responsibilities scientists now carry." [10] Yet, a number of scientists, social and natural, are questioning whether the scientific establishment is in fact made up of such uncommitted and objective scientists. Catherine Roberts, a biologist, has written what she calls "a deliberate attack upon the conventional scientific outlook" which she perceives as dominating world thought.[11] She protests the idea that the pursuit of scientific truths should be blind and unenlightened. The alternative she proposes would place humanistic ideals rather than scientific knowledge at the center of scientific inquiry. Roberts was profoundly influenced by Polyani, who has insisted that detached scientific objectivity is a delusion that threatens not

only science but other human activities as well.[12] Moreover, he
contends that despite its worship of the objective and neglect
of the subjective, science's most significant visions have
emerged from the scientist's intellectual passions and personal
commitment to a search for truth.

Within sociology, the source of the largest proportion of
theories influencing the delivery of services to the poor and minority groups, the Union of Radical Sociologists, was formed in
1969. Composed primarily of young, white, Marxist-oriented
students and professionals, it has pressed mainstream sociology to develop a more relevant sociology.

There has been, in addition to the creation of professional organizations with radical orientations, an increasing number of
journals and books with radical perspectives as well as panels
and symposia at national meetings devoted to the issues raised
by the emerging radical sociology. The issues center around
certain themes which are recurrent in radical writing and
speaking. One theme is the rejection of "positivism" in contemporary sociology, which is the view that "in the social as well as
in the natural sciences, sense experiences and their logical and
mathematical treatment are the exclusive source of all worth-
while information." Another theme is that sociology has been
nothing more than a tool of the corporate state, providing
skills, techniques, and facts meant to be used by the dominant
power structure to manipulate and control the masses.

In operation, radical sociology has two faces, either of which
may be perceived to constitute the sociological presence. On
the one hand there is political radicalism which embodies a
position that challenges the established structures supporting
the technocratic society; on the other hand, there are the professional radicals who want to shake up the conventional
modes of scholarship in their disciplines, to redefine what is
appropriate scientific methodology and to realign the status hierarchy in regard to "ways of knowing the world." It is the
former group that represents the strongest allies for those in
black communities struggling for change in the basic distribu-

tion of power in this country. It is the latter that is likely to have the greater impact on the clinical practitioner searching for specific knowledge to increase his effectiveness in helping individuals and groups in these communities with the personal and social problems they encounter there.

Forsythe warns, however, that there is an inherent limitation in radical sociology's approach to blacks.[13] This limitation is in the tying of blacks to a universal category of the oppressed. White radical sociologists, like white bourgeois sociologists, have been too far removed from the black situation to be able to understand blacks as a unique social category. Furthermore, Marxian theory, the central theoretical position in radical sociology, is in essence ethnocentric despite its universalistic posture. His writings are replete with attacks on the cultural values, community structures, and personal characteristics of Third World peoples, as shown by his contention that the rise of the bourgeoisie had made possible the dominance of inferior societies by superior ones: "Just as it has made the country dependent on the towns, so it has made barbarians and semibarbarian countries dependent on the civilized ones, nations of peasants on nations of bourgeois, the East on the West." [14]

Sociology is not the only discipline among the behavioral sciences that has felt the sharp attack from within in regard to methodology and content. Child has pointed out that a basic defect in psychological research is the restriction of topics considered suitable for inquiry to those amenable to application of the more precise and objective methods.[15] More serious, in his judgment, however, is the attempt to exclude experience and awareness from the subject matter of psychology. Again the recurring theme among radical scientists as among counterculturists is the validity of the subjective, the personal, the unique in the search for truth. Maslow's strong convictions in this regard are expressed as follows:

> If there is any primary rule of science, it is, in my opinion, acceptance of the obligation to acknowledge and describe all of

reality, all that exists, everything that is the case. Before all else science must be comprehensive and all-inclusive. It must accept within its jurisdiction even that which it cannot understand or explain, that for which no theory exists that which cannot be measured, predicted, controlled or ordered. It must accept even contradictions and illogicalities and mysteries, the vague, the ambiguous, the archaic, the unconscious, and all other aspects of existence that are difficult to communicate. At its best, it is completely open and excludes nothing. It has no "entrance requirements." [16]

Radical scientists have for the most part been sympathetic to the protest movements emerging out of black communities, as they have generally supported criticism against tradtional science. However, the deep antagonisms in black communities against scientific theories, and the research that generates them, requires more than the support of a set of minority caucuses within the social research establishment in order to dissipate the antagonism. The demands made by blacks themselves emphasize two more radical changes in the status quo: (1) the inclusion of the black perspective in the development, implementation, and interpretation of research, and (2) community control of the research conducted in black communities; the latter is seen as a means of insuring the former.

Most of the increasing numbers of blacks in the social science professions could be considered ideologically a part of radical groups. In fact, Forsythe makes the point that blacks have for the most part always been radical and it is only in recent years that whites have moved to more radical positions.[17] Black social scientists have over the years brought into the scientific arena issues and perspectives which otherwise might have remained unconsidered. The primary target has been the research process itself, that set of activities through which scientists hope to achieve the goal of knowledge-building. Perhaps the heightened sensitivity of blacks to the foibles and fallibility of research comes from their own recognition of the lack of congruence between the social world which they have experienced and the world described in the findings of academic social science research.

Knowledge which has been derived from social science research, as pointed out earlier, may have its most direct application either to broad social policy or to individual and small-group change efforts. The criticisms of research which are frequently encountered in black communities are due to inappropriate or inadequate applications in both areas. The changes which are most often proposed to remedy the perceived abuses of research activities in or related to black communities are twofold: the inclusion of the black perspective in every stage of research from the formulation, implementation, and the community control of the research activity in terms of sanction and evaluation. These proposals have been perceived for the most part as a threat to the integrity of scientific research and a step in the direction of a form of community-based totalitarianism.

SCIENCE AND THE POWERLESS
An intensifying criticism by black social scientists and black community residents alike is that white social science is biased, and therefore research conducted in black communities or about black people should be implemented with a black perspective. The rejoinder is usually that blacks themselves are biased and lack "objectivity" required to study their own community. Science, after all, is not in the business of creating ideologies—even though ideologies might have positive value at a given point in time for a specific social group—and therefore a rigorous application of its methodologies is the best insurance against distortion and subjectivity.

It is clear that science has had its share of biased scientists. Some have been outright racists, those who attribute negative characteristics to a particular race on the basis of preconceived notions and despite the lack of evidence to support these notions.

Other social scientists have been guilty of more subtle distortions based on lack of experience with black life styles and lack of understanding of the symbols, norms, motivational patterns, and interactional processes which characterize these life styles.

Black social scientists have not escaped the influence of the intellectual climates in which they worked and produced, so that their value systems impinged on their research in a somewhat different way. In their thrust to obtain scientific support for changing conditions in black communities, the specific emphases or content of their studies reflects to a large extent the changing concerns within black communities regarding their position in the American ethnosystem. The earliest period continuing through emancipation was one where change efforts and their theoretical supports focused on proving that blacks were indeed human and therefore subject to the protection of their human rights; the second period, roughly from the turn of the century to the civil rights movement of the 1960s, was concerned with proving that blacks deserved equal status in society; and the period since that time has seen less emphasis on equal status and more on the right to be different, therefore on proving the significance of black culture and its place in a pluralistic society. It is not surprising then that scholars who were writing in different periods might seem curiously out of step in another. Ideas have to be evaluated within the context of their times. The definitions of reality change swiftly. Rose has catalogued some of the turnovers as he questions:

> Who would have thought that Bayard Rustin, the old socialist who accused W. E. B. DuBois of conservatism, would be marked as a sell-out while DuBois would become the hero of the militant Left? Who would have believed that James Farmer, the founder of the Congress of Racial Equality, would be the first black to join the administration of a Richard M. Nixon? One wonders what might have happened had William Styron published his confessions of Nat Turner ten years earlier, at a time when he might well have been praised by black

critics for making a Nat Turner a Mosaic-like figure. (He was too late—Che was the revolutionary hero of the day, not Moses.) Daniel P. Moynihan might have been lauded instead of damned. (Kenneth Clark was praised. He said pretty much the same things in *Dark Ghetto,* relying on many of the same sources.) [18]

BIASED PRIORITIES

Research has been carried out primarily under auspices of institutions of higher education. The faculty and researchers are ninety-eight percent white. It should not be surprising then that the problems selected to study have come out of the perspective of middle-class white America rather than out of what may be a different set of perspectives—those of minority group persons themselves. For example, major research emphases have been placed on the study of black responses to prejudice and discrimination; pitifully little has been done on the study of white implementation of racist attitudes. The concentration, in fact, of social research on the attitudes, motivational systems, and response pattern of blacks implies that understanding these phenomena is tantamount to understanding the problematical relationships between blacks and whites. This is analagous to studying the relationship between weather conditions and the growth of corn by only studying the corn and ignoring the weather!

Tillman and Tillman have pointed to several such biased priorities in social science research relating to racial or interracial issues.[19] For example, a stream of studies have had as patent goal the discovery of ways by which blacks could be *lifted* to functional parity with whites in regard to education, employment, or housing. Another stream has been devoted to studies of the extent to which blacks are integrated or segregated from basic American institutions (with the value assumption being that these institutions; e.g., the predominantly white schools, church, country clubs, etc., are desirable and desired). Another group of studies are merely gross reporting of attitudes and perceptions of blacks by whites or of whites by blacks, which may be of questionable significance given other research which indicates frequent disparity between attitudes and behavior. What is obviously missing, then, is research which studies the dynamics of racism as a functional component of the social system. Perhaps even more Important would be studies aimed at identifying *intragroup* relationships in order to provide the insights needed to develop cohesive social organization of the black minority. Yet such research would inevitably clash with the core culture values of cultural homogeneity rather than cultural difference and the priority given individual over collective needs.

It is not only in the choice of research topics but in the very conceptualization of research problems that the researcher bias is evident. Hare has pointed out that most of the concepts utilized in sociological research on race relations indicates a "white-European-immigrant fixation." [20] Thus words like ghetto, minority group, accommodation, assimilation, etc., are based on theoretical models which were developed in the study of immigrant groups and the processes associated with their entry into American society and their subsequent interactions with mainstream American culture. These conceptualizations, e.g., ghetto, are used to refer to the situation of blacks in this country despite the fact that their manner of entry and subsequent experiences have clearly not followed the pattern of other immigrant groups. The disinterest of researchers in developing different concepts to deal with different realities is a blatant disvaluing of multiple realities. Even the argument that knowledge building is a process of utilizing what is already known as a starting point from which to generate new knowledge is an indictment of that process if it is inflexible in the face of evidence indicating that the prior knowledge is irrelevant to some present phenomenon.

The claim that research methods are by their very definition unbiased and objective has been attacked from several sides.

Methods utilized in a given research effort can and often do reflect the value biases discussed above. A case in point is the now infamous study of the treatment of syphilis conducted at the Veterans' Administration Hospital, Tuskegee, Alabama. The study was experimental in nature and experimental methods enjoy the highest status of any in the scientist's armamentarium. In the classical experimental design a control group is imperative; i.e., random assignment of subjects (1) to an experimental group which is exposed to the treatment, and (2) to a control group which is not exposed. Williams has described the application of this most prestigious of research designs at Tuskegee:

> What we know of the Tuskegee syphilis experiment is a shocking disclosure of clear-cut scientific racism. During a 40-year federally funded study, scientists in Alabama used 600 black men as human guinea pigs. The men, victims of syphilis, were denied treatment even after the discovery of penicillin, so that scientists could study the progress of the disease. . . . To make this act of moral pauperism worse, scientists already knew the effects of long-term untreated syphilis from data obtained from a Norwegian study that was conducted from 1891 to 1910. Syphilis is a highly contagious, dangerous and debilitating disease that left untreated can cause sterility, blindness, deafness, bone-deterioration, nervous system degeneration, heart disease and eventually death. The experimenters tricked these poor black men into participating in the experiment by offering them transportation to and from the hospital, hot lunches, medical care for ailments other than syphilis and free burial.[21]

The methods used in the collection of data, i.e., the research instruments themselves, may reflect bias. Questionnaires developed using language with which blacks may be unfamiliar; interviews done by white interviewers toward whom the respondents may be hostile or reluctant to expose true feelings, attitudes, etc.; participant observer methods with participant observers who are white—these methods may lead to invalid, unreliable data which nevertheless is accepted as valid and reliable and a basis on which to make judgments about the phenomenon studied, whether it is a level of participation in political activities, sexual behavior, or child-rearing practices.

Phillips has pointed out the frequency in scientific research that similar or identical findings are given different interpretations by different scientists.[22] This difference, when it occurs in research done in black communities, often reflects the racial bias of the investigators. A clear example of conflicting interpretations of similar findings can be seen in studies of self-concept and self-esteem among blacks. Several excellent critiques of the research literature in this area exist.[23] These critiques emphasize not only the methodological inadequacies of some of the studies (e.g., Kardiner and Oversey, Grier and Cobb)[24] in which generalizations about self-esteem among blacks is made on the basis of pitifully small and nonrandom samples. However, also apparent is the difference in the interpretation given to the findings by different investigators. For example, Baughman makes the point that the fact that so many blacks learned to *act* subservient and inferior when in the presence of whites should not be perceived as conclusive evidence that they actually *felt* inferior.[25]

The significance of these differing interpretations of the determinants of behavior represents weak points in the theoretical substructures upon which professional practice supposedly rests. Certainly service priorities may be determined by whether you think that behavior (e.g., perceptions of male-female roles) is a consequence of cultural tradition or a consequence of the manner in which major social institutions function. The Moynihan controversy can be used as a final illustration of this point. Moynihan found a statistically significant difference in the incidence of one-parent families among blacks when compared with whites.[26] His interpretation of this finding was that efforts to bring about positive change for blacks in this country must stress increased family stability; efforts must be directed toward influencing blacks to adopt mainstream family pattern in order to improve the social status of the group. The cries of consternation from the black community were the consequence of another explanation of the significance of the Moynihan findings; i.e., the "system" itself helps to produce more one-parent black families, and therefore efforts should be placed on changing the "system" rather than directing blacks to a "pull yourselves up to our level" philosophy.

It is clear that weak spots exist throughout the substructure of behavioral science theory. There is even difference of opinion about how much "knowledge" actually exists in a field like sociology. Phillips, for example, contends that "the evidence concerning the extent to which sociological variables are able to explain the variation in other variables is unimpressive." From his point of view more misinformation than information has been gathered on many subjects in sociological research. The same can be said with varying degrees of documentation in other behavioral science fields as well, e.g., anthropology, psychology, economics, or political science. Even in a field such as history, there is considerable lack of consensus about just what is a historical "fact." Furthermore, Phillips asserts that the influence of behavioral science theory on decision makers has been highly overrated; as a matter of fact, there has been very little use made of knowledge developed in the behavioral sciences—even when it has a high degree of validity, and therefore fears of potential harm to come from improper utilization of research is unfounded.[27]

Despite Phillips's disclaimer, however, there is considerable evidence that social science theories have been used to support social policy decisions—both on the right and on the left. It is a generally accepted notion that Myrdal's massive study of blacks in the United States published in 1944 was a major part of the evidence which led to the Supreme Court decision on integration of schools in 1954.[28] More recently Jensen's research comparing black-white intelligence has been used to justify termination of support for compensatory education programs for black children since the differences between black and white

IQ is primarily hereditary (80 percent) and therefore cannot be influenced beyond this hereditary potential by environmental modification.[29] It is therefore not surprising that distrust of research and the academics who carry it out runs deep and strong within black communities. The demand now heard is for community control of the research done in it.

THE ISSUE OF COMMUNITY CONTROL

It is imperative to recognize the deep antagonism toward research that has emerged in black communities all across the country. To many in these minority communities, research is synonomous with "survey," and myriad surveys have been made ostensibly to identify needs so that program planners could tailor services to meet these needs. Yet few programs have actually been implemented. Thus an attitude now prevails that there has been enough research in black communities and no more is needed to point out the obvious. More directly, community persons have demanded that proposed research to be done in their community guarantee some benefit to the community or else access to the community will be denied. In 1970, concerns such as these led to the establishment of the Community Research Review Committee of the Black United Front of Greater Boston, which had as its major objective the formulation of principles and guidelines for the conduct of all research within the black community of metropolitan Boston. Other such efforts of black communities to control the nature of the research undertaken within them have been documented in the literature. Most of these efforts have sought to develop commitments from researchers and monitoring procedures which would assure the protection and progress of the community without endangering the scientific integrity of the research itself.

It is perhaps too easy to explain away the current hostility in black communities toward research as an expression of fear of the unknown, not unlike that shown by any primitive or naïve people when confronted with a phenomenon they do not understand. Since many of the central figures in these protests have been "indigenous" leaders or paraprofessionals without the credentials of membership in the scientific brotherhood, accusations have also been made that the protest against research is militant rhetoric designed to demonstrate the protesters' courage to confront the perceived oppressors. The most common criticism of all—because it is so easily proved— is that the protesters are self-styled community "leaders" who in fact do not represent the total community. Rarely can anyone be identified in any community who is a representative of all its factions.

It is more difficult, however, to reject completely these criticisms of community involvement in research when there are a growing number of social scientists, black and white, who argue *for* that involvement. Smith asserts that the determination of ethnic minorities to control their own affairs and destinies can be linked with the processes of scientific investigation for the purpose of preventing research abuses and advancing the course of responsible knowledge-building that will serve minority people.[30] Others lay emphasis on community involvement to insure "benefit" to the community although the nature of that benefit is described loosely as "a commitment to assist the people of that community to positively change the conditions under which they live" or pointedly as "the provision of something the community needs. [31] The issue of community involvement in the research process is not a simple one. The many agendas that operate simultaneously in the mix of community persons and academicians, blacks and whites, activists and theoreticians, can in fact have traumatic consequences. The involvement of community people in the work of scientists will undoubtedly at times make those social scientists trained in another tradition intensely uncomfortable. However, if flexibility and openness are present, the rewards may far outweigh the disadvantages. It is also clear, however, that the process of community involvement will be more effective if it is rationalized, defined, and systematized at the inception of the research so that, if later conflicts arise, there is a policy for dealing with those conflicts before there were vested interests in opposing points of view that would influence how governance is perceived.

LIMITING PROPOSITIONS
IN APPLYING SCIENTIFIC KNOWLEDGE

Science is not inherently racist or oppressive—not even behavioral science in which the scientists, even racist scientists, are inextricably a part of the human situation they are studying. In contrast to what many people in minority communities believe, science does not impose definitions of reality upon people living that reality. Careless, sometimes racist scientists and unsophisticated, sometimes racist politicians and just plain people join at times to impose such definitions. It *is* clear that behavioral scientists have been used in the service of racist or oppressive social policies as much or more than they have in support of humanistic social policies. Yet, rather than reject a powerful method for "knowing" the world, it would be far wiser to define a set of limiting propositions which will be useful in considering applications of the methods of science in black communities.

Scientific method is only one of the ways available to practitioners for learning about the world. The basis of all scientific method is epistemology—the ordering and classification of phenomena. Yet, the individual experience cannot always be neatly classifiable in mutually exclusive categories which then become either antecedent or consequent variables in some explanatory system. Sometimes this is because the phenomena under question are inaccessible to scientific investigation; e.g., marital behavior that the couple wish to keep private may be studied only secondhand without actual empirical evidence to document their verbal statements. More often, however, it is because the phenomenon of concern is a unique personal experience and attempts to classify it into some general category of behavior would not only be difficult but meaningless.

It must be recognized that science is not value-free. This is particularly true in the behavioral sciences. Thus, the values which illuminate a specific scientific enterprise are implicit if not articulated, and the value context is an important consideration in the analysis of the findings and the projection of their implications. For example, an important feature in the investigation of a scientific hypothesis is the a priori selection of a test of significance and the level of significance at which the hypothesis will be accepted or rejected. The choice of a level of significance determines the risk the investigator wants to take (1) that he will reject the hypothesis when it is in fact true, or (2) that he will accept the hypothesis when it is in fact false. In the case of the hypothesis that there are no genetic differences in the intellectual capacity of blacks and whites, I may believe that the former risk is by far the greater, i.e., the consequences of being wrong are likely to be so harmful that I will want a statistical test to show that the risk is *extremely* unlikely before I would accept the hypothesis. On the other hand, a value-free scientist would supposedly accept the hypothesis when evidence supported the decision on conventional grounds alone. Yet, the fallacy lies in the fact that the implication that the scientist is willing to accept the greater risk and the consequences which might accrue if he is wrong, are in effect a statement of his values.

The sociobehavioral sciences have sought to emulate the natural sciences in objectives and methods, particularly physics. However, *whereas physical phenomena—such as rocks, prisms of light or molecules of oxygen—may be governed by general laws which are deducible; social phenomena such as families, courts, or social welfare programs are less likely to be controlled by equally deducible general laws.* Even propositions which have been stated as laws such as "the law of supply and demand" or the "law of diminishing returns" tend to proliferate exceptions as attempts are made to apply them in problem-solving situations.

An overriding criticism of the research literature is that it is full of generalizations which become stereotypes and only serve to perpetuate myths already held by biased investigators and generated by biased methodologies. However, *generalizations are patently developed for the social scientist and not for practitioners.* In the language of research, these generalizations are estimations or approximations of reality based on laws of probability. Yet practitioners have often lifted these generalizations from the research literature as explanations of reality when in fact they never refer to an individual case but to a set of probabilities based on infinite observations "in the long run." Furthermore, the set of probabilities can be viewed most rationally by the practitioner as a set of alternative explanations, from most likely to least likely, with the practitioner still having the task of using practitioner skills—not research skills—to determine which possibility holds in the individual case. For example, generalizations have been made about the matriarchy as the predominant pattern of family interaction in black families. No matter how one may castigate the researcher's faulty interpretations which produced the generalization, the practitioner must take full responsibility for translating it into practice strategies that have ignored black husbands and fathers in planning services for families on a routine basis, without considering the individual case and the need to use the *experience* in the human encounter as final determinant of what is reality.

Thus the knowledge that science offers to practice is in the illumination of alternatives, varieties, diversities rather than in the presentation of central tendencies or generalizations. Certainly the practitioner needs to be aware of the total range of expected or probable events, behaviors, or conditions in given social situations, not merely the most likely. This distinction has been described as the difference between linear thinking and multidimensional or branching thought processes. De Bono has defined the two poles similarly as lateral or vertical thinking.

> With vertical thinking one concentrates and excludes what is irrelevant, with lateral thinking one welcomes chance intrusions. With vertical thinking categories, classifications and labels are fixed, with lateral thinking they are not. Vertical thinking is a finite process, lateral thinking is a probabilistic one. Vertical thinking follows the most likely paths, lateral thinking explores the least likely. . . .[32]

The inevitable frustration experienced by social workers who cannot shift from vertical to lateral thinking is demonstrated in the case of the Jackson family (as described by a social worker).

> I know a family living in Jordon Downs—a public housing project. I have known the Jackson family for four years. Knowing them, I have puzzled over the fact that even under the most "negative" of conditions (according to the books), there are mysterious forces at work in family functioning that often lead to unexpected results.
>
> The Jacksons are a nuclear family. There is a mother and a father and five children are still living at home. Mr. Jackson has held a job off and on in a factory where he works the night shift. He has a former wife and three children living in a town about a hundred miles away. He manages some support for the children and visits them a few times a year. However, this angers his present wife who suspects that his real interest is in his former wife, who has not remarried. Mr. Jackson is a heavy drinker. He regularly beats his wife and abuses the children when he is drinking. As a parent, he is authoritarian. Mrs. Jackson is often angry with her husband and gets into loud arguments in which both of them curse profusely but for the most part she appears helpless to deal with her husband.
>
> The Jackson children group together and help each other. The older children have rebelled against their father and against their helpless mother. Donna is sixteen and is a talented singer. Her younger sister, Elizabeth, is fourteen and

makes most of the clothes worn by her sister and her mother. Both girls are highly intelligent and make good grades when they attend school regularly. However, Elizabeth has run away from home several times and initiated proceedings in court to have herself declared incorrigible so that she could be placed in a foster home. When she was placed in a foster home, however, she became lonely for her brothers and sisters and returned home after two months. The boys have more indepen dence and have not found it necessary to run away. When their father is on the rampage, they usually disappear to return only after he has sobered up.

There are many elements in this family's functioning which is considered pathological and destructive by professionals in human services. Yet in *all* the Jackson children, there is a spark of something rare and special. They are not merely bright and aware, they have strength and wholeness. . . . If we agree that certain kinds of families *often* produce certain kinds of children, we also have to recognize the complexity, the mystery of the interaction of innate talent, family functioning and the influence of the community and the dominant society.

The paradox inherent in this example is that on the basis of vertical, logical thinking, the Jackson children *ought not* to be so healthy, so strong and whole. Lateral thinkers, coming out of a systems perspective with profound appreciation for the principle of macrodeterminacy, would have little problem with "explaining" the Jackson family. In fact, the level of family functioning would be viewed as only one of the less likely outcomes in a whole set of outcomes associated with the "negative factors" in the psychosocial environment.

The hope for more effective problem-solving activities in black communities is not the destruction of scientific efforts to understand the problems but for the incorporation of the scientific technology in a broader perspective on the relationship between man and man and between man and his environment. The propositions presented here provide a basis for such incorporation to occur. Yet, it is clear that there are no models for practice inherent in the set of propositions. On the other hand, it is possible to evaluate more carefully the extent to which existing models or models to be proposed are congruent or incongruent with the philosophical orientation presented here.

SUMMARY
Practitioners in the helping professions have made a heavy commitment to a scientific base for their practice. Although scientific knowledge may be conceived of as "power" which the practitioner makes available to the client for use in problem-solving, there is considerable evidence that the knowledge does not always lead to viable solutions. Scientific explanation is in fact only one of several alternative types of explanation and other explanations may be more useful in some kinds of problem-solving. In exploring the nature of explanation, it was shown that explanation by definition, explanation by empathy-building, or ideological explanation may be more effective than scientific explanation (e.g., in solving the problem of obtaining support for a social welfare program).

There are groups in society who have rejected the "power" of scientific explanation as currently practiced. This power is perceived as essentially unethical and often corrupt. These groups—the counterculturists and the radical scientists—are pseudopowerless to the extent that there appears to be a negative valuation of them and their values by mainstream society. For example, their concern for subjectivity and the unique human experience is not shared by the scientific community in general. However, this negative valuation does not stem from science's identification of the counterculturists or the radical scientists as a stigmatized collective but rather from the stigmatization of science by a self-identified collective. In contrast, the truly powerless people such as the black racial minority in the United States have been again and again stigmatized by the findings of objective science acting to reinforce the negative valuations of society at large. Therefore, the goal of empowerment must include the uncovering of the extent to which supposedly unbiased scientific research in fact reflects biased priorities, biased methodologies, and perhaps most significantly the fact that most research conducted in black and other minority communities has almost always been by scientists from outside the community and with minimal capacity to understand its dynamics.

Some limiting propositions in regard to the application of scientific knowledge were proposed: (1) the scientific method is only one of the ways available to practitioners for learning about the world; (2) science is not value-free; (3) the social phenomena with which helping professionals work are rarely governed by the kind of general laws that have been devised in the natural sciences; (4) generalizations are the tool of social scientists and not practitioners; and finally, (5) the value of science for practitioners is in the illumination of alternatives and diversities rather than as the source of universal laws.

experiential exercise

The following exercise has been designed to illustrate the importance of different kinds of explanations for different purposes.

If answers are conceived to be "explanations," for which of the following questions are there alternative explanations? Of the alternative answers for a given question, which would relate most closely to the goal of empowerment for blacks, i.e., to the reduction of the effects of negative valuation?

> Example: What has been the effect of slavery on the family life of black people in the United States?

> *Empathy-building* answer: It has made black families vulnerable to the same extent that any family whose ancestors experienced terrible oppression would be vulnerable.

Ideological answer: It has created a cohesive brotherhood of those who even today are committed to the concept of "black power" as the ultimate weapon against the oppression of racist America!

Scientific answer: Research indicates that contemporary pressures such as discrimination are more important in shaping the behavior of black Americans than any heritage from the slavery experience.

The following questions have been adapted from a problem suggested by Postman and Weingartner in *Teaching as a Subversive Activity* (New York: Delacorte 1969). They aim to provide an opportunity to experience the idea that there are many ways to "know the world." Study them carefully.

1.

If black culture encompasses the "real" virtues in our society—e.g., emphasis on the extended family, collective rather than individual good, cooperation rather than competitiveness, free emotional expression rather than puritanical self-control, etc., then why are so many blacks caught up in lives of violence, crime, drug addiction, and "rippin' off" other blacks?

2.

If we insist on blacks' controlling and operating the major social and economic institutions in their communities, how do we justify any provision for blacks to control or operate social and economic institutions *outside* predominantly black communities?

3.

If schools do not have economic success as a primary goal for education then what would be their relevance for black communities which suffer so greatly from economic deprivation?

4.
What is the difference between accepting the fact that there are differences between individuals and the fact that there are differences between races?

5.
Are you in favor of or opposed to bussing to achieve integration of schools?

6. How do helping professionals deal with the fact that black people often perceive social agencies as systems to be manipulated or exploited rather than as sources of help?

7.
Is it possible that problems like foreign policy problems, energy problems, or economic problems can influence the effectiveness of strategies we may devise to deal with racism in our human service organizations?

8.
Who are the five most important blacks in the United States?

9.
When do you think the United States will elect its first black President?

10.
How can we make existing social and psychological services more effective in helping people in black communities to cope with their problems?

NOW ANSWER THE FOLLOWING QUESTIONS

(a) Which of the above questions can you answer with absolute certainty?

(b) How can you be certain of your answers?

(c) What information will you need to answer other questions with absolute certainty? Where will you get the information?

(d) Which questions require the greatest amount of definition before you answer them?

(e) Which questions require the testimony of experts? What makes one an expert?

(f) Which questions assume the answerer is the expert?

(g) Which questions may have false assumptions?

(h) Which questions require predictions as answers? What kinds of information may improve the quality of a prediction?

(i) Which questions restrict you to giving factual information? Which do not? Which require no facts at all?

part three

power blocks
in negative
images of black

A major contribution of Sigmund Freud was his identification and analysis of those forces within us all which go unnoted but are of such magnitude that they often push us and pull us through life like hapless dust particles in a windstorm. Perhaps, more importantly, Freud recognized that self-knowledge or "insight" reduces the power that these forces have over us and keeps us from some endless treadmill of ungratifying, repetitious behavior. Insight into the black experience has been limited to the extent that the repressive forces of racism have employed all the traditional mechanisms of defense in order to stave off the anxiety-producing truth as others have seen it. In order to appreciate the operations of what has been referred to as negative valuation of a racial group, it is important to understand the defensive distortions that are negative images of black which persist in diverse segments of social life.

Each of the five chapters in Part III presents evidence of these negative images—in genetic myths, in perceptions of black families, in peer groups, in schools, and in organizations.

chapter five

. . . in genetic fiction

It is ironic that in a nation in which individualism is a bedrock value, the negative valuation of a collective is so often based on belief in the individual's incapacity to transcend some set of inferior characteristics inherited from his endless line of ancestors. Hirsch has provided an excellent discussion of the genetic mythologies that have come clothed in the cloak of science and supported subtle prejudices and discriminations at best and gross atrocities at worst.[1] The perpetrators of this assault on collectives include some of science's most famous names: Karl Pearson (1856–1936), whose massive contributions in the field of statistics are almost overshadowed by his shoddy and poorly designed research on Jewish immigrants to Britain on which he based his conclusion "Taken on the average, and regarding both sexes, this alien Jewish population is somewhat inferior physically and mentally to the native population";[2] Joseph de Gobineau (1816–1882), who wrote the four-volume *Essay on the Inequality of the Human Races* and in it espoused the superiority of the white race.[3] The United States has had its share of these scientists whose racism transcends and confuses their scientific objectivity.[4] Since negative valuations in individuals based on membership in the stigmatized collective inevitably refer to some supposedly inviolate laws of inheritance, it is important to look at the issue of black genes, white genes, and gene pools, as these relate to the potential of individuals, black or white.

Genetics is defined as "the science that explains why like begets like and why cats always have kittens." [5] In its insistence on defining the process by which living things follow certain programs laid out in genetic materials at conception, it has attracted vocal advocates who would twist its tentative and modest propositions about the process of genetic inheritance into iron-clad laws of racial inequality ordained by nothing less than evolution or the human condition. It is no wonder that in black communities, genetic issues tend to be perceived as perpetuators of negative racial stereotypes and unseemly pessimistic determinism in regard to what blacks can achieve. Rarely is genetics considered to be a source of understanding and effective helping. The influence of biological racial differences upon personality and behavior patterns has been overemphasized by racists to justify discrimination and mistreatment of racial minorities.

Yet it cannot be denied that every animal, including man, has a specific genetic pattern which determines specific attributes such as visual acuity, rate of metabolization of glucose, range of tone perception, or structure of hair follicles. [6] The crucial questions for helping professionals are: To what extent is human behavior a consequence of such genetically determined characteristics and to what extent are these characteristics differentially distributed among racial or ethnic groups? These are not merely questions of academic interest—like whether the Romans were able to get more favorable prognostications by consulting chicken livers than did the Incas who looked at the lining of llama stomachs. Contemporary questions regarding the role played by genetics or family relationships or random events in the etiology of human problems are bread-and-butter issues. Thus, it is important to ask to what extent the solutions to such problems are constricted by biological "givens." This means that in black communities it is necessary to confront head-on such questions as "What is race?" and "What is black?" and then to consider what difference being black makes in problem-solving efforts. More specifically, How does being black affect intelligence, health, and emotional stability—the basic resources for success and achievement in American society. This chapter will deal with those questions, in the hope of providing adequate responses for those practitioners who are constantly bombarded with conflicting opinions and data and an inner struggle between what appears to be sound logic and the contrary evidence provided by one's own instincts.

WHAT IS RACE?
Race has been defined as "a breeding population characterized by frequencies of a collection of inherited traits that differ from those of other populations of the same species." [7] These inherited traits are usually described as skin color, eye shapes, hair, or other such obvious features. However, internal characteristics, qualities inaccessible to the eye, also serve as important racial indicators; some of these internal characteristics which are differentially distributed in breeding populations include types of ear wax, capacity to taste certain substances, blood types, and tendency to excrete certain chemical substances in the urine. It is obvious then that race is a group concept; it has no meaning in terms of single individuals—except when certain inherited traits appear more often in some groups than in others. This means that an individual categorized in a given race may not have all the traits that collectively characterize his racial population. When we attempt to place all members of the human species into groups based on physical characteristics, we find no hard and fast boundaries so that categories are mutually exclusive. Instead, we find much overlap and blurring at the edges, so that sometimes it is difficult to decide where a particular individual should be placed.

In spite of much disagreement among social scientists as to the variations in racial categories, almost everybody's list will include the three large groups (classical anthropologists refer to these as the three main racial stocks) Mongoloid, Caucasoid, and Negroid. Yet, it is clear that within each of these three major groupings there is diversity of breeding populations so that each should more properly be referred to as a racial conglomerate rather than a racial group. In regard to the Negroid group, Maquet has written:

> A black race is an illusion if one means by it a homogeneous group with common anatomical and physiological characteristics. Actually, it is a group of races, comprising in Africa, four races and several subraces. Of course, this classification is open to question, but it is certain that one can find among the blacks a number of groups, each characterized by a cluster of hereditary features. Finally, the blacks have nothing more in common than a more or less dark skin and kinky hair. A limited base to account for the cultural unity of Africa! Especially since there are blacks outside Africa: in Asia there are the black peoples of India and in Oceania the Negrito and Melanesian peoples. . . . Africanity then is not based on the community of a common race.[8]

Within any of the three major races, we find a tremendous amount of variation. Not the least of this variation is due to gene flow in large-scale hybridization of breeding populations. Recent studies have come up with a figure of 20 percent of the gene pool among American blacks as having some from European sources while 80 percent has been contributed by African sources.[9] This has been reported with the additional projection that after thirty or forty generations of random mating, i.e., mating in which race was not a factor in the selection of a marital partner, the average color of the American population would be only slightly darker than today while the American black would have disappeared from all but the history books. These statistics serve to illustrate the source of much of the concern in black communities where it is well known that race is as much a social designation as a physical one and that racial extinction, deliberate or not—is a distinct possibility.

The helping professional is likely to encounter in black communities as many different attitudes about the physical characteristics of race as there are in the textbooks. There are blacks who are very dark-skinned who, with the advent of the "black is beautiful" thrust within the community, have been able to construct for themselves positive self-images and pride in their dark skins. There are others who are dark-skinned and are able to say that they are proud of it but because of their earlier socialization have not yet been able to accept emotionally the fact that white is not better and that the lighter one's skin the more attractive he or she is. This dissonance between what is said and what is felt is uncovered in classicical Freudian slips or persistent habits such as using bleaching creams (but only because it is so effective in moisturizing the skin) or admonishing a child not to play with a very dark child (because he is bad or "not the right kind of playmate"). There are fair-skinned blacks who whites would consider black because of their ancestry but who "pass" because of their perception of black as inferior status and white as providing greater privileges. At the same time, there are fair-skinned blacks who take special pains to constantly refer to themselves as black so that no mistake will be made in identifying them. In some instances, these fair-skinned blacks will present a depressed affect because they feel unaccepted by black friends and at the same time hate the white world and feel no sense of identity with it. It is very obvious then that race is for most people something that is felt and not something that is defined by anthropometric terms.

Betty and Harold Phillips, thirty and thirty-two years old respectively, are a middle-class black couple who applied to an adoptions agency for the adoption of an infant. The family history, taken as part of the adoptions process, indicated that Harold Phillips was an engineer with the same company for nine years and was now in a responsible management position while his wife was an elementary schoolteacher. They had been married for seven years and had no children of their own. They were buying a house in a well-established integrated, upper middle-class neighborhood and had managed to build up a substantial amount of savings, including stocks and municipal bonds. Harold was a member of a well-known black family which included a judge, several physicians, and a Congressman. He was very fair-skinned with dark-brown, almost straight hair, worn rather long, and dark eyes. He expressed disappointment that they had not been able to have a child of their own but stated, "I am sure that I can love any child that I care for from infancy." His wife, Betty, was slim, rather petite, with light-brown skin, dimples, and curly hair cut short. She stated that she had come from a large family and at first had thought that she did not want children because of all the turmoil and struggle she had experienced in her own family. However, she stated that, like her husband, she had come to realize that she really did want children and that "it would be shameful for us who have so much not to share it with a child."

The white worker assigned to the home study quickly approved the couple, for it appeared that they more than met the qualifications for adoptive parents and "with so many little black babies needing good parents, we should not waste a minute." The next stage of the process, however, did not go well at all. The worker called the Phillipses when it appeared that a suitable infant was available and arranged a "showing." The Phillipes at first seemed pleased with the baby—at least, Mr. Phillips did—but decided to talk it over before making a final decision, and a few hours later telephoned to say that they did not think the infant would do, or as Mrs. Phillips put it, "I just didn't get the feeling that this baby could have been ours." After virtually the same script was acted out two more times, the worker asked to see Mr. and Mrs. Phillips in consultation before proceeding further. Mrs. Phillips agreed that they would come into the office, but at the appointed time she came alone, explaining that her husband had some business emergency to take care of and could not come.

The worker confronted her with the fact that their behavior indicated lack of real commitment to adoption and that therefore the agency was considering whether the application should be terminated. Mrs. Phillips began to cry and said that it was all her fault. She had been the one who had not found the infants suitable and her husband had merely gone along with her feelings. The worker pressed for more explanation as to what Mrs. Phillips had felt about the babies and finally Mrs. Phillips blurted out, "They were just too dark." The worker was surprised, since she had thought that it had been agreed that a baby "halfway between the two of them in color" would have been reasonable. Mrs. Phillips went on to explain, that all her husband's family were "very fair" and they had in fact not wanted him to marry her because "I am too black." However, she was the lightest one in her family and her brothers are "black as the hinges of hell." She had been afraid that a child of her own might be much darker than herself, even though her husband was fair. Her fears had been so great that, without her husband's knowledge, she had had her gynecologist insert an IUD so that she would not get pregnant. She has never told her husband, and only after much pressure on his part did she agree to apply for adoption. This, she felt, would be one way to be sure of getting a very fair baby that "my in-laws would not reject."

The worker was not sure how to deal with this information and told Mrs. Phillips that she would have to discuss this with her supervisor before coming to a decision. Mrs. Phillips said that she would withdraw the application rather than tell her husband what she had done. "He would say that it does not matter to him; but I know what his relatives would do and it would hurt him and I love him too much to see him hurt!"

At the supervisor's suggestion, the worker presented the case to a staff conference attended by the agency's seventeen workers, including four black staff members. The worker indicated to the staff that she was inclined to accept Mrs. Phillips' strong need for a fair-skinned child in the same way that the agency took into consideration any prospective parent's preferred physical characteristics in an adopted child. Furthermore, it appeared that Mrs. Phillips had accurately perceived the kind of rejection the child might incur from her in-laws and that she should not be forced to rear a child who would be estranged from its grandparents.

The black workers, however, expressed strong criticism of Mrs. Phillips and insisted that she had, in fact, rejected her own heritage and shown no indication of any real capacity to help a black child, dark or fair, to have a positive self-image. One black worker pointed out that there could be no assurance even that a very fair child of one or both black parents would in fact not become darker as it grew older and, under those circumstances, would Mrs. Phillips expect to be able to return the child to the agency? Another black worker indicated that Mr. Phillips seemed to be more secure in his identity than his wife and her decision to withhold her real feelings about having a child could be perceived as a negative indicator, i.e., an inability to risk open communication. The white worker was uncomfortable with the criticism of Mrs. Phillips and said that she thought she had been able to establish rapport with her and could help her work through her feelings so that she could express her real feelings to her husband. It would then be a joint decision as to whether they would insist on a child as fair as he or accept one that was not. The black workers were dissatisfied with this solution but commented that "because of the tremendous need for homes for black babies" it was perhaps the best thing to do.

The genetic issue of the probability that Mr. and Mrs. Phillips would have a child of their own darker than either is of relatively small consequence here. The risk may actually be much smaller than Mrs. Phillips fears. However, the more significant issue is whether Mrs. Phillips' negative attitude toward a darker child would impair her capacity as a parent.

RACE AND INTELLIGENCE
On the basis of all evidence currently available, there can be no other conclusion but that *intelligence as measured on IQ tests*

is a highly heritable characteristic. There are questions that remain, however, that have overriding significance for helping professionals. These questions include, "How much is heritable? Is that which IQ tests measure *really* intelligence? Even if it is intelligence, is intelligence highly correlated with success in life? Is the difference in IQ scores between blacks and whites more a function of environmental factors than hereditary ones? If in fact, *as a group,* blacks have a lower mean IQ than whites *as a group,* then what does this mean in regard to the characteristic problems encountered in black communities?

Arthur Jensen published a study in 1969 that has perhaps cause more furor in academic and lay circles alike than did Copernicus' shift of the center of the universe or Darwin's audacious account of man's evolution.[10] Jensen's study seemed to prove that about 80 percent of our intelligence is due to genetic inheritance and only about 20 percent to the environment. Thus the fifteen points difference between IQ scores of black and white populations in the United States which the cumulative record of educational research has unearthed would seem to suggest that whatever part of that difference is due to heredity is irreducible and not amenable to any "compensatory education" strategies to change. Just how much of that difference is due to hereditary factors is a matter of bitter controversy; proponents of the hereditary view have suggested that allowance for gross difference in the income and cultural experiences of the races would reduce the difference from fifteen to eleven points. On the other hand, the advocates of the environmental view propose that if somehow culture, history, and motivation could be sufficiently equated, then the interracial difference would be reduced to parity.

One might say that this has little significance to the helping practitioner who must deal with individuals or even communities of individuals, since even if Jensen's position were accepted, the goal would still have to be the creation of an environment which would support maximum realization of intellectual potential for every individual. However, from the moment of publication of Jensen's findings there has been evidence that the findings would be used in a far different way. For example, the environmentalist point of view was the basis upon which many social and educational programs of the 1960s had been based, from Head Start to Job Corps. The idea was to remove environmental disadvantage and thereby raise the level of achievement of poor, mostly black youth. The failure of these programs, i.e., the fact that they had not resolved the differences between blacks and whites in regard to academic performance, employment rate, or income level, could be placed squarely on the Jensen scapegoat—innate characteristics, inherited and therefore immutable. This completely ignores the fact that other influences could have brought about the failure to obtain significant changes—ineffective or inappropriate teaching methods, cultural bias by potential employers, mismanagement of programs, etc. These factors, however, difficult to prove and even politically dangerous to attack, could be swept under the proverbial rug now that Jensen has provided an easily acceptable and even "scientifically" documented explanation; thus it could be said that these programs failed because they called for the impossible—the elimination of differences that are based on genetic inheritance! Therefore, a caste-like structure of educational system was proposed by Jensen and his supporters to give recognition to the fact that the belief in human equality was patently false. Hernstein deplored the fact that the emphasis on equality could lead to "rigid, inflexible expectations, often doomed to frustration, thence to anger . . . [instead] we should be trying to mold our institutions around the inescapable limitations and varieties of human ability." [11]

It can be conceded that *individuals* do inherit a potential in regard to the construct defined as intelligence—which, by the way, will depend on environment to reach its maximum. Furthermore, it is also conceded that, given both the heritability of intelligence and the racial isolation and consequent racial inbreeding that assures that individuals whose potential has been systematically depressed by the racist system will breed primarily with individuals also disadvantaged, significant differences are likely to occur when IQ scores are compared with those of the dominant oppressors. What is not conceded, however, is that this can be used to rationalize punitive, nonsupportive practices *because* it implies that the situation is hopeless. This is not purely from the standpoint of methodological issues in regard to the research which generated the findings, although there is much evidence that the metholdology left much to be desired. It is much more closely related to the need to look for variations among groups rather than central tendencies as the basis for planning strategies of intervention to deal with problems.

The crunch comes to the helping professional who is faced with Mary M., a black unwed mother who wants desperately to be able to support herself and her children. The social history, however, reveals that she is a grade-school dropout with poor grades, erratic employment, and now has two children born out of wedlock. According to Jensen and his supporters, you would more than likely perceive this young woman as having less than average intelligence, so that encouraging her to fulfill her aspirations can only lead to frustration and anger. How does one determine whether Mary M. is truly limited in potential or has experienced limited opportunity and inadequate social support. The traditional IQ tests would more than likely confirm her low intelligence, even those tests that are supposedly "culture-free." Considerable effort has been spent in developing such culture-free tests; however, Jensen contends that even on such tests his differential between blacks and whites holds.

There are several reasons why Mary M. might do less well on the test than her true intelligence should reflect. As to the test-taking situation itself, there are many instances in which black children are made afraid of the test since it is rarely positive or gratifying in terms of feedback. It is more than likely to report

negative information; therefore, to expect *best* performance of
Mary M. under such conditions would be absurd. Even more
importantly, people who do well on IQ and achievement tests
do not necessarily perform better than average in most jobs.
There have been a multitude of studies of the nature of the
relationship between IQ scores and job performance on a variety of jobs using all sorts of techniques for rating performance.
In general, the findings show that IQ accounts for less than 10
percent of the variation in actual job performance. It might be
argued that persons holding particular jobs tend to be close in
IQ since the selection process, whether by educational qualifi-
cation or merely cultural bias of the person responsible for hiring, will tend to hire to fit whatever stereotype is held regarding
the intelligence needed for the job; i.e., bright persons might
not be hired in menial jobs even when presenting themselves
because they might not "fit"; on the other hand, persons who
are not particularly bright might not be hired for jobs which do
not necessarily require high intelligence because of an
"image" it is desired to project. However, it is unlikely that
Mary M. will ever take an IQ test. Yet the effects of Jensenism
and its view of blacks *as a group* as less intelligent than whites
as a group could nevertheless influence her negatively since
teachers, employers, and social workers would expect that any
failure on her part was due to basic low intelligence rather than
to other possible factors.

Mary M. is a real person who grew up in rural Louisiana, the
oldest of seven children of sharecropper parents. Mary M. did
not go to school much after she was nine or ten since
her mother always seemed to need her at home to help with the
younger children. Consequently, she was never able to pass
from one grade to the next as she should and she finally
stopped going.

She felt as if her mother only wanted her as a workhorse,
thus she was vulnerable to the attentions of a twenty-year-old
neighbor when she was only sixteen. When she became preg-

nant, he married her and she went to live in his widowed mother's house with her husband and nine of his brothers and sisters. When an uncle of her husband's in Chicago told him he could get him a job in the factory where he worked, they went north. Her first child was born three months later in the charity ward at a hospital larger than any she had ever seen before. The marriage was rocky and full of battles. She worked in a laundry, as a nurse's aide in a nursing home, and in various and sundry domestic jobs. Finally, after a fight in which her husband beat her so badly she could not see out of her left eye for a week, she left the baby with her sister-in-law and returned to Louisiana, saying that she would get him as soon as she regained her health and earned some money.

She went to her parents' house and again began to work as a domestic and to help with the younger children—an endless treadmill of washing and ironing and cooking and cleaning. She soon became involved with another man but this time when she became pregnant there was no question of marriage, since he was already married with several children. Her twins were born in her mother's house. Her husband's mother told him that she had the babies and he wrote her a vitriolic letter threatening to kill her if she ever returned to Chicago and that she should forget their son, because if she ever tried to get him, he would have her declared an unfit mother. Mary M. cried and nursed her babies and cried some more, and when they were only a few weeks old, she resumed the sorry treadmill of household chores for others.

Her mother had an aunt in Los Angeles who had "married well" and Mary M. wrote and asked if she could stay with her until she found a job. The aunt agreed, and Mary M. "caught a ride" with a family that used to live in her hometown and had returned for a visit. For helping with the driving and paying for part of the gas, she was able to get to Los Angeles. The children were left behind with her mother. Mary M. found a job as a housekeeper two days after she arrived, and for the next five years she worked in eight different households. The white women she worked for treated her much better than the rural white ladies in Louiana, and she earned much more than she had there or in Chicago. She found a nice apartment in the middle of the ghetto, but in Los Angeles even the ghetto was nicer than in Chicago. She had a nice "boyfriend" who ran a catering truck during the week and served as a minister on Sundays in his own little storefront church. He helped her to buy a small car so that she would not have to stand on the corners waiting for the bus to take her to Beverly Hills or Westchester or Brentwood.

In addition, she supplemented her earnings with welfare when her twin daughters came from Louisiana to live with her. Of course, she did not tell the welfare workers *all* that she made and she did not say that her husband "somewhere in Chicago" was not the father of her twin daughters, although in the eyes of the law he was indeed the father since there had never been a divorce. So Mary M. told her employers that she was doing as well as she ever had in her life and did not intend to marry her "boyfriend" because it would be expensive to get a divorce and anyway, he would probably treat her better if they were not married.

One of the women she worked for, a social worker, frequently pointed out to her that she was thirty-two years old and should be looking for some kind of job with more of a future than domestic work. She said there were training programs Mary M. could get into that would teach her things like data processing or clerical work. Sometimes she would tell Mary M. about civil service openings for the city or county, such as in the housekeeping department of the city hospital. The wages were better than she earned as a domestic worker and there were vacation days and health insurance and other fringe benefits. But Mary M. said no thank you, she did not want to work with a whole lot of people telling her what to do; in the houses, most of the ladies were gone all day and she worked at her own tempo and she knew how to do it well. She didn't want to go to school either because "I never done well in

school." So most of the ladies decided that she had low aspirations, and was probably limited in intelligence, and what could
you expect?

It came as a complete shock, therefore, when Mary M. an-
nounced to all the ladies she worked for that she would not be
coming back again. At first, they thought she was just being ir-
responsible and wasn't thinking about the future. Therefore it
shocked them even more to hear that she was opening up a
secondhand store in her neighborhood. She had been working
in it already but a sister was there full time. She had seen what
good things the ladies gave away that they were not using
anymore and she knew that the people in the ghetto could use
them at a price they could afford. She had talked to people who
had secondhand stores and found out how to go about getting
merchandise, and she was able to rent an empty store from an
owner who had his own store in the same block and was tired
of bad tenants. She had convinced him that she would keep a
nice place with no rowdy loiterers and pay her rent on time.

Mary M. had gotten off the welfare some time before when
her husband had been killed in an automobile accident in Chicago. She had gone back to try to get her son, but he said he
wanted to stay with his aunt; she told him that if he ever
wanted to come to her he could. But she knew about social security and that her daughters were eligible for survivors' benefits because, by law, they were her husband's children. She
applied and began to receive the social security benefits. She
laughed with her friends over the fact that even after writing to
inform the welfare department she no longer needed assistance, she received checks four months in succession because
"the computer couldn't understand what I said." But she carefully returned each check with a note, repeating her statement
that she was no longer eligible.

The question of Mary M.'s IQ is almost unanswerable in
terms of Jensen's tests. "The assumption generally is that IQ
tests a single measurable capacity underlying other skills; it is
stable, conferred in the first fifteen years of life, and it sets a

limit on what a person can learn to do." Yet, there is considerable evidence that what a person with almost any IQ can learn
or do depends upon what he wants to do and what kind of education and training he has had. Mary M.'s capacity to survive
under horrendous social, educational, and cultural disadvantages might well be superior to that of a "well-brought-up"
middle-class white woman who suddenly found herself without
support of family, money, or skills and knowledge valued by the
majority in society. Yet, on the traditional IQ tests, Mary M.
would score lower than her white counterpart.

If the question of genetic determination of intelligence works
to the disadvantage of the individual in the ordinary encounters
he or she has with established social institutions and their
functionaries, certainly the disadvantage is compounded when
it is in the form of social policy affecting the entire group that is
considered genetically inferior. Jensen and his adherents have
proposed more rigid tracking systems in our public schools
adapted to the supposedly inherited differences in groups and
have also suggested before congressional committees that
money spent on compensatory education programs aimed at
increasing the academic achievement of blacks is wasted,
since they will never be able to reduce the gap created by
genetic differences. Shockley, who is perhaps the "farthest
out" of the Jensen supporters, has even suggested that nature
has color-coded groups of individuals so that the pragmatic
man on the street can make statistically reliable predictions of
their capacity for intellectually rewarding and effective lives.[12]
In its least radical form, this view would propose that the un-
derrepresentation of blacks in certain occupations—stock-
brokers, lawyers, nuclear physicists, etc.—is as expected
because the pool of black individuals with the necessary intelligence is proportionately lower. Furthermore, low achievement scores by blacks in a school or in a school system, when
compared with whites, is no cause for alarm because, again,

this difference would be expected because of the inherent genetic differences. The negative effect for the group, then, is that little attention is given to the fact that other differences between the groups that are manageable—racist bias of teachers, etc.—may be contributing to the low scores. The central tendency trap opens up again and thousands of hapless victims fall in who might have been helped if the fatalistic view had not prevailed.

The dissatisfaction with IQ tests does not lie solely in black communities where they have been used so destructively. They have proved similarly unacceptable and inappropriate when used on the general population as well. The British, for example, are attempting to develop a substitute for the Wechsler and Stanford-Binet tests developed in America which will give far more weight to creativity than is seen in these standard tests.[13] Creativity is the ability to generate new ideas where the idea of a right answer is irrelevant or highly personal. On the new British test, children will be asked to generate many different ideas from a single starting point, e.g., how many possible ways can you think of to use a frying pan (or an old tire, or a bucket)? The test will be longer-timed too, since many persons who get right answers but too late on timed tests may not be mentally slow but are able to think of many more alternatives to be weighed and counterweighed before making a decision. Similarly, when children or adults know that a test is timed they tend to answer impulsively and maybe incorrectly, whereas if they are made to stop and think they will get it right even within the allotted time. Thus, the British test is seeking not to come up with an IQ "score," which is the old linear model, central tendency bugaboo, but rather to generate a "profile" of abilities which describe patterns of dealing mentally with the world, patterns which may have differential desirability given the nature of the environmental situation or context.

RACE AND OTHER GENETICALLY BASED
CHARACTERISTICS

The evidence supports the notion that the heritability of intelligence is a valid, acceptable principle of human growth and
development that has been resisted primarily because of the
way it has been used for political or racist purposes. Intelligence is not the only human characteristic that has been so
manipulated. All individuals possesses inborn differences that
are due to special patterning of brain structure, endocrine
glands, and anatomy which, like other human beings in gross
outline, are never the same. When a husband and wife cannot
agree on the temperature at which to set the thermostat in the
bedroom or the right intensity of the lighting or the volume on
the stereo set, it is evidence of their inborn differences in physiology of the senses. It is when the inborn distinctiveness of individuals is transformed into generalizations about the distinctiveness of entire groups or races that the mischief is created.
Thus, the literature contains supposedly scientific treatises af-
firming that blacks have greater insensitivity to pain, greater
ability to tolerate manual labor, and lesser control of the emotions when compared to whites. This extreme school of biological determinism has not achieved intellectual respectability for
many years, but it still has been a strong theme in the laymen's
perspective in racist societies.[14] This is of considerable importance in the helping professions, since the kind of helping
strategies that biological determinism supports have been
characterized by Rainwater as "benign totalitarianism."[15]
Thus, there is considerable emphasis on control over the activities of those deemed biologically inferior because they are not
capable of judging what is best for themselves. The paternalistic strain in welfare programs is an example of how the attitudes influence helping professions. The tendency to judge as
"normal" in blacks the kind of behavior that would be considered an indication of the need for help in whites—e.g., apathy,
emotional lability, etc., is another instance of such negative influences.

The fallacy concerning genetic inferiority in the black population has insidiously affected the consideration of life expectancy. It has been clearly established that blacks have a shorter life expectancy in the United States than whites, but this is more likely due to environmental factors rather than genetic ones.[16] The complexity of these factors is enormous. For example, many respiratory ailments such as chronic bronchitis, emphysema, and certain forms of asthma have been shown in some industrial areas to be more prevalent among inner-city residents whose homes are close to the sources of air polluted with industrial contaminants. Blacks are also found increasingly in high-risk occupations. At the same time, death by accident is significantly higher among blacks than among whites. Perhaps one of the most significant differences in death rates of black males is the high risk of murder. Bims states:

> No discussion of statistics come close in conveying the sheer prevalence of murder in many of America's black communities, where men are being slaughtered in unprecedented proportions. In Detroit, where the murder percentage is the highest in the nation, eight young blacks were slaughtered one night in an incident believed to have been associated with a drug war. They shared the fate of nearly 700 persons who were murdered in the city in 1971—nearly 600 of them black.[17]

That murder is also more prevalent among lower socioeconomic groups and among young people, and that blacks have both a higher proportion of young persons and persons in the lower socioeconomic group than whites, contributes to the disparity but does not entirely explain the difference. Aggression is a complex phenomenon of perhaps multiple sources, and violence is its bitter fruit. Moyer asserts that the two major theories on aggression are both inadequate: i.e., the idea that aggression is a biological phenomenon built into the gene structure and the idea that man has no inborn impulses to violence but learns it.[18] Moyer insists that the evidence supports a physiological model of human aggression; i.e., "the brain contains inborn neural systems . . . when these systems are active *and* the appropriate stimuli are present, the person will act aggressively. The aggression system has varying sensitivity (i.e., varying levels at which it is activated) influenced by a number of factors—heredity, blood chemistry, learning, etc. Most importantly, "the person who inherits a low threshold for hostility will find many targets for his aggression if he lives in a deprived, frustrating, and stressful environment. However, if he is surrounded by love, and exposed to little provocation, his aggressive behavior will be sharply limited." Thus, even if low aggression threshold were randomly distributed among all ethnic groups, those persons or groups of persons living in stressful environments could be expected to exhibit more violent behavior.

Not all such perceptions of the genetic pool of blacks are in the direction of deficiencies or negative characteristics. Attempts have been made to provide scientific evidence that there are genetic differences between blacks and whites resulting in athletic superiority of blacks in sports.[19] These supposedly inherited factors included a basically elongated body structure that enables blacks to function as more efficient heat dissipaters than whites; a greater ratio of tendon to muscle resulting in "double-jointedness"; longer legs, wider calf bones, and greater arm circumference, all of which supposedly give blacks greater athletic capability. Yet, the research on which these generalizations are based has been attacked as methodologically indefensible. Harry Edwards points out, for example, that there were no probability samples of black Americans to compare with white Americans or even random samples of white and black athletes.[20] Supporting data were taken primarily from black athletes of proven excellence and from other uncontrolled selection procedures. He demonstrates that there is no attention given to the fact that "sports participation holds the greatest promise of escape from the material degradation of oppressed black society."

The true nature of a racist society, however, is apparent in the fact that although a proportionately larger numbers of blacks excel in professional football, until recently there have been almost none in the quarterback position, which is the indisputable leadership position on a football team. Chrisman, in a particularly perceptive analysis of the psychosocial dynamics of professional football, has placed this paradox as inherent in the nature of the game.[21] If football were only a sport, "the black quarterback might well be integrated into that position just as he has been in all the others, for a team can attain its peak only through the unrestricted use of the best players at each position." However, Chrisman maintains that football in the United States is one of the leading expressions of American culture and its attendant value system in which white supremacy is still a persistent and viable component. Blacks, therefore, after having been excluded until the second half of this century, were perceived as suitable primarily for the bruising, physical positions on the team and not the "thinking" positions. Chrisman states, "The standard clichés were trotted out. . . . Because blacks lack intelligence, courage, leadership and crowd appeal, they could not be winning quarterbacks. On the other hand, the brutal force, the speed and the grace of a running back, tackle or cornerback did not contradict—in some cases even corroborated—the vision held by many whites that blacks are superphysical but a little deficient upstairs." In the ritual which is football, cherished American values are acted out and the quarterback is the superstar who can be a swaggering Errol Flynn type or a puritanical Gary Cooper type but never the black descendant of abject slaves. The generalizations of genetically based racial differences that make blacks physically superior but whites intellectually superior have their origin in the racist fantasies of American society rather than in sound, scientific research.

Although certain characteristics may be differentially distributed in gene pools of different racial groups, for the most part the differences have not had functional significance except as they provide support for political opinions held by various groups in society. Blacks, themselves, have chosen at times to identify genetically based racial differences that support their aspirations for building a more positive collective identity and subsequently a redistribution of the power in social relationships which have been withheld from them on the basis of supposed differences. Frances Cress Welsing, for example, has identified a significantly greater capacity in blacks to "feel" emotion as compared to whites, which is embodied in the concept of "soul." [22] More interesting, perhaps, is her concept of whites as "color deficient", i.e., the absence of color is defined as a negative attribute which is at the root of compensatory behaviors in whites who unconsciously recognize that they are missing something important.

Despite the temptation to attribute particular physical, emotional, or psychological characteristics to population groups— positive or negative, depending on whether you are a member or not—there is always greater support for a complex of determinants of observed differences between groups which are simultaneously genetic and environmental, historical and contemporary.[23] Many slaves survived because of physical strength and toughness, but many others did so because of high intelligence and shrewdness. The construction of ideology of spurious bases of genetic endowment foreshortens the powerful influence of the collective experience and reduces that experience to something less than it should be.

SICKLE-CELL ANEMIA: THE BLACK DISEASE
Whereas there is little sound scientific evidence to support the view that blacks are more emotional than whites or have superior athletic ability, there is considerable evidence that the frequency of certain physical characteristics such as skin pigmentation, shape of hair follicles, or amount of space between teeth are different when blacks are compared with whites. Furthermore, there are significant differences between the two groups in regard to at least two disease entities: Sickle-cell

anemia is considered to be definitely genetic in origin; the other, high blood pressure, may be due to environmental stresses imposed by an oppressive society. Given this difference in the presumed causal nexus of the two disease entities, it is interesting to note the manner in which prevention and treatment have been carried out.

Sickle-cell anemia is caused by an abnormality in one of the genes that regulates the manufacture of hemoglobin, the substance in red blood cells that binds and carries oxygen to the tissues. Those individuals who have the defective gene produce red corpuscles which become sickled instead of the normal doughnut shape whenever there is a reduction in the oxygen content in the environment. The sickle-shaped cells cannot move smoothly through the capillaries and pile up, preventing vital substances such as oxygen from nourishing surrounding tissues. This condition is known as a sickle-cell crisis and it is extremely painful. In addition to the crisis itself, the genetic abnormality, or sickling cell phenomenon, causes slowed growth and development and increases susceptibility to infectious diseases. Most who have the disease die before twenty and there are few who live past forty. Actually, the disease occurs only when there are two sickling genes present in the individual, one from each parent. Thus sickle-cell anemia is known in genetics as an autosomal recessive disease. The individual who has only one sickling gene and a normal gene will not have the disease but will be a carrier who is considered to have sickle-cell "trait." There are few symptoms present in the case of individuals with sickle-cell trait except perhaps discomfort and pain at high altitudes or in unpressurized airplanes. The risk for these carriers is that they may marry a carrier and thereby produce one child in four with not only the trait but the disease itself, with all the painful symptoms and limited life expectancy that this implies.

Until the early 1950s there was little recognition of sickle-cell anemia since it is primarily a disease occurring in blacks. However, the civil rights movement was one in which there were demands to recognize everything about blacks as an essential component of American social life and anything that was indicative of neglect of black concerns; e.g., ignoring sickle-cell anemia as an important disease entity, was to be decried. Powledge points out that:

> The sudden burgeoning of interest in sickle-cell disease is the result of the convergence of three factors: charges of neglect, an infusion of money, and a ripening technology. Diagnostic techniques have also made its contribution, inexpensive, relatively easy, mass testing procedures are available that can reliably reveal the presence of abnormal hemoglobin in a small blood sample. The tests detect both the trait and the disease.[24]

The attention given to sickle-cell anemia, however, was perceived by many in the black community as additional evidence of the racist orientation of helping professions which perceived a genetically based disease as having higher priority than lead poisoning from peeling paint in substandard buildings or iron-deficiency anemia from malnutrition in an affluent society. More dramatically, the killer has proved to be "strokes" or bursting blood vessels due to the abnormally high blood pressure, a known characteristic of blacks. It soon becomes evident, however, that the high blood pressure is not genetic in origin but perhaps "overdetermined" by a variety of social as well as physical conditions.

However, the genetic and medical facts about sickle-cell anemia cannot alone explain some of the consequences of an increased public awareness of sickle-cell anemia as a "black disease." There has been a proliferation of laws passed in several states concerning screening for sickle-cell trait. Some of these laws require that blacks be tested for it as well as for veneral disease before a marriage license is issued. Some are as biologically inaccurate in their implications, as in Washington, D.C., where it is defined by law as a communicable disease.

These laws place an emphasis on the identification of defects in the black population rather than on the treatment of the disease, which is real rather than potential. Yet there is no denying the impact of a disease that sentences a child to recurrent pain and limited life span and creates tremendous emotional consequences of guilt, anxiety, and depression through the entire family. Helping professionals should be aware not only of the need for genetic counseling as a preventive measure (and the counseling should leave the couple involved with the right to determine whether they want to risk the one-in-four chance of bearing a child with sickle-cell disease) but also of the need for adequate medical treatment and emotional support to children with sickle-cell anemia and their families.

The message from the field of genetics is clear enough for unprejudiced minds to comprehend. Each of us is unique (except for the proportionately small number of twins and other multiples), and our particular collection of genes is specific to ourselves. Furthermore, no racial or ethnic group has a monopoly on the "good" genes or escapes completely the "bad" genes. For example, blacks are the primary group afflicted with sickle-cell anamia, but Caucasians get cystic fibrosis, Eastern and Central European Jews have Tay-Sachs disease; and Mediterranean stock get Cooley's anemia. However, the whirlwind advancement of "the new genetics" with its breezy assumptions regarding control over biological inheritance has raised again the specter of past excesses. One recalls Charles Davenport, (1866–1944), who labored in the vineyards of social eugenics and warned that the principle of equality was a biological absurdity and the efforts of social workers, and even public health workers, were contrary to the direction of evolution.[25] It is not far from there to Shockley, Hernstein, Jensen, and Eysenck, who declare that they have solid evidence that blacks are intellectually inferior to whites and no amount of federal support for programs aimed at closing the intelligence gap between the two groups will do any good. Practitioners in human services would do well, then, to heed the warning sounded by Etzioni as he considered the hazards of genetic engineering:

> Is the newfound popularity of biologistic interpretation anything more than a reaction, maybe an overreaction, to the previous excessive reliance on education and social reforms as a propellant of change and to the view of man as highly pliable? And will we not, in one or two decades from now, overreact again to the overreaction, after many millions of people may have been affected by what looks to be the next fad, biological engineering? Is there a way to avoid, or at least reduce, this gross oversteering, these enthusiasms, as bases for public policy, and to gain a better grasp of the potentials and dangers involved before we change course? [26]

SUMMARY

This chapter has presented considerable evidence that genetics has been a favorite vehicle for negative valuation of blacks. The physical differences which characterize the different racial groups have been grossly expanded to include differences in mental ability, emotional stability, and a host of other dimensions along which groups can be placed differentially.

Race has been defined as "a breeding population characterized by frequencies of a collection of inherited traits that differ from those of other populations of the same species." Three main racial groups have been identified—Caucasoid, Mongoloid, and Negroid—but there are tremendous variations within each. Therefore, the helping professional is likely to encounter wide differences in so-called racial characteristics—e.g., hair texture, skin color, etc.—in black communities as well as many different attitudes about their value based on the extent to which individuals have or have not incorporated values of the larger society.

Race and intelligence and their relationship has been discussed in some detail, since this relationship is one of the more controversial of our times. Although some researchers insist that there is a genetically based inferiority in regard to intelligence of blacks, strong evidence to the contrary exists. Furthermore, there are strong ethical as well as scientific reasons which would reject political decisions to deny some group in the ethnosystem opportunities based on preconceived notions of their genetically based capacities to take advantage of those opportunities.

Even when genetically based racial differences are proposed as favoring blacks—such as athletic superiority—it has an underlying negative message; i.e., physical ability is an inferior ability to intellectual ability—more animal-like and not demanding use of high-level reasoning or other intellectual skills. Despite the fact that certain characteristics may be differentially distributed in the gene pools of different racial groups, for the most part the differences have not had functional significance.

Finally, sickle-cell anemia is identified as a genetically based disease which has been given greater attention than some other more evident problems in black communities, such as heart disease. Some feel this is because the genetic etiology of sickle-cell anemia can be perceived as indicative of "genetic inferiority," whereas heart disease or respiratory problems are more likely to be the result of factors associated with poverty and/or poor environmental conditions.

experiential exercises

1.
In a mixed racial group meeting for the first time, ask each member to state his or her name. Then ask the members to write down all the names they can remember *except those known prior to the meeting*. The hypothesis is that members

will more often remember the names of persons of the same racial identification as themselves; i.e., the cues obtained from facial characteristics as well as familiarity with certain ethnic names combine to increase the likelihood that this will happen.

    (a) To what extent is this hypothesis supported?

    (b) If it is supported, what are the implications for helping professions?

2.

In a mixed racial group, ask each group member to identify those characteristics of self which have generally been described by his/her family members as his/hers inheritance from parents or earlier ancestors.

    (a) Which characteristics are most frequently identified?

    (b) Is the heritability of these characteristics supported by evidence from the field of genetics?

    (c) To what extent can beliefs about the heritability of these characteristics influence an individual's social functioning?

    (d) Are there differences in the kind of characteristics identified among the racial groups represented?

3.

Interview a black member of MENSA (an organization of persons who score very high on IQ tests).

    (a) How was the IQ score discovered, and by whom?

    (b) To what extent does he or she believe that there have been opportunities available to put his or her intellectual capacities to maximum use?

4.

Interview agency staff regarding their perception of the capacity of the client described below to engage in a problem-solving process.

> Mrs. Gray is a thirty-seven-year-old widow with four children. She has been receiving social security supplemented by public assistance since her truckdriver husband died three years before. She has a high school education but has not worked since her marriage at eighteen. She and the children live in a low-income housing project and rent is based on a sliding scale according to ability to pay. She enrolled in a training program for mental health paraprofessionals but has been having difficulty in adjusting to the trainee role. Although the program provides child care, she cannot seem to get to the training program on time; when confronted with her frequent tardiness, she lashed out in an almost uncontrollable rage and insisted that she was not losing much by being one to two hours late. She does not participate in class discussions and has had great difficulty in carrying out written assignments although her completed work indicates a better than average competency in written language. Because of her somewhat puzzling behavior, project staff have referred her to a community mental health center for psychological counseling, a supportive service provided trainees in the program.
>
> (a) Ask workers, "To what extent would you evaluate the probability that this woman could make maximum use of a psychotherapeutic relationship aimed at resolution of the problems she has presented in the training program?"
>
> (b) After their response, interject: "Oh, I forgot to mention that Mrs. Gray had been given an IQ test and has tested at 140." How does this additional statement change the nature of the expectations in regard to this client's capacity for utilization of psychotherapy as a problem-solving tool?

chapter six

. . . in black families

Perhaps more has been written about the families of black people than any other aspect of growing up black in America. Social science perspectives on black families have traditionally emphasized differences in form and processes when compared with white families. However, perceptions of the source and consequences of differences have varied widely, depending on the point of view of the observer. For example, some have maintained that black families are ineffective at best, pathological at worst in regard to their impact on children growing up in them. Some scholars have attributed this to the operations of the oppressive and racist society which warps and distorts black families into dysfunctional forms; Frances Welsing, psychiatrist on the faculty of Howard University, in an interview published in a black women's magazine, stated:

> Black people do not have families—we have survival units. That is all that we are allowed to have. A family plays a specific role in the organization of any social system. A family in a viable society has a particular role and then they have little social units called children to be functional people to carry out the natural development of the group. As oppressed people, we are not supposed to be maximally developed. . . . We hear a lot of discussion by black scholars . . . praising the strength of black families. Nonsense! You can't talk about strengths and then talk about oppression.[1]

In these remarks, Welsing joins a host of other behavioral scientists who have characterized black families *in general* as dysfunctional as a result of racial discrimination and prejudice inflicted consistently since the forced removal of blacks from the African continent. Yet, perhaps more pernicious in the scheme of things are those scholars who also view black families as dysfunctional but perceive this fact as the *cause* of all the behaviors which prevent blacks from succeeding—crime, violence, alcoholism, drug addiction, gambling, prostitution, etc. For example, in his infamous description of black family life as a "tangle of pathology," Moynihan advanced the notion that these problem behaviors are so much a part of black life styles that they have become self-perpetuating and thus do not need white oppression or discrimination to perpetuate them.[2]

In recent years, there have been some attempts in the literature to balance the view of black family life. Robert Hill has attested to strengths that exist in black families.[3] Other black social scientists have emphasized the fact that black cultural values and family patterns are based on survival needs and for the most part are more humanistic and have greater validity than the hollow values of middle-class American society.

Rainwater has referred to this point of view in regard to the poor, who also have at times been perceived as living more authentic lives than "hung-up" middle-class people as the apotheosizing perspective, i.e., "this perspective tends to emphasize the heroic quality of the life of the disinherited . . . heroic not just in the sense of being able to cope with adversity and still maintain life but in the sense that as a result of adversity, the disinherited have been able to create a way of life that has beauty and virtue."[4]

The helping professional who becomes immersed in the literature of the black family therefore has a wide variety of perspectives which in many instances are so contradictory that one could well wonder whether the same families are being described. Actually, the families studied in order to derive theoretical postulates have often not been truly representative of all black families. Billingsley writes:

> There are four tendencies in the treatment of black families in social science scholarship. The first is the tendency to ignore black families altogether. The second is, when black families are considered, to focus almost exclusively on the lowest-income group of black families, that acute minority of black families who live in public housing projects or who are supported by welfare assistance. The third is to ignore the majority of black stable families even among this lowest income group, to ignore the processes by which these families move from one equilibrium state to another, and to focus instead on the most unstable among these low income families. A fourth tendency, which is more bizarre than all the others, is the tendency on the part of social scientists to view the black, low income, unstable, problem-ridden family as the causal nexus for the difficulties their members experience in wider society.[5]

Efforts have recently been made to study middle- and upper-class black families. However, for the most part the emphasis remains on the "ghetto" family as the prototype of *"the* black family." Again, for the helping professional it becomes important to be able to understand the rich diversity of family structures, family relationships, family processes and family outcomes as they are encountered in black communities. Whereas the academician is trying to find explanations for observed differences (statistical) in the distribution of certain behaviors among different groups, the helping professional is fortunate to be able to deal with much smaller social systems and, since these are never identical, it is understanding variation and its implications which mark the successful practitioner.

MULTIPLE FAMILY STRUCTURES
Billingsley has described twelve types of family structures among blacks in the United States. First, there are three types of nuclear or primary families in which the marital pair and

their children have no other persons living with them. These may be *incipient* when there are no children, *simple* if composed of the couple and their children, or *attenuated* if there is a single parent and children with no others present. Second, there are extended families in which these are other relatives or in-laws of the marital pair who share the same household with the primary family. Extended families may also be incipient, simple, or attenuated depending upon whether children are present or whether there is only one parent. Finally, there are augmented families which includes nonrelatives in the household. There are at least six possible types of augmented family depending on whether there are children present, whether it includes relatives as well as nonrelatives, and whether there is only a single parent as head of household.[6]

The single-parent family, which has borne much of the criticism of those who perceive family structure as crucial in socialization of children and two-parent families as the ideal, can be broken down into subtypes according to whether the single parent is male or female and whether he or she has never been married, is married with an absent spouse, legally separated, divorced, or widowed. Only about 6 percent of black families are *attenuated* single-parent families, despite a common notion that this is characteristic of black families. None of these family types constitute the majority of black families, so the search for a central tendency would fail to identify a "typical" black family and would necessarily emphasize a multi-modal distribution; i.e., nationally about 36 percent of all Negro families are of the simple nuclear type, nearly 20 percent are incipient nuclear families, whereas the remaining 38 percent are extended or augmented families of one kind or another. Thus, even to point out that the commonest type of family structure among blacks is the ideal nuclear family of parents and their children does not convey the variety of structures that exist and the need to understand the dynamics inherent in all of these structures as they relate to the family's effectiveness in fulfilling its major social functions.

There are other aspects of family structure which may have significance as a determinant of the behavior of those growing up within it. For example, it is a reality factor that a black child is much more likely to grow up in a large family than a white child. Since there is a negative correlation between income and family size, it can be assumed that these larger families will have fewer financial resources to insure adequate health care, education, or cultural enrichment experiences. Within black communities, however, there are conflicting points of view about the desirability of large families. Some suggest that family planning to reduce family size is an important prerequisite for improving the status of blacks since it will make possible a higher standard of living. Others insist that such family planning efforts are covert attempts at genocide. Furthermore, if blacks are to gain any political power in this country, it will only be where they are in large enough numbers to provide a power base from which black leaders can obtain leverage within the system. It is clear, however, that neither of the polar extremes of these views contains much hope for improvement of the position of blacks in this country. Severe reduction of the birth rate among blacks, in fact, is likely to occur as it has among whites in the middle and upper socioeconomic classes where there is now more chance of obtaining adequate material and cultural resources. On the other hand, even if family planning programs succeeded in reducing the birth rate among low-income blacks there is no reason to believe that more money will be spent on education or other activities leading to a higher socioeconomic level.

The stereotype of the single-parent family as characteristic of black families is based on the assumption that a circular process is in operation whereby black males historically were subjugated and emasculated and the woman was the only stable factor in slave families. Black women, therefore, continue to function in a domineering relationship to the male so that black husbands leave their wives to avoid either the responsibilities they have never been socialized to shoulder or to avoid the

subordinate role forced upon them by their wives. This stereotype, like most, does not begin to identify the complex nature
of the relationships which exist in black families between marital partners and between the marital partners and the children
as well as between the nuclear and extended family systems.
The terms "single-parent," "female-headed," "matriarchal," or
"matrifocal" households have often been used synonymously,
although each has a different referent in regard to family structure and process. Single-parent, for example, may refer to a
household headed by male or female parent. Although the majority of such households—among both white and black—are
headed by females, a substantial number are headed by men
and therefore could by no stretch of the imagination be considered matriarchal. However, matriarchy in the strict sociological
sense denotes a kind of family structure in which lineage is determined by the maternal rather than paternal family; i.e., "a society in which some if not all of the legal powers relating to the
ordering and governing of the family are lodged in women
rather than in men." [7] It has been suggested that the female-
dominated household described by sociologists in terms of informal decision-making power may be termed more accurately
"matrifocal." However, Stack has observed that neither the
concept of matriarchy *nor* matrifocality accounts for the variety
of family strategies found in urban America. In a study conducted among blacks in a major metropolitan community,
Stack and her associates found that domestic functions were
carried out by clusters of kin who may or may not reside
together.[8] The basis of these cooperative units is co-genera-
tional sibling alignment, the domestic cooperation of close
adult females, and the exchange of goods and services between the male and female relatives of those females. Thus
older females in grandparent roles might perform important
roles as resource persons, particularly in regard to child care,
but rarely did they have major decision-making powers.

  Black females have always exceeded black males in number
and the ratio of black males to black females has been stead-

ily declining. For example, in 1850 there were 99.1 black males for every 100 black females; however, by 1970, there were only 90.8 males for every 100 females.[9] The fact that men are relatively scarce puts black females at a distinct disadvantage in the distribution of power in their relationship. It is therefore ironic that despite the fact that most blacks—like whites—perceive marriage and the nuclear model as an advantage and that the competition for black men is fierce, the idea persists that black women somehow are in control and able to perpetuate matriarchal family systems. Murray has written:

> As long as she (the Negro woman) is confined to an area in which she must compete fiercely for a mate, she remains the object of sexual exploitation and the victim of all the evils such exploitation involves. In the Negro population, the excess of girls is greatest in the 15 to 44 age group which covers the college years and the years when most marriages occur . . . The explosive social implications of an excess of more than half a million Negro girls and women over 14 years of age is obvious.[10]

The competition for mates is intensified by the fact that some men are unwilling to marry at all and an increasing tendency for Negro men to marry white women. The following case demonstrates the problem encountered by many middle-class black women who have thoroughly incorporated the society's normative expectations regarding the manner in which family life is established.

> Sara L. was a thirty-two-year-old black woman, single, who was employed as a reading specialist in a large, Midwestern city. It was the same city in which she had grown up and she was surrounded by a host of relatives and friends. However, she had in recent years become increasingly subject to spells of depression and moodiness. Normally, she had a sunny disposition; she was not pretty but her friends referred to her as nice-looking. She had been an honor student in high school, had gone to a well-known predominantly black university and later earned a master's degree in a large state university in the

East. Her parents had died in an automobile accident while she was in graduate school and she had returned to live in the house she grew up in, but alone. She had an older sister and a younger sister. Both were married and lived in other cities, too far to visit regularly, but they considered themselves close and talked often by telephone. The older sister had married a physician; the younger sister had married a much older man, a wealthy businessman who was often featured in *Ebony* magazine as an example of a black man who had "made it."

Sara's friends were almost all married but they still included her in most of their activities. During college she had been engaged but had broken it off when her fiancé insisted on joining the Air Force. She did not think that she could tolerate such a nomadic life. At first, there always seemed to be at least one man around who was interested in her but somehow none of them seemed to be quite right. However, now there were fewer and fewer single men her age or older and she often found herself the "extra" at her friends' parties or else paired off with some embarrassingly young man. A number of times, she had found herself almost "involved" with married men who "forgot" to mention their marital status or with divorced men whom she couldn't help thinking of as "marital failures." Sara's friends often told her that "thirty-two isn't so old; you've still got a chance," or "a lot of girls these days are deciding not to get married." But Sara knew that she did want to get married and she became more and more despondent as her chances seemed to slip away. She began to suffer from headaches, back pain, and lack of energy. She was spending a large portion of her income on medical bills and finally her doctor suggested that she see a psychologist since he could find no physical basis for her complaints.

Sara somewhat reluctantly accepted the referral but really did not intend to follow through with it until she found that the psychologist was also black and female. She did not feel that her problems were psychological but she was curious about the psychologist and decided to make an appointment. Thus began an eight-month course of psychotherapy which turned out to be extremely useful to Sara. The psychologist was able to help Sara articulate and then examine her attitudes about marriage and the extremely narrow definition she had of "suitable" men which was related to her competitiveness with her sisters, with schoolmates for honors, and now on her job. Most importantly, she was able to help Sara to understand the limited options black women have as a group due to the excess of females over males and to reduce her growing negative self-image as her failure to meet "the right man" was being blamed on her own "lack of worth as a woman." Much discussion in her therapy sessions concerned her attitudes about sex, particularly premarital sex. Although she had had intimate relationships with a few men with whom she had become serious, the circumstances had always been strained and ungratifying because she had felt that "it wasn't right." Furthermore, she dreaded pregnancy, and she described the kind of girls who had to drop out of high school and even college, and it was clear that Sara saw them as having low status, not very intelligent, and certainly having none of the characteristics she would use to describe herself. She had never been able to welcome sex without marriage as the goal. She was asked by the psychologist to think of men she liked but would not marry. This made it possible for Sara to admit that there were many men that she felt sexually attracted to but avoided because they were not "suitable" for marriage. Much later she was even able to admit that there might be the possibility of an intimate relationship with a man which might not end in marriage. Sara was convinced, however, that she would not feel free to follow her inclinations in the city where she had grown up and "everybody knows me and anything I did would be spread all over!" As a consequence, Sara began to look outside the city for other opportunities and applied for and got a job with a book publishing company in the East.

At the termination of psychotherapy, she told the psychologist that the fear of remaining single had dissipated since she could now see that "if I don't get married, it may be because there are too few men and not because there's something wrong with me." She also implied that although it still would not be easy, making a life independent of friends and relatives might also open up the possibility of alternatives to marriage if marriage didn't happen.

Ladner has pointed out that very often it is white women who initiate sexual advances toward black men.[11] Throughout history black men have been lynched when white women, angered because their advances had been refused, cried rape. At the same time, black women were completely vulnerable to the sexual assaults of white men, forced to bear their children, denied the right to keep their children if the master wished them sold. The minuscule number of interracial marriages even in today's climate of eroding legal obstacles to such alliances may be attributed to this historical reality. The fact that, of black-white marriages reported in the 1970 Census, 60 percent were black husband and white wife while only 40 percent were black wife/white husband, might indicate the different dynamics at work because of the different historical experiences for black males and females. Whereas the relationship that is no longer forbidden can be perceived as affirmation of masculinity for black men, the relationship with the white male is more likely to be problematical due to the society which has placed white womanhood as a value (reinforced by Madison Avenue and the mass media which are more likely to associate "sexy" with white and "domestic" with black) at the same time that for black women history has identified white men as rapists rather than lovers.

There is evidence that in black families the marital relationship is strongly influenced by the attitudes of the external environment. The myth of the matriarchy, despite its weak documentation, is a part of the network of ideas to which all of us are exposed in due course by virtue of being a part of this society. The increasing aggressiveness of black males as they have sought to establish their rights to the same privileges given to any citizen and, in the process, to erase the myth of the passive, apathetic, black male image from the eyes of the nation has found the matriarchy notions threatening, to be discredited whenever the opportunity arises. Thus many black men are insisting that "aggressive" black women have no place in the new scheme of things where the black male is finally ready to move into positions of authority and responsibility and needs support from black females, not competitiveness.

It is clear, however, that the definition of black males and black females, as in competition to see who will be No. 1, is a red herring in the struggle for equality for all blacks. It may also be indicative of a peculiarly American value structure which has been incorporated by blacks despite the fact that it is antithetical to what existed in Africa prior to slavery. Nobles points out that kinship controlled all the relations in the traditional African communities and the survival of the tribe was a primary principle of social relationships. Furthermore, when there was a forced separation of tribal members, it merely meant that there was a reorganization of the definition of who was included in tribal boundaries, i.e., a reorganization of the tribal affiliation. Thus, according to Nobles, slaves in America moved closer and closer to the definition of black people as the tribe, thereby encompassing all blacks under the tribal mantle.[12] However, in contemporary times, the dominant culture reinforces members of black families for living as individuals. Thus black men can see other black men and black women not as part of the collective in which the members have a shared fate but rather as threats to their personal aspirations. The attempt to make black women the causal agent in the subjugation of black males during and after slavery is absurd. Yet, the subtle and not so subtle images of "castrating" black females has in fact seeped into the relationships between some black males and some black females to distort the fact that now as in the past their fates have always been inextricably intertwined and that the greatest threats lie outside their attempts to cope with that external environment. Furthermore, insofar as their attempts to cope with that external environment are characterized by divisive competition rather than unity and cooperation, to that extent failure to cope successfully is a foregone conclusion.

In addition to the threat to effective family functioning posed by conflict between the sexes, there is also the illusion that black families can be categorized according to social class and that families in different categories have little in common—certainly not enough to provide the basis for cooperation in the efforts to obtain more equitable distribution of power when black communities are compared with white. There is a strong feeling that blacks are moving more and more into the great American middle class and as such they have a different value structure from their lower-class counterparts. Furthermore, since class is a more powerful determinant of behavior patterns and life style than race, there is little basis for the development of the collective or "tribal communality" that Nobles suggested. Therefore, in community organization efforts, for example, allies are more likely to form along class rather than racial lines.

An example of difference when black middle class and black lower class are compared is in the area of sexual attitudes. Middle class blacks are less permissive in regard to what is considered acceptable sexual behavior than are lower income blacks; however, they are still more permissive than middle-class whites. Staples suggests that possible reasons for this include the fact that most middle-class blacks have come from lower-class origins and thus constitute the first generation of middle-class family members. Furthermore, the racial isolation of most residential communities has meant that lower-class and middle-class blacks have often lived in close proximity to each other and as a consequence middle-class black children have been exposed in greater numbers to the permissive sexual attitudes of their lower-class peers. Warnings from middle-class parents regarding what is appropriate sexual behavior often was not reinforced by the child's peer group. Furthermore, the rewards for "acting middle-class" are obviously fewer among blacks when such behavior does not even guarantee the right to live outside of the same residential areas as lower-class persons.[13]

Bernard has proposed that the only determinant of class differentiation in black communities is income level.[14] Furthermore, differences in patterns of behavior in black families, particularly in regard to the marital relationship, are not based on class but on the extent to which they have internalized institutional norms relating to marriage and the family. Those who conform to the institutionalized norms of American society because these have become an intrinsic part of their personality and who would adhere to them even under considerable stress are defined as "acculturated." Those who do so only as a matter of external adaptation and not because of any internal conviction are referred to as "the externally adapted." These two groups contain all income levels, since "the difference between them is not based on income but on ethos, not on money but on acceptance of conventional standards of behavior— especially in relation to sex and work." Despite the stated wish of Bernard to avoid any value label or pejorative terminology, the use of "acculturated" and "externally adapted" still appears to place a clear indicator on which is more valued given that "externally adapted" is associated with such terms as "superficial," "no depth," etc., while to be acculturated is associated with the notion of social skills and social functioning. The significance, however, of the manner in which each of these adaptations at a given time may be valuable for the persons involved is easily discernible. For example, if a husband and father leaves his wife and children so that they can be taken care of on welfare at a higher level than he can afford, this nonadherence to norms of family life may in fact lead to a higher level of social functioning for the family. There is the case of the middle-class minister who refused to marry his long-time girlfriend because she would be unacceptable to the congregation as a minister's wife (despite the fact that the liaison was common knowledge) and there was no other occupation in which he could earn a comparable standard of living. These are, in Bernard's terms, "externally adapted" individuals in terms of norms of marriage and family life but may very well represent the best possible solution at the moment to the particular situation. Rodman refers to this phenomenon as "value-stretch" which occurs when a group shares the general values of society with others but in addition has developed alternative

values when implementing the general values are beset by obstacles.[15]

It is clear that black families, like black individuals, are like all
other families in the United States, like some other families,
and like no other families all at the same time. They have
shared American cultural values to the degree that in many
cases their family forms and processes are Indistinguishable
from any other American families. On the other hand, there are
experiences that black families must deal with—obstacles in
making a living, finding suitable housing and good schools for
children, helping children to understand and deal with racism,
and the negative self-images it places in front of them, etc. Finally, there is the fact that each family is a unique entity, like no
other family, and the particular combination of personalities
creates consequences for each of its members that can be attributed to that alone. It is important, then, to move beyond the
issues of family forms and differential family behavior patterns
to confront some critical questions regarding the role of the
family in problem situations characteristically encountered in
black communities.

PROBLEM BEHAVIOR

The implication inherent in much of the behavioral science literature is that the family is the causal agent of almost any
problem producing behavior an individual might present.
Thomas and Sillen point out that:

> The intense focus on the family as the determinant of pathol-
> ogy or health may encourage serious misconceptions—the
> assumption for example that a certain type of family pattern
> always has the same consequences. Actually of course, there
> is no one-to-one relation between family structure and per-
> sonality development. A family may have a weak father and a
> dominant mother; yet in each situation the impact on children
> of different temperament may be quite diverse. The broken
> home does not necessarily breed delinquency; nor does the

intact home assure socially approved behavior. Loving
mothers may have emotionally disturbed children, and disturbed mothers may have well-adapted children who are apparently immune to the mother's pathology and erratic patterns of care.[16]

It is certainly clear that if there were such a simple, linear
relationship between family processes and type of outcome in
terms of personality and behavior, there would be a far greater
proportion of blacks who are mentally disturbed, criminal, or
hopelessly ineffectual in day-to-day living. Yet, the majority of
black people live relatively successful lives. Therefore, it seems
that greater interest should be placed on why so many blacks
who, in spite of family patterns that are associated with dysfunctional lives, have escaped the consequences.

An example of a family pattern usually defined as "deviant"
is the female-headed household. In situations where a role
partner in a social relationship is absent or cannot perform the
functions of the role, it may be necessary for the other partner
to perform both roles. Such cases of role synthesis has been
described in other societies and perceived as an important
adaptive capacity. Yet, as Staples points out, the female-
headed household among blacks has been defined as pathological. Americans perceive something inherently wrong in a
female-headed household but there has been no clear linkage
made between this particular family structure and particular
problem situations.

There is evidence, however, that some of the interpersonal
dynamics in black families, as in other families, often lead to
problem-producing behavior. There are many instances, particularly in low-income ghetto communities wherein the combination of survival pressures, and consequent ineffective parenting
produces individuals whose own emotional needs are so un-
satisfied that it becomes difficult for them to "give" to another
person, whether to a lover or child. If there is any self-perpetuating feature of black low-income family life it is this situa-

tion in which parents cannot give emotional security to their children because of their inability to obtain physical, social, or psychological supports for themselves. It would be a mistake, however, to assume that all blacks, low-income parents, are ineffective and emotionally deprived individuals who are therefore inept in helping their children develop emotionally stable personalities. Spurlock has pointed out that "a mother who appears to be ineffective, limited, apathetic, tired and overburdened in an agency setting which is alien and peopled with unfamiliar types, may in fact when viewed in her own setting come across very differently, i.e., warm, able to handle frustrations and set limits." [17] There are parents who are highly creative in dealing with the limitations of their environment and therefore highly *effective* in spite of it; other parents who are under a minimally supportive environment would be quite adequate in the parenting role but have been overwhelmed by the magnitude of the set of frustrations, traumas, and crises with which they have been faced and therefore become ineffective; still other parents do not have the emotional or economic resources to be able to give their children the kind of help they need in learning to cope with the world but have been blessed with a variety of close relationships—relatives, neighbors, friends—who have compensated for this lack in themselves so that the children do splendidly well in managing their personal and social environments.

Spurlock has also pointed out that the majority of black children seen for psychological evaluation because they are not achieving academically display depressive symptoms which appear to be related to feelings of helplessness and "giving up." [18] These are related to a sense of inferiority which is generally reinforced as they come into more and more contact with the broader society and the psychic energy expended to deal with defending against these unacceptable feelings leaves nothing left over to deal with the demands of academic learning. This issue of negative self-image of blacks is perhaps one of the most controversial in the social science literature relating to the black experience. The implication in Spurlock's statement in regard to the etiology of depression in black youth and its relation to difficulties in academic achievement is that either the family does not provide a strong enough image of self to be able to withstand the negative indicators encountered outside the family in the racist environment or, in another way, these negative messages from the environment are so powerful that families cannot counteract them or prepare a child to deal with them adequately.

The significance of whether or not negative self-image is a commonly encountered phenomenon among black children as well as adults is related to whether or not the self-concept of a person is antecedent of particular behaviors. Nobles has provided an excellent review of psychological research relating to black self-concept and notes the equivocal findings.[19] Some research indicates that not only do blacks come to identify with the aggressor and take on his disdain for the racial group which is then expressed at some level as disdain for himself but that the family plays a central role in the transmission of those values and attitudes of society. Through the family, the child learns what he cannot do, all the blocks and barriers he must face, and most of all the futility of trying. Other researchers have questioned whether many blacks find emotional satisfaction in complying with the demands of white society. Still others have emphasized that a sense of group identification and group belongingness can act as a shield against the buffeting of the broader society. Thus, there needs to be greater understanding of the mechanisms whereby some blacks have a strong, positive identification with their racial group while others perceive it as a negative, shame-bearing association.

Pouissant and Atkinson have described studies of self-image which show a high correlation between self-image and achievement.[20] They perceive the need for achievement developing in both black and white Americans, as this society grants considerable approval for the ability to achieve success. Thus, the demands for academic achievement of black youth and their parents are often exceptionally high; yet the actual achievement levels of the youth are not commensurate. This is attributed to the practice in black families of laying down verbal rules and regulations to children about how they should behave in the classroom, with punishment meted out for any detected transgressions; however, there is little guidance and encouragement given in the area of verbal-symbolic mastery which is the key to success in academic situations. Whereas this may be true, it does not mean that blacks lack *capacity* to master abstract verbal symbols but they lack the constant practice in manipulation of these symbols that characterize the dominant culture out of which they were primarily derived. In fact, there is growing evidence that difference is not deficit. Thus lower-class black children have a fully developed, fully structured language. Houston has pointed out that much of the educational research on black cognition is pervaded by misconception and mythology since it is usually carried out by persons without the appropriate background in modern linguistic and psycholinguistic theory.[21] A great deal of work has to be done in the field of education to determine how the existing linguistic systems to which blacks are accustomed can be utilized to the same extent that standard English is utilized to develop cognitive skills and the informational systems required for effective functioning in major occupational and other social roles.

Language is an extremely important aspect of self-concept and the damage to that self-concept when it is deemed unacceptable by the larger society is perhaps incalculable. On the other hand, there must be some middle ground between the obviously unlikely solution to have middle-class society accept as valid the linguistic forms commonly found in lower-class black families. What appears to be required is (1) the indication in schools that there are many linguistic styles for expressing ideas; (2) at times one linguistic style is more appropriate than another; e.g., at home, the lower-class black mode of communication which has been developed in the family but in the world of middle-class institutions and occupational settings, standard English is preferred and therefore more appropriate; and (3) the goal of the public schools is to make the student comfortable and highly skilled in the use of his own as well as the standard linguistic systems. It is apparent that there is immediately a shortage of teachers who have the bicultural orientation to develop curriculum based on such a perspective. This may well be the reason for failure in ghetto schools. This will be discussed in greater detail in chapter 8. However, it is clear that there is a disjunction between family and school demonstrated in the internalization of educational and occupational values and goals by many black children and their parents but a lack of clear connection of the goals to specific behaviors which are effective in achieving these goals.

THE FAMILY AND THE ENVIRONMENT
In the traditional social science literature dealing with socialization of individuals, the family is perceived as the primary socialization agent, with school next in importance. However, families and schools exist in a social environment which not only influences their socialization efforts directly, i.e., by defining the values which are to be incorporated by the individuals, but which also influence the individual directly through communication systems that may or may not be mediated by families or schools. It is clear, however, in the writings of Welsing, Frazier, Chestang, and others, in contrast to those of Moynihan, that the external environment is perceived as playing an even more significant role than the family in shaping behavior. For example, Chestang has proposed that the black experience—characterized by social injustice, institutionalized disparity between "words and deeds," and powerlessness to influence the environment—has resulted in "the development of two parallel and opposing thought structures, each based on values, norms, and beliefs and supported by attitudes, feelings,

and behaviors, that imply feelings of depreciation on the one hand and push for transcendence on the other. Effective social functioning and environmental reality require that black individuals incorporate both these trends into their personalities—the one to assure competence in dealing with reality, the other as an impetus for transcending reality." [22] Chestang suggests that problems occur for the individual when the depreciated character is dominant and in isolation from the transcendent or when the transcendent character is dominant and fragmented from the depreciated. The former situation exists when the individual gives in to feelings of worthlessness, hopelessness, and helplessness . . . he sustains the stereotypes from the larger society. The latter case is illustrated in the "oreo" individual who has failed to maintain contact with the past and takes on the pseudo-identity of the dominant society. Although Chestang points out that this formulation in regard to personality formation among blacks is admittedly hypothetical, he thinks there is enough empirical evidence supporting it to serve as a basis for further exploration along these lines. Furthermore, it can be perceived as a common expression of any situation in which a group in society "must negotiate a hostile environment." [23] It is clear, in any event, that these formulations are presented as universal in such situations as were the formulations of Freud and Erikson and Maslow. The family then may determine whether an effective unity between the two personality structures will be achieved or whether a preeminence of one at the expense of the other will create a problem-producing situation. Differential family structure and process therefore can still be perceived as having positive or negative consequences in regard to social functioning of the individual.

Perhaps the most influential environmental force in the determination of behavior is the mass media—television, movies, and to a lesser extent newspapers and magazines. A phenomenon of the 1970s has been the bursting on the scene of the so-called "blaxploitation films." These films feature black characters who swirl in atmospheres of violence, sex and drugs. They are usually giving the message—if any can be found—that success can be had with nothing less than hip talk, flashy clothes, cars and weapons. Pouissant notes that:

> These movies glorify criminal life, and encourage in black youth misguided feelings of machismo that are destructive to the community as a whole. These films with few exceptions damage the well-being of all Afro-Americans. Negative black stereotypes are more subtle and more neatly camouflaged than they were in the films of yesteryear, but the same insidious message is there: Blacks are violent, criminal, sexy savages who imitate the white men's ways as best they can from their disadvantaged sanctuary in the ghetto.[24]

Pouissant goes on to differentiate the effects on different individuals in black communities. Mature adults and average, middle-class black youths may easily regard these films as nothing more than fiction and fantasy. However, poor young blacks with no real models to emulate and impoverished family life may perceive the fiction as reality. Furthermore, since in many of these films the black heroes are not only selfish, egotistical, and unscrupulous, and are as likely to inflict destructive violence upon other blacks as well as whites, there is no support for black unity and cooperation. Expediency and exploitation—whether directed against neighbors, families, or friends—are the rules of the game. These images are evidently having their impact on black youth in ghetto communities.

Television is increasingly adding more black faces in commercials as well as in on-going series; and certainly the fact that it is in the home and families are more likely to see it more often than movies indicates its importance as a part of the social environment that influences behavior. There has long been the criticism that television watching has reduced family interaction and thereby the quality of family life; an even more recent criticism has been that young people are reading and writing less and looking at television more, so that they are losing these critical skills in the immersion in the audiovisual me-

dium. Blacks on television have moved from the traditional ste-
reotyped roles as maids, shoeshine boys, etc., and are shown
as affluent, family-centered, and policemen rather than criminals. However, there are deep divisions within the black community regarding the effects of the "image" of blacks in almost
every television show in which blacks perform.

For example, one of the most acclaimed television movies of
1974 was "The Autobiography of Miss Jane Pittman," the story
of a one-hundred-year-old black woman whose life spanned
the years from the Civil War to the civil rights movement of the
1960s. Yet, writing in the *Black Scholar,* Ramsey states that this
television drama was in fact an insidious kind of propaganda,
nothing more than "history again filtered through white lens—
constructed to keep black truth from passing through with integrity." [25] Ramsey was especially incensed because the narrator in the television version was white although in the novel,
written by a black author, the narrator was black. Ramsey
attributes this change in the script to the overseer mentality of
whites who "need to stand watch over our lives, direct our activities, interpret our experiences." Perhaps most significantly,
however, the script changed the memorable last scene in the
novel where Miss Jane Pittman, a centenarian, joined with the
militant black youth, supported by the black community, to
walk together up to a "whites only" fountain to drink. The television version showed Miss Jane walking *alone.*

It is the portrayal of black family life, however, that has provided the greatest controversy in both television and the movies, perhaps out of the sensitivities in the black community to
the mythology which has plagued black people regarding their
family forms and life styles. A television show, "Julia," was
praised for showing a middle-class black nurse and her little
boy in something other than a ghetto environment, but it was
damned for making her a widow and therefore perpetuating the
"image" of the black family as characteristically single-parent,
female-headed. Another television show, "Good Times," was
praised for showing a two-parent family with good family rela-

tionships but panned because it was in the ghetto; the man was usually unemployed and the mother was often the sole support of the family—stereotypes raising their ugly heads again. "That's My Mama" was praised for showing more clearly middle-class family images but panned for making "Mama" a heavy, domineering mother who rules her son with a powerful, matriarchial hand.

A movie made in 1970, "Sounder," depicted a Southern black farm family with the emphasis on the deep love of the black man and the black woman and their incomparable instincts for survival, yet an editorial writer for the Los Angeles *Sentinel,* a black weekly, was prompted to write: "Those who seek images via . . . Sounder are lost in a fog . . . they are missing the real gut fight . . . people can become powerful when they provide for the mediocre and average among them. Any people who are forced to overemphasize the top never deal with the full human reality. . . . Black America has functioned on the talented tenth theory too long."

Perhaps, all of this shows most of all that the mass media are a significant part of the environment to which black families must respond in their efforts to develop their children. On the other hand, the depiction of black families in the mass media reflects the multiple images of these families that exist and the response to any single image often asks the impossible . . . that somehow it embody the whole.

SUMMARY
This chapter has reviewed the negative images of black family structures and processes. Sociological as well as psychological perspectives on the family have served to delineate differences in black and non-black family structure and process. Furthermore, the differences identified have tended to reinforce the negative valuation of the black collective. Black social scientists themselves have shown considerable difference of opinion

as to whether black families are characterized by pathology—
albeit a consequence of system pressures—or by strength generated from an almost universal struggle with forces of oppression in society.

An analysis of the often conflicting research on black families revealed some consistencies which appear to contradict
the negative mythology. First, there are multiple family structures among blacks with no particular structure comprising a
majority of all black families. Second, unique characteristics in
regard to the relationship between black males and black females have been distorted to emphasize the conflict elements
in their relationships rather than the mutual support elements.
Third, despite the fact that there are differences in values and
life style of low-income and middle-income black families,
there are also similarities when compared with each other and
differences when compared with white families at the same income level. Therefore neither class nor race alone is sufficient
to serve as a predictor of behavior patterns or life styles—the
two must be considered simultaneously.

Perhaps the most important factor in the role the family has
played as carrier of society's negative valuation of black people
has been the strong connection between characteristics more
common in black families and "problem" behavior; i.e., single-
parent households, marital instability, even poverty have been
identified as primary factors in the etiology of problem behavior. However, direct, linear relationships between family process and problem behavior have not been clearly demonstrated.

Finally, sources external to the family but which serve to
characterize black families have been identified as reinforcers
of society's negative valuation of blacks. These negative
images of black families can be found in various presentations
in the mass media. However, much of the negative impact
comes not so much from inaccurate portrayals of black family
life but from the tendency to perceive *any* portrayal as "typi-

cal," and therefore more diverse portrayals are needed to reflect the actual diversity in the form and content of black family life.

experiental exercises

1.
Visit a park in a low-income black neighborhood and another in a middle-income black neighborhood. Are there observable differences in the following: number of family groups proportionately using the park; nature of the activities; kinds of facilities available for use by families; quality of family group interaction. Talk to park and recreation personnel to determine the extent to which the parks are utilized by people in the neighborhood, the activities most popular, and the extent to which there are planned, family-centered activities. Repeat this kind of observation in a low-income white neighborhood and a middle-income white neighborhood. What appears to be the most powerful determinant of differences observed—class or race?

2.
Identify an agency which provides a program for youth in a low-income black neighborhood and seek answers from staff to the following questions: Are parents involved in providing support for the youth program? If so, what kind of support? What strategies have been used by the agency to obtain parental support for agency programs? What familial characteristics appear to be associated with parental involvement or noninvolvement in programs serving their children?

Given the situation in this agency in regard to parental involvement, what modifications would you make in an attempt to improve parental involvement and strengthen family life in the community the agency serves?

3.

Identify an agency which provides a similar program for youth in a middle-income black neighborhood and another in a low-income white neighborhood and repeat the questions above. On the basis of the sets of responses, how would you characterize similarities and differences in parental involvement in low-income black, low-income white, and middle-income black neighborhoods as well as in the strategies required to increase parental involvement and, perhaps most importantly, *the purpose of parental involvement to begin with?*

4.

The Association of Black Social Workers has taken a position in favor of the development of "Black Family Service" agencies similarly to Catholic and Jewish family service agencies. However, these sectarian agencies have been moving toward the opening up of their programs to non-Catholic and non-Jewish families. The issue seems to rest on whether such variables as ethnicity or religion influence family processes to the extent that a person will need specialized knowledge in order to assist with family problems or that families will prefer to go for help to sources that are identified with their religious or ethnic group.

Suggest the following question to a local black community newspaper for a reader opinion survey: "Resolved: A black or Afro-American family service agency should be established in our community."

> (a) As measured by reader response, how significant would you say this issue is as compared to others on which reader opinion has been sought?

(b) Are most readers "for" or "against" the proposed agency?

(c) What factors appear to be associated with support or non-support of the proposed agency?

chapter seven

. . . in peer groups

The adolescent youth of contemporary American society have been the focus of a seemingly unending stream of literary production attempting to describe their activities, dissect their values, and determine their significance for the direction of future social change. In this orgy of analysis, black youth have paradoxically been both under- and overstudied. In regard to the processes of growth and development, there has been a tacit assumption that the descriptions based on studies primarily of middle-class groups define the "norm"; furthermore, these descriptions are at a level of abstraction that indicate little about the particular behavioral content. For example, the Group for the Advancement of Psychiatry in its integration of biological, psychological, and cultural perspectives on adolescence declared:

> In the transition from childhood to adulthood, the adolescent finds a temporary way station with others of his kind. The peer group provides a sense of belonging and a feeling of strength and power that is very important to him. In order to gain acceptance by the group, the youngster often tends to conform completely in modes of dress, hair style, musical taste and the like. The peer group, greatly expanded by modern means of transportation and communication, today constitutes a culture which has its own language, customs, social institutions, modes and methods of solving problems, and philosophies.[1]

This is an essentially accurate profile of most adolescents in our society. However, it reveals little of the specific content of the black adolescent's experience. Thus, it fails to give attention to the concrete expressions of "language," "modes of problem solving," or "social institutions" which are not identical but vary among the ethnic teen-age subcultures. On the other hand, whereas black youth are conspicuously absent from descriptions of normal adolescence, they are over-represented in discussions of deviant patterns. Juvenile gangs, promiscuous and drug-taking teen-agers are more likely to be perceived as black due to the social science preoccupation with such forms of deviant behavior in black communities.

The power of groups as determinants of individual behavior has been fully recognized by theoreticians and practitioners alike. Hartford has described four generally accepted effects of groups on those who participate in them; socialization, the development of identity and self-concept, education and learning, and the formation or modification of values, beliefs, and attitudes. This means that the group is a particularly versatile opportunity system which can be used intentionally in a wide variety of change efforts. However, it is the informal group—notably the peer group—which is either prototype or starting point for the conceptualization of more formal or planned groups. The primary focus of research and practice interests in regard to the peer group process has been during the pre-adolescent, early adolescent, and late adolescent periods on the basis of evidence which would suggest that children at earlier ages are essentially egocentric whereas older individuals shift into social clubs or organizations in which there is less intimate involvement.

The informal, neighborhood groups are of particular significance in low-income black neighborhoods where parental authority often is eroded due to the limited time available to give to older children because of more insistent demands of younger children in large families, the long hours spent on ungratifying jobs that generate frustrations which can be projected onto children, and the absence of planned family-centered recreational activities. In some instances this has led to the emergence of juvenile gangs; the "gang problem" is considered to be characteristic of high-density, inner-city communities. Yet, not all adolescent peer groups in black communities are violent and involved in criminal activities. Furthermore, since neither the process nor consequence of involvement in neighborhood peer groups is the same in black communities as in white, it is important to understand the difference.

SOME THEORETICAL PERSPECTIVES
Sociological definitions of the group are as varied as are definitions of community. These definitions differ in terms of their respective stress on the nature of communication, the social relationships members hold to each other, the degree of organization, the manner in which membership is determined, the nature of the functions it performs, and a host of other variables.[2] The one characteristic that is seemingly common to all definitions is that a group refers to more than one person. The peer group refers to one in which the members are about the same age. Most importantly in our consideration of adolescent peer group is the fact that these groups are also reference groups, i.e., a group with which an individual feels identified and from which he derives his norms, attitudes, and values. Certainly, the force of family interaction is still highly significant in most individuals in this age period; however, the peer group takes on similar and sometimes greater significance. Reference group theory holds important clues as to peer group dynamics as well as adolescent behavior problems in general. In addition, it suggests those directions in which the experience of black and white adolescents are similar as well as different.

Whereas it is clearly understood by most what is meant when the peer group is referred to as a reference group, the much broader conceptualization of reference group is rarely appreci-

ated. Clark has summarized much of the social science literature on reference groups and has identified both groups and
nongroups to which the term has been applied.[3] *Groups* that
generally serve as reference groups range from Boy Scouts to
juvenile gangs, from informal friendship networks which are
based in the neighborhood to other friendship networks which
have no territorial base. However, it is recognized that in order
to qualify as a group, the boundaries must be somewhat fixed,
i.e., it should be known at any given time who are members and
who are not. There are other reference groups which can only
be described as *collectivities,* since there may be no face-to-
face interaction but there is a sense of solidarity derived from
shared values and a sense of obligation to behave in a particular way. Thus, honor students in a school, cheerleaders, football players may feel a sense of kinship and pattern their behaviors by what is perceived as an unwritten "code" embodying
their shared values, e.g., courteousness or bravado, aloofness
toward nonmembers, or instant friendship with another
member of the group upon first meeting. In addition, *social categories* serve as reference groups in spite of the fact that individuals in them may neither engage in interaction nor share
common values. These social categories may be in terms of
race, sex, age, criminal record, or age period. Perhaps the most
difficult to accept under the rubric of reference group is the individual who serves as an ideal or model. Role theorists
distinguish between the *reference individual* who is used as a
pattern for a total life style and the *role model* who is a point
of identification for a single role, such as employment role or
familial role. Thus, given this broad conceptualization of reference group, it is apparent that the peer group is both a reference group itself and utilizes other reference groups as a
source for the development of normative attitudes and behaviors.

The peer group—like the family—is an interpersonal environment giving its members an opportunity to initiate and respond
to interaction with other human beings and, in the process, to

construct a stable identity consistent with that as prescribed by the reference group network. The individual acts, the group responds; the group acts, the individual responds. In this complex social rhythm, the ego-identity as described by Erikson emerges. In this process, there are some principles derived from reference group theory which are useful in any attempt to describe peer group in black communities and to compare them with their counterparts in non-black communities.

It is almost self-evident that an individual is unlikely to accept as reference group those persons or groups who reject him or who he feels have rejected him. Thus, in black communities where children are often weaned on stories of white oppression, it should be unlikely that whites as a social category would be utilized as a reference group. The simplicity of this principle is deceiving, however, since it is immediately apparent that there are some blacks who do in fact use whites as a standard against which they evaluate themselves as well as others. Even more unfortunately, due to lack of intimate exposure to much beyond the surface image of white life styles—particularly among black youth—there is a tendency to distort the reality so that the negative becomes supernegative and the positive likewise becomes superpositive. How does this happen if it is perceived that blacks have been rejected by whites? In these instances, it appears that the message received is not that whites have rejected blacks and therefore *them;* whites have rejected certain characteristics or behaviors of black people and by avoiding the taboos (nonstandard English, illegitimacy, sexual permissiveness, low educational aspiration, etc.) rejection can also be avoided.

If there is both an attraction toward and rejection of the white group as a reference group for black youth, it can be said that the same ambivalence is discernible in the attitudes of white youth toward blacks. For example, the popularity of black music aimed at teen-age audiences transcends racial lines. Black youth are quick to point out the white imitators of such well-known black entertainers as The Jackson Five or Aretha

Franklin. There is evidence that blacks are perceived as less inhibited, more free to move about without the stifling constraint of adult controls. Despite the fact that the intermittent rebellions of adolescence allow some lack of conformity to parentally prescribed behavioral norms, these are not permanent. The seductive images of black freedom from controls are crushed beneath more powerful images of the inferior status given to blacks and the result is a more consistent rejection of values (extended kinship bonds), attitudes (toward religion) and behavior (wearing flashy clothes) which are associated with blacks.

A principle closely related to that of not accepting as reference groups those who reject you is the one which states that the individual must feel that a reference group to which he does not belong is at least a realistic aspiration for him. Thus the social category "white" is unattainable as long as it is defined merely in terms of skin color or ancestry; on the other hand, if white is viewed not as a condition but as a constellation of values, attitudes, and behavior patterns, it becomes as attainable as any social category. If a certain "consciousness-raising" occurs, however, even those who would ordinarily accept this latter meaning of white in the United States can be made aware that no matter how a black person conforms to white norms, he remains black from the racist perspective. Thus, it *is* essentially skin color and ancestry that are crucial. Very rarely can a black become so wealthy he can afford anything he wishes without encountering some seller who prefers not to sell to a black; or so highly educated that there is no job for which he is qualified that cannot be refused him out of racist considerations; or so circumspect in his behavior that a racist cannot point to his taste in cars, use of language, or attitude toward the political system as evidence of some negative characteristics differentiating a black mentality. Today's black youth are more acutely aware than any previous generation since slavery of the disparities between the promises of the American social system and the actuality of black citizens.

Thus, it is rare to find evidence that the peer groups in black communities consider the values or behavior patterns of the white group as reference for them, although less rare among middle- than lower-class black youth.

The peer group is an important aspect of anticipatory socialization into adult roles. It makes it possible for certain rehearsals to occur which increase the individual's capacity to perform the adult role. For example, the Group for the Advancement of Psychiatry describes the adolescent's involvement with dancing, an important activity in peer-interaction during this age period:

> Dancing has occupied a central place in the customs of many cultures. The rythmic bodily activity of dancing satisfies a number of needs. There is the delight in physical movement for its own sake, and the feeling of release which comes with the discharge of the tensions in activity. On the other hand, dancing provides a means of expressing more specific sexual and aggressive urges both in symbolic form and in action . . . the "rules" of these dances require that the dancers seldom touch and never embrace each other. Sexual urges can be expressed and coitus can be symbolically enacted, but the youngsters are protected from the danger of close physical contact.[4]

In essence, the peer group activity permits a limited erotic experience without the tremendous responsibilities incurred in the full sexual experience.

In the more structured adolescent peer groups, it is possible to act out the roles of leader, group clown, critic, information seeker, mediator, etc., which tend to parallel roles adults perform in their organized activity sets. This also permits adolescents to "try out" a variety of roles before settling in to the package role identities which are most compatible with the individual's self-concept. The significance of the ability to be sensitive to cues for behavioral expectations and to behavioral requirements of a variety of situations cannot be overestimated in regard to the socialization process. The peer group is often an opportunity system for such learning, even though it is clear that the family is still an important factor. For example, Short and Strodtbeck have written:

> The family does not equip the child with role-playing facility adequate to the demands of such institutions as the school; and unsatisfactory experiences in school further narrow the range of role-playing opportunities which later facilitate job success—"getting along" with employers and fellow workers, and more than this, getting along in new and strange situations generally. The ability to move easily from one role to another and to adjust rapidly to new situations is a much cultivated art in modern urban society, particularly among upwardly mobile persons.[5]

Short and Strodtbeck then view the delinquent gang as ineffective in helping its members to develop this behavioral repertoire. Thus, the opportunity for "trying on" various roles appears to be associated with formal structure and is not as available in the more informal peer group situation.

From the standpoint of the practitioner, perhaps the most useful principles to be derived from reference group theory are those relating to the dynamics of peer group influence over individual behavior. For example, one such principle suggests that the individual's behavior can be controlled to some extent by influencing his choice of reference group. It is perhaps clearer to think of reference groups as independent variables, i.e., affecting the behavior of the individual through the medium of its normative structure. On the other hand, the reference group may also be a dependent variable; i.e., the individual can contribute to the stability of his self-identity by choosing a reference group(s) or interpersonal environment which is compatible with it. In this sense, then, the helping practitioner places emphasis on work with the individual so that, for example, a juvenile probationer can be convinced to attempt to become a part of an on-going group in a neighborhood service center. If, however, the peer group is determined to be an independent variable, influencing the individual's behavior, then it may be important to learn the structure and nature of that group and, if at all possible, change the normative content of the reference groups with which the individual is now identified. This is the detached worker or street worker approach. It essentially involves establishing a relationship with the members of the group and using the influence of that relationship to direct group energies into gratifying but nondelinquent activities.

These theoretical perspectives provide a gross outline of the nature of the structure and dynamics of reference groups during adolescence. However, it is clear that individuals will have differential commitment to group involvement and different groups will have varying capacity to develop cohesion, consensus, effective leadership and consequently the loyalty of its members. As a result, some adolescents grow up with the peer group as a primary life force whereas others experience the group only in a minimal, barely perceptive way. One of the variables that appear to make a difference is class; another is race. The following sections will describe those factors which appear to differentiate low-income black peer groups from other low-income adolescent groups and middle-income black peer groups from other middle-income adolescent groups.

LOW-INCOME COMMUNITIES
Perhaps one of the most salient characteristics of adolescent peer groups in low-income black communities is the extent to which they support a precocious, even precipitous rush into adulthood. For the young black males—particularly those growing up in families without fathers, there is early introduction into a responsible, adultlike role in which other family members come to depend upon him for services usually obtained from the father; e.g., contributions of money from part-time jobs, responsibility for assisting the mother with younger

children, etc. Thus, "mama's little man" finds it easy to rationalize peer behaviors that imitate adult behaviors; e.g., drink-
ing, intimacy with the opposite sex, joy riding in automobiles
(sometimes stolen). Illegal activities to obtain money are even
closely related to the pressure to get "bread" to support many
of these adultlike behaviors.

Short and Strodtbeck have done extensive research on nine
black and six white gangs in the Chicago inner-city area.[6] Definite racial differentials in gang behavior were observed.
Whereas delinquency of the white gang appeared to involve
protest against conventional family obligations, there was no
such protest observed in black gang members. The black gang
members were more likely to participate in domestic chores
such as baby-sitting and running errands for their families. The
authors conclude that participation in the "good" aspects of
lower-class black life (responsibility in domestic chores and
organized sports activities) is closely interwoven with bad
aspects (conflict, illicit sex, drug use, and auto theft). As compared with lower-class white communities, delinquency among
lower-class blacks is more a part of a total life pattern in which
delinquent behaviors are not as likely to create disjunctures
with other types of behavior. What is apparent in comparing
delinquent gangs and other peer groups in low-income communities is the greater incidence of "social disabilities" in the
former; i.e., an emotionally impoverished family life, low academic achievement, limited cognitive skills, etc. Some fortunate youth in low-income communities have few such social
disabilities and others have almost all that can be imagined.
Yet there is a direct relationship between the number of social
disabilities and involvement in delinquent activity. There is still
in low-income adolescent, non-gang peer groups the appearance of precocious adulthood as young mingle with old in daytime as well as at night. Ladner has observed in regard to girls
in low-income urban housing projects:

> At the age when girls outside the community are playing with
> dolls and engaging in all those activities which reflect child-

hood, girls within its borders are often unable to experience this complete cycle. . . . Parents in the black community are often unable to protect their young children from harsh social forces which protection would insure that they grow up in this "safe period" emerging relatively unscarred. One of the consequences of these pervasive community influences upon the child is that they superimpose emotional precocity on the girl that often exceeds her chronological years. This precooity often enables her to enter networks of individuals and situations wherein traditionally unacceptable behavior for her age group takes place . . . for example, the thirteen-year-old who can pass for sixteen or seventeen in certain circles not only becomes exposed to but takes part in behavior that would normally be beyond her range of experience and therefore beyond her ability to manage herself adequately.[7]

The following is an excerpt from a social worker's report of group work with teen-age girls in a low-income black neighborhood:

. . . the girls are often looking for not a role model but somebody who can be a significant other person in their life because they are lacking the older mother, older sister, aunt, with whom they can have just friendship and closeness. We were able to incorporate the philosophy that the lives of one set of people have no more validity than the lives of another. What's important is to be able to have some choice about your life; to be able to weigh alternatives, to think things through, and to make choices which satisfy us and those who matter to us. For example there was Vivien, age 13, who was extremely promiscuous. She's never been pregnant, but she'd had venereal disease so many times that she can't even remember how many times now. In one session, the group members started joking and laughing, which had become an indication that they're getting ready to get into something pretty deep, and they would like me to be aware of it. They frequently started off with, "She's breaking the school record" . . . then there would be the joking. At this session somebody's comment hit Vivien. She said, "If I could get attention any other way, I would, don't you think I would?" The whole room got quiet. Vivien continued, "If I could be maybe an A student, or an athlete, or a cheerleader, then I could get to be a teacher, or a psychiatrist." And I said, "Why couldn't you just be a girl who didn't just jump into bed with every fellow, but when you did, you were good at it, and you didn't catch VD?" They all looked at me. I didn't want them to think that their road is a bad road, and that the only way to get their lives straightened out is to make a complete switch and go in the entire opposite direction. Just being a therapist doesn't give one the option to establish a scale for priorities of life styles. It's just bad to have VD because you're sick and that isn't a consequence one relishes.

Vivien started the discussion very puzzled, saying, "Well why would you say that?" I started off with, "What does VD do to you?" And she said what it does to her. "Does it make you feel good?" "No, it makes me feel bad." "Do the fellows like you afterwards?" "No, they don't like me afterwards." "Do you enjoy sex?" "Yes, I enjoy sex." "Would you like to have one man or a couple of men?" "Well, a couple, I'm not ready to settle down." She'd answered her own thing. She didn't want VD. She didn't want especially to be promiscuous . . . she was asking just for a way out of the situation which would be a little more acceptable to herself and others.[8]

The fear of supersexuality among black youth is an often unspoken factor underlying white opposition to integration of public schools. In the middle 1970s it was disconcerting to many blacks and whites to hear an octogenarian, a long-time member of the Los Angeles school board, express the feeling that black youth were two to three years ahead of white youth in regards to sexual maturity and that mixing of the races in sex education classes would lead to trouble. Despite the outpouring of citizen protest against these remarks, they can be considered representative of a sizable number of persons in the white community who still accept the stereotype of black communities as being hotbeds of rampant sexuality. It is not denied that there is considerably more exposure to sexual matters in low-income neighborhoods than middle-income neighborhoods, and a larger proportion of blacks are low-income than whites. Furthermore, at every income level there is greater permissiveness toward sex among blacks than among whites.

However, to use this as evidence of inevitable sexual aggressiveness of blacks toward whites in an integrated school situation leads to some unlikely assumptions. The first is that permissive attitudes toward sex are necessarily "bad"; perhaps the notion that there is intrinsic pleasure to be obtained from sexual relations without guilt or anxiety is as avant-garde in terms of our social relations as was the "new" idea in the post-Victorian era that it is not true that only "bad" women enjoy sexual relations. Certainly it is also less likely that the natural values long associated with sex in black communities will prove destructive of the social fabric than some of the new patterns of sexual relations, manifested in unhealthy ways when a group, restrained in its sexual expression for years, becomes obsessed with seeking new sexual thrills. Another unlikely assumption is that the values of a low-status minority will inevitably come to dominate those of the majority in an integrated school situation. This could only occur if there were a strong tendency to accept these values already existing in the majority group. Efforts to isolate the white students from black students may be perceived as any previous attempt by authoritarians in power to protect the masses from "subversive" ideas.

Suttles, who also studied the social organization of urban ethnic neighborhoods—blacks, Italians, Puerto Ricans and Mexican Americans, found that only in the black neighborhoods had girls evolved gangs.[9] This is only one of several instances in which adolescent cross-sex relations differed in an ethnic neighborhood when compared to the stereotypic patterns attributed to American youth in general. Suttles described the general pattern as well as the observed differences in each ethnic neighborhood. Suttles noted:

> Among the Italians there were no named girls' groups, and in general young girls steered clear of the boys lest they be compromised. The boys practiced equal avoidance lest they be taken as having overly serious intentions, unless the girl had gone so far as to be considered an "easy lay" . . . In view

of both the local Italian boys and their parents, girls who joined named groups were being so forward as to invite sexual attention. The local Italian gangs themselves regarded the girls as so inferior to them that they ridiculed any attempt of the girls to claim a corporate identity. In turn, girls who attempted to join groups or associate themselves with some of the boys' gangs were subject not only to ridicule but to outright physical abuse. In the eyes of the local Italians, this sort of treatment was inevitable if not altogether desirable, and it seemed the appropriate reaction in a community where men were noted for their exercise of unvarnished power.[10]

The Puerto Ricans made up only a small proportion of the population; in fact, it was so small that everybody knew almost everyone else in the community by their first name and as a result gangs were late in developing since the basic factor in their formation—the need to establish an identity and define it territorially—was missing. Understandably then, the teen-age Puerto Rican girls had not formed any named groups. Like the Italian and Mexican girls, they usually associated with other girls who acted as mutual chaperones. In turn, the boys were likely to speak of "our girls," meaning all the local Puerto Rican girls for whom they seemed to feel some paternalistic obligation. Although similar in some respects to the Puerto Ricans, the Mexican Americans provided another variation:

> Among the Mexicans, cross-sex relations were somewhat equalitarian, and the Mexican girls possessed four named street-corner groups of their own. Each of these groups, however, was explicitly affiliated with a boys' group and expressed these in joint names with feminine suffixes. The girls regarded the boys' group as their protector, and in turn the boys referred to them quite explicitly as "our girls." Although the association between these male and female groupings was quite firm and durable, it did not necessarily extend to a pairing off of couples. The girls seemed quite ready to hover in the protective shadow of the boys' groups, and although they were not as confined to the home or to all-female company as were the Italian girls, there was little doubt of their subordinate status.[11]

In the black neighborhoods, on the other hand, still another variation was observed:

> Not only did the black teen-age girls possess two street-corner groups of their own, but these girls' groups were totally detached from the boys' groups. Their names bore no resemblance to that of the boys' groups, and the girls themselves derided the idea that there was any connection with the boys. In fact, the two girls' groups tended to be more durable than those of the boys and, as the girls reached young adulthood, their groups outlasted the two oldest boys' groups by a year or two. The black boys practically never spoke of "our girls" in a paternalistic sense, but sometimes a black boy and girl would couple off and refer to one another as "my girl" or "my boy." All in all, then, cross-sex relations were quite equalitarian. . . .[12]

Despite the emphasis in the literature on the deviant nature of adolescent peer groups in low-income black neighborhoods, some added perspectives are needed before the actual shape and process of peer group functioning become evident. For example, much of what is considered deviant and even illegal behavior when carried out by a juvenile is not so when engaged in by adults. Thus, not going to school, leaving home of one's own free will, being "sexually active," etc., are acceptable behaviors for those legally of adult status but not for so-called minors. Thus youth in these communities find themselves pushed into the precocious adulthood by lack of parental protection, by the failure of public schools to attract the necessary commitment to enable the development of cognitive and social skills required for effective adult functioning, and by the integration of intergenerational activities that permits a close involvement with adult behavior. Yet, the reality is that any youth that does not conform to dominant social "norms" of behavior for his age period is likely to be stigmatized and further alienated from mainstream activities and therefore from mainstream values and normative pressure. The peer group operating in such an environment is likely to submit to the formidable pressure to move into more and more delinquent circles until it becomes a full-fledged gang with name, dress style, and formal acknowledgment in the community.

The extreme stress on families—usually in the category of "working poor"—who are attempting to rear children in low-income black neighborhoods and to help them to incorporate the values of the larger society cannot be overestimated. In fact, the instability and disorganization of many of these neighborhoods is exacerbated by the high transiency of the population, particularly the upwardly mobile. As has been pointed out in regard to the hundreds of low-income housing projects in this country, they tend to be only a momentary stopping place for the more well-adjusted socially skillful families who quickly move away so that most of those who remain for any length of time are "losers." This greatly decreases the possibility of such neighborhoods having positive adult role models for youth. Thus, these stable, black families often think that the only way to remove their children from the influence of negative peer control is to move prior to the junior high school stage and the rapid formation of identifiable peer culture. However, in recent years, particularly with the advent of bussing programs in which students from minority neighborhoods are given an opportunity to go to school in middle-income predominantly white areas, a problem has been created for parents who find that the youth who can thus "escape" for a while at least the negative influence of neighborhood peer groups must come face to face almost daily with hostility and rejection because of "trying to be white." The question then becomes that of how to deal with the dilemma of improving the youth's chances for adequate education without making unbearable most of his waking hours spent in the neighborhood. The following is an example of this kind of problem and how it was handled with the help of a community worker from a neighborhood service center.

Mrs. Parker, a depressed-looking black woman in her early thirities, asked to see an intake worker at the neighborhood service center a few blocks from the apartment she shared with her thirteen-year-old son Michael. She told the worker that she needed to know what to do about the "bad" kids in the neighborhood and how to keep them "off Michael's back." She knew that they had been giving him a terrible time, calling him "sissy," trying to get him into a fight. She had bought him a bicycle three different times and every time it had been stolen. She thinks that Michael knows who stole his bicycles but won't tell "for fear of getting in trouble." The intake worker introduced Mrs. Parker to Paul, a community worker who "knows a lot about the boys in this neighborhood." Paul told Mrs. Parker that he had grown up in the neighborhood and was now attending college at night, and that he enjoyed his work because he believed his own experiences could help other kids "make it" too.

Mrs. Parker said that the best thing she could do was leave the neighborhood, but she couldn't afford anything better on her small salary as a department store clerk. "At least I'm not on welfare." Michael's father had deserted them when Michael was less than a year old and she was only eighteen. "I have devoted my life to Michael. I am determined that he is going to get a good education and be able to leave this neighborhood!" It was soon apparent to Paul as she described her situation that she had already begun her program to remove Michael from the neighborhood. When Michael was twelve and ready to enter junior high school, she had been approached by his elementary school principal and offered an opportunity to bus Michael to a school in an affluent all-white community about twenty miles away. This opportunity would be given thirty children from the ghetto neighborhood and she had jumped at the chance. This was Michael's second year and she was proud of his achievement. Not only was he doing well academically but he belonged to the Little Theater group and had appeared in two school plays. Since most of the children in his junior high school could swim they had swimming pools or access to one; she had enrolled Michael in a weekend swimming class in the same community in which he attends school. This was a terrible strain on her since she had to take him herself to any after-school or weekend activities. However, she did not mind because "it's going to mean a lot to have him out of this neighborhood environment with its gangs and prostitutes and god knows what else!" However, Mrs. Parker admitted that Michael was beginning to worry her because he seemed to be losing interest in his school work and it was getting harder to make him study. He daydreamed a lot. She thinks it's because of all the teasing he gets from the neighborhood boys, although she had told him to stay away from them. "I know he has to play, with somebody. He can't make too many friends out where he goes to school because it's too far to visit much." When Paul asked about the other children in the bussing program, Mrs. Parker said that there were only a few left—about eleven— most of them had dropped out in the first year and the school system had not opened up the program again. In fact, some of the worst kids were those who had dropped out of the bussing program and were now jealous of Michael. Most of those who were still in the program were girls and Michael "isn't really interested in girls yet."

Paul agreed to help Mrs. Parker with her problem. But it was quite clear that her aspirations for her son were bringing him into conflict with his own identity and relationship with his peeers. This was confirmed for Paul after he got to know Michael and succeeded in developing a big brother relationship with him. His major contribution to the problem posed by Mrs. Parker was in making her understand how important it was for Michael to be "bicultural"—adept at relating to people in both the black and white communities. Thus, he convinced her that Michael could do as well by taking swimming lessons in the neighborhood YMCA; and when Michael proved to be a potential standout on the Y swimming team, it enhanced his neighborhood image. Furthermore, Mrs. Parker was able to join a Parents Without Partners group sponsored by the neighborhood service center and begin to recognize that her life should include more kinds of gratification than that obtained from "devotion to Michael."

MIDDLE- AND UPPER-INCOME NEIGHBORHOODS

In the sometimes frenetic criticism launched against the black middle class, it is often overlooked that it was the youth primarily from this background who dramatically confronted the white system of segregation in the United States in the 1960s and inaugurated the civil rights movement. It was not the masses of undereducated, poorly motivated, understandably violent youth of the ghettos who engineered the sit-ins and began to shape the concept of "black power." It is important then to consider the peer associations among these youth who were able to develop the skills necessary to utilize group process as an instrument for effecting social change. It is important again to point out that middle-income families in black communities would often not be characterized as such in white communities, but would be defined as working class. However, in regard to aspirations, particularly for their children, values and behavior patterns, these families headed by postal workers, beauticians, and skilled workers would have to be placed in the mainstream of middle America. Whereas many of their white counterparts would not have thought it possible to send their children to college, these families did so and in the process contributed to the resulting advancements in the area of racial equality.

As pointed out above, many of these stable, even middle-class families are trapped in deteriorating neighborhoods and negative social influences. On the other hand, many have moved into more solid, middle-class dominated neighborhoods where the physical and social environment is much more positive. As one moves further up the income ladder, there is an increasing likelihood that the neighborhood will be predominantly white; yet the social distance from the low-income ghetto is often smaller than the physical distance would indicate. For example, black families who live in predominantly white neighborhoods may still return to their former neighborhoods to go to the barber shop and beauty parlor or to church. Furthermore, many of the social organizations to which they belong insure social contacts that extend into almost all of the geographical areas in which blacks are in the majority. This is an important factor to recognize in any consideration of associational patterns, even during adolescence.

Middle- and upper-income black adolescent peer groups are never identified as gangs, but this is also true of white middle-class adolescent peer groups. However, for a time during the hectic 1960s, it appeared that white, middle-class adolescent gangs—known variously as "hippies," "groupies," "tribes," etc.—would become a greater threat to American society as it is currently defined than the delinquent gangs of the lower classes. Although their deviance was of a relatively innocuous sort—smoking marijuana, running away from home, not taking baths, jeering at the sacred values of materialistic society—this struck great fear into the white establishment. After all, a shoot-out between gang members in Watts or Harlem only resulted in some dead "niggers" while the middle-class groupies were the potential inheritors of the political, economic, and social power of the nation and their corruption represented a powerful danger. Whereas from time to time individual middle-class black youngsters infected with the same sense of alienation and disillusionment with their parents' life style would appear among the migrating alliances, there was rarely an instance of such alliances made up predominantly of black youth. There is evidence that the fires of protest among white middle-class youth have died down and it is not clear in what direction this group will move in the immediate or long-range future; however, it is obvious that there has been little attempt to imitate the "groupie" life style among middle-class black youth.

Among middle-income black families, there tends to be a much greater degree of control over the activities and associations of their children. There is no "street-corner" society and consequently friendship networks tend to be relatively small and loosely structured. Since these youth tend to do better in school than their lower-class counterparts, there is more emphasis on school-related activities and associations. Parents are more active in school affairs and teachers are more likely to grant special interest and status to these youth whose family patterns, values, and aspirations are consistent with their own. This appears at first glance to be a picture very like that of middle-class white youth; however, again as in the case of lower-class adolescents, there are some major racial differences.

The middle-income black parent who is eager to have his children attend integrated schools, compete successfully with white children and to have friends who are white is at the same time painfully aware that most integrated situations are extremely superficial and there is only "so far" his child will be permitted to go in social contact with whites. Therefore, despite moving into integrated neighborhoods and integrated schools, these parents tend to promote social contacts with other blacks, particularly during adolescence; however, considerable effort is made to insure that these contacts will be with the "right kind." They are willing to sponsor YMCA, YWCA, Girl Scout and Boy Scout groups, and to closely monitor the membership. Of course, integrated groups are preferred but if not possible at least the groups should include only youth from families of similar income and/or educational level as theirs. This effort is even more pronounced among upper-income black parents who have developed national groups (e.g., Jack and Jills; Top Teens, etc.) whose major purpose is to provide a constant stream of social and cultural activities for the children of its highly selected member families. Picnics, dances, swimming parties, trips to various parts of the country and even abroad are planned by the youth but often in conjunction with a corollary social event for the adults. Museum trips, theater parties, special educational workshops, etc., are also usually included to expand cultural horizons. This strategy is highly effective in reducing boredom which constitutes the most intense problem faced by most adolescents in a society which prolongs the period between childhood and adulthood. Unfortunately, it is available to far too few adolescents in black communities.

The push for integration in adolescent activities poses for black middle-class parents an often distressing dilemma. The mother who is anxious for her son to be exposed to the white world, and to obtain the educational and social skills necessary to wrest from it a privileged status, is usually not at all happy about the possibility that this will extend to marriage to a white girl. Although the problems likely to be encountered particularly from white parental opposition are given as major reasons for the resistance, undeniably the sense that such an act reflects a rejection of the black woman and consequently the mother is also a factor. Even more stressful is the fear that the black adolescent girl in a predominantly white neighborhood and school will develop a lowered self-image as she is constantly faced with white standards of female beauty. The ultimate rejection for her is to observe the black male adolescent gravitating to relationships with white girls but to find no white male adolescents showing a similar level of interest in her. This kind of situation threatened to disrupt the entire educational process in an integrated suburban high school which had in a short period experienced a dramatic increase in black enrollment.

When riots among black and white students broke out at Brentwood High School in the spring of 1969, most of the community was stunned. Brentwood was located in a medium-size suburb of a Midwestern city which was essentially a middle-class bedroom community with a history of good race relations. However, in the past few years, the small black population of Brentwood had begun to swell, with the advent of new job opportunities in an automobile plant nearby and stronger enforcement of fair housing laws. Most of the new black families in Brentwood were embedded firmly in the middle class: skilled workers, teachers, government workers, and a small but affluent professional group—physicians, lawyers, and businessmen. Their children apparently had little difficulty moving into the public schools and there were no "ugly incidents" such as accompanied many other situations in which blacks moved in larger numbers into predominantly white schools. The school population at the time of the riots was approximately 3,600 with about 700 black students.

The riot reportedly started when a group of black girls "jumped on" two white girls in the school cafeteria. A group of white boys came to the assistance of the white girls and almost immediately the black boys joined the battle and a full-fledged black against white melee ensued. Plates, utensils, and chairs began flying across the cafeteria, and while teachers, administrators, security guards, and even maintenance staff tried to intervene, it soon became apparent that the police would have to be called. The police, using fire hoses, finally broke up the battle and arrested some seventy students, most of whom were black, including eighteen girls. Twelve students had to be treated for cuts and other minor injuries. The news media gave full coverage to the incident and there was much concern in both the white and black communities that the causes be determined and steps taken to see that it was not repeated. Although no formal fact-finding group was formed, the school administration made an effort to interview those involved, as well as teachers and parents, for information regarding the precipitating cause or causes. A fairly clear picture emerged.

The black girls who were identified as having started the fight were close friends and had transferred only that year from a predominantly black school in a middle-class neighborhood close to the inner city. They had been accustomed to leadership roles, as they had been cheerleaders, involved in service organizations, and held offices in student government. This year, however, they had found themselves constantly frustrated as they had attempted to enter the same kind of activities in the suburban, predominantly white school. They suffered lowered self-esteem, became less interested in school and more "militant" regarding their status as blacks. They were friendly with a number of the black boys but loudly proclaimed their disinterest in having whites as friends. They soon became aware, however, that the white girls were more interested in the black boys anyway, particularly since several of them were star athletes on the football, basketball, and baseball teams. The night before the riot, there had been a dance in the school gymnasium. Although there was some pairing off, most students attended these school dances in groups that tended to form into closed systems once the dance was underway. A group of black males had been quickly incorporated into a group of white males and females, and almost all dancing was intragroup; it meant that the boys danced almost exclusively with the white girls. The black girls, on the other hand, were effectively excluded from interaction with black males or white males and spent most of the evening talking to each other, feeling angrier and angrier, and engaging in more and more provocative verbal assaults on nearby groups of white students and black male students. It was this same anger and frustration that had spilled over into the cafeteria scene which had escalated into a pitched battle between the races.

The principal of Brentwood was familiar with a consultation program in the local community mental health center and took the problem there in order to obtain assistance in devising a strategy for dealing with the problem. A team from the center was assigned to the school, and after a sequence of meetings with school personnel, parents' advisory group and some students, a multifaceted approach to the problem was devised. Several encounter groups were started, most involving both males and females and black and white students. However, at least one encounter group was developed for blacks only at their request. "There ought to be some place in this school we can talk without Whitey listening in!" In addition to these efforts to improve communication between the groups, there were also sessions held with school personnel involving sensitivity exercises to uncover elements of institutionalized as well as individual racism. After a year, the reports of all participants were mostly favorable. The all-black group had served as a place where the black males and females could work through some of their feelings—many of which were distorted—toward each other as a necessary prerequisite to dealing with the larger interracial system. The group finally evolved into a Black Culture Society, whose primary aim was the introduction of black cultural forms in music, theater, historical and contemporary literature into the mainstream of the school's academic and extracurricular life. Out of the other interracial encounter groups, new friendships were formed across racial lines and participants reported greater understanding of the feelings of those outside their own group even though in some instances these feelings were considered irrational or a matter of "over-reacting." Finally, the school administration and faculty were able to create an environment in which such efforts could be realized; e.g., forming a student-faculty committee to review textbooks and make suggestions regarding those that appeared to be racist or deficient in providing a pluralistic perspective, expanding the opportunity system for broad student participation so that it would be possible to include more students in status-giving activity, such as a Girls' Booster Club for all the school's athletic teams, not just for the football team. Thus, the fierce competition for membership in a group in which twenty-five had been designated the maximum was reduced when there were five groups and the number of possible members increased to 150! Similar expansion of opportunities for involvement in other areas of school life were accomplished.

The black middle-class adolescent is not likely to come to the attention of helping professionals in the gang context as do low-income, ghetto youth. However, the problems they experience in growing up in our society are similarly derived from and must be resolved in the context of group experience. The rap group described above was created to make use of the powerful influence of peers and the shared experiences of the group members to deal with a sensitive problem for the girls, the school, and even the society. Furthermore, the presenting problem may have been couched in the concept of search for identity or the problem of self-esteem with which all adolescents must struggle. Yet the specific content of the struggle is a unique aspect of the black experience.

VOLUNTARY ASSOCIATIONS
The continuing importance of the peer group into adult life has been overshadowed by the intensity of the adolescent peer-group experience. Yet, the significance of group membership

throughout the life cycle for understanding social behavior at the community level has been well-documented. For example, most sociological studies of communities include some reference to the voluntary associations that exist within them. These studies have been the source of a negative comparison frequently made that black communities are more disorganized than white communities. The implication is that there are relatively few voluntary associations that have significance in black community life. This negative valuation is not borne out by studies that have looked more deeply into the social structure of black communities and have not equated "significance" with "having importance for whites." If we consider voluntary associations to mean large or small formal organizations in which membership is optional, then it can be demonstrated that such organizations abound in black communities and have been created for a variety of purposes that cannot be served as easily by informal friendship networks.

Babchuk and Thompson reported findings from a survey of blacks in Lincoln, Nebraska, that indicated that 75 percent belonged to at least one voluntary association.[13] This was considerably higher than the 25 percent reported in a national survey conducted by the National Opinion Research Center.[14] Perhaps the most extensive survey of black membership in voluntary associations was made by Ross and Wheeler in Tampa, Florida in 1967.[15] These researchers found that 44 percent of their probability sample of 1,086 respondents belonged to at least one voluntary association. These included church-related organizations, lodges, veterans groups, political clubs, professional, business, and service groups, sports and athletic clubs, civil rights or social action groups, and social clubs. Although professionals were more likely to report membership in at least one voluntary association than any other group (85 percent), even the unskilled and the unemployed indicated a fair amount of involvement (37 percent for both groups). These associations—except for the professional associations—were overwhelmingly monoracial. Membership in churches and unions

were not included in this study since membership in these organizations is at least to some extent involuntary.

Linking voluntary associations in communities is a common
strategy in community organization practice in pursuit of community-wide goals. Warren, however, has provided research
data from Detroit's black neighborhoods which suggest that
these neighborhoods tend to be heterogeneous and therefore
group conflict is more likely when associational linkages are
sought.[16] Furthermore, indigenous leaders are likely to be individuals whose participation in organizations is made at considerable sacrifice. At the same time, the leaders' commitment to a
single neighborhood group or special purpose organization is
often undermined by the high demand for their talent by many
groups in the market for scarce black leadership.

Black voluntary associations have experienced the same vulnerability to negative valuation from the larger society as have
black individuals. In the case of service organization, this negative valuation is likely to stem from the fact that these organizations are largely invisible to the larger society despite laudable
achievements. For example, a black organization provides the
major financial support from the community to the largest private adoption agency in Los Angeles and a national black so-
rority operates one of only three successful job corps programs
for women in the United States. Yet, despite the fact that neither of these programs is exclusively or even primarily for
blacks, the organizations are scarcely known outside the black
community. This virtual invisibility of black organizations to the
larger society contributes to the image of black organizations
as feeble, comic-opera imitations of white organizations.

A more destructive kind of negative valuation is encountered
by social action organizations, especially if they threaten to
challenge successfully the status quo. These organizations
have at times been unfairly attacked and rendered powerless
by accusations that they are militant and support violence, by
accusations that their funds have been mismanaged, and by
direct manipulation of leaders and/or members to create dis-

sension and conflict. The more often this voluntary association seeks recognition and support from outside the black community (e.g., funding for projects or alliances with non-black organizations), the more likely it is that messages scoring its deficiencies will be received.

Social workers have been intensively involved in community action efforts involving black communities; yet, there is an appalling lack of solid research data regarding the interrelationship among type of community, type and strength of leadership available, nature of resistances to community-defined change goals, and the relative utility of various types of voluntary associations in working to achieve these goals. Warren's research is an important initial step in the development of this type of programmatic research. Sensitive measures of neighborhood heterogeneity, levels of resistance, and strength of voluntary associations would appear to be crucial next steps.

SUMMARY

This chapter has described the paradox that black adolescent peer groups in the ethnosystem have been both overstudied and understudied. On the one hand, they have been over-represented in discussions of deviant patterns of adolescent behavior—juvenile gang activity, drug use, promiscuity, runaways, etc. In these discussions, negative images of blacks abound. The black adolescent peer group therefore becomes another vehicle for the negative valuation of blacks. At the same time, there has been little specific study of black adolescent growth and development. This would include considerations of *variations* among black youth in regard to expressions of language, modes of problem-solving, and the adaptive social structures and processes they create. Thus, the particular similarities and differences between lower-income and middle-income blacks were described. Some differences in the adolescent experience of black males and females were also noted. An emphasis was placed on the impact that pressures

from the larger social system have on the day-to-day existence
of adolescents.

The final section in this chapter was devoted to an examination of voluntary associations—the adult equivalent of the juvenile peer group. The large number of such associations in
black communities contradicts an important negative stereotype of black communities—i.e., these communities are disorganized and therefore provide little opportunity for residents to
develop skills in collective action. However, evidence was presented indicating that the ineffectiveness of a voluntary association in the implementation of collective action is based on two
important consequences of the effects of society: negative valuation of blacks. First, the limitations placed on where blacks
can live have resulted in greater heterogeneity of residents in
black communities in terms of socioeconomic level, values,
etc., which reduces the likelihood of consensus. Secondly,
these associations rarely have connecting links to organizations in the larger society which control important resources—
e.g., publicity, money, access to foundations, etc. In pursuit of
the goal of empowerment for black communities, what is vitally
needed are the skills of social workers in reducing the negative
effects of heterogeneity in group process and in creating links
to needed resources.

experiential exercises

1.
Identify six to twelve "high achieving" high-school seniors in a
low-income black community where gang activity is a problem.
Bring them together for group discussion of the following:

> (a) How do *they* define their "peer group," e.g., who belongs,
> how is membership determined?

(b) What activities are engaged in as a *group*? What activities are engaged in by individuals but influenced by the group?

(c) What pressures have they experienced as a result of being "high achievers"?

(d) In their opinion, what could be done to reduce such pressures?

(e) Who are the adults who could be most useful to them in dealing with these pressures?

2.

Repeat the above exercise with six to twelve of the following:

(i) black teen-agers who are bussed to schools outside of a low-income community;

(ii) a mixed group of black and white teen-agers who attend a predominantly white school.

3.

The following vignettes involve perceptions of black adolescent peer groups as negative influences on members and in the community. If utilized as a basis for role-playing, an opportunity is provided to explore the possibilities of reducing the negative and increasing the positive effects of the peer group on its members:

Vignette 1. Teachers at an all-black high school requested consultation from the local community mental health center to help school personnel understand and deal with the tremendous problems of apathy, violence, and open rebellion among students. The problem had now begun to spread among girls, whereas heretofore they had been confined for the most part to the male students. The social work consultant assigned to the school decided to hold "rap sessions" with the girls to explore their attitudes, values, and aspirations and to determine whether more socially approved behavior patterns could not be encouraged. The following is an excerpt from one of the group sessions:

WORKER (to group in general): How much do you girls consider yourselves to be like the kids in the neighborhood?

MAE: I'm not really like them but I think that some of the things they
do are really all right. I wouldn't sit around and talk about
them stealing . . . it's all right and I wouldn't mind my boyfriend stealing . . . I would be scared he might get caught
and put in jail, but stealing is just a way of getting some
money.

WORKER: You are saying that sometimes it's necessary for people to
steal?

MAE: I think it's all right to steal when you can't get a job and don't
want to join the Army and get sent to Vietnam or something
like that.

PHYLLIS: I got a fine pants suit last week off this dude who I know
took it out of Sheldon's Department Store, 'cause I saw it
there a month ago.

WORKER: Does your mother care if you buy them?

PHYLLIS (laughs): She buys 'em all the time!

MAE (pointing to another girl): Hey, Sandy. You tell 'em about stealing.

SANDY (looking around grinning): Hey, what do I know about stealing? (after a lot of laughter)

MAE: How 'bout those welfare checks . . you must *own* the welfare
department by now, kid.

SANDY: I mean, I worked for that bread. I sit up and *plan* things like
that. I really do. I have to draw little pictures on paper . . . you
know, hallways and doors I can get out of and stuff like that!

If you were the social worker, how would you respond?

Vignette 2. You are a social worker representing the staff of the
community mental health center at a meeting aimed at developing a position statement relative to gang violence in the
schools. Also present are school administrators, teachers,
parents, and representatives from other organizations such as

SCLC, CORE, the Urban League, the Black Muslims, the NAACP, etc. A school principal has made a strong statement indicating that the administrator who has just spoken is "a tool of the honky establishment" and that the whole gang problem has been blown all out of proportion in an effort to justify "coming down on us with their tanks and guns and wiping us out." He goes on to say that all the talk about *stopping* the gangs ought to be turned to talk about *using* the gangs to deal with the white power structure in order to "get them before they get us." After this outburst, there is a great deal of heated response from those attending—both pro and con.

You think that a statement is desperately needed to reduce dissension and move the group to constructive action. You rise to speak. . . .

chapter eight

. . . in schools

If the Supreme Court decision of 1954 in the case of *Brown vs. the Topeka Board of Education* was perceived by segregationists as a stunning blow to the principle of racial separation in the public schools, the evidence in 1975 is that they should not have worried nearly so much. Furthermore, blacks who considered that decision as the beginning of the end of prejudice and discrimination in the United States have now to deal with the painful reality, which is that desegregation has occurred only in halting steps; that when it has occurred, it has not always brought positive consequences in terms of achievement and racial harmony; and perhaps most painful of all, that school may not be the certain route to middle-class status and escape from the ghetto as was once believed. The fact is that public school systems are complex, unwieldy bureaucracies, riddled with "power" games, filled with gaps through which requests and suggestions constantly fall, hopelessly ineffectual in dealing with incompetence and only sluggishly responsive to innovation and creativity. Black children—and as recently shown, many non-black, poor children—have found that the promises held out to them in the preschool years about the joys of leaving the parental nest and entering the exciting world of public school have not been kept. The situation is a critical concern of helping professionals in black communities who must constantly come to terms with both the dream and the reality.

Clausen has defined the aims and functions of formal education related to socialization of the child as "transmitting knowledge, norms and values along with the orientational and motivational underpinnings that this requires; and recruiting or
channeling people into programs of preparation for social positions allocated on the basis of achievement." [1] This formal socialization process has been broken down into many subgoals;
e.g., development of specific cognitive skills such as reading,
arithmetic, and writing; the mastery of information systems
which at the same time commit the child to such mastery as a
value; overcoming serious deficits in preparing for the educational program; and developing more general skills relating to
paying attention, sitting still, and participating in classroom activities and transmitting the dominant values and goals of the
American core culture. Yet this crisp delineation of societal
goals to be achieved by means of a public education system
fails to take into account the fact that abstract social goals—
like liberty, equality, or cognitive skill—are like old explorers'
maps which roughly approximate vast territories but which are
in many ways distorted and lacking in important details. It is
not surprising, then, that our educational system in the United
States has been viewed by some as a royal road to success
whereas others call it an utter failure in that respect.

Those who support education as the basis for social improvement and progress for lower-class people maintain that
the successful acculturation of immigrant groups came as a
result of their ability to utilize free education to gain the needed
values and skills. This same opportunity system therefore is
open to blacks *if they have the capacity and the motivation to
use it effectively.* Greer points out, however, that at the turn of
the century—the only time when both foreign-born immigrants
and Negro migrants left their traditional rural cultures and
moved in large numbers into Northern urban areas—the experience for blacks and immigrants were very different.[2] If, in fact,
there was "equal opportunity," it is strange indeed that the
black remained on the periphery of the system sometimes as a

"strike breaker" and menial while the other ethnic groups "successfully joined the on-going society and proceeded to grow with it and adapt to its demands." This is true despite the fact that the majority of school pupils—immigrant and native born—were dropouts and the immigrants and their offspring were encouraged to become truants, even during their elementary school years, by the ready employment to be found in an expanding economy. Students remained in public schools only until some acceptable school-leaving age had been reached, i.e., compulsory education laws for those beyond fourteen years of age only applied to those who were not permanently employed. In fact, the factory and the union were the primary socialization agents, not the public schools. Furthermore, educational advancement came *after* economic advancement rather than before so that it was a consequence of economic improvement and not the means to obtain it.

In Greer's thesis that economic stability for a group precedes its ability to use the educational system as a vehicle to middle-class status, it clearly suggests that the schools are not to blame for the failure of blacks to achieve at the same level as whites; it is the differential in economic stability which imposes on blacks a dispr/ortionate number and variety of obstacles to school achievement, e.g., poor nutrition, inadequate environment for studying, etc. This is the thrust of the "Coleman Report" which found almost no significant differences between schools attended by blacks and schools attended by whites, whether in regard to physical facilities, teacher characteristics, or formal curricula.[3] Perhaps more importantly, whatever variations exist in the resources—physical or educational—of schools, it appears to have no relationship or very little to students' eventual achievement in reading and verbal and calculative skills. Since the publication of the Coleman Report there has been wave after wave of controversy—not as much over the validity of the findings as in regard to their implications. Furthermore, the implications are in terms of two "gut" issues: the value of racial integration as a social policy and the significance of educational reform in increasing the achievement level of blacks and other racial minorities in this country.

These issues are far from academic. Hodgson has reviewed the reverberations from the Coleman Report and concludes that it provided a basis upon which Jensen and his supporters could contend that intelligence variation "explains variations in school achievement to a much larger degree than does discrimination or inequalities in education." [4] It provided conservatives in the Nixon administration, particularly in the Office of Management and Budget, with justification for cutting the budgets of educational programs, and it provided the courts with new interpretations or definitions of equal opportunity and discrimination. Given then the influence of these efforts to discover the content and consequences of education for black children as compared to white, it is important to deal with these "gut" issues which have been raised as they relate to implications for the black communities in this country.

BLACK ACHIEVEMENT IN SCHOOLS
The idea that education "makes no difference" in regard to lifetime success as gauged by income appears at first blush to be so ridiculous as to be unworthy of further discussion. Obviously jobs that require little education, like janitor, domestic service worker, or nurse's aide, also pay very little, while jobs requiring a great deal of education, like physician, lawyer, engineer, or certified public accountant, pay a great deal more. Furthermore, there is a consistent and direct relationship between total lifetime income and years of schooling; i.e., the more years of schooling you have, the greater the total income over your lifetime you can expect to earn. However, this begins to make sense as one realizes that whereas the menial jobs mentioned command menial wages, there are also jobs requiring more education which also command menial wages; jobs requiring high school graduation, e.g., clerical work or gas station attendant, do not pay much more. Everyone is aware of

truck drivers, plumbers, salesmen, or business proprietors who do not have college degrees but earn far more than teachers, librarians, or nurses. Thus, in the analysis of *all* persons in occupational roles, there is little capacity to predict income if educational achievement is known without a significant degree of error. Total lifetime income, however, is an average of all persons at each educational level as defined by number of years of schooling. However, it may still be true that range of individual incomes at each level of schooling is so wide and overlap from one level to the next to such an extent that it would be difficult to predict income on the basis of educational level or vice versa.

We have then the paradox of "no relationship" between variables when one statistical technique is used and a clear relationship when another statistical technique is used. It is necessary to see the underlying rationale of the statistics to tease out the meaning in each case. For example, the fact that total lifetime income is likely to be greater for each year of schooling obtained suggests that it is important to encourage education as a means of obtaining economic security. On the other hand, the fact that educational level alone is not a good predictor of what income will be (although income level is perhaps even less accurate a predictor of educational level) suggests that educational achievement may be neither a necessary nor sufficient condition to obtaining economic security.

It is necessary therefore to understand the conditions under which education is most likely and least likely to be associated with economic status. For example, in an expanding economy, there might be very slight relationship as persons with limited knowledge and ability are brought into jobs and taught the necessary skills. On the other hand, in a tight economy when there are many more people seeking jobs than jobs available, there might be a very considerable relationship between educational level and economic status, as the employer can demand more education for jobs that do not require it as a way of reducing the number of persons qualifying for scarce job openings. Education is a more important variable related to income if you are black, but education alone does not equalize differences in income between blacks and whites. Certain jobs that do not require high educational achievement but do in fact lead to higher than average incomes, e.g., certain skilled trades, have by exclusionary union practices successfully kept blacks out, and therefore again among blacks there may well be a more direct relationship of education to economic status than among whites.

In view of the findings regarding the relationship between education and income, the implications of helping practitioners depend upon the target of intervention. If the target is at the community level, these findings do not negate the need for continued efforts to make public school education more effective in raising the achievement level of black children. Achievement here is defined broadly to include not merely the cognitive skills of reading, writing, and arithmetic but achievement of a positive sense of self, social skills, ability to mobilize one's resources to deal with a changing and often hostile environment, capabilities in entreprenurial or managerial roles, etc. The assumption is that there is a uniformly high association with achievement in cognitive skills and achievement in these others, so that analysis of achievement in the cognitive areas will make possible inferences about achievement in the others. However, it may be true instead that a *minimum* level of achievement is required for these other skills, e.g., ability to feel good about one's self or managerial skills, and increasing this level thereafter has little real effect. Yet, in the broadest sense, achievement in all these areas is an important goal of education. To let it be merely a means of higher income is to limit severely the concept of what education is really about.

Jencks, in fact, does not perceive that because his data prove no direct relationship between expenditures on schools and achievement that this could indicate a need to spend less on schools; indeed he wants larger expenditures. Schools are often depressing places and since people spend nearly a fifth of their lives in them, a school should offer an interesting, comfortable, and pleasant environment.[5] Although this does not indicate a belief in the theory that schools are meaningless, it does indicate a belief in their insignificance as instruments for raising the achievement level of a group. Social interventionists interested in this latter objective would be advised to leave the schools alone and concentrate efforts on targets more likely to influence such achievement. Clark has written:

> . . . it is difficult to comprehend why or how a group of social scientists who are experienced in educational research could publicly define the primary function of education almost exclusively in terms of economic reward. Unfortunately, nowhere does the Jencks report seriously discuss the educational goals of social sensitivity, respect for justice, and acceptance of differences among human beings. And Jencks and his associates missed, or deliberately ignored, the chance to define as important the need of our educational system to reinforce in children their potential for empathy and dignity.[6]

Whether or not these other objectives of education can be achieved without additional expenditures appears to have been rarely explored. In fact, money spent for the schools, which may be a large concern of a community organizer, seems to have been justified strictly in the kind of cost-benefit terms in which the benefit is achievement in regard to cognitive skills.

ROLE OF THE TEACHER
Perhaps one of the most telling blows to efforts to increase spending in the area of education has come from Moynihan, known for his analysis of black families as source of problem behavior in black communities. He suggests that there is a law of diminishing returns in regard to educational expenditures and that the efforts of many liberal, middle-class teachers, administrators, or others in the educational establishment are in fact class interests. Therefore he wrote:

Any increase in school expenditure will in the first instance accrue to teachers, who receive about 68% of the operating expenditure of elementary and secondary schools. That these are estimable and deserving persons none should doubt but neither should there be any illusion that they are deprived. . . . increasing educational expenditures will have the short-run effect of income inequality.[7]

This is not too far removed from some of the criticisms that have been made of teachers in black communities; i.e., they are more concerned with maintaining their middle-class status than in teaching children. This criticism has been leveled at both black and white teachers but is particularly bitter when referring to white teachers in black communities. There is a strong feeling that the low achievement of many black schools in urban centers in the North has been the result of indifferent, culturally deprived (in terms of black culture) and ineffectual white teachers who usually are in the majority in these schools. Yet the Coleman Report and the analyses that followed did not find that black students in schools where most of the teachers were black did better in terms of standardized achievement tests. There is no way of knowing, however, whether they indicate significant differences in regard to other achievements, e.g., social skills or positive self-image. There are research findings, however, which do indicate that black students in Southern high schools had made higher level of self-image and sense of fate control than did black students in Northern high schools.

It is clear that the role of the teacher as a factor in the student's performance is a controversial issue. Postman and Wiengartner have proposed that students do not fail, only teachers; i.e., when students do not develop satisfactory achievement levels in regard to mastery of curricula, the teacher has in fact failed a primary obligation.[8] It is important then to consider the situation of black children and their teachers in schools. This is complicated by the fact that there are multiple types; e.g., predominantly black or all-black body with predominantly or all-black teachers; predominantly or all-black student body with predominantly or all-white teachers; integrated student body with predominantly white teachers; a small minority of black students with predominantly or all-white teachers; or, finally, a few token or "atomized" black students in an ortherwise white school in terms of both students and teachers. The case of integrated student body and integrated teaching staff is of course the ideal that is rarely approximated in real life. Other rare situations are a predominantly or all-white student body with predominantly or all-black teachers; integrated student body with predominantly or all-black teachers, a minority of black students with predominantly or all-black teachers.

This reflects the operation of a combination of factors—the small proportion of black teachers when compared to the total number of teachers in public schools and the power of the white community to successfully resist any situation involving their children in which there will be a loss of cultural dominance. Thus the specific set of relationships that exist between the black students and the teacher may well be determined by the specific situation in regard to congruence or incongruence of the ethnic distributions of students and teaching staff in a given school. This will be further influenced by the interaction of other variables as socioeconomic status of both students and teachers, geographic region, and size of the community. Despite the considerable source of variation, it is important to consider how some of these interactions can, in fact, influence the academic performance of black students as well as the development of social skills and capacity to function effectively in the social environment.

The most important factor here appears to be that the teacher's aims and activities can appear very differently to children of different cultural backgrounds. Yet, teachers often do very little to clarify these aims for children (everybody knows that we have to be quiet in school!). Futhermore, it is almost axiomatic that children will learn only what they want to learn, i.e., what they perceive to have some value either because it gives them pleasure or because it brings them approval from significant others in their social environment. Groups differ in regard to what is perceived as interesting, stimulating, and certainly in what will elicit approval from parents at home. Most importantly, however, there is a growing body of evidence that there are ethnic differences in learning patterns which need to be identified if learning is to be maximized. Stodolsky and Lesser found such differences among Jews, Negroes, Chinese and Puerto Ricans in regard to four abilities considered as tools in learning more complex kinds of knowledge: verbal ability, reasoning, number facility, and space conceptualization.[9] On verbal ability, Jewish children ranked first (significantly better than all ethnic groups), Negroes second, Chinese third, and Puerto Ricans fourth. On space conceptualizations, Chinese ranked first, Jews second, Puerto Ricans third, and Negroes fourth. The patterns not only differ as to patterns observed in each ethnic group but, once the pattern specific to the ethnic group emerges, it is consistent regardless of social class variations within each group. The authors suggest that "if the maximum educational promotion of particular patterns of ability accentuates the diverse contributions of different ethnic groups, this gain in pluralism seems another legitimate aim of education." [10] Unfortunately, despite the emphasis on a learning "profile" rather than some absolute and unidimensional conceptualization of learning ability, there is danger here that overenthusiastic supporters of the notion of diversity in learning patterns presented by different ethnic groups may still tend to stereotype *individuals* from these groups whose learning profile may not match those of the norm for the group.

The danger of stereotyping by teachers was dramatically reported in a study reported by Rist concerning the influence of social class of children on expectations of teachers.[11] In a kindergarten classroom, a group of children who were observed to possess those attributes which are considered by middle-class adults to be associated with future success were selected by the teacher as being potentially "fast learners." In the same manner, those children who did not display these character-istics were called "slow learners"—despite the teacher's lim-ited experience with children who had just been enrolled in kindergarten. The placement of children within the various classrooms into different reading groups was supposed to be based on the promise of future potential in kindergarten, but the clearest criteria for the fast learning group appeared to be cleanliness, interest, eagerness to engage in interactions with adults, display of leadership within the class, and coming from homes which were not on welfare, with parents who were edu-cation achievers, etc. On the other hand, the unpromising group of "slow learners" were for the most part those children who were dirty, smelled of urine, did not actively participate in class, spoke nonstandard English—i.e., different from that which the children, the teacher, and other students were used to—and came from poor homes generally supported by wel-fare. Rist has written:

> In relation to the "fast learner," the kindergarten teacher de-veloped expectations regarding certain students as possess-ing a series of characteristics that she considered essential for future academic success. Second, the teacher reinforced through her mechanism of positive differential behavior those characteristics of the children that she considered important and desirable. Third, the children responded with more of the behavior that initially gained them the support and attention of the teacher. Fourth, the cycle was complete as the teacher focused even more specifically on these children that con-tinued to manifest the behavior that she desired. A concurrent behavioral process appeared to occur between the teacher and the slow learners. The students came into the classroom possessing a series of behavioral and attitudinal character-istics that within the frame of reference of the teacher were perceived as indicative of failure. Second, through mecha-nisms of reinforcement of her initial expectations as to the fu-ture performance of the student, it was made evident that he was not perceived as similar or equal to those at the table of fast learners. In the third stage, the student responded to both

the definition and actual treatment given to him by the
teacher which emphasized his being an educational failure.
Given the high degree of control-oriented behavior directed
toward the slow learner, the lack of verbal interaction and encouragement, the disproportionately small amount of teaching time given to him, and the ridicule and hostility, the child
withdrew from class participation. The fourth stage was the
cyclical repetition of behavioral and attitudinal characteristics
that led to the initial labeling as an educational failure.[12]

This is similar to the findings in a controversial study in
which a teacher was told that a certain group of children were
fast learners and another group of children were slow learners,
although in actuality the test scores of the identified slow learners were higher than those of the group identified as fast
learners.[13] After a period of time, however, the teacher who had
been told that she had a class of fast learners reported at the
end of the period that the students were above average and the
teacher who had been told that she had slow learners reported
that they were below average and that the grades of this group
were substantially lower than those of the other group. Thus,
the self-fulfilling prophecy appeared to be at work. However,
critics of the research have argued that it was far more likely to
be a situation in which the teacher did not want to appear to
contradict "experts" and without this dimension might have
been more likely to indicate the "true" performance rankings
of the children.

It is clear, however, that despite the fact that the studies mentioned here are for the most part "single sample case" (i.e., a
single classroom), it does suggest that labeling and stereotyping occur in school settings. These studies cannot attest to
how often it happens and what factors relating to school,
teacher, ethnic distribution of the student body and/or faculty
appear to govern it. The vulnerability of lower-class black children to this negative labeling process is also clear. It is con-
ceivable that at some time, individual black children, particularly in a predominately white school, or the entire group of black

children might be given certain privileges by teachers who "favor" them. However, this favoritism can soon be shown as another shade of labeling. It occurs whenever there is a tacit acceptance of inferior capacity with the result of lowered expectations.

From the standpoint of helping professionals interested in a maximizing achievement of children in low-income black communities the crucial issue is to what extent are the teacher or parents the more powerful influence in regard to effective socialization. In middle-class white communities where reading scores and physical facilities are invariably superior, there is also a higher level of involvement of parents in the actual operation of the schools, a more positive relationship between parents and school staff which are in turn based on a greater congruence of cultural values and life styles between parents and school personnel, so that the school actually becomes an extension of the home situation. This is extremely different from the situation in most low-income communities where home life and school life are distinct and separate entities and often in actual conflict, e.g., when home emphasizes relative values and the school emphasizes absolute values. It may well mean that the task of the social interventionist is to help create this kind of relationship where it is lacking. In that case, the problems of discipline, low motivation, etc., which haunt the schools in low-income black communities can be greatly reduced if not completely eliminated.

RACIAL INTEGRATION OF SCHOOLS
AS SOCIAL POLICY
At one point in our history, there was no question that the liberal view of education demanded the integration of schools as the required condition to fulfill the promise of equal educational opportunity and to reflect a truly democratic society. The 1954 decision outlawing segregation appeared to be the mighty push needed to catapult the nation to the achievement of that

goal. However, the growing awareness of the depth of resistance in the white community to making the changes required to truly desegregate schools—bussing, open housing, etc.— and the simultaneous recognition that desegregation and integration were not the same thing, helped to push black people away from racial integration as a goal and into a "black nationalist" or at least a "black pride" stance in which racial integration was not only not a goal but actually perceived as a destructive effort to reduce the collective strength of black communities.

The creation of racially or ethnically mixed schools is a matter of social policy concern since in the ordinary course of events in a racist society the inevitable reflection of that society will be in the racially and ethnically homogeneous public schools located in their racially and ethnically isolated communities. The fact that there are so many differing opinions about the consequences and therefore the desirability of racially mixed schools may be due in large measure to the many ways in which such mixing may occur. In addition to the unlikely "natural" mixing based on racial integration of neighborhoods, some racial integration can be achieved by redefinition of district boundaries, to gerrymander in some cases and in others not, in order to provide the desired mix. Some racial integration can also be achieved by bussing students to schools outside their neighborhoods—a strategy which has created perhaps the greatest consternation among whites. But within these general structural models there are almost infinite variations in specific situations based on socioeconomic status of blacks and whites involved in integration efforts, history of a community's race relations, competence of teachers and administrators, level and nature of parental involvement, and opportunities for racial integration and cooperation in other areas of community life. The complexities of these multiple variables acting in concert to bring about consequences to the implementation of even more variable designs for integration have meant that there is evidence supporting almost any consequence that you might predict—chaos or smooth transition, rapid improvement of minority achievement or deterioration in minority achievement, no change or improvement in achievement of white students or deterioration in their achievement, more positive racial attitudes or more negative racial attitudes.

The social policy issue that is generated by the equivocal results of research in this area is equally perplexing. In essence it revolves around the question of whether racial integration or enriched school services is the more effective mechanism for raising the achievement level of black children. As pointed out in the previous section, there are those who feel strongly that pouring money and services into schools in black communities has had little real effect in raising achievement levels. Others, however, indicate that neither does racial integration substantially improve academic performance of black children. Armor published a study on whether forced bussing to achieve integration resulted in enhanced black achievement, self-esteem, race relations, or opportunities for higher education.[14] Using data from four bussing programs, his conclusions were that the evidence did not support the notion that bussing is an effective policy instrument for improving academic performance of blacks or for improving interracial relationships. Coleman's study, done a few years earlier, had shown that such benefits did accrue from racial integration:

> School integration . . . is the most consistent mechanism for improving the quality of education of disadvantaged children. Integration alone reduces the existing gap between black and white children by 30%. All the other school factors together don't add up to nearly that much.[15]

Still, among blacks themselves there is growing opposition to bussing, as well as a growing conviction that the solution to the problems of low achievement levels among black public school students lies in the control of schools in black communities by blacks themselves. To push for racial integration is perceived as accepting the subtle implication that blacks cannot learn unless in the presence of whites. On the other hand, one could consider this idea system as being unmindful of the fact that experience has demonstrated that racial separation and racial mistrust are mutually reinforcing processes so that whites and blacks who grow up in isolation from each other are most likely to fear and hate members of the other racial group. It is suggested that proponents of ghetto control or ghetto enrichment strategies are motivated by frustrations met in efforts to achieve integration and the belief that obtaining resources to strengthen community institutions within the black community are more likely to be forthcoming from an essentially racist political system than integration remedies. However, the dollar cost of a genuinely effective enhancement effort would be great, requiring massive increases in per-pupil expenditures, in the supportive psychological health and remedial education programs, in teacher retraining in the development of new curricular materials and revision of teaching methods. Thus, it would be difficult to demonstrate that such an effort is anymore politically realistic than efforts to achieve integration.

Carlson has pointed out that the issue of integration versus better school services is not an either-or proposition. The fact of the matter is that "equalizing educational opportunities and integrating schools should prove to be reciprocally reinforcing processes. As money becomes available to poor students, rich parents will be less reluctant to have their children integrated with these students. And integration itself assures more equal distribution of education funds." [16] A powerful argument regarding the question of why blacks achieve at higher levels in integrated situations is related to the fact that generally this means going to school with white children of a higher socioeconomic level. Silberman writes, "The benefits of integration come almost entirely from the fact that integrated schools tend to be middle class. Placing black students in lower-class white schools does not help their achievement at all." [17] In light of this fact, some concern has been expressed that integration of

poor blacks into white middle-class schools is logistically impossible since there are probably not enough white middle-
class schools to meet the demand. Carlson disagrees:

> Lest one be concerned that there not be enough middle class
> schools to absorb poor blacks and poor whites, one should
> know that the social class structure of the United States is no
> longer pyramidal; now, in fact, there is a big bulge in the
> middle. The problem is finding ways for those on the bottom
> to penetrate the hard underbelly.[18]

Clearly, the issue is not only whether to integrate or not to integrate; rather, *if* integration, then, under a given set of circumstances, what is the most effective strategy for achieving it? If
not to integrate but retain the racially homogeneous school in
the black community, then under what circumstances can this
have the most positive consequences for achievement of academic, social and psychological competence?

ALTERNATIVE SCHOOLS IN BLACK COMMUNITIES
Considering the gross ineffectiveness of public school education in black communities, it is not surprising that there have
been efforts to create alternatives to that educational system.
What is surprising is that such alternatives have been so few
and of such limited success. Essentially, there are two types of
alternative schools which have struggled to provide a different
kind of education than black children receive in their neighborhood public schools. The first is the same kind of "free
school" that has emerged in white middle-class communities,
generally operated by young white counterculturists who believe fervently that education should be individualized, unstructured, and unoppressive. The other type has been the black-
oriented alternative which places primary emphasis on learning
from a "black perspective," filling in the gaps in regard to
black history, black culture, and black values that are present
in the regular school curriculum.

In regard to the counterculture model, there is ample evidence that it does not meet the needs of black communities in the same way that it does those of white communities. Powers has described the problems arising in one of the original free schools established in 1966 in Ann Arbor, Michigan, and in which a number of black parents brought their children. Despite the fact that the founders of the school were anxious to include black children, according to Powers, they "rejected the terms on which the black parents wanted their children to be helped." [19] These terms included some strict attention to the development of essential skills in reading and math even at the expense of some free expression, Kozol comments in this regard:

> There's not much that a poor, black 14-year-old can do in cities like New York or Boston if he cannot read and write enough to understand a street sign or to read a phone book. It is too often the rich college graduate who speaks three languages with native fluency, at the price of sixteen years of high-cost, rigorous, and sequential education who is most determined that poor kids should make clay vases, weave Indian headbands, play with Polaroid cameras, and climb over geodesic domes.[20]

The other type of alternative school which emphasizes black culture is less likely to fall into this trap and does not reduce attention to such essentials as reading and writing and arithmetic but are more likely to teach these subjects using examples from the immediate environment of the black community than the white middle-class images contained almost exclusively in the textbooks of the public schools. In some of these schools, particularly those operated by the more militant black organizations, children are likely to get political lessons as well as cultural lessons, i.e., indoctrination in political philosophies consistent with a black nationalist stance. The most successful of these schools appear to view their content as supplementary, even compensatory, to public school education rather than a substitute for it. This is consistent with the view that blacks in this country are essentially bi-cultural and therefore are able to function at maximum effectiveness when they are skillful in both cultural milieus and clearly understand when it is appropriate to deal from the perspective of one rather than the other.

Perhaps the most chilling aspect of the debates raging across the country in regard to education in black communities is that the solutions proposed are based at best on considerations of present-time economic demands and social relationships. There is recognition of the diminishing requirements in a highly industrialized society for unskilled laborers and therefore the obsolescence of unskilled human beings. Thus, black students are exhorted to stay and conquer the educational system in order to qualify for jobs requiring technical and professional skills. There is little hope held out for those who do not. What is not recognized, however, is that to the extent that we are moving into a post-industrial era, there may even be little hope for those who do.

Toffler in his *Future Shock* declared that we do not even know what "Johnny must learn" in order to function in our future. "To create a super-industrial education, therefore, we will first need to generate successive, alternative images of the future—assumptions about the kind of jobs, professions, and vocations that may be needed twenty to fifty years in the future; assumptions about the kinds of family forms and human relationships that will prevail, the kind of ethical and moral problems that will arise, the kind of technology that will surround us, and the organizational structures with which we must mesh. It is only by generating such assumptions that defining, debating, systematizing, and continually updating them, that we can deduce the nature of the cognitive and affective skills that the people of tomorrow will need to survive the accelerative thrust." [21]

If Toffler's admonition is true for society in general, it is even more critical for those concerned with the education of blacks and the future of black communities. It is inevitable that the image of the future will be shaped in large measure by the racist distortions of the present. Furthermore, to the extent that blacks anticipate the direction of "accelerative thrust" it will be possible to outrun obsolescence.

SUMMARY

Schools have been shown to reinforce society's negative valuation of racial minorities both through their portrayal in course content and their treatment in the classroom. Schools also serve, however, as a mechanism for the development of skills and mastery of knowledge that makes possible a high level of social functioning and consequently to experience positive valuation. It is this latter characteristic of schools which is generally accepted by critics and supporters of public school education alike. The supporters contend that the success of immigrant groups that came in earlier generations was due to the values and skills learned in our free public schools. Critics, however, point out that it was the factory and the unions which provided opportunities for economic advancement to these groups and that educational advancement came later. Furthermore, the schools have not provided the values, knowledge, and skills needed by most poor people regardless of racial or ethnic background to advance to middle-class status. At the same time, much of the educational content and process serves to perpetuate the negative valuation of racial minorities which contributes in large measure to their feelings of powerlessness and their subsequent inability to function at a high level in society's major social institutions—e.g., the schools and the labor market.

In light of the contradictory perceptions of the effect of schools on blacks, the achievement of blacks in schools was explored in some depth. The role of the teacher in the achievement of black children was examined. Although the operation of a self-fulfilling prophecy in the negative performance of black children has been identified, the severity of this problem has been challenged. Evidence of a strong association between the level of cooperation between parents and school and the achievement level of the children was provided. The advantages and disadvantages of racially heterogeneous and racially homogeneous schools was discussed. Since it is unlikely that massive changes in current racial imbalance in the schools will be forthcoming it is imperative that an emphasis be placed on identifying and developing conditions which support achievement of black children *regardless* of the racial distribution of students in the school. These conditions are likely to be different, however, given the specific nature of that distribution.

Finally, alternative schools were discussed in terms of their potential relevance for black communities. Alternative schools as a substitute for regular public schools—with some rare exceptions—have not been particularly effective in meeting the needs of large groups of black children. Alternative schools which consider themselves supplementary or adjunctive to the regular school program have been more effective and more viable than substitute schools.

experiential exercises

1.
Arrange to visit an alternative school in a black community. Observe the nature of the interaction between students and teachers. How are the following needs of children met by the school: (a) need for a sense of identity; (b) need to feel competent; (c) need for positive reinforcement of one's self-image; (d) need to develop basic cognitive skills, e.g., reading, computation, etc., and (d) need to be exposed to competing values.

Select another alternative school—this time, in a predominantly white community. Explore for answers to the questions posed above.

(a) To what extent are the schools similar or different?

(b) How would you assess the quality of education provided children in each of these schools?

2.
Interview five teachers who teach in a predominantly black school and discuss with them their perceptions regarding: (a) the relative intellectual capacities of blacks and whites; (b) the factors associated with school achievement; (c) their perceptions of community resources available to assist black children with problems they encounter and whether these resources are different from those available to white children; (d) their perceptions of the extent to which schools achieve societal goals versus personal or individual goals; and (e) what they predict they will be doing in ten years; in twenty years.

Select five teachers who teach in a predominantly white neighborhood. Explore the answers to the same questions as posed above.

(a) To what extent are there similarities and differences in the two sets of responses?

(b) On the basis of the responses, to what extent do you expect that schools in predominantly black *or* predominantly white neighborhoods will constitute a positive environment for black lower-class children? Black middle-class children?

chapter nine

. . . in organizations

If a sense of shared fate is the glue which holds communities together, then organizations constitute the energy which provides the developmental thrust and therefore determines whether the community will merely survive or whether it will grow and prosper. Hage and Aiken have written, "The ubiquitousness of organizations is easily explained; they are the major mechanisms for achieving man's goals. Whenever there is some specific objective to be accomplished, the realization of that goal requires the development of an organization." [1] Even more specifically, the level of development of a community is generally defined by the complexity and efficiency of the network of organizations required to carry out such basic functions as production, consumption, or social control.

Whereas primary groups, particularly the family, have been given major responsibility for early socialization of the individual, as he grows older, progress toward social maturity requires involvement in more and more complex organizations in order to develop and utilize required social skills. Whether encountered in the educational system, the economic system, the health care system, the judicial system or the social welfare system, the forceful influence in the person's life is an organization. A simplistic statement of the source of problems in black communities has been the indictment of the family for its ineffectiveness in assisting its members in socialization tasks. Probing analyses have been made of the deficiencies that exist in black primary groups and myriad strategies proposed to "treat" the dysfunction. On the other hand, the deficiencies and failures of organizational structures which are instrumental in determining the individual's capacity to function effectively in society (e.g., schools, business and industrial organizations) or in assisting the individual if problems are encountered which limit capacity to function effectively (e.g., medical care organizations, public assistance agencies, juvenile court system) are less likely either to be studied intensively or indicted for ineffectiveness. It is important to understand, however, that blaming the family for problems experienced by its members fails to take into account the fact that families are embedded within a network of interlocking systems-within-systems and therefore are constantly being influenced by the other human aggregates that abound in the total society. Furthermore, families that are simultaneously operating in an ethnic community, a geographical community and a total society or nation-state must necessarily adapt to norms governing the interrelationships of these interlocking subsystems. The purpose of this chapter is therefore to describe the nature of organizational structures operating in black communities and the manner in which they function for good or for ill of those residing within them.

Stafford maintains that considerable pressures are being placed on black social scientists to study the complex organizations with territorial jurisdictions in black communities for the purpose of formulating solutions to the problems they present; however, if carried out, these studies must be illuminated by a detailed knowledge of the functions and goals of organizations, of the interrelationship of black communities and the total society, and a commitment to observe and criticize organizational oppression.[2] Unfortunately, practitioners are confronted with the need to engage in problem-solving long before definitive answers come to us from the social science of the future which has been imbued with the black perspective. However, this merely means that it is necessary to weigh existing knowledge along with experiential evidence, discarding in the process that which appears to be patently in error or distorted, and creating for ourselves the "working hypotheses" which may assist the social scientist along the way to proof.

ORGANIZATIONAL PROCESSES
The large number of blacks who fall into the lower socioeconomic category has meant that larger number of blacks demonstrate characteristics associated with lower-class status. Rainwater has pointed out that lower-class people are not socialized to work toward the solution to problems through the mechanism of organizations; but neither are working and middle-class people.[3] Most activity in the cultural life of this country is pursued on a private and individual basis. On the other hand, in the middle class, importance is given to organizations which belie their relatively limited impact. For example, middle-class people tend from childhood to be involved in organizations from Boy and Girl Scouts to various committees and governments related to school settings at all levels. Yet, for most middle-class persons, organizations—even the American Legion, Future Farmers of America, are for most of the members "sources of entertainment, of a sense of belongingness and ideological indulgence, rather than a major avenue to the solution of problems of adaptation."[4] Organizational strategies to deal with major social problems have had only limited success when engaged in by middle-class persons so that the expectation that lower-class persons will perceive such strategies as relevant to their own needs and wishes is highly unlikely. However, even in instances where an organizational strategy might be selected to deal with a problem being experienced by lower-class persons, there are real obstacles to their participation. Very frequently, lower-class persons tend to feel that any attempt to be a part of an organization will result in their being looked down upon, manipulated, and exploited. Sometimes lower-class persons do not perceive themselves as

problem-ridden to the same extent as professional helpers and therefore have no motivation to become part of an organization aimed at relieving problems. Even if problems are perceived, it may be difficult for lower-class persons to perceive any relationship between organizational activity and prospects for change.

Finally, some of the apathy of lower-class persons is merely a matter of being overwhelmed by the day-to-day issues of survival with no energy left over for organizational activity. Thus, organizational membership by low-income blacks as a mechanism for problem-solving has to be viewed as a strategy of limited potential. Whether or not they themselves participate in organizations to achieve their own ends, organizations are embedded in the structure of black communities, usually as instruments of the larger society designed and operated by middle-class persons ostensibly to achieve lower-class ends. Therefore, the credibility, viability, and effectiveness of these organizations are crucial issues in the human service arena. There are characteristics all organizations hold in common. Yet, the influence of environmental context is an intervening variable which affects all of these characteristics. For example, all organizations develop a process to deal with change efforts; however, whether change or innovation is easy or difficult may be determined by the degree to which change is customary or whether the pull of tradition prevails within the community.

Organizations are for the most part bureaucracies and it is extremely difficult to find anything else when one observes the structure of complex organizations. Bureaucracies require clearly articulated rules which govern purpose, function and practice in the organization and supposedly insure efficiency and continuity. It is pyramidal in shape, with most of the power residing in the executive level at the top and going downward to the line worker. And there is no doubt that bureaucracies have made it possible to accomplish tasks which less impersonal, informal structures would not achieve. In this organizational structure, the individual is placed in a position according to the principle of division of labor. Furthermore, the various positions that go to make up the organization are molded into a vertical hierachy with the boss at the top and extending down to the lowest menial laborer. Individuals in the organization, therefore, accept a set of obligations in return for a specified set of rewards, e.g., a certain salary, vacation days, more intangible or social prestige. Yet, as has been pointed out in earlier chapters, blacks, particularly in low-income black communities, tend to eschew the impersonal bureaucratic relationship for the more personal relationship. Thus, it has been seen by the dominant society as an indicator of deficient socialization. On the other hand, it might very well be that the impersonal bureaucracy is *not* the prototype of all complex organizations which are effective and that new organizational structures which may be more compatible with low-income black community life may be over the horizon.

Toffler suggests that ". . . there is evidence that bureaucratic hierarchies, separating those who 'make decisions' from those who merely carry them out are being altered, sidestepped or broken." [5] Toffler goes on to describe the organization of the future as the "ad-hocracy." This new type organization is the result of rapid acceleration of social-technical change moving away from the demand for tasks that are routinized and predictable to a demand for temporary role structures to deal with novel conditions; new arrangements of people and tasks which break sharply with bureaucratic tradition. At the opposite pole from the pyramidal, highly bureaucratic organization is the "collegial" agency based on the principle that all staff are considered to have equal status, responsibilities, and qualifications. Kahle points out, however, that this type of organization is only mythical since it is virtually impossible to achieve or maintain such a "leaderless" social system. ". . . no organization or agency with a publicly sanctioned purpose and function can operate without direction, control and responsibility, and it must be able to move quickly in decision-making to meet a wide variety of changing situations." [6] Thus,

Kahle acknowledges that the collegial agency does not permit the flexibility that Toffler finds in his ad-hocracy despite the fact that it supposedly erases the rigidity and overpowering rules of the bureaucratic organization which ironically also serves as an obstacle to quick response to new problem situations. Kahle suggests, therefore, a combination of the pyramidal-collegial structure so that it becomes "a broad rectangle topped by a flattened pyramid." Thus, it retains the basic managerial control of the pyramidal system but allows the freedom and two-way communication of the collegial system.

The bureaucratic structure has provided a rather safe and secure context out of which the definition of professional and professional roles in the organization can be clearly described. A major problem in agencies in black communities has been the conflict generated in the interaction of professionals and paraprofessionals in the same agencies who have found their working relationships impaired by the coming together of people with disparate views about the structure of organizations. First, there are the professionals who perceive themselves as having "earned" the right to hold certain privileged status within the organization and the rewards that accrue therefrom. This is in keeping with bureaucratic structure. However, paraprofessionals entering the system have had to define themselves in one of two ways, either of which stir up criticism. In the first instance, they perceive themselves as entering career ladders with quickly incorporated aspirations to move on up. Their models are the professionals (both those who trained them and those they work with) and so it is not surprising that the paraprofessionals do not change or even modify bureaucracies but begin to fit comfortably within them as they accept and even admire the hierarchical structure and those at the top. On the other hand, the paraprofessionals may come in really wanting to bring about change in the organization and fully expecting that they were hired because of their identification with the community and the desire to have that different perspective represented in the delivery of agency services.

Therefore, the message received is that the agency is collegial rather than bureaucratic and that they are peers of other staff. This is easily said, however, but there are covert, even unconscious resentments when the paraprofessionals actually begin to *behave* as if they are peers of the professionals. The consideration that respect and deference go along with certain positions in the hierarchy remains a powerful force even when the hierarchy—at least in theory—ceases to exist.

The Catch 22 situation that paraprofessionals find themselves in is only one more example of the disparity between what is said to be right and just in society and what is done to many blacks, and most paraprofessionals have been minority group persons. Yet, in confronting the middle management of the agency—generally, the immediate supervisor—regarding this or other discrepancies between words and deeds, the paraprofessional is likely to run into the "intimidation rituals" described by O'Day as the organizational response to protest.[7] Thus, the protest from the paraprofessional can be suppressed in two stages. The first, or stage of *indirect intimidation,* has two parts. The first step is *nullification;*i.e., he will receive the assurance of the immediate supervisor that his accusations or suggestions are without foundation—in fact, the result of misconceptions or misunderstanding on his part. An investigation may even be undertaken which always proves that his accusations are groundless. However, if he persists, his supervisor will find a way to separate him from the rest of his co-workers, thereby softening his overall effect on the organization and insuring that he will not gain allies. This step is *isolation.* It may mean a less visible position in the hierarchy, reducing access to rsesources and people, or merely a systematic unresponsiveness to his criticisms and suggestions. The temptation here is to confront the administrative unresponsiveness in some dramatic but ultimately self-defeating way, since an overreaction can provide ample evidence that the protester is psychologically defective. If this indirect intimidation does not work, it becomes necessary to move to the stage of direct intimidation. The third step then is *defamation,* in which there might be efforts to influence potentially sympathetic persons by attributing his criticisms to questionable motives, psychopathology, or incompetence. The superiors hope that this will force the protester to retreat into passivity or leave the agency of his own accord. If he does neither but persists in his efforts, the way prepared for the final step is *expulsion.* O'Day observes that:

> To understand the effectiveness of organizational intimidation one must examine the reasons why peers and subordinates usually fail to support the reformer, withdraw support, or even actively resist his efforts. Their passive or active resistance may indicate an increased desire or struggle for an organization's scarce resources (material benefits or status, power or prestige—or even dependency). It may also indicate that they perceive themselves as cast in an unfavorable light by the reformer's enthusiasm and heightened activities in pursuing present or changed organizational goals. Members of the organization may secretly believe that the reformer's efforts will be successful, and fear its implications for the position in the organization.[8]

There is an apparent futility about this formulation which can be expressed in the statement, "You can't fight City Hall." However, O'Day suggests that the appropriate time for the protester to push for change is during a period of crisis. In that kind of situation, there is usually enough anxiety and uncertainty that members will be open to adopting new structures that promise relief.

Black professionals in organizations have found themselves facing several dilemmas. They have had to accept the idea that education and achievement in this society places one above those who do not have it; yet, particularly in the wake of poor, despised blacks attacking the systems of which the black professionals have fought so hard to enter and are still fighting to climb above bottom rungs, there is an enormous amount of guilt which gets projected in many ways; e.g., a denial of the importance of "credentials" and a cynicism about the value of their professional education or the utility of their professional skills, particularly in dealing with characteristic problems encountered by blacks. Some black professionals go to the other extreme and insist that any black can achieve what they have if they work hard enough and save instead of frittering earnings away foolishly. Other black professionals insist that their professions must be more relevant, accountable to black people, but have few positive suggestions as to how such relevance or accountability is to be achieved. And still other black professionals are committed to the identification, formulation, and dissemination of knowledge which does have relevance for working in black communities and exclude almost any other aspect of their role in the organization from their consideration.

Whatever specific stance is taken by the black professional, there are likely to arise any number of conflicting situations within the organization based on the interaction of black professionals with each other and with white co-workers if it is an interracial organization. These situations include problems relating to supervision: the supervisor who has difficulty in confronting workers who belong to another racial group with deficiencies in performance due to fears of being accused of racism; problems relating to definition of competence, e.g., black workers who feel that they are not given access to the same promotional opportunities as white workers, etc; problems relating to level of identification with agency versus black community, e.g., the public assistance agency has been a primary target of black community recipients who perceive it as a bureaucratic nightmare and suspect anyone who works for it. This is also true, however, of black professionals who are employed by the Bank of America, major oil companies, police departments, or any of the organizations in America which have a reputation for racism and oppression. The question inherent in this suspicion is, Why would someone who professes to be on the side of the oppressed work for the "enemy" unless salary means more than integrity? Yet this suspicion as well as suspicion over many areas could be avoided if black professionals were to follow some basic principles.

First, it is clear that black professionals cannot drift along with the prevailing winds without defining a direction in which they are going. This means that black professionals have to be ready to answer the sticky questions about their role in the organizations of which they are a part. Furthermore, since in almost every instance—particularly when operating within organizations which are located outside the black community—this role is controlled by the power structure and not by the black professional, it is important for black professionals to indicate that this is a reality of which they are not ignorant. There should be recognition of the exploitation and often unique status given the black in the organization; e.g., low status in terms of the organizational chart but high status when the federal staff concerned with Affirmative Action is making site visits to the organization. It also means that black professionals have to be constantly aware that regardless of how well they have mastered a discipline and demonstrated competence, an inescapable intervening variable in their evaluation and the response made to them by peers and others is that they are black. In some instances it may mean preferential treatment based on excessive white guilt or it may mean discriminatory treatment based on unconscious white racism. In any event, it would be naïve to consider that race is meaningless in the dynamics of organizational behavior.

The white worker in the black community is also suspect, but of course for different reasons. There is evidence to support the notion that many white professionals who practice in black communities are persons of lesser skills or who merely want to "mark time" until they can find preferred jobs in the larger community. When whites are placed in administrative roles over black workers, it is extremely difficult to convince the blacks that the choice was not made because of racism and that the oppressive master-slave relationship is not merely being continued in more sophisticated form. If that were not

difficult enough, the attitudes regarding interracial relationships, particularly among black male staff members, black
female staff members, and white female staff members are
likely to become pronounced under certain conditions, such as
if white female administrators appear to give preference to
black male staff or if a black female staff member is promoted
over a black male staff member.

In addition to intra-organizational problems created by racial
attitudes, there is the critical question of the relationship between organizations in black communities and external systems. Any dependency at all on support from organizations,
public or private, outside the community and controlled by
whites is considered to reduce the credibility of the organization's commitment to the priorities of the black community. Essential in the consideration of an organization's relations to
other systems is the concept of power. Blau defined power as
"the ability of persons or groups to impose their will on others
despite resistance through deference either in the forms of
withholding regularly supplied rewards or in the form of punishment." [9] Certainly if the "regularly supplied rewards" are in
the form of financial support without which the organization
could not survive, the significance of this for autonomous behavior by the organization is crucial. Thus, whether federal
grant money, municipal revenue-sharing funds, allotments
from United Way or Community Chest, or payments from clientele outside the community, the possibility of conflict between
the priorities of the community and the external sources of
support cannot be overlooked. The most ideal situation, of
course, is where (1) there are varied sources of support so that
no single external source is crucial; (2) the pressures to provide support are generally created by abstract sense of social
or moral obligation and not by expectations of conformity to
some specific set of behaviors; and (3) the basic ideological
perspectives of the sources of support are for the most part
consonant with those of the black community and the organization.

Traditionally, the consumers of the services of an organization control the production and distribution of goods and services through their ability to purchase them. Yet there is often conflict between the needs and demands of clients and those of the members of the organization, and there is considerable question as to whether an organization is really serving its clients or merely in the business of self-maintenance at the least possible level of service. Furthermore, as organizations have become more complex, there has been greater separation of the consumer and control functions traditionally held by the client group. The greatest separation and therefore the least control exists in the case of large public monopolies where the consumer has no choice but to accept the services rendered and control is in the hands of commissions that may have little responsiveness or sensitivity to consumer demands. On the other hand, the largest degree of control and the least separation is in the case of the consumer dealing with a small business firm. It is a complex issue, that is, the degree to which consumer control of an organization's services is desirable. We are all aware of the "Madison Avenue" success in manipulating consumers to indulge themselves in useless and even worthless products. In many instances, particularly in human service organizations, it may be necessary to have the control function exercised by some other authority such as governmental authority to insure social justice.

It should be pointed out, however, that clients of organizations are not totally inept and powerless, particularly when they create organizations themselves in order to gain more control over the organizations ostensibly in the business of serving their needs. Thus, they may be able to create countervailing power either through their ability to exert pressure through political authorities to act on their behalf against the organization or more direct application of power in the form of consumer boycotts, publicity through the various mass media, or even in extreme cases disruption of business to highlight their protests.

Organizations may differ in their internal and external processes due to significant differences in the types of clients they serve. Blau and Scott have characterized complex organizations as (1) business concerns which benefit owners; (2) commonweal organizations which theoretically benefit the general public; (3) mutual benefit organizations which benefit the members of the organization; and (4) service organizations which benefit their clients.[10] Harshbarger has pointed out, however, that this classification is more output-oriented and does not take into account other important sets of organizational variables which may create important similarities and differences among organizations.[11] For example, whether a business benefits its owners and a mutual benefit association its members may be of less concern than the fact that the success of the business depends upon the trust customers have in the product, whereas the success of the community cooperative buying service may depend upon the trust the members have in each other. In organizations serving black communities, the overriding problems of survival have influenced their operations regardless of the particular target group for which they were created. Thus, it is often difficult to operate a business without concern for service to the community or to set up a service organization without consideration of the economic support to maintain it, which might mean the development of a business enterprise whose profits are earmarked for the service function. Mutual benefit organizations also are often business and service operations as well. For the purposes of discussion here we will consider those organizations in each of these categories on the basis of *primary* rather than exclusive concerns.

COMMONWEAL ORGANIZATIONS
There are other interrelationships between Blau and Scott's categories of complex organizations which have special significance in black communities. The commonweal organizations have been defined in terms of the benefit supposedly accruing

to the total society, which may embrace many different communities; e.g., police and fire departments, public utility companies, etc. However, these organizations have been notoriously discriminatory in their policies regarding service delivery to minority communities. It is a common complaint in neighborhoods that have changed over time from all white to increasing numbers of black that, as the whites leave, the services become more and more slipshod. Garbage is collected less often, police protection decreases, and so on.

Purcell and Specht have recounted the case of "The House on Sixth Street" and the overwhelming evidence of the inefficiency and insensitivity of the network of commonweal organizations in the delivery of services to a poor minority community.[12] A twenty-three-year-old black, single mother of four children had come to a neighborhood service center to complain that there had been no gas, electricity, heat and hot water in her apartment house for more than four weeks. Part of the difficulty she and the other tenants in the deteriorating building was related to the intricately connected but almost never clearly defined organizational network necessary to deal with problems of "commonweal" services. Purcell and Specht write:

> In order to redress a grievance relating to water supply (which was only one of the building's many problems) it is necessary to know precisely which city department to contact. The following is only a partial listing:

No water	Health Department
Not enough water	Department of Water Supply
No hot water	Buildings Department
Water leaks	Buildings Department
Large water leaks	Department of Water Supply
Water overflowing from apartment above	Police Department
Water sewage in the celler	Sanitation Department.[13]

This was further complicated by the fact that an unscrupulous landlord might deliberately withhold these services from tenants in order to force their moving so that he can renovate the building for higher income or let it deteriorate completely and then sell it to an urban renewal agency.

Helping practitioners who want to aid people who have problems with commonweal organizations are required to have in-depth knowledge of the often obscure policy regulations governing the delivery of thoir servicns. Much of the frustration visited upon minorities in their own communities derives from the inability to deal with these organizational structures which are located for the most part outside the community and even if physically within it are controlled by persons whose loyalties, sense of obligation, and first priorities in service delivery are in other directions. Most middle-class persons, regardless of race or ethnicity, have had to deal with the horrendous problems indicated on the list above and certainly not more than one at a time. Therefore, the disabling entanglements experienced in dealing with commonweal bureaucracies are scarcely realized. This means that the power which can be exerted by the affluent but not by the poor never is applied to bring about change. But this does not mean that it is futile to attempt to bring about such change. It does mean, however, an understanding of how and from what sources power is derived in social situations and how to use this knowledge to assist individuals and groups in the community to achieve solutions to social and personal problems.

The difficulties with public utility companies are only one dimension of the problem with commonweal organizations in black communities. Perhaps the best known and highly publicized problems arise in dealings with police departments. Mottoes of police departments (e.g., "to protect and serve") are often the target of derision. A 1967 survey of the racial composition of police forces in major cities in the United States revealed that in all cases, blacks are vastly underrepresented.[14] For example, in New York City, the estimated percentage of non-white population was 16 percent but only 5 percent of the police force was non-white. Atlanta, often considered the South's most progressive city in regard to race relations, had a population that was 38 percent non-white with only 10 percent of the police force non-white. Even Washington, D.C., besides being the nation's capital and the only major city with a population of 63 percent non-white, had police force with only 21 percent minority personnel. It is no wonder that the system of public safety is singularly unresponsive to the needs of residents in black communities.

It is interesting to note that in most analyses of police-minority community relationships great attention is given to the unusually high crime rates which tend to characterize them. The more politically conservative analysts emphasize the propensity of community residents to engage in nonlegal activities and lay much of the responsibility for this factor onto deviant values which sanction such behavior. The more politically liberal analysts are likely to attribute the high crime rate to the adverse social conditions which breed crime, such as high density, low income, deteriorating neighborhood, family breakdown. Yet little analysis is made of the primary organization aimed at providing public safety and protection—the police department—in order to determine whether its conceptualization and implementation of its societal function renders it so ineffective in reducing crime in these communities.

There are several organizational characteristics of police forces which may well influence the negative outcomes in minority communities. For example, police departments are bureaucracies and, like all bureaucracies, in order to operate successfully they must attain a high degree of reliability of behavior as well as a high degree of conformity with prescribed patterns of action. Therefore an inordinate importance is given to discipline. However, discipline can only be effective if the ideal patterns are supported by strong sentiments which presuppose devotion to duty, the recognition of the limitation of one's authority and competence, and unvarying performance of routine activities.

Policemen are socialized to have strong feelings of "we" versus "they," to take orders well because there are increasing amounts of wisdom and competence as one climbs the organizational hierarchy. The strong bond of loyalty to the organization, which is an ingrained part of police culture, therefore works against efforts to change the basic principles of operation in order to ameliorate grievances which have grown up between the force and the community. The nature of these grievances has been cogently described by Rose:

> Ghetto residents frequently perceive the police as members of an occupying force, who are present in the ghetto to protect the interests of a nonresidential white population whose value system they conform to and uphold. The police who are most often selected from working class segments of the population view the present structure of American society as highly desirable. Persons possessing attributes which deny that they have absorbed the principal dimensions of middle class American culture provoke suspicion and are subject to careful police scrutiny. Blacks possessing lower class life styles, which are expressed overtly in a variety of ways, are logical objects of suspicion, given the way the police culture operates.[15]

Most large urban police departments have initiated programs designed to either increase the sensitivity of police to the feelings of persons in black communities toward them in particular and life in general. Other attempts have been made, such as the creation of community relations divisions within the department which have as major focus the improvement of relationships between police and persons in minority communities. However, it has been patently clear that these efforts do not extend much beyond the officers directly involved in the community-relations function, and without deeper penetration of the organization nothing much in the way of change can be expected.

Black policemen have had a particularly difficult time in adjusting to an almost untenable situation in which to be accepted by their white counterparts they must come across as even more hostile and rabidly out to support law and order. However, there is some evidence that black policemen are beginning to form their own associations—for which there is ample precedence among other ethnic groups of policemen—and that this new breed of black policemen is willing to protest improper or intemperate conduct on the part of fellow officers directed against black communities. This factor may be important in recruiting efforts in black communities where young blacks have not perceived a police career as desirable.

Another view has been given by Rosen, who argues that in his analysis of data collected in five systematic studies of major urban police departments in regard to police behavior and attitudes in regard to black communities. He concludes:

> . . . the best available evidence on police behavior fails to support any assertion of widespread and blatant racial discrimination on the part of contemporary urban police. This does not mean that there have not been individual acts of police discrimination; quite clearly, such acts have undoubtedly occurred. But in the aggregate, and as a characteristic of the police system, major patterns of discrimination have yet to be documented. Finally, there is no denying that policemen are somewhat insensitive to the desires and needs of blacks, but it also seems likely that the black community has also tended to be insensitive to the problems of the police. And this seems to be the real tragedy: Police and blacks caught in an escalation of conflict, distrust and hatred. In this vicious circle it is extremely difficult to determine who is the hero and who is the villain.[16]

The real issue, as indicated earlier, is whether or not the police departments of our large cities perform effectively given the nature of their organization and the kind of social context in which they must exist. The proponents of community control believe otherwise and have insisted that black communities must run their institutions. Before a truly community-responsive organization can be achieved, James Q. Wilson, one of the strongest opponents of the concept of community control over police, points out that in the era in American politics when local precinct houses were oriented more toward ward politicians than bureaucratic superiors, they constituted a focal point for bribery, third-degree interrogations, and prison shakedowns. In contrast, we have the modern police department—not immune to the inroads of racism, brutality, or corruption, but these occur much less often than formerly, and least of all in the more highly professionalized departments. Honesty and effectiveness are functions of professionalism which, in turn, depends upon largeness of scale and insulation from politics, neither of which conditions would be met in a situation of community control.[17]

The community control advocates point out that no matter how professional a police department is, it is almost stymied when there is no community support for its activities. Furthermore, it is difficult to consider honesty as more problematical with police controlled by the community than with the present situation in which blatantly illegal activities in the black community are overlooked. Altshuler wonders:

> Would actual corruption be greater in community-controlled than in city-wide police forces? Tight central control and frequent transfers may be one way to limit corruption, but another is to conduct frequent outside audits and undercover investigations. White journalists and legislators would be waiting to blow every scandal out of proportion and to use it as a pretext for takeover. Being aware of the precariousness of their autonomy, Negro neighborhoods would be especially zealous in their own efforts to avert scandal.[18]

This model of community control presupposes a decentralized system in which local, territorially defined communities are responsible—apparently through some community board for day-to-day operations of the police. It is clear that a variety of models might be constructed with this condition as the essential core but with interrelatedness to a central system of supportive laboratory training and computerized record-keeping services. Despite the fact that most proposals regarding

community control, particularly in regard to the police function, are not taken seriously by the power structure in our
urban centers, there are a few instances in which the gain of
political control has created an opportunity for community control of other systems as well. Some such communities have
achieved this on the basis of abdication by whites, as in Newark or Compton, and to a lesser extent Atlanta or Washington, D.C.

BUSINESS ORGANIZATIONS
When the black ghettos of the United States exploded in rebel-
lious upheavals characterized by violence, burning, and looting, many white businessmen could not understand why they
should be the special targets of attack. Their lack of comprehension can only be laid to the "invisible" nature of the black
experience to whites, as so eloquently described by Ralph Elli-
son, since the reasons why are so obvious, so pervasive, and so
painful to blacks. It is also due to ignorance of history which
permits all racial rioting to be seen as similar if not identical
phenomena, so that Los Angeles in 1965 and Detroit in 1967
were considered the same as Chicago in 1919 or East St. Louis
in 1917. Indeed, those earlier riots were occasioned by black
challenges to the status quo of segregation and discrimination
and white determination to maintain it. The later riots, however,
were not black armies against white armies fighting to establish a position; rather, it was blacks against the system represented by the police and the white business establishments.
As Fogelson points out, "The Negroes were looting to acquire
goods most Americans deem their due and burned to even the
score with unscrupulous white merchants." [19] The truth is that
the business system in America has since blacks first arrived
made it abundantly clear that "free enterprise" was "for whites
only."
    The history of attempts by blacks to gain a foothold in the
world of business is replete with examples of constant con-

straints being imposed by the dominant white society. The earliest enterprise developed to any appreciable extent by blacks was the catering business. Jones writes: "As far back as 1780 northern black caterers were making fortunes, and the men and women who entered this line deserve to be called the true pioneers of black-owned business. Perhaps the nature of catering was the reason for the initial success. Since the black man had spent most of his life in serving white masters, catering was a logical and practical way to show his business skills. It represents an opportunity to make money from work that had previously been considered menial." [20] However, waves of white immigration and the entry of these and even native-born whites into an obviously profitable business, coupled with the increasing utilization of white restaurants by the luxury trade, spelled the demise of the more affluent catering businesses owned by blacks. This process was repeated over and over again in the North and South, i.e., blacks were successful in establishing businesses but were never able to expand. Abram Harris attributed this failure to: (1) the difficulty of obtaining capital and credit; (2) low wages, competition for jobs, and immigration; (3) mob violence; (4) occupational restrictions; (5) prohibitions against owning certain types of property; (6) denial of the right to sue; (7) restrictions against settlement in the West; and (8) civil and educational handicaps.[21] It should be noted that another important factor may be relative lack of support from other blacks who had incorporated the white attitude that "white is better."

The years after slavery witnessed extensive and intensive efforts by blacks to crack the walls of the American business establishment. There were some notable successes and many, many failures. Burrell and Seder, in an exploration of successes, come to the following conclusions:

> Every man whose story we have told is an exception. Most of them have exceptional intelligence. All of them have extraordinary patience, endurance, imagination, energy, drive and

luck. All of them had to sweat and strain and struggle many times as hard as their white counterparts for every sale, every achievement, every dollar. . . . In America, lots of ordinary white people make it. Why shouldn't an ordinary black man of average ability be able to make it too? Why should he have to rise to heroic achievements in order to share in American life? That's what black people are complaining about.[22]

The general absence of blacks from business continues into the contemporary era in which the largest black industry, insurance, is made up of fifty companies, less than 1 percent of the national total. Despite the constraints imposed on black business enterprises, there are still those who point to other minority ethnic groups such as the Chinese, the Japanese, the Jews as evidence that discrimination is not enough to rationalize black failure. The invidious comparisons suggest for the most part that blacks lack business acumen and potential—otherwise, they, like other minority groups, would have established much more successful business organizations.

Ivan Light, in a masterful, scholarly analysis of ethnic enterprise, has shown that other forces than differences in inherent potential account for the observed differences in business success.[23] A powerful factor was the cultural tradition of rotating credit associations among Chinese, Japanese, and West Indian groups which permitted them to counteract racist trends in the society which served as obstacles to development of business enterprises in minority racial communities. However, the success of these rotating credit associations was based on cultural ties and traditional values that had been erased among blacks in the United States by slavery and its aftermath. Light wrote:

> The persistence of the rotating credit associations among Chinese, Japanese, and West Indians provides tangible support for E. F. Frazier's contention that tradition played a critical role in the business success of "other alien groups" and that a lack of traditions inhibited Negro-owned business in the United States. Moreover, it makes possible an under-

standing of why racial discrimination in lending affected American-born Negroes more deleteriously than it did Orientals and foreign-born Negroes. Unlike the Chinese, Japanese, and West Indians, American-born Negroes did not have the rotating credit tradition to fall back on as a source of capital for small business enterprises. Hence they were especially dependent on banks and lending companies for credit; and when such credit was for one reason or another denied, they possessed no traditional resources for making do on their own.[24]

The practice of rotating credit was variously referred to as "susu," "partners," "chitty," "syndicate," "huis," "tanomoshi" according to the ethnic group and its place of origin. However, the general model was always one in which a small group of people paid into a common pool a given amount on a regular basis. At a specified date all the money so collected would go to one member and the procedure would be repeated until all members benefited in turn. Partnership portions—relatively large amounts of cash to the individual designated to receive it—could be used to capitalize small businesses; invest in real estate; or pay for the transportation of relatives wishing to immigrate—in which case it assured the continuation of a close-knit, often kinship group held together by obligations which could serve as the basis for an even larger group of "partners."

In the mutual associations described by Light, obviously they were a necessary precondition to the development of actual business enterprises in the racial or ethnic communities.

It can be pointed out that the programs of the Great Society placed a major emphasis on increasing the participation of blacks in the major business and industries in this country as well as providing greater opportunities for blacks themselves to develop new businesses. Yet there has still been utter insensitivity to the special problems of blacks and minimal commitment to overcoming these problems. Jones provides an illuminating case history showing what is required if these problems are to be resolved:

In the summer of 1965, Kenneth Sherwood, a successful furniture salesman, visited the manager of the U.S. Small Business Administration office in Harlem, New York to present his business proposal. It was a bit different from most, for he was buying an established retail furniture business from a Jewish merchant. The furniture store, long famous in Harlem, was grossing a bit less than a million dollars a year. (The figures were taken from tax returns.) An analysis of income and expenses over several recent years and a review of the current financial situation revealed that the business had done very well. It had, in fact, been the means by which the owner had become a multimillionaire.

Sherwood was offered what one might fairly call a good deal. For $200,000 in cash and the assuming of a $110,000 mortgage on the real estate, he would become owner of a sizable inventory, along with equipment, vehicles and real estate. The building—five stories plus basement (totaling 60,000 square feet of space)—was situated on the main business street in Harlem. (The value of the location was increased intangibly because most of the businesses on the street were owned by whites. For many, many years a black man could not even rent a business office on this street; and even in 1965 it was almost unbelievable that a black man should be able to purchase a building there of that size.)

After a visit to the business with the applicant, the manager concluded that the deal was sound and necessary; it would be a breakthrough for a sizable black business in one of the country's largest urban communities. The basic question remained. How was the applicant to raise the money to make the most of this opportunity of a lifetime? The applicant had only $20,000 in cash savings (partly raised by refinancing his house), and SBA's lending policy was to grant loans only on a one-to-one basis: for each dollar he borrowed, the applicant would have to have one dollar of matching equity in the business. It seemed to be an impossible requirement. Nevertheless the deal was made because the SBA manager found a way. Here's how. The applicant, analysis showed, would realize an appreciated value of close to $170,000 the moment the transaction was made. The total cost of the business deal was $310,000. An appraisal of the real estate gave it a value of $350,000 (assessed at $325,000) and the value of the equipment and inventory was $130,000 for a total of $480,000. The difference between the $480,000 and the purchase price of $310,000 represented an appreciation of $170,000. Adding the applicant's $20,000 to the $170,000 in appreciated value, SBA's one-to-one ratio requirement would be met close enough.

The next move was to find a bank to participate with SBA on a $200,000 loan. A black-owned commercial bank (Freedom National Bank of New York) agreed to assume a participation of 25% ($50,000) and after a few weeks of negotiating and processing of documents, the loan was arranged. (It was, to that time, the second largest loan made to a black business in this country.) This case illustrates more than mere ingenuity and scrambling. Clearly, if the loan officer and the regional director of SBA had not been black, this business would not be in existence today. For the white officials at the SBA office said at the time that it could not be done. But the black officials knew the SBA regulations, and they had the imagination to find a way. It wasn't a fault in the SBA regulations that discouraged the white officials; it was a lack of desire to help and a lack of interest in black-owned businesses.[25]

Although it is clearly better to have committed black brothers in positions of power in the organizations of the dominant society, it is equally clear that this alone will not provide major impetus for business development in black communities. In seeking more powerful alternatives, it might be well to look at two models—one from the past and one from the present as source of insights.

The role of religion in supporting the secular aspects of black community life has been scarcely appreciated until recent efforts to strip away the biased layers of social science dogma and the revelation of the black experience beneath. Genovese, in his monumental epic of slave life, describes religion as "the organizing center of their resistance within accommodation."[26] Unfortunately he failed to see essential differences between the doctrinaire religion of the slaveowners and the ingenuous modifications of that religion made by slaves. The power of religion as a spiritual force in black life has been chronicled but its influence in the nonreligious sphere has only been faintly outlined. It is not surprising then to find the religious movement of Father Divine—a phoenix-like phenomenon rising out of the misery and frustrations of the Great Depression, to create a finely woven mixture of spiritual, social, and economic factors within an organizational framework.

Coleman has indicated that a most important asset to a community is the presence of mutual trust among its constituents.[27] In groups in which there is little economic capital, collective community enterprises, as shown by Light, can be initiated through the development of mutual-help associations based for the most part on trust. The transiency that plagues so many black communities in urban areas and the all-consuming involvement of blacks in the struggle for bare survival have strongly inhibited the development of organizations based on trust. But Father Divine was able to overcome these obstacles to an amazing extent.

Father Divine was born George Baker in Georgia about c. 1882. He began his preaching career in the South, but after some conflict with local whites he perceived that it was time to move North c. 1915. He spent several years in Baltimore, Maryland, where he was an off-and-on store-front evangelist, and then moved on to Harlem. In 1919 he moved to Sayville, Long Island, with a band of twelve disciples and there established his first "heaven." It was here that the dogma of divinity began to emerge as basic to his relationship to his followers and he took on the identity of "God" and his followers became his "angels." He operated a licensed employment agency out of which his angels were sent out to work primarily in domestic service. They soon established a reputation for dependability and hard work so that jobs were not difficult for them to find. All of their earnings, however, were contributed to "heaven" and they were doled out allowances as well as room and board.

The movement expanded rapidly as Father Divine made the services of his employment agency free to all who needed it and his followers used the opportunity to proselytize. Perhaps his most impressive act was to bring busloads of people from

Harlem to his Long Island "heaven" and feed them tremendous banquets with the implication that his ability to do this in the middle of the Depression was due to divine powers. As the Depression deepened, thousands of blacks from Harlem made the trip to Long Island, feasted at the tables of Father Divine and ended up joining his flock. This was despite the fact that some very stringent conditions of membership were imposed. There was to be celibacy and chastity; old names must be given up and a heavenly name taken, like Blessed Quietness, or Happiness Sunshine; regular attendance at services was required, and all money earned had to be put into the common pool. Despite these heavy requirements, the Peace Movement Mission prospered during a time when the security it offered far outweighed the insecurity and even starvation that many saw as the alternative.[28]

So many "angels" joined Father Divine's Peace Mission that the little employment office was insufficient to keep every one employed, particularly in a tight job market and even with the reputation of the workers. Father Divine's solution was to encourage the establishment of businesses of all kinds which would create the jobs needed. The regulations governing the operation of the businesses were as stringent as those governing the religious component—i.e., no profits were to be taken by the individuals except for bare maintenance. All the services and all the monies earned were perceived as due the collective and not the individual. Light has described the Divine business operations in the following excerpt:

> In starting a business, local Divinities pooled their funds and their labors. Divine Peace Mission Movement Cooperatives spread into every small field of endeavor. Between 1933 and 1937, Father Divine became Harlem's leading landlord. His followers leased three apartment houses, nine private homes and three meeting halls with upstairs dormitories. Followers also operated several grocery stores, ten barber shops, ten dry cleaning establishments and twenty to thirty huckster wagons featuring fruit and fish at evangelical prices. A coal

business shuttled trucks between Harlem and Pennsylvania coal fields. In addition Divine's followers acquired similar interests in Newark, Jersey City, Bridgeport, and Baltimore. Laundries and restaurants were, however, the most numerous of Divine enterprises. Father's twenty-five restaurants in Harlem made a significant contribution to the relief of misery in the Depression. His restaurants sold thousands of wholesome ten-cent meals to the unemployed; in addition his restaurants dished up 2,500 free meals a day in Harlem alone.

After the Depression, Divine's business expansion continued although membership decreased. By 1953, Angels operated hundreds of cooperative Peace garages, laundries, meat markets, grocery stores, barbershops, construction and painting firms, tailor shops, furriers, restaurants, hotels, boardinghouses and photographic studios in major cities from New York to Los Angeles.[29]

Thus, small business was the route chosen by Father Divine to deal with the problem of maintaining a heavenly host here on earth. Yet, deep within its radical ideology was the strong force of the Protestant ethic. Followers of Father Divine could not accept public assistance; hard work and independence were the gifts he offered those who believed in him. Thus business success and staying off welfare were achievements of Divine's followers that blacks in general have often been unable to duplicate. It was owing to the fanaticism underlying the religious sect that created the solidarity required to initiate and maintain myriad business enterprises as well as autonomous social service institutions for members.

On the contemporary scene, the nation of Islam—the Black Muslims—have adopted the strong religious base on which to construct secular institutions, notably business enterprises. Clearly, ideology and organization are a more powerful resource system from which to develop business than individual motivation and skills. Unfortunately, no successful integration of a secular philosophy has had the holding power for people in black communities that could generate the solidarity needed to move into business ventures. So far, it appears that nothing short of religious fervor will accomplish this.

The Community Development Corporations are a current response to the problems of economic development in black
communities. Like the religion-based organizations, this model
attempts to integrate economic and social welfare concerns
into a single framework. In 1968, a bill was proposed to
Congress which would establish community corporations that
would, among other things, expand economic opportunities
through the purchase and management of properties and
businesses. It was also suggested that profits from the corporation could at the discretion of the management use its profits
to pay a "community dividend" rather than a return to stock-
holders. This community dividend could be used to support or
develop health centers, housing projects, or day care centers.
Although this element of community concern lifts it out of a
classical capitalist mold, the idea, in contrast to the communal
socialism of Father Divine, is imbued with the capitalist spirit.
The idea is to promote entrepreneurship in black communities
so that more capitalists are created whose major pursuit is a
profit from business enterprises which would accrue to stock-
holders primarily and the collective community secondarily.

The limits of black capitalism have been stated:

> Federal credit and technical assistance should be extended
> and discrimination against Negro enterprises in such matters
> as surety bonds and other forms of insurance should be dealt
> with—if necessary through federal legislation. Much can be
> said for a federal program to assist support and assist ghetto-
> based community development corporations that will have
> power to operate or finance commercial and industrial en-
> terprises. But even with all these kinds of encouragement, to
> suggest that Negro entrepreneurship can produce much more
> than a token number of new jobs for the hard-core unem-
> ployed, at least for a long time to come is pure romanticism.
> Even if the ghetto markets could be walled off, in effect,
> through appeals to Negroes to buy black, the market is not
> big enough to support significant manufacturing, and the
> number of white employees who could be replaced by black
> workers in retail and service establishments is limited.[30]

Obviously, a segregated "black capitalist system" operating within a larger "white capitalist" system is untenable. However, it would be unwise to view business in black communities entirely in terms of whether it should be patterned after capitalist or socialist models. Actually, neither model operates in a pure form anywhere, and if the entire nation can utilize elements of both ideological positions when it seems wise to do so, certainly communities need even less not be locked into some rigid prescription of how business should be structured. What does appear valid is the historical exclusion of blacks from business enterprise except in a most limited way so that the positive outcomes of participation in the business establishment have not accrued to black communities. Of course, the most obvious is the standard of living it makes possible and the position of blacks as a group on any socioeconomic scale can attest to the impact this exclusion has had in that regard. Closely allied to standard of living are the resources for supporting the service sector so that the absence of funds in black communities from community-based business enterprises has meant a limited base for the development of community-based social services, as has occurred in Jewish communities. Finally and most importantly, there are many kinds of power that comes from business success and the sense of powerlessness that permeates black communities indicates how important it is that such power be experienced for the psychological health of those within it.

There is technical power that accrues from involvement in business enterprise. As Selekman and Selekman point out: "The power of nature, released by science, is translated by business into energy-producing machines, tools, and services built and operated by men of varied skills in structured daily tasks—machines, tools and services which carry forward the chain of activities that operate the many-layered entity we describe as modern industry." [31] Certainly this involves the effective management of complex components of a continuing flow of activities directed toward the smooth operation of the organization. The technical power of economic administration spills over, however, beyond the limits of the organization to provide expertise in everything from United Way fund-raising drives to political campigns to powerful governmental advisory bodies. A community that lacks this power lacks a powerful mechanism for wielding influence that can have positive outcomes for the community.

SERVICE ORGANIZATIONS
Although the organization is a social entity with universal characteristics that transcend specific function, there are unique aspects among organizations of different types. Human service organizations are geared to deal with the personal and social problems that continually emerge in complex societies and are defined as "abnormal" in the sense that their presence indicates that something—individually or collectively—has gone wrong in the social system's processes. Despite the ubiquitousness and the significance of these organizations, they have received relatively little attention in the literature of organizations, and practitioners seeking to understand them have had to utilize principles and criteria developed out of the study of other organizational forms. The study of a broad spectrum of human service organizations includes such diverse areas as income maintenance, aging, physical and mental health, correction, public housing, family planning, schools, day care, drug treatment, and urban redevelopment. These agencies in many ways constitute the conscience of society and it is not surprising that personnel stress commitment to improving the quality of life for minorities and the poor to an extent not found in the more clearly business-oriented or even commonweal organizations. Both on the basis of empirical observation and logical prediction there is much less racial animosity and much more genuine racial openness among helping professionals than may be found in industry or even in departments of government. It is perhaps paradoxical that despite this fact, the

human service organization in black communities can be as oppressive and racist as the most profit-oriented manufacturing concern.

Zweig has attributed the paradox to a basic dynamic of ambivalence which distorts perceptions and therefore elicits irrational responses from human service organizations.[32] The ambivalence is experienced by organization personnel as vacillating between advocacy of black clients and their situations on the one hand and the maintenance of policies and practices which handicap them on the other. Thus organizations located entirely or partly in black communities often espouse a position of support and advocacy for practices "relevant" to the community but the rhetoric is not followed up with meaningful change in agency procedures and practices. This can be attributed to a number of factors in the larger social environment.

Shifts in political priorities and related funding priorities over the past several decades have created a sense of impending crisis in service organizations so that survival transcends pressures to recognize oppressive practices for what they really are. There are myriad examples of the way that individual needs generally take precedence over the needs of the collectivity in contemporary American society. Values are not absolute but are arranged in a hierarchy, and the value hierarchy of individuals in a given society tend to be associated markedly with those of others in that society but among subsystems the degree of association drops. For example, a white person in this society may value racial integration and be willing to live in an integrated neighborhood. But when he is offered twice the value of his home by block-busting realtors, he may put a higher value on material gain than living in an integrated neighborhood. Similarly, a black professional may be closely identified with the black community and value it as a place to live in; however, if the schools deteriorate and become useless in the education of his children, the value he places on good education for his children may be higher than the value he places on remaining in the black community. Within organizations the helping professionals who do in fact want to provide effective services to black communities find that they must make a choice between delivering poor or marginal services and keeping a job. The job generally takes precedence—not, however, without some effort at rationalizing to avoid cognitive dissonance. Thus, the helping person defines his position in such terms as, "As long as I am inside the system, I have some hope of influencing change; if I leave, probably someone without my commitment and good intentions will replace me"; or "I'm going to be a spook who sits by the door, and I am merely waiting the propitious moment to lead the insurgency against the repressive system." It is certain, however, that the shakier and more vulnerable the organization appears in regard to its continued existence, the less likely that staff will press for major change. The fear of upsetting the delicate balance and pushing it into a position where its enemies can justify its final demise is too clear a possibility.

Another problem which makes service organizations in black communities ineffective in dealing with institutionalized racism is the frequent demand placed on these organizations to fulfill both a helping and a social control function. Thus, even community mental health centers get caught up in the problem of receiving many referrals from probation departments which make going to the center for "therapy" a condition of probation. The probation officer is torn between his utilization of counseling skills in rehabilitation efforts and the police functions pressed upon him by the courts. Perhaps the most frequent experience of conflicting norms in the professional role is observed in welfare departments. Zweig has written:

> For the welfare worker attempting to serve both helping and police ends in carrying out his agency's mandate, an intolerable dilemma is imposed. Should the welfare worker emphasize the helping or police functions? The helping functions are likely to get good responses from the client, but charges from the agency of being "soft" or "too identified with the

client's interests" or "disloyal to agency policy." The police functions are likely to bring agency approval, but charges from clients that the worker is a "stooge for the establishment" or a "cop in disguise." Obviously, the dilemma creates conditions of ambivalence for welfare workers, and especially salient in terms of minority communities which most welfare workers know to be alienated, disenfranchised and in need of special opportunity.[33]

When welfare agencies are put in the position of defending both the helping and police functions, the result is enormous dissatisfaction of both the client system and the policymakers, not to mention a tremendous loss of morale for all employees required to function in the context of conflicting expectations.

Service organizations, much more than business or even commonweal organizations, are subject to criticism regarding the criteria for determining competence of its personnel. Whereas business competencies—accounting, marketing, personnel administration, etc.—are technical and measurable with considerable objectivity and clear-cut outcome measures, the competency of the human service practitioner is largely psychosocial and despite the existence of a knowledge base underlying practice, the translation of this knowledge into specific techniques which can be uniformly applied in a given set of conditions to achieve a specific outcome has not been accomplished to any great degree. Accountability is much more likely to be considered in terms of the number of hours, number of cases handled, etc., rather than the number of problems actually resolved or ameliorated. The helping professional is therefore more vulnerable to charges of incompetence. This has particularly been true in black communities where the intensity and perseverance of social and personal problems logically call into question the competency of those who must solve them.

The cyclical, pendulum-like swings relating to the delivery of services in this country, like almost all other social phenomena in this technological age, have grown faster and faster so that in a single generation we can perceive the thrusts toward polar extremes along continua that formerly took several generations to be traversed. Thus, the solutions proposed in the 1940s in regard to the problems encountered in black communities were implemented in large measure in the 1960s, and now in the seventies have been evaluated as ineffective and even destructive. The criticisms of service organizations remain essentially the same: Agencies are inaccessible, bureaucratic, too specialized, impersonal, concerned primarily with organizations survival. The answers which have been proposed and tried with remarkably little effect have been neighborhood-based services, generalist family workers, the use of paraprofessionals, the use of vouchers for the purchase of social services, the use of community-based evaluators to be funded directly from federal sources, etc. There are several reasons why these efforts have failed to visibly change the overall level of functioning of individuals in black communities including the fact that many of these efforts were only half-hearted, underfunded, and in minuscule proportion to the immensity of the problems.

Up to now nothing new has been successful in increasing the impact of direct service agencies on the social and economic conditions of individuals and families in black communities. However, this should immediately call forth a consideration of the interrelationship between direct service agencies and two other types of human service organizations: the social action agency and the planning agency. It cannot be assumed that incremental innovations in the structure of direct service programs can overcome the effects of poverty and racism without the necessity of dealing with such problems directly. The social action agency is concerned with promoting collective action in the effort to resolve or mitigate social problems such as poverty and racism. There are two alternative positions taken in organized social action efforts. The first is the reform approach which essentially attempts to identify those organizations or even total social institutions (e.g., the criminal justice system) which are at the root of the problem and then to bring about change in these organizations or institutions to improve the condition of those who have suffered. The objective is not to destroy the offending institutions but to change them through utilization of a variety of tactics including confrontation, negotiation, as well as public appeals and coalitions. The second approach is revolutionary and the objective is not merely to change the target systems—it is declared malignant regardless of the intent of its leaders—but to eliminate them as root causes of social and personal distress. This system destruction can be sought by political means or by violent means. Kotler has classified all change strategies as either coercive, persuasive, or reeducative.[34] A power strategy is unconcerned with beliefs and attitudes of the target system and tries to change behavior through such sanctions as legal authority (school desegregation), force or threat of force, or payment. A persuasion strategy, on the other hand, is one that attempts to convince the change target that the desired behavior serves his best interest—i.e., racially integrated schools provide better educational environment for whites as well as for blacks. Finally, a reeducative strategy is one that attempts to bring about a lasting change in the behavior of the change target by promoting internalization of new beliefs or values. This educational or "therapy" approach is the least direct and most difficult strategy. In fact, it is unlikely to be effective when dealing with the total public or offending institutions.

Kotler has also defined the major roles required in the establishment of a social action agency.[35] There are the *directors* who start or head the organization and who wield the power. It appears that charisma, integrity, and organizational development skills along with almost total absorption in "the cause" are the primary qualities of this role. There are *administrators* who are responsible for the day-to-day business of the organization making sure that people and material resources are deployed in the most effective manner. The *organizers* are those who have effective skills in enlisting the support of others to the cause, operating primarily in personal influence channels (mass meetings, lobbying, personal phone calls, negotiation teams, etc.). The *technicians* provide consultation or service to the agency either in paid or volunteer positions. These include professional fund raisers, lawyers, advertising practitioners, public relations specialists, and management consultants. Although these roles are crucial, other less apparent roles are also necessary if the social action agency is to survive. *Advocates* are needed who will use the power of the pen or their status as a public figure—politicians, entertainers, athletes, etc.—to speak out for the agency and its cause. The *financial supporters,* who may be small donors or full-fledged backers, are required to keep the organization operating. This is particularly important since it is unlikely that governmental funding is going to be placed with an organization which may be dedicated to destroying components of the power establishment, which in turn controls in large measure the political process.

There is often a need for *volunteers* dedicated enough to the objectives of the agency to give their time to it. This is particularly difficult to achieve in black communities where those most affected by the desired change are also caught up in the struggle to survive and have little time for volunteer work. In fact, getting dedicated and competent persons to fill all these roles in agencies aimed at social action in black communities is so difficult that it is clear why such agencies have not been easy to organize. The question of whether direct services or social action is the approach with the greatest potential for effecting positive change in social and economic conditions in black communities has been resolved to a great extent. We now accept the conceptualization of *dual* requisites which together are mutually supportive but exclusively would be asking black communities to make do with the proverbial half loaf. This is eminently reasonable also when one considers that both types of organizations are needed rather than overburdening a single organization with both functions. Where this has been attempted, the problems of limited resources and the need for two sets of professional skills rarely encompassed in a single professional almost imposes the requirement that service organizations choose service or action as its major program goal. Grosser, in evaluating six community organization programs aimed at helping youth, found that:

> . . . social action and service components may exist either as part of a comprehensive project, or more desirably, as separate cooperative entities. The cooperation of the services and action functions into discrete organizations is suggested because the two functions are frequently in disharmony . . . and because the dispensers of public agency services are congenitally unable to distinguish between the protest and service function when practiced by the same organization.[36]

The third type of service organization is the planning agency. In contrast to the distinction made between service and social action agencies, planning can be viewed from two perspectives—either as an administrative tool required of all organizations or as a basic activity engaged in by organizations dedicated exclusively to planning. Perhaps the crux of the community control debates lie here, in the issue of who plans for the delivery of services in black communities. Whereas some inroads have been made in providing opportunities for community input into single organizations such as a neighborhood service center, community mental health center, or day-care centers, the community persons taking advantage of these opportunities have often found to their dismay that the *real* policies are made by United Way, welfare planning councils, county boards of supervisors, or some agency within the federal Department of Health, Education and Welfare. This is apparent when questions are raised regarding certain agency policies or practices and the response is "The feds require it" or vague allusions to "the political reasons" that won't allow change. It then becomes clear that the planning agencies themselves have considerable impact on what happens in black communities and therefore involvement of persons from black communities is imperative in their policymaking process, whether at staff or board levels.

Ironically, those professionals in the helping services who accuse black communities of "inability to work together," i.e., to work collectively to achieve common goals, have no better track record in cooperative planning to make the delivery of their services through the maze of agency networks more rational, efficient, and effective. The reasons are plain. Planners often tend to state planning objectives or goals in such precise terms that there is little room for differing perspectives. Planners often make the mistake of excluding from the planning process those who they feel will be in disagreement with their objectives, which is an open invitation to destructive criticism. The planner's lifeline is constructed of information, "hard" and "soft data" which give the graphic picture of the reality with which the planner must work. Thus, access to high quality, i.e., valid and comprehensive information is a sine qua non of the planner's responsibility. The planner must constantly anticipate the unintended consequences of alternative planning goals, e.g., closing down a housing project, developing a community advisory board to participate in the policymaking process for public health facilities in the community, or removing some residential housing for a playground and recreational center. If the planner is on the staff of an organization with planning as its major activity, it is necessary to help that organization develop credibility as a legitimate change system with the power to bring about action on the recommendations which emerge from its activities. Fogelson and Demone suggest that:

> Dissent may be massive, nondirected, or aimed at specific elements of the innovative change. In such cases, strategies of neutralization of conflict are necessary. The planning body must engage in a series of ever-changing flexible coalitions. The nature of the coalition is directed by the particular problem at hand, rather than by overall identification with the goals or aspirations of any particular segment within the action system. To the degree possible, it must preserve its neu-

trality throughout the planning process. Alliances must be calculated to strengthen the organization, not to weaken it.[37]

SUMMARY

This chapter has explored the role that complex organizations perform in black communities and in the empowerment of black individuals. The organizing principle for the content included was provided by Blau and Scott, characterization of complex organizations as (1) business concerns which benefit owners; (2) commonweal organizations which are established to benefit the general public; (3) mutual benefit organizations which benefit the members of the organization; and (4) service organizations which benefit their clients.

Commonweal organizations have been notoriously discriminatory in their policies regarding service delivery to minority communities. These include public utility companies, police departments, fire departments and other organizations serving the general public. The major thrust of proposals aimed at reducing the negative effects of discriminatory policies is toward increased control of these organizations by territorially defined communities. A variety of models for community control can be constructed without destroying an interrelatedness to a central system of supportive administrative services.

Business organizations in black communities have historically been at the mercy of constant constraints imposed by the dominant white society. Light suggests that the lack of a cultural tradition of rotating credit associations also has served as an obstacle to development of business enterprises in black communities. However, religious groups such as Father Divine's Peace Mission cooperatives and the Black Muslims have been relatively successful. The Community Development Corporations are a current, government sponsored effort to deal with the problems of economic development in black communities. The importance of such efforts is based on the recognition that economic power is an indispensable mechanism for social development in these communities. Human service organizations are geared to deal with the personal and social problems that continually emerge in complex societies and include such diverse areas of concern as income maintenance, aging, health and mental health, corrections, public housing, family planning, schools, day care, drug treatment, and urban redevelopment. However, shifts in political priorities and related funding priorities have resulted in the transdendence of issues of survival over issues relating to oppressive practices.

No innovation in the operations of human service organizations up to this point in time has been successful in increasing the impact of direct service agencies on the social and economic conditions of individuals and families in black communities. However, the importance of social action agencies and planning agencies in the achievement of these goals must be recognized. Thus the direct and indirect service objectives are mutually supportive.

experiential exercises

1.
Many organizations operate in many different racial, ethnic communities but tend to take on characteristics in Black and other minority communities which reflect negative valuation of those communities. Obtain photographs of the following organizations operating in both a black community and a white community (with income level held constant) which may reflect this variation.

____Branch bank	____A chain supermarket	____A fast-foods outlet
____A police station	____Fire station	____Public library
____Service station	____Playground	____Public school

When differences are noted, request an interview with a central administrator to discuss the organizations orientation to "community relations." In the process of the interview, seek to determine the *stated* reasons for variations in the presence of the organization in different communities.

2.

Many organizations operating in ethnic communities attempt to reflect the life style of people in the community, others offer a "standardized" concept of the organization which is considered appropriate regardless of the nature of the community in which it is located. Identify five organizations in a black community in each of the two categories. Examples may be restaurants specializing in soul food versus restaurants that do not; bookstores that specialize in black literature versus those that do not; a district office of a public agency that has large numbers of black staff members versus one that does not; a community mental health center that offers a traditional mental health program versus one that perceives of itself as geared to community life styles, etc.

3.

The affirmative action programs have led to more blacks moving into management level positions in organizations, particularly those operating in black communities. These "new" black professionals, by definition, are considered middle class—which may have some implications in regard to their performance in the organization. Although there is evidence that social class distinctions are not sharply defined among blacks an opposing view is that middle-class blacks are more insecure in that status than middle-class whites and therefore the tendency is to identify and protect that status with more intensity. To gain insights into this and related issues, arrange to interview personnel in three types of organizational settings: business, commonwealth, and social service:

(a) To what extent do managers perceive their interaction with black and non-black staff as similar or different? Is the perception related to race of the manager?

(b) To what extent do managers perceive their concerns regarding black versus non-black clients as similar or different? Is the perception related to manager's race?

(c) To what extent do staff perceive their interaction with black and non-black managers as similar or different? Is the perception related to race of the staff member?

(d) To what extent do staff perceive their interaction with black and non-black clients as similar or different? Is the perception related to race of the staff member?

(e) Are there significant differences among the three types of organizations in regard to perceptions of black and non-black managers and staff? For maximum information the comparisons of the three kinds of organizations should be made (i) in a community in which the client group is predominantly black and (ii) in a community in which the client group is predominantly non-black.

4.
The following is an "in-basket" type exercise which illuminates the difficulties involved for administrators of human service organizations in black communities who must struggle with the problems of black communities and the problems of providing services in a manner adjudged competent by standards of the profession. Utilizing simulation of the administrator's response to the memos in his "in-basket," it is possible to highlight the specific components of the dilemma and to generate discussion of creative alternatives to dealing with this dual perspective.

FROM THE ADMINISTRATOR'S DESK
The Southeast Neighborhood Service Center is located in a predominantly black neighborhood in the Los Angeles area. The neighborhood it serves contains approximately 125,000

people, many in substandard housing with limited access to most health, social, or recreational services. The Center provides a wide range of services including educational, health, employment counseling, job placement, housing, recreational, consumer education, and legal aid services.

John Crane, the director, is a thirty-five-year-old trained social worker (MSW) who considers himself to be a "democratic" leader committed to effective social change in the community. He also considers the involvement of indigenous residents of the community on the Center staff and in its program as vital to its success. Thus he has hired twelve indigenous "community aides." In addition there are nine trained social workers and two social work supervisors. Each supervisor has both social worker and community aide supervisees.

For the past several months, there have been growing signs of intergroup conflict in the Center among various levels of staff. However, the director has taken no action to deal with the problem and recently took a three-week vacation leaving one of the supervisors, Mrs. Millie Adams, in charge. Upon his return he found the following memos and letters on his desk.

If you were John Crane, how would you handle each of these communications?

To: John Crane, Director
From: Mary Houston, MSW
Re: Loretta Gaines, Community Aide

On Tuesday, June 18th, I requested a community aide to take Mrs. Pearl Henderson (File #34765) to County Hospital for a clinic appointment. Millie Adams, supervisor, assigned Loretta Gaines to take Mrs. Henderson for her appointment. On the basis of subsequent conversations I have had with both Loretta Gaines and Mrs. Henderson, it appears that en route to the clinic, Mrs. Henderson mentioned that she would be moving soon into a board-and-care home which I had helped her to find. However, she would rather stay in her own court apartment and would do so except for the fact that she needs a ramp to get her wheelchair up and down her front steps. Whereupon, Loretta Gaines informed her that she has seen her steps and is sure that her brother can fix a ramp for her and will do it without cost as a favor to Loretta. Mrs. Henderson got very excited and accepted Loretta's offer. What this means, however, is that *seven months of sensitive case-work with Mrs. Henderson has gone down the drain!* I spent that time working with sweet, senile, 85-year-old Mrs. Henderson to get her to consider moving to housing where she can get proper attention. (The last time I visited her she put a dish-towel on the fire instead of the pot she had in her other hand!)

I have reported this to Millie Adams. However, she refuses to take any action against Loretta Gaines due to the fact that she made Mrs. Henderson a legitimate offer of help! I have indicated to both Millie and Loretta that I would be bringing this to your attention.

To: John Crane, Director
From: Millie Adams, Supervisor
Re: Henderson Affair

I am sure that you will be receiving a memo from Mary Houston regarding Loretta Gaines and the problem that came about when Loretta offered to have a ramp made for Mrs. Henderson so she could stay in her present apartment. I have reprimanded Loretta since it was made clear in her orientation and in subsequent staff meetings that any intervention on behalf of a client is to be cleared first with the social worker to whom the client is assigned. Loretta is aware that she was in error and is terribly afraid that she may lose her job over it. However, I am convinced that she has learned her lesson and such a lapse of memory will not happen again.

On the other hand, Mary Houston is still boiling and would prefer for Loretta to be fired as a "lesson" for the community aides who, "if they don't follow the rules and regulations can ruin people's lives." I sympathize with her but I do not see any real value to be gained by firing Loretta. For the most part, she is a good worker who has tremendous potential.

P.S. I had Loretta tell Mrs. Henderson her brother could not fix the ramp after all. Mrs. Henderson's distress was punishment enough for Loretta.

Mr. John Crane
Southeast Neighborhood Service Center
1111 East Trinity
Los Angeles, California

Dear Mr. Crane:

I am a member of the Citizen's Task Force on Urban Problems and the owner of the only black-owned Cadillac dealership in the country. I am a lifelong resident of this community and have spent a good deal of it working to bring about equal opportunities for our people. The Task Force on Urban Problems is concerned about the many problems in our community such as lack of decent housing, unemployment, lack of recreational facilities, poor schools, and family instability. At our meeting last Monday night, we had representatives, as you know, from various community groups, business organizations, and social agencies in this area to discuss their views on the scope of the problems and what the most effective solutions might be. Three representatives from your agency were at the meeting. One of these representatives was Mr. Fred Dudley who I understand is a community aide at Southeast Neighborhood Service Center. In all of my years of serving on various community projects, committees, task forces and boards, I have never heard such foul language used to express what should have been ideas relevant to the issues at hand. Mr. Dudley poured out profanities in such profusion that it was hard to follow his train of thought. However, if one could discern any message in all the filth, it seemed to be that all the "m-f do-gooders" including those in the agency he was representing are doing more to hurt the community than the "pigs" and the "honkies" from outside.

I do not know what Mr. Dudley's function is in your agency but I would suggest that whatever it is, he is no credit to the agency. He, in fact, turned off almost every leader in the room who might have at some time been interested in supporting your efforts. I hope that you will see this letter as merely the opinion of someone who, like you, is interested and involved in trying to make our community a better place in which to live. In my opinion, Mr. Dudley is of absolutely no help in that cause.

Sincerely,
Mr. Victor Thompson, President
Thompson Motors, Inc.

Dear Mr. Crane,

You don't know me but I have seen you sometimes when I have been to the Neighborhood Center and I think you would be a fair person. I have had several problems that I have gotten help for there at the Center and my worker was Miss Baker. I have another problem and I came in there last week but they told me I had to see Virgie Lee Johnson who is aide there. Virgie Lee used to live around the corner from me over on McKinney Street and I could tell you some things about what all she's done that would make your hair straight! But I'm not trying to get anybody in trouble, so my main point is that I would like to see Miss Baker again. She is a good social worker. I would like to see somebody anyway who can help me when I come over there and not have to see somebody who has more problems than I do.

> Thank you for your kindness in this matter.
> Mrs. Lucille Wisdom

To: John Crane, Director
From: Enid Carrington, Chairman Community Aides of Southeast Neighborhood Service Center
Re: Monthly Meetings for Community Aides

We, the twelve community aides at Southeast Neighborhood Service Center would like permission to meet in our own group—without other staff—once a month on the fourth Friday. We know that we also attend the regular staff meetings but we feel that we would like to discuss some of the kinds of things we want to see happen in the community as well as some of the problems that we as a group have been having here in the Center. We would like to do this without feeling that we are being judged (or misjudged!) by the other staff. We feel that it is important for us to be able to do this on agency time so that it is clear that we are involved in the business of the Center and not out "plotting" against it in the community.

We would appreciate hearing your answer as soon as possible since the fourth Friday of this month is next week.

part four

strategies of empowerment

The four chapters in Part IV are concerned with the specific activities engaged in by practitioners and client systems in pursuit of empowerment. Since each human encounter is a unique mosaic of shared and unshared experiences, attitudes, interests, values, and goals, the possibilities of any given set of interactions for any given set of participants in the encounter are infinitesimally small. In essence, this almost totally unpredictable state can be transformed into an increasingly stochastic one by the continuous introduction of new information about the participants and the context. Thus, the knowledge that the encounter is one in which a person with a problem comes or is sent for assistance to a helping person drastically reduces the interaction possibilities. If it is learned that the person with a problem is black and the helping person is white and a social worker rather than a stockbroker or funeral director, we have reduced the possibilities even more. Although never reaching the point of total predictability, it is soon possible to identify some distinct probabilities as our information increases.

Therefore, when black people who are subject to a sense of powerlessness by virtue of their membership in a stigmatized collective requests or requires assistance from a social worker, some distinct probabilities emerge in regard to the helping process. The four chapters in Part IV deal with the contents of that encounter which—on the basis of current knowledge—would appear most likely to lead to a reduction in the client's sense of powerlessness and achievement of the client's goals. Experiential exercises are not included in these chapters since, in this instance, continuing practice with black clients is itself the most effective means of "experiencing" the chapters' contents.

chapter ten

characteristics
of the nonracist
practitioner

The criticisms of helping professionals has indicated that there
is a great difference of opinion as to what constitutes a "nonracist." There is the point of view that everyone in our society is
racist, since we have been socialized to incorporate its racism
into our personal belief systems. There is another point of view
that race is irrelevant if the practitioner is a humanist, i.e., a
firm believer in the basic worth and dignity of all human beings, regardless of race, color, or creed. Both of these views
say everything and nothing; by their all-inclusive nature they
deny the reality of differences that in fact makes a difference.

Conventional textbooks on the helping process always give
at least some attention to the desirable characteristics of the
helping person; however, rarely does this include explicit reference to the matter of racial biases. Caseworkers are ad-
monished that the client's ability to use help will depend upon
"the worker's true interest in helping him, his objectivity,
warmth, and his acceptance of the client and respect for
him." [1] This is translated from the perspective of behavior modification into the worker's need to "maintain conventional, culturally patterned civility . . . our cultural background and context require such civility." [2] Truax and Mitchell reviewed
studies involving the relation of therapist interpersonal skills to
outcomes in therapy situations and found that positive outcomes were almost invariably associated with therapists who
demonstrated accurate empathy, nonpossessive warmth, and

genuineness.[3] Accurate empathy "involves the ability to *perceive* and *communicate* accurately and with sensitivity both the feelings and experiences of another person and their meaning and significance." Nonpossessive warmth means a warmly receptive and nondominating attitude, while therapist genuineness refers to his ability to be "a real person in an encounter, presenting himself without defensive phoniness, without hiding beside a professional façade or other role." The practitioner who is warm, empathic, and authentic with clients who belong to the same race or ethnic background or class as himself could well be constrained, cool and mechanical with other clients who did not fit into that social category. The picture of the racist practitioner comes clearer, however, when it is detailed with the practitioner's typical responses to situations involving persons from cultural contexts different from his own.

Those authors who have attempted to deal with indicators of racism in helping encounters have generally identified the tendency to adopt stereotypic explanations for behavior and stereotypic choices of helping strategies. For example, some helping professionals demonstrate the illusion of "color-blindness" or the attitude that the black person is just another person; on the other hand, the opposite error is made that all the black person's problems are somehow related to being black and that frustration and hostility toward whites is the core conflict of his personality structure. Some clinicians are likely to avoid discussion of race because of the discomfort they feel, while others want to talk about it continually as if not to do so would be indicative of insensitivity. Some clinicians dismiss a black person's criticisms of him as merely "transference" and therefore without foundation when in fact his racist attitudes are the basis of the distrust and critical attitude. Others view this same criticism as evidence of paranoia and distorted perception of reality when in fact it may be only a characteristic transference reaction. Many practitioners believe blacks are nonverbal, nonpsychological-minded and therefore not given to introspection or amenable to psychotherapeutic intervention. Still other practitioners believe that blacks are more spontaneous, emotionally expressive, and therefore more open to people with whom they may become involved in a helping relationship. The picture that emerges is, at least for the white practitioner, one expressed by "damned if you do, damned if you don't," as the many faces of racism appear to reside even in opposites.

It is perhaps not too farfetched to consider the possibility that a dialectical method in which the contradiction of opposites is resolved in synthesis may constitute a mechanism for removing the dilemma. Thus, the antithetical extremes of "blacks are more expressive" and "blacks are less expressive" may be resolved in a Hegelian synthesis representing a higher plane of truth, e.g., "Blacks who are expressive differ from blacks who are less expressive in some specific aspects of their life experiences." However, the particular content of the synthesis arrived at may be colored by prejudice, e.g., "Blacks who are expressive differ from blacks who are less expressive in that the former have more White genes than the latter." The fact that the evidence may not bear this statement out is irrelevant—prejudice by definition ignores evidence that is contrary to the belief. Since the practitioner must constantly employ knowledge that extends beyond the limits of experience, opportunities for racist attitudes to contaminate the knowledge base for practice abound. Yet, there is indication that the application of four specific skills on the part of the practitioner would reduce the likelihood of this contamination.

First, the practitioner should possess the ability to perceive in any behavior, others' or one's own, alternative explanations for that behavior, particularly those alternatives which the self might most strongly reject as false. This skill requires utilization of existing knowledge from the behavioral sciences that help to illuminate the experiences of different subgroups in the ethnosystem—their differences as well as their similarities. This knowledge often comprises conflicting generalizations about behavior in these subsystems as well as conflicting generalizations about the interrelationships that characterize their interaction. It is tempting and easy to seize that generalization which best fits our own predilections without adequate appraisal of the alternatives; as a consequence, practitioners far too often select and utilize an extremely limited and stereotypic set of generalizations about black clients and their problems.

There are means of drawing inferences about client systems which tend to reduce the extent to which they are stereotypic. Sarbin, Taft, and Bailey have proposed the utilization of the categorical syllogism as a model for making inferences about clients from a theoretical framework.[4] The syllogistic form utilized is the one in which both the major premise and the minor premise are universalistic and affirmative. (A syllogism always involves two statements combined in such a way that the truth of the third statement can be determined.) For example:

Major premise:	Black students in predominantly white schools develop poor self-images.
Minor premise:	Ann-Marie is a black student in a predominantly white school.
Conclusion:	Ann-Marie will develop a poor self-image.

It is recognized by Sarbin, Taft, and Bailey that there are almost no universals in the complex interactions that take place between human beings and their environments. However, they have designed the syllogism so that the premises are stated as universals but probabilities are assigned in recognition of the fact that they are not universal. These probabilities of major premises are based on research findings, relevant theories, or practice wisdom; the probabilities for minor premises are derived from direct contact with the individual client or client system. The conclusion is assigned a probability derived by the multiplication theorem in probability theory, i.e., the probability of the joint occurrence of two independent events is the product of their separate probabilities. Therefore, we can provide the following example:

> Major premise: Black students in predominantly white schools develop poor self images. (.65)

The indication here is that an analysis of the research literature on the subject, the theoretical material from social psychology dealing with the development of self-image, and/or the practice experience with black students in predominantly white schools suggests that this statement has a probability of being true (hypothetically) 65 percent of the time.

> Minor premise: Ann-Marie is a black student in a predominantly white school. (.90)

The indication here is that in my contact with Ann-Marie I have discovered that the school she attends fits my definition of a predominantly white school in nine out of ten defining characteristics. For example, although there are relatively few black students or teachers, Ann-Marie has an opportunity to take some classes each week in an excellent school that is predominantly black as part of an exchange program.

> Conclusion: Ann-Marie will develop a poor self-image. (.58)

The indication here is that our risk in using this theory in planning any type of problem-solving efforts involving Ann-Marie is about four times out of ten of not achieving success.

This deductive model which has been expanded by Bloom is an approach "in connecting portions of the scientific knowledge base to the events in the client's life even though it requires numerous assumptions to make the model operative." [5] More importantly, this deductive approach moves the practitioner away from merely selecting generalizations as stereotypes to a more critical analysis of any generalization in order to determine some level of probability. The client also is not seen as representative of a "category" but again as possessing attributes of a category to some greater or lesser degree. Individualizing the client is therefore crucial. Furthermore, the conclusion is also a probability statement which alerts the practitioner to the chance taken that some alternative conclusion is true. Thus, the tendency to lift generalizations about blacks from the research or theoretical literature—even if positive—and then to utilize them uncritically and stereotypically in planning helping strategies is avoided.

A second skill required by the nonracist practitioner is the ability to collect objectively through the senses those verbal and nonverbal cues which would help to single out of all possible alternatives the one that is most likely or most probable for a given client. For the nonracist practitioner, no stimuli is closed off from awareness by preconceived notions regarding its validity or utility. It is the total of these stimuli which are sorted out and patterned in order to determine their significance in the problem situation. This skill is essentially the implementation of an inductive process. This inductive process as described by Bloom provides a systematic way for a number of cues or facts to be connected to form an explanation or several alternative explanations.[6] Probabilities are then assigned to the alternative explanations. Finally, on the basis of the *most likely* explanation, an action hypothesis is developed which is immediately testable in the helping encounter.

An example of this inductive process can often be seen in social planning efforts. For example, a low-income black community in a large Southern city has a record of chronic health problems. Of the city's eleven public health districts, the district encompassing this community is first in regard to incidence of almost every public health problem—venereal disease, tuberculosis, infant mortality, etc. Social planning, which has been described by Rothman as one of the basic models of community organization practice within the social work profession, is concerned with the technical process of problem-solving around specific community issues.[7] The practitioner or social planner usually develops a plan that would serve to reduce or eliminate a given problem and then develops a strategy to "sell" the plan to the community. This approach is based on the idea that change in a post-industrial society requires highly trained experts who are able to negotiate the complex bureaucratic organizations and guide the change process. The planner on the staff of the Comprehensive Health Planning agency gathered facts about the community in order to devise a plan aimed at reducing the extent of the health problems. The facts included the following: an inordinate number of run-down, multi-family housing; high rate of alcoholism and veneral disease; infrequent garbage pick-up, large numbers of rodents, mosquitos, flies, and other pests; frequent seepage from the city sewage system into open ditches; the large number of female-headed households; and, of course, the large number of individual residents suffering from chronic illnesses. On the basis of these facts the following hypotheses were developed:

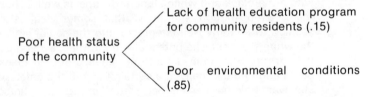

The probabilities assigned were on the basis of consultation with various community agencies knowledgeable about the community and its problems, health service consumers, and health care experts. On the basis of this process, the planner identified poor environmental conditions as the major contributor to the community's poor health status. His action hypotheses was that "the development of a plan to increase city services, e.g., garbage pick-up, pest control, and enforcement of building codes by the Housing Department would, if adopted, lead to a substantial reduction in the health problems of the community. This hypotheses was immediately testable since the plan was developed by the Comprehensive Health Planning Agency, presented to the city council and approved. Subsequently, there was a reduction in some of the health problems in the district, particularly those that were attributable to poor sanitary conditions; however, the veneral disease statistics, the acoholism problem, etc., did not show significant decreases.

This inductive process can also be utilized in the one-to-one modality as is demonstrated in the following case example:

> Ann is an attractive seventeen-year-old black high-school student who was referred for counseling because of her increasing depression and nervousness since she began attending a new school. She was an only child, living at home with her mother and father, who had recently moved into the new neighborhood as a consequence of the father's job transfer. The school she had attended before had been predominantly black. The new school was racially mixed, although a majority of the students were white. Ann told her counselor that there was a great amount of discrimination at the school, both within the black and white student groups as well as between them. Even though she knew that *some* black students seemed to be fairly well integrated into the social network of the white students, she personally did not feel accepted by either group. She noticed that one small group of black students congregated daily at a certain table in the cafeteria, yet she was holding herself back from introducing herself to them. Ann expressed to the counselor who was also black her feelings of isolation and confusion as to what was happening to her in the school and what she wanted for herself.

> The counselor reviewed the facts as perceived and presented to her by Ann. Two hypotheses or "choice points" stood out:

> Ann was being discriminated against at school. (.60)
>
> or
>
> Ann was experiencing isolation, tension, and stress from the move, complicated by her own fears and expectations of others. (.40)

> The counselor decided to develop an action hypothesis based on the first hypothesis, particularly since it was highly likely that by doing so, the issues present in the second hypotheses would emerge and could be taken care of at that time. The ac-

tion hypothesis was described by the counselor in this manner: "If I focused in our counseling sessions on having her specify more concretely how and by whom she was experiencing discrimination, then Ann would become more aware of what she could *do* under the circumstances."

In subsequent sessions, the action hypothesis was implemented. Ann indicated that she felt she was being discriminated against by a large number of white students, evidenced by snide remarks about her hair or body odor as she walked in the halls, being pushed and shoved while in line for nutrition and lunch, and having students get up and change seats after she sat down next to them. In the process of having her define what was happening to her, she indicated that these things might not happen to her if she were not a "loner." At first, she was not very clear about her position with the other black students. When the counselor inquired whether she felt that other black students were also being discriminated against by white students, she replied that she did not know because she was not in contact with any of the black students. She spoke about being different from them, specifically in terms of her "conservative" clothes and the fact that she did not use the "hip" jargon that the other students did. The counselor asked her to exaggerate her "differentness" and try to convince her (using a Gestalt technique) that she was so very different from the other black students that she could not hope to be their friend. As she tried this, Ann eventually concluded that she was not as different as she thought she was. She then spoke about the cafeteria activity and of her fear to approach the small clique of black students who gathered there daily. The counselor had her bring the cafeteria experience into the present and make it explicit by role-playing it in the office. Ann experimented with different ways to approach the group, for example by asking a question about a class assignment, or making a statement that she wanted to meet them. At this point, the counselor developed another set of choice points:

> While discrimination was a realistic issue in Ann's life, she was generalizing it to include everybody and consequently was not approaching those black students who might be interested in meeting her. (.90)

or

Ann's belief that everybody was discriminating against her was probably correct. (.10)

Again the counselor developed an action hypothesis: "If I suggest that Ann make contact with other black students where she could begin to establish a social network for herself through a collective identity, then I expect that Ann's feelings of isolation and being discriminated against would be significantly reduced and she would begin to feel an increased sense of her own significance and ability to handle the school situation."

The counselor followed the action prescribed and Ann agreed to try. She succeeded in making contacts with other black students and learned that many of them were also victims of racial discrimination. The students began discussing ways of actively dealing with this problem as a group. Ann also joined an ethnomusicology course on campus which taught African drumming and had both black and white students enrolled. Thus, Ann's success in establishing contacts with others, her efforts to "do something" about the issue of discrimination, resulted in reduced isolation and tension and depression. The counselor discontinued sessions upon mutual agreement but with the understanding that counseling was available at anytime Ann thought she could use it to meet a need.

A third skill that is characteristic of the nonracist practitioner is the ability to feel warmth, genuine concern, and empathy for people regardless of their race, color, or ethnic background. Many practitioners openly acknowledge that there are clients with whom they personally have difficulty relating at a warm, empathic level, e.g., the truly narcissistic, the severely depressed, or the alcoholics. This is acceptable—up to a point. Acknowledgment of the difficulty should be the first step in a process whereby the practitioner moves from self-awareness to self-control, i.e., the ability to control heretofore unconscious aspects of one's personality which have served as an obstacle to establishing warm, genuine, and empathic relationships with certain kinds of people. The next steps in the process are less likely to be taken if those certain kinds of people are rarely encountered or can be avoided. However, the next steps are imperative if a certain kind of people belongs to a particular racial or ethnic group. This is not only because their need for human services brings them into service systems in much larger numbers than their proportions in the ethnosystem would suggest but, more importantly, because professional ethics *require* that professional skills not be denied individuals or groups on the basis of race or ethnicity.

The following is an account written by a student which demonstrates an ability to relate on a warm, empathic, level with a client of a different racial background. Perhaps more importantly, the empathy permitted this student to experience the significance of feelings of powerlessness in the lives of powerless people:

> Mrs. Smith had been referred to me for assistance with a variety of problems relating to her husband's surgery for progressive tuberculosis and her own struggles to maintain her emotional equilibrium under the financial, social, and emotional stresses that his illness had imposed. For six months during his hospitalization, we worked on these problems and I was continually amazed at her resilience in the face of so many difficulties, the closeness of the relationship between Mrs. Smith and her husband, so much that she made the 40-mile round trip from their home to the hospital almost every day for that entire period! Finally, I was notified by Mr. Smith's physician that a team meeting was to be held, at which time Mr. Smith's prognosis would be discussed. The entire interdisciplinary staff was present. I was asked to present my assessment of his condition and to report on my work with the family. During that meeting, it was decided that Mr. Smith was no longer an appropriate rehabilitation candidate since he was not progressing and the doctor's did not know why. Their immediate solution was to have him discharged to a nursing home within the week! I stated that the staff seemed to be acting hastily in view of a six-month hospitalization. I asked for more time to work for the family, particularly with Mrs. Smith, to help her prepare for the transition. Furthermore, both she and Mr. Smith had wanted to try having him stay at home. The

staff stated that he was in no condition to do so. I suggested that Mrs. Smith should at least be given a choice in the matter.

When Mrs. Smith was ushered into the meeting, the matter of choice never came up! She was preemptorily told what the plan for her husband was as made by the staff—to a nursing home and that was that! At that moment I shared with Mrs. Smith the terrible powerlessness inherent in our positions. Mrs. Smith is black, poor, and relatively uneducated. I was a social work student—perhaps the least influential of all the persons in the room, not only by student status but by virtue of the secondary role of social work in a medical setting. Some of the staff had expressed their hostility toward me openly before the Smiths were brought in. The head nurse questioned whose needs were being met by my suggestion that Mr. Smith have the choice of returning home if he wished. I decided to explore some issues with the Smiths later. The odds against us were too great in that staff meeting.

Mrs. Smith left the room crying and I followed. Spontaneously, I began to cry with her. We went to my office where we talked and drank coffee and cried some more. She indicated that she wanted to get back to her husband who had been returned to the ward because she knew he would be upset and would not want to talk to anybody but her. I agreed that she should go but also indicated that I was willing to help them do whatever *they* wanted to do.

The Smiths still indicated that they wanted to have Mr. Smith home on a trial basis. After fighting administrative red tape and continuing staff hostility, plans were made for Mr. Smith to be discharged to his home. He was able to spend one night at home with his wife, having dinner with her, touching the things he remembered and loved. In the middle of the night, he had a respiratory attack and had to be rushed to an emergency hospital. He was transferred to a nursing home several days later and one week later, he died. Sometime later, Mrs. Smith called me to let me know how much she appreciated the fact that her husband had been able to have that one night at home and how devastated she would have felt if he had died in a nursing home never having been home again at all. It was as if the fight against the institutional power block (which became less powerful as she began to realize her strength, i.e., her "rights" and her ability to obtain support from me and my supervisor in the struggle) had given her new confidence in her ability to survive without her husband. Her last comment to me was: "I'll always miss him, but now I'm not as depressed as I was. I'm taking care of myself, and things are going to be alright."

Finally, the fourth skill that characterizes the nonracist practitioner is the ability to confront the client when true feelings of warmth, genuine concern, and empathy have been expressed but have been misinterpreted or distorted by the client. The misinterpretation or distortion of feelings communicated in a helping encounter is an important ingredient to be used in the pursuit of heightened self-awareness and competence in interpersonal relationships. Yet, there are many practitioners who find confrontation of issues that may have racial connotations to be so threatening that the issues are denied or avoided. Thus the client is denied an opportunity to learn something about himself and how he relates to others.

> The case of Margo V. demonstrates how effectively a social worker may utilize the misunderstanding to open up important areas for exploration. Margo was a sixteen-year-old pregnant girl living in a home for unwed mothers. She was seen in weekly interviews by the staff social worker for a variety of problems including chaotic family situation, the need to make critical decisions about her life with a new baby she was determined to keep, and a poor self-image which severely reduced her willingness to perceive herself as anything but a victim. During one of the weekly sessions, the social worker remarked that she had seen the mobile that Margo was making in the crafts class:

SOCIAL WORKER: It is really lovely what you were able to do with those tin cans, empty spools, and a few scraps of ribbon and felt. I think it will be just lovely over your baby's crib!

MARGO: Humph! (Scowls and turns to look at the pictures on the wall.)

SOCIAL WORKER: What's the matter, Margo? You don't like your work?

MARGO: (Still looking at the wall.) I just did it because Miss Cohen said I had to do something. I'm not puttin' any ole tin cans over *my* baby's bed! I'll bet you wouldn't do it. It's OK for some little ole black baby like mine, but I bet you woudn't want that ole thing over *your* baby's bed! (Turns around and glares at social worker.)

SOCIAL WORKER: I should have realized that it would be important to you to have new things for your baby—store-bought things! You know, I *did* put a mobile made by one of the girls over my baby's bed three years ago. But that just makes what you just said that much more important. You know why?

MARGO: (Shakes head no.)

SOCIAL WORKER: It's because no matter how much I may hate it or you may hate it, we *do* live in different worlds. So, I can live in *my* world and not know how much you and other black girls want brand new, store-bought things for your baby; and you can live in *your* world and not know how much a lot of people in my world care about hand-made things.

MARGO: I see all those pictures of white folks and their babies in the magazines and I don't see no hand-me-downs! Everything is new!

SOCIAL WORKER: But that's it, Margo! It's in the magazines like that because they are trying to sell you new things. It's all selling. And I'm not saying that new is not good. I just don't want you to think that I am praising something you're making for your baby because I think that is all you ought to have! I think black people should have what they like just like white people should have what they like!

MARGO: Seems to me that blacks have to take just what they can get.

SOCIAL WORKER: All blacks?

MARGO: Well, most I know.

SOCIAL WORKER: Well, let's see what we can do about seeing to it that Margo doesn't fall into that "most" category. If *some* don't, then let's make sure that Margo is in *that* category. How about that?

MARGO: (Smiles.) Right on!

At the point that Margo indicated that the social worker's praise was being interpreted as an indication of her low es- teem for Margo and her unborn baby, the social worker could

have quickly denied it, told her that she was "silly" for thinking it, demanded to know why she felt that way, or moved on
to another topic. None of those options, however, would have
made it possible for Margo and the social worker to clarify
how each felt about the other's race and to build a foundation
for future exploration of even more sensitive matters involving
racial differences.

SUMMARY
This chapter has considered criticisms of practitioners as "racist" and identified specific practitioner behaviors that are associated with racist attitudes, e.g., the tendency to adopt
stereotypic explanations for the behavior of a particular racial
or ethnic group. At the same time, it was recognized that identical practitioner behaviors may be interpreted positively or
negatively in regard to the degree that they reflect racist attitudes and, in addition, contradictory and/or totally antithetical
behaviors may be identified as reflective of racism. Four specific skills were suggested as characteristic of nonracist practitioners: (1) the practitioner should possess the ability to perceive in any behavior—other's or one's own—alternative
explanations for that behavior, particularly those alternatives
which the self might most strongly reject as false; (2) the practitioner should possess the ability to collect objectively through
the senses those verbal and nonverbal cues which would help
to identify out of all possible alternatives the one which is most
likely or most probable for a given client; (3) the practitioner
should have the ability to feel warmth, genuine concern, and
empathy for people regardless of their race, color, or ethnic
background; and (4) the practitioner should be able to confront
the client when true feelings of warmth, genuine concern, and
empathy have been expressed but have been misinterpreted or
distorted by the client.

chapter eleven

engaging black client systems

The first step in making an elephant stew is to catch the elephant. The first step in empowering a people is to catch their imagination, i.e., to communicate a mental image of the helping person as a means to a desired end. The image held by residents of black communities is much more likely to reflect the minister, the fortuneteller, or a friend rather than the social worker, the psychologist, or the psychiatrist. There is in fact considerable evidence that existing agencies disseminating contemporary brands of professional help are not attracting those who most need such services to be able to construct more effective lives for themselves.

There are myriad ways in which clients may present themselves to one or more of our social or mental health agencies: They may come because they perceive the agency as a source of material assistance, or assistance in decision-making regarding some personal or interpersonal problem; they may have been sent by some agents of social control such as the courts, the doctor, or the schools; or they may come because a social worker has "reached out" and offered assistance that the client is not yet sure will be forthcoming. Despite the extremely limited data available on the numbers of residents in black communities who come to these agencies for assistance relative to those who may need it, it is safe to suggest that most come because they perceive it as a means of obtaining some needed material assistance or because they have been sent, pushed, or driven by agents of social control who have defined a problem which the clients themselves have not defined. Although much can be done to create a climate in which those who need help will feel comfortable in actively seeking it, the most powerful attraction of all is a good product. Therefore, the key to the positive evaluation of social and mental health services in black communities may well be the extent to which these services successfully counteract the myth of negative valuation and reduce feelings of powerlessness for black clients. To achieve this goal, consummate attention must be given to engaging the client in the problem-solving effort. This does not refer merely to those activities which relate to the initial offering of services and the beginning of the helping relationship. It also refers to the on-going efforts to insure that the client's strengths are recognized, held up for mutual consideration, and utilized in almost every step of the helping process. These activities can be categorized in four groups which may not be sequential and which, although most important in the initiation stages, may be operative throughout the entire process: (1) establishing rapport; (2) establishing the practitioner's expertise; (3) assessing accurately the client's strengths; and (4) establishing the client as causal agent in achieving a solution to the presenting problem. It is the contention here that these are crucial emphases in achieving the engagement and commitment of the client in the problem solving effort.

ESTABLISHING RAPPORT

Vontress has defined rapport in the counseling relationship as the "comfortable and unrestrained relationship of mutual trust and confidence between two or more individuals . . . the existence of a mutual responsiveness which encourages each member to react immediately, spontaneously, and sympathetic to the other." [1] This rapport is extremely difficult to achieve across racial lines since it presupposes a willingness to let another person know what you think, feel, or want and such disclosures have often resulted in negative consequences for blacks.

Self-disclosure is likely to occur only in a context of trust and blacks have had little reason to trust whites as a consequence of the racism which has effectively poisoned their relationship. Knowledge of how to build trust in spite of this obstacle is imperative in any cross-racial helping encounter. It may very well require different approaches to a black client from white and black helping professionals.

O'Shea has described three years of work by white therapists with eight young blacks who were delinquent, dropouts from disrupted homes.[2] The matter of establishing a trusting relationship in which dysfunctional behavior patterns could be changed was problematical from the first. It became evident that such trust is not created immediately by some incantation of magical words on the part of the therapists or by some mystical conversion on the part of those seeking help.

The opportunity for involvement in a therapeutic group had been offered boys at a continuation high school and in the words of one of the boys, "these two cats, gray studs from the university, came down to offer 'discussions' . . . and we stood'em up and we tried to shock them." In the beginning the resistance was high and attacking. "Derisive shouts greeted any therapist's comments. Mimicking of the two therapists accompanied the noise. Any specific comments of the therapists were denied." Yet, over time specific incidents occurred which gave the therapists opportunities to build the trust required for meaningful change.

> The group proceeded in a rather random fashion, only sometimes serious until about the *fifth month*. Then we had a *crisis*. Eddie had been in a fight in the streets. He and a partner had been attacked, pushed around, and told to "get your ass out of town before you're going to get killed." He came to the group session frightened and agitated, and sought partners to "go down with him to get'em." . . . It was finally decided among the group that the fight could be

avoided, that it really ought to be avoided. Eddie was "rapping" to get partners because he felt that he needed them, but this wasn't the answer, and this was the end of the "fight." Now the group was able to recognize that this was the first "gift" of treatment: that resolution is one of the aims of discussion, that this is the "good stuff" of coming to the psych clinic.

Another crisis followed. The boys in their wanderings around the university campus had become conspicuous . . . the dress was exaggerated, the "process" jobs on the hair was extreme, they had an extreme "thug" appearance. One day, three of the boys arrived a few minutes late to the group therapy session to be followed immediately by a uniformed university policeman and an off-duty, part-time university student policeman who sought to protect the integrity of the alma mater. . . . The policemen were immediately ushered out by the therapists, at which time [the incident] was turned [over] to the group for discussion. The boys, in effect, took it passively. This kind of thing happens all the time. It will always happen. Both therapists verbalized that they were furious, that this shouldn't happen, that the therapists will make sure that it won't happen. The police here, at least, cannot float in to question about specific charges. This anger and defense of the group by the therapists later proved to be crucial in the formation of deeper trust.[3]

It may very well be that black therapists would not have required more than five months before this trust could be established. On the other hand, middle-class blacks often have to indicate *their* ability to understand and appreciate the concerns of their lower-class brothers since they are frequently viewed as "oreo cookies," i.e., black on the outside and white on the inside. This often demands a fluency in the normative communication patterns of both middle- and lower-class persons. For example, Claudia Mitchell-Kernan reports an incident in which her ability to do anthropological research in a black community was appreciably enhanced by her ability to "signify," i.e., to construct and convey messages with multi-level meanings—an art that is skillfully practiced in low-income black communities. She writes:

The following interchange took place in a public park. Three young men in their early twenties sat down with the researcher [R], one of whom [I] initiated a conversation in this way:

I: Mama, you sho is fine.
R: That ain't no way to talk to your mother.
   (Laughter)
I: You married?
R: Um hm.
I: Is your husband married?
   (Laughter)
R: Very.
   (The conversation continues with the same young man doing most of the talking. He questions me about what I am doing and I tell him about my research project. After a couple of minutes he returns to his original style.)

I: Baby, you a real scholar. I can tell you want to learn. Now if you'll just cooperate a li'l bit, I'll show you what a good teacher I am. But first we got to get into my area of expertise.
R: I may be wrong but seems to me we already in your area of expertise.
   (Laughter)
I: You ain't so bad yourself, girl. I ain't heard you stutter yet. You a li'l fixated on your subject though. I want to help a sweet thing like you all I can. I figure all that book learning you got must mean you been neglecting other areas of your education.
II: Talk that talk! (Gloss: Ole!)
R: Why don't you let me point out where I can best use your help?
I: Are you sure you in the best position to know?
   (Laughter)
I: I'mo leave you alone, girl. Ask me what you want to know. Tempus fugit, baby.[4]

Although in this instance, the researcher was *seeking* help rather than *offering* help, the ability to demonstrate familiarity with life styles and life experiences of someone seeking help may be just as important for practitioners in their effort to establish rapport. Given the racial isolation that exists in our society, it is much more likely for middle-class blacks who themselves have had ghetto origins to be able to communicate in the idiom of the black lower-class than it is for lower- or middle-class whites.

There are different and often conflicting ideas regarding the significance of language in the helping relationship: One idea is that you must attempt to "speak the language" of the client and this will help establish the rapport required for effective helping relationship. However, carried to an extreme, you may have the paradox of a middle-aged, white female social worker, conservatively dressed and sitting austerely behind the pro forma desk in her office, sprinkling her conversation with a young, black male client with phrases like "right on" and words like "groovy" or an occasional "shit." The result is ludicrous and serves as the content of a longtime game played by blacks and called "ridiculing whitey." On the other hand, there is nothing gained when a "professional," black or white, bombards such a client with such choice verbal morsels as "ego capacity," "separation anxiety," "narcissistic gratification," or "passive aggressive behavior." This is often related to a second idea which is that talking the language of the client is patronizing and "brings you down to his/her level." Yet, language that fails to communicate or accentuates social distance is not effective in establishing rapport.

The important factor here is *authenticity*. The white worker who has not been involved in the black community, particularly the black, lower-class community, will find the language and life styles foreign and discomfiting. The significance of authenticity is especially important when the practitioner is in the role of advocate, broker, planner, or organizer, i.e., when it is required that he relate both to the black client and to representatives of the societal institutions impinging on the client's life, when he may have to operate both inside the black community and in the larger ethnosystem. As Kahn points out: "Whatever style of speech an organizer uses, it should be one he can maintain comfortably and in all situations. If an organizer has been talking country with the poor people and Harvardese with the power structure, he could be in an awkward situation if he had to talk with both groups at the same time." [5]

The inability of white working professionals to work in black communities is not some reverse racist thrust in service organizations in black communities but a rational recognition of the ineffectiveness of working with persons who are strangers and who are enigmas in terms of the most basic kinds of communication, i.e., what are their desiderata in life? what do they feel about the blows life has dealt? who are the significant others in their lives? etc. This is not an identical situation with black professionals and white clients since the racist society has decreed that blacks, to make it in the system, must do so on white criteria. Consequently, they have had to learn the values, life styles, norms of white America. The same has not been true of whites who have not had the same pressure to learn what it means to "live black." Thus, the white worker who has truly been able to get inside black communities and experience the texture of life inside has no difficulty with being authentic when communicating with the black client. There is a sensitivity, a use of language, that is not stilted but true and an easy familiarity with the physical and social reality of the black community which could earn the title "blue-eyed soul brother."

Black professionals have another kind of challenge in establishing rapport. Many, in order to incorporate the values and behavior patterns of the dominant society, find the impressions of their earlier, predominantly black interactions fading and thereby reducing their capacity to relate effectively to black clients and their characteristic problems. More importantly, however, the black practitioner may fall into the same trap that awaits many white practitioners—that is, stereotyping blacks who come for help and consequently stereotyping approaches to establishing rapport. For example, these approaches may be based on the mistaken notion that all blacks would be equally responsive to indications from the practitioner that (a) the cause of their problem lies in the oppressive white-dominated system; (b) blacks have to "stick together" in their opposition of white institutions; (c) "talking black" is the language of the ghetto and not the university; (d) all blacks have been poor and feel inferior; (e) blacks respond negatively to anything "middle-class"; or (f) blacks do not have the same negative response as whites to profanity, sex, or the free expression of emotions. These stereotypes may well generate initial behaviors in the helping process which poison it irrevocably. The antidote is a constant recognition that there are heterogeneous life spaces, life styles, and value hierarchies among blacks as well as among whites and there should be a constant effort made to understand and experience as many of these as possible. Out of this familiarity with "where the client is," it is possible to develop a skill in demonstrating your appreciation for those aspects of his life space, life style, or value hierarchy (which you in fact *do* appreciate) as a means of establishing rapport. It may be appreciation of the frustrations felt over typical negative responses from those in authority as demonstrated by the therapists with the group of young, male dropouts or it may be appreciation for a skill unrecognized by the dominant society—"rapping"—as demonstrated by the researcher. In both instances, authentic entry into the life space of the help seeker was the critical prerequisite to successful intervention.

ESTABLISHING EXPERTISE
The tendency for powerless people to perceive social workers and other helping professionals as extensions of the powerful institutional forces which negatively value them is unquestionably prejudicial to the development of an effective problem-solving process. Even the matter of what to call that process as it is implemented in black communities is fraught with the dual hang-ups of the professions and oppressed people. For example, the tendency to refer to professional intervention aimed at resolving problems which include an emotional component

as "therapy" or "treatment" has been viewed as a perpetuation of the medical model which is inappropriate and irrelevant for most "problems in living." "Social casework," "social group work," "community work," all identify particular methods of practice defined by the nature of the client system; however, they are far more familiar to the practitioner than to client systems. Many receiving those services would not be able to state that they had received them. "Counseling" is a more generally acceptable term easily modified by "individual" or "group" depending upon the number of persons involved in the help system. When the total community is the target for change, "community organizer" is heard but is more often encouched in another role—project director, community analyst, or program specialist.

Unfortunately, almost the least positive of all practitioner designations in black communities is "social worker," which is only a little more positive than "welfare worker." In fact, the two are often used interchangeably. Although we might want to make the distinction between the trained "social worker" and the "welfare worker," there is at this time little hope for such a massive attitudinal change when it has been reinforced by years of negative experience.

The job titles to which persons are usually referred can be changed fairly easily, however, to identify the particular nature of the problems that the social worker is competent and expected to handle, i.e., employment specialist, mental health specialist, educational specialist, health care specialist. It is also extremely easy to substitute "aide" for "specialist" in the case of practitioners without professional training. These changes may be more important in black communities where the designation social worker has such negative connotations and the need to identify expertise related to specific problems is most acute.

There needs to be some consideration of the relative effectiveness of different methods of practice—the one-to-one versus group versus community modalities. There is, in some cases, a perception in black communities that the so-called one-to-one or casework or psychotherapeutic mode has little value in black communities, i.e., the practitioner skilled in that modality has bankrupt expertise. The data from the help systems in black communities do not bear that perception out. Lerner's extensive research in a community mental health center indicated that indeed positive outcomes in regard to presenting problems could occur through use of the one-to-one approach.[6] However, she warned against a tendency to think in either/or terms regarding practice methods when in actuality our methods should be custom-tailored to suit the divergent needs of individual clients and client systems.

At the same time, however, it should also be pointed out that in pursuit of the goals of empowerment, group and community methods may provide a richer context or opportunity system for reducing powerlessness in our clients. The value of these modalities lies in the ease with which the sequential process of negative valuation and the response to it can be reproduced, permitting counteracting strategy to be developed, implemented, and evaluated. This is suggested by Perry, who has stated that community action agencies have been most successful not so much in the significant change wrought in the communities but "by investing in the development of human leadership capital (however unintentionally), they produced a new resource for the poor neighborhoods—a pool of individuals with the social vocabulary of experiences and skills necessary for moving through the system to secure opportunity for their neighborhood."[7] Thus more powerful individuals in that sense can be perceived as the building blocks of more powerful communities.

ASSESSING CLIENT STRENGTHS
Many potential black clients are ruled out for any but the most concrete services and with the limited quantity of such services available, it is no wonder that there is an underutilization of

agencies by black people with social and/or psychological problems. Thus, engaging black client systems is related not only to the motivation of black clients to utilize the services offered but also to the service-provider's assessment of the potential client's capacity and the recognition of opportunities available in his social and physical environment—including the opportunity represented by the help system itself.

There is a strong relationship between the concepts of power and the concept of motivation. The various forms that power, as a force in interpersonal relationships, can take are richly divergent. Personality characteristics that are valued in a particular situation, such as aggressiveness in seeking information needed by a community group to document its case for some social reform, may be considered as a form of power. Other forms include good credit, access to information, physical strength, the ability to speak well or organize people and materials effectively, a particular position within a communication network, popularity with an influential group or organization, technical skills that can be placed in the service of others (such as typing or carpentry)—all of these and many more forms of power can be utilized by people in search of solutions to their problems. It is apparent that clients bring differential amounts of power to a problem-solving situation and moreover, the inability to solve the problem without professional help usually points to some considerable power deficit. In some instances negative valuations of them have made them insensitive to the power that is available to them. If these negative evaluations have been accepted and incorporated into the selfsystem of the person, he is generally described as "unmotivated," i.e., he perceives no reason for his situation to be different. On the other hand, if he has not accepted these negative valuations—at least not entirely—he does not perceive the status quo as his "due" and is interested in exerting whatever power he can muster to change it. This person would thus be described as "motivated."

Motivation to work on a problem can therefore be defined as

the amount of pressure a client feels to effect change in his problem situation. The pressure stems from both the perceived gap between what "is" and what "ought to be" and from perceived possibilities for closing the gap. French has described motivation similarly as a combination of the push of discomfort and the pull of hope.[8] From that perspective, considerable discomfort in one's life situation is important for motivational push while some hope that the problem can be solved provides the motivational pull.

A racist notion encountered in helping professions is the notion that situations and events which would constitute problems for other people are not experienced as problems by black people. Supposedly they have become accustomed to deprivation and distress and have developed ways—although sometimes deviant ways—of coping with these negative conditions. In contrast, whites have not developed these emotional callouses and can be expected to demonstrate a more sensitive response to adversity. Yet, to consider that such a difference exists between the racial groups based on their differential experience of lifelong deprivation and stress denies a generally accepted fact of human behavior, namely, the fact that persons who have had adequate physical and emotional gratification during early psychosocial development are better able to tolerate severe trauma and deprivation later on than are those who have been deprived of such early gratification.

Once the fact is established that blacks do indeed feel the push of discomfort, it is necessary to identify factors associated with the pull of hope. It has been discussed that people in black communities are not particularly hopeful that helping professionals can really assist them in dealing with their problems. It should be pointed out that hope is likely under certain conditions, e.g., hope is more likely when there has been a successful experience in utilizing helping systems. Furthermore, success in achieving long-range and ultimate goals require the incremental achievement of smaller, more immediate goals.

Therefore, it is understandable when clients with long histories of failures, inadequacies, and deprivations are unimpressed with promises of vastly improved living conditions as a consequence of their participation in citizens' groups or a therapy group or a community survey for a planning organization. The proposed reward is so nebulous and unreal that it does nothing to relieve anxieties regarding participation and self-exposure. On the other hand, more specific objectives of the helping process which promise some tangible benefit over a limited period of time and within a specially limited cost will perhaps raise the level of motivation. Motivation, therefore, would be higher if the goal were to help the client to stop beating his wife rather than the global objective of strengthening family life. In like manner, community improvement is a far less motivating force than obtaining street lights in an area plagued by criminal activity or removing a reactionary and racist principle from a high school in the community.

Hope is more likely if the helping person appears to have expertise in the probem area. Thus, the hopeful client is not only one who has had some experience in achieving resolution of a problem but also one who encounters a helping person who can demonstrate success too in dealing with the presenting problem. This moves beyond the issue of establishing rapport to the issue of competence.

A follow-up study of couples who had received premarital counseling from a social agency revealed that most couples had "liked" the social workers who had done the counseling and had found no difficulty in relating to them.[9] However, the majority did not feel that if problems in their marriage were to arise they would consider counseling as a problem-solving resource. They were not convinced that the social workers were truly competent to deal with such problems. This was an important finding since one of the objectives of the premarital counseling program was to give the couples a positive experience with counseling which would encourage them to use it if problems emerged later in the marriage.

In order to increase the hope of clients in black communities it may be necessary to develop "testimonials" in the form of films, group meetings, or other instances in which persons who, from the community or otherwise similar in socioeconomic background to the prospective client, attest to the effectiveness of help they have received. It is interesting that the black church has understood the importance of "testifying" as a technique of encouraging converts and maintaining commitment of members. Thus, the church has been a much stronger force as helping resource than traditional agencies and the helping practitioners.

Closely associated with the matter of competence is the fact that hope is more likely if the individual's definition of the source of the problem suggests that the helping person can influence or effect change at the source. As pointed out in chapter 3, persons in black communities often attribute problems to fate, luck, or a supernatural being and therefore are likely to look for helping persons who have some relationship to or control over such forces. It is difficult to convince such persons that the traditional helping professions are in any way connected to or have control over fate or the supernatural; this is the realm of the preacher and the fortuneteller, not the psychiatrist, rehabilitation counselor, or teacher. Not all blacks, however, are superstitious and it becomes imperative then to use the experiences of those who have benefited from traditional sources of help to be utilized in dispelling superstition among others. At the same time, it is important that professional helpers do not ridicule or attack the belief systems that exist or the result will be alienation of the individuals with problems. It is recognized however, that the opportunities to demonstrate effectiveness in black communities are limited since traditionally helping agencies have not provided adequate services to black clients or have excluded them from receiving services altogether.

A client who is motivated to work on his problem situation is in a position to begin to use those forms of power described

earlier which can be appropriately applied to his problem-
solving effort. This conceptualization of client power is extremely close to the definition of "capacity" as developed by
Ripple, Alexander, and Polemis in their family agency studies.[10]
These studies aimed to determine the relationship between motivation, capacity and opportunity and the effect of that interrelationship on continuance in treatment. Capacity was used
to identify "those abilities that the individual has at his disposal
to use in coping with the current problem situation." From our
perspective, however, client power involves a much broader set
of factors than "abilities," including such additional assets as
access to information, position in a communication network, or
reputation in the community. At the same time, two important
classes of ability usually included in considerations of capacity
require our attention. The first relates to functional intelligence,
i.e., the ability clients have to think logically, perceive cause-effect connections, and verbalize ideas and feelings. The second
relates to the presence or absence of crippling defenses which
serve as a block to problem-solving. In the assessment of both
these capacities, blacks have been subjected to individious
judgments.

Functional intelligence has been emphasized here since
there is rarely an instance in social work practice when results
of an IQ test are crucial in determining the course of the
problem-solving process. On the other hand, there are multitu-
dinous instances when accepted indicators of intelligence, e.g.,
verbal ability, are used to provide the basis upon which decisions as to "suitability for individual psychotherapy" are made.
The implication is that therapy requires a certain ability to see
the facts of a problem and to connect those facts according to
logical principles; but illogically, the inability of practitioners to
understand the clients communication is used to indicate the
limited intelligence of the clients rather than the practitioners.
Adequate assessment of intellectual capacity often requires not
intelligence testing but the patience to establish rapport coupled with observation of the client in his own world where he is

unconstrained by the repressive formality of the agency setting.

Lerner describes a poignant example of the racist assessment of capacity in the evaluation of black schoolchildren by white psychologists.[11] The procedures called for each child to be permitted a half hour of unstructured play with blocks, Tinker Toys, or beads, followed by a brief discussion with the psychologist regarding what he (or she) had made. However, when the psychologist asked the child what he had made and the child responded, the psychologist rarely understood the response because of his unfamiliarity with black dialect, particularly coming from a fidgety, playful child. As a consequence the psychologist repeated his question, arousing increased anxiety in the child who was not being understood, until finally the child found a simple word that the psychologist could understand—"sticks"! Having found it, he repeated it anytime he was asked what he had made—and so did all the other children who had been observers of this interchange. After all, it is better not to frustrate the poor, limited psychologist with articulations that he cannot understand. Yet, it is on the basis of such experiences that these children and others like them have been evaluated as having limited intelligence, limited capacity to verbalize ideas, or limited ability to conceptualize. The irony is that this preposterous notion is held of people with a rich oral tradition—expressed in song, speech-making, signifying, rapping, and in a host of other ways.

Recent literature dealing with racism in mental health professions has emphasized the extent to which blacks are considered poor candidates for mental health services based not only on deficiencies in ego strengths aleady discussed (intelligence, motivation, etc.) but also on the presence of defenses which, although necessary for adaptation and survival in a racist society, are destructive of any attempt at traditional therapeutic process. This seeming paradox has its origin in the conceptualization of defense mechanisms as responses to anxiety. Instrumental responses actually achieve reduction through the elimination of the conflict or frustration. The father and husband who has been unable to find a job may leave home so that his family will be eligible for welfare. In that sense, his response is intrumental in that it achieves a higher level of support for his family than he could manage if he remained. This is particularly effective if he also manages to maintain contact and a warm relationship with his family in spite of his "leaving" to establish their eligibility for welfare services. On the other hand, "flight" as a defense against the anxiety elicited in a therapeutic situation is counter-productive and noninstrumental. Therefore, the same defense mechanism can be both instrumental and noninstrumental depending upon the particular circumstances.

Grier and Cobb have suggested several defensive postures that can be identified in the social interaction between blacks and others in the ethnosystem: (1) cultural paranoia, which develops out of a profound distrust of whites and of the nation so that the expectation is that every white man will potentially mistreat him and every social institution will operate against him unless he personally finds out otherwise; (2) cultural depression and cultural masochism, which develop out of the actual suffering he experiences yet at the same time needs to live in spite of it; and (3) cultural antisocialism, which develops out of his experience with laws, policies, and institutional procedures which have no respect for him as an individual or blacks as a group so that he in turn has no respect for or sense of obligation to conform to these laws, policies, or procedures.[12] It is obvious that each of these postures should be viewed as a continuum with one polar extreme representing the individual who has no adequate perception of his reality, operating therefore in an "as if" situation, i.e., as if the world were a just and benign place for him. At the other polar extreme is the individual so absorbed with the deficiencies and excesses of his life situation that he is blocked from perceiving avenues of partial escape.

Chestang has encapsulated some of the flavor of this aspect of black experience in his formulation of black character development.[13] He suggests that blacks have dual personality components as a result of personality development. One is related to the depreciated character, i.e., the part that recognizes the frustration, hypocrisy, and low status that society decrees for him and responds with feelings of worthlessness and hopelessness On the other hand, there is that part of the personality which seeks to transcend the position in which he has been placed and seek union with nature and actualize his existential potential. Thus, blacks have both a depreciated and transcendent component to character development and if either dominates, there is likely to be difficulty in social functioning. The "depreciated only" character conveys apathy, hopelessness, and complete acceptance of the social role of victim—even deserving victim. On the other hand the "transcendent only" character denies the reality of the social depreciation that is his lot and not only for himself but usually for all blacks. He is then accused by his transcendence-deficient black brothers as an "oreo cookie."

The participation of blacks in a therapeutic process may generate resistances that are very much related to their experience in a racist society and which interfere with that process. Thus, denial of problems, paranoid feelings of persecution, tardiness, nonpayment of bills, missed appointments, silence, or impaired memory of past events, blaming the system as totally responsible for whatever happens to them, are frequently encountered by therapists in their encounters with blacks. Pinderhughes writes:

> . . . several of these resistances sometimes represent indirect expressions of hostile aggression on the part of persons in whom more direct expression has been inhibited. Several reflect a sense of victimization, pessimism and fear which make denial of problems or passive surrender to them safer than an assertive attempt at problem solving. . . . Blacks in the system of segregation and slavery showed indirect rather than direct aggression by responding rather than initiating, by reading the thoughts of other persons while hiding their own,

and by engaging in accommodating-subordinating ritualized behavior designed to make as few waves as possible in the system. Psychotherapy methods which encouraged discussion of thoughts, feelings, and problems in an open manner with a white person could not easily bypass a lifetime of conditioning in the opposite direction.[14]

Resistances are a part of any therapeutic encounter and their management is an important consideration in the counseling process. Furthermore, in most instances, the persons involved in the counseling process are not black so that resistances cannot be used as a rationale for assessing black incapacity to make use of counseling services or justification for not engaging them in a counseling-type process.

The fact that restrictive physical, economic, and social conditions which hamper large numbers of blacks in their efforts to cope with their life situations have been fully documented in the social science literature. However, what has not been made clear is the nature of the intervening variables which often cushion the impact of negative conditions or exacerbate their effect. The impression received from much of the literature is that they operate in a consistent manner, are relatively unmodifiable, and therefore limit the opportunity for blacks across the board to deal effectively with problems of living. Yet there are sufficient examples of blacks who have been able to rise above negative conditions, solve tremendous personal and interpersonal problems and achieve success in the dominant society that the presence of such intervening variables appear to be confirmed. What is also suggested is that the assessment of opportunity afforded by the physical and social environment must always be based on an opportunity profile, i.e., weighing relative obstacles represented by environmental deficits along with relative compensations from other environmental supports. For example, the negative effects of low income, poor and overcrowded housing, and limited educational resources may be offset to some extent by a large and supportive extended family network or recent admission to a training program which would indicate prospects for being able to support a higher standard of living in the future as well as a possibly responsive political climate in which there is willingness to act on obvious instances of inequality. The failure to see these compensatory factors may lead to an inappropriate pessimism regarding the possibility of change. The pessimism of practitioners often gets transmitted to clients and instead of "hanging-in" to obtain assistance in maximizing available opportunities, they "drop-out" and create another example of a self-fulfilling prophecy.

Another kind of opportunity is provided by the helping system itself and it has been noted that this system has excluded, discriminated against, and generally performed inadequately in regard to the enhancement of social functioning for black clients. For example, Thomas and Sillen have described psychiatrists who take a nihilistic view of the potential of blacks to make use of mental health services. The reasons given are that it is hopeless to treat persons who live constantly in pathogenic environments or that the problems presented by blacks are so wrapped up in the oppression of the racist White power structure that no attempts at help can be successful until racism itself is eradicated. Thomas and Sillen contend that it is dehumanizing to take this attitude that blacks unlike other human beings do not experience the conflicts, ambivalences, or vulnerabilities stemming from innumerable hazards of life.[15] The implication is that they are responsive to a single although complex aspect of interpersonal relationships. The insistence that nothing can be done for blacks experiencing personal distress until major social problems are solved has been compared to an insistence that nothing be done about the casualties of war until war itself is eradicated!

ESTABLISHING THE CLIENT AS AGENT OF CHANGE
In the theoretical presentation on the dynamics of powerlessness in chapter 1, it was pointed out that activities aimed at reducing powerlessness in our clients must make it possible for the client to perceive of self as causal agent in achieving

the solution to his problem rather than as hapless victim. This is perhaps the essential paradox of the helping encounter with black clients—the need for simultaneous recognition that although the power shortages in their lives stem in large measure from negative valuations made of them by others, empowerment for themselves can only be achieved through their own efforts. Thus, it is crucial for the practitioner to elicit a beginning "contract statement" from the client in which the nature of that effort is confirmed and accepted. The contract statement may take one of several forms depending upon the theoretical perspective of the practitioner.

Practitioners whose perspective on practice emanates from psychodynamic or psychosocial theory may seek a statement from the client similar in form to: "I must try to understand how my life experiences have led to this problem; if I can understand that, then I will also understand what to do about it." This provides sanction for exploration with the client of past and present interplay between the client and significant others to find etiological explanations for the current problem situation. This exploration further aims to pinpoint the power deficits which have led to inadequate, ineffective, or inappropriate social functioning and from that point to move toward removing the blacks which have led to powerlessness.

In the problem situation practitioners whose perspective is essentially a behavioral or social learning one, will elicit the contract statement similar in form to: "If I can discover what events precipitate or maintain specific problem behavior, then I will be able to manipulate those events in order to control the behavior." This approach is not concerned with underlying causes in the sense of how the problem started but rather contemporary mechanisms which maintain it. Practitioners whose orientation is from a client-centered or "humanistic" perspective will elicit a contract statement which is similar to: "If I can come to truly know and understand myself and how I relate to others, then I will understand what to do about my problems."

The common theme in each of these statements is the "I will

understand what to do about my problem." Thus, it is clear that the problem is to be solved by the client and not by the social worker. The social worker is facilitator, sensitizer, resource person, advocate, teacher—but not a person who will solve problems for the passive and the powerless.

The following is an excerpt from an initial interview with a young, black client who has had her son removed from her home because of child abuse. The worker is providing the client with the counseling which had been mandated by the court before the child's return home could be considered. It demonstrates the manner in which the contract statement may be elicited even from an initially hostile client.

CLIENT: Are you going to be the one to decide whether I get my child back or not?

WORKER: The court will ask my opinion about how you and your child will get along if he is returned.

CLIENT: How will you know anything about that?

WORKER: I hope *you* will let me know something about that.

CLIENT: O.K. I'll tell you. It's going to be great so you can go tell the court to let him come back.

WORKER: But I don't know that it will be great.

CLIENT: I just told you, didn't I? You said that if I let you know . . . didn't you?

WORKER: Just listening to what you say is all I need to do to understand what happens with you and Jimmy?

CLIENT: Yes. ,

WORKER: Then, I think you need to say a good deal more.

CLIENT: I still don't understand what good talking is going to do. I told that other social worker who did the investigation for the protective services people that I didn't mean to hurt Jimmy. I wouldn'a hurt him either if he hadn't tried to pull away from me so hard. That's why his arm got dis . . . dis . . . ."

WORKER: Dislocated.

CLIENT: Yeah. Dislocated. But I caught him stealing from next door. He could grow up to be an armed robber and what would the court think about that? They'd throw him in jail for life, that's what! But they'd rather pick on parents who're just tryin to make kids grow up decent!

WORKER: It sounds as if you feel that you're damned if you do and damned if you don't.

CLIENT: Damned right!

WORKER: Are you also wondering what *I* can do to change all that?

CLIENT: Damned right!

WORKER: Well, I guess the answer is not much—not nearly as much as you can.

CLIENT: What d'ya mean? *You* can tell the court to give me back my child! *I* can't get him back by myself!

WORKER: I can tell the court that I think you know how you got into a situation where the court thought it necessary to remove your child from your home and I can also tell the court that I am convinced that because of that knowledge, it won't happen again. But I can only say that if I really am convinced and that can only come from what you tell me.

CLIENT: You want me to say that I lose my temper sometime with Jimmy and I have learned how to control it?

WORKER: I don't want you to say anything that is not true. I am only saying that it has to be true that you know how you got into this situation and that you have figured out how to prevent it from happening again.

CLIENT: (suspiciously) Suppose I say that I got into it because that no-good, used-to-be friend of mine called the protective service people and lied on me because I wouldn't loan her money. And suppose I say it won't happen again because I'm goin to beat her ass for her if I ever catch her!

WORKER: Then I would want to talk about that plan of yours to see how workable it is. For example, how do you know some other "no-good friend" won't call the protective service people on you the next time you accidentally hurt Jimmy? Can you be sure that you won't accidentally hurt him again? How can you deal with his behavior so that you won't need to punish him or maybe not so often? How can you deal with trying to raise a kid in a neighborhood where so many things can go wrong? How can you deal with friends who hit on you for money and then do you dirty first chance they get?

CLIENT: I sure hope you got the answers to all that cause I sure don't.

WORKER: I think that you do! And may be if I can help you get at your answers, maybe you'll find out that you *can* prevent what has happened from happening again.

CLIENT: That's a pretty big order.
(Silence)
But I think that I would like to try. I want my kid back and I don't want to lose him again.

WORKER: Can you tell me what It Is that you're saying you want to try?

CLIENT: Well, I guess I'm saying that I'm going to try to talk about all those problems I'm having and maybe if I can understand what's happening, I'll know how to handle Jimmy better . . . because, if it seems that I can, then you'll let the court know it so I can get him back.

WORKER: That sounds like a good place to start . . . maybe we can start with whatever problem of the many you mentioned, *you* think is the most important in terms of what happened between you and Jimmy.

For those individuals, groups, or communities that have been subjected to negative valuation to such an extent that deep-seated feelings of powerlessness have resulted, the most common resistance to change efforts is disbelief in either their own capacity to effect change and/or the likelihood that those who do have the power to effect change will be interested in doing so in their behalf. The client in the above situation had identified the "causes" of her problem in systems over which she felt she had no control—the neighborhood, the court, the "no-good" friend. On the other hand, she did perceive the worker as having influence with the court. This influence was perceived, however, as discretionary, i.e., to be determined by the worker on the basis of arbitrary, subjective, or even capricious response to the client.

Particular theoretical approaches to practice hold particular dangers when the worker is attempting to engage black client systems. For example, when the client already has located the source of the problem *and its resolution* outside himself, it may appear to be foolish and bureaucratic nonsense for the psychodynamically oriented worker to explore his life situation—even that aspect of it which is directly related to the presenting problem. Furthermore, this exploration of the client's life situation—instead of the general impact of an oppressive court system or pathology-burdened neighborhood—could result in undue responsibility for the etiology of the problem being placed on the client which would only serve to reinforce the negative valuation experienced over the lifetime. To avoid this danger, the exploration of the client's life situation must begin with an acceptance of the client's identification of the source of the problem and exploration of ways to deal with that source. For example, in the case of the mother whose son has been removed from her home by the court, and who has identified her problem as the oppressive court, the deteriorated neighborhood, the treacherous friend, the issue is what is the effect of these negative life aspects? what is the difference in her life situation as compared with those who escape these negative effects?

It is generally assumed that behavioral approaches eliminate the stigmatizing effect of having to define behavior as deviant or pathological in order to prescribe a "treatment." However, in the case of people suffering from severe power deficits in their ability to function effectively in their social environments, there is another risk perhaps as inimical as stigmatization—the depersonalization of self or perception of self as object and product of the environmental forces rather than as subject and creator of that environment. Thus, the subtle distinction must be made between a conception of self as controlled by conditioning and reinforcing events in the environment and a conception of self as controlling those events to achieve self-directed behavior change. For the person with strong feelings of powerlessness, there is a heightened possibility that even successful modification of problem behaviors will be viewed as something that was done *to* him rather than something done *by* him. The behaviorally oriented worker must take every opportunity to identify the "client as controller" rather than the "client as controlled."

Even the client-centered or humanistic approach has risks involved when attempting to engage the black client. This is perhaps the most difficult approach to rationalize to persons suffering intense feelings of victimization by others. The emphasis on the need for self-understanding often appears to the black client to be an idiotic waste of time. This may be due to the inherent nature of this approach as delineated by Carkhuff and Berenson in their analysis of Rogers' client-centered therapy: "However active or passive the client-centered therapist, there are many not so subtle indications that the process is a rather precise reflection of a polite middle class, and will function most effectively with persons who share the attitudes, the values, and the potentials of the polite middle class." [16]

Of course, few social work practitioners adhere strictly to the client-centered techniques as evolved by Rogers and his adherents. However, the inappropriateness of an approach which suggests that self-understanding is the royal road to solving personal and social problems for persons who have experienced so many life events over which they had no control should be recognized.

SUMMARY
This chapter has described the unique issues involved in engaging black clients in a helping process. An underlying assumption is made that most residents of black communities who come to social agencies for help have been sent by schools, correctional authorities, or other agents of social control and do not have firm convictions that the practitioners in the agencies have skills they can use in solving their problems of living.

Establishing rapport between client and worker is an important requirement in the initial stages of a helping process and it is particularly difficult when it is attempted across racial lines. Yet, knowledge of how to build a trusting relationship with black clients in spite of this pervasive distrust of whites as a category as well as of the established agencies has been developed. The practitioner should be able to indicate familiarity with the communication patterns, life styles, and life experiences of black people. At the same time, the practitioner should present an authentic "self" to the client—including a use of language that is not stilted or alien but true.

Black clients rarely expect that expertise in dealing with *their* problems in living can be found in established social or mental health agencies since these same agencies have been perceived as accepting and perpetuating the negative valuation of blacks that is endemic in the society. Furthermore, "social worker" is almost inevitably translated as "welfare worker" and all the odious associations that blacks have in regard to the welfare system as also attached to "social worker." Consideration should be given to having social work practitioners as well as others in black communities identified as problem area "specialists," e.g., family relations specialist, educational specialist, employment specialist, etc. Expertise can also be identified in terms of practice methods, i.e., expertise in working with individuals, groups, or community groups.

An important aspect of engaging black client systems is the assessment of motivation, capacity, and opportunity since it is often as a consequence of the assessment of these factors that blacks are not permitted access to help systems or are dropped out of them. For example, the criteria used to measure motivation in other subgroups in the ethnosystem may not be valid when used with black clients. Knowledge of the black experience provides us with clues as to how motivation can be increased (e.g., develop "testimonials" regarding services of agencies and the value of those services), capacity can be more adequately assessed (e.g., by observation of the client in his own life space), and opportunity can be more objectively identified (e.g., the careful weighing of the obstacles represented by power deficits along with the compensations available from environmental supports).

Finally, it was pointed out that an essential requirement in engaging the client is some kind of contract statement in which the client accepts at least to some extent that he is *the primary causal agent in achieving the desired change.* This "contract" statement may vary with the specific theoretical approach but should be included regardless of which theoretical approaches as they may be utilized in pursuit of empowerment for black clients were presented.

chapter twelve

empowerment
and the role
of the practitioner

There is an awesome distance from the point an elephant is captured to the point where his captors enjoy an elephant stew. Often, it is an equally immeasurable distance from the point where a client becomes actively engaged in seeking solutions to his problems with a professional person and the point where the problem is considered solved. Empowerment as a practice goal when working with black clients, or other minority clients for that matter, can shorten the distance. Earlier it was suggested that empowerment as a goal for the client implies the client's perception of his own intrinsic and extrinsic value; the client's motivation to use every personal resource and skill, as well as those of any other that he can command, in the effort to achieve self-determined goals; and finally, a conviction that there are many pathways to goal attainment and as long as one makes the effort, failure is possible but the more effort one makes, success is probable.

This chapter is concerned with empowerment as a component of the problem-solving process itself, regardless of the theoretical approach which gives it its shape. Our interest here is in the identification of those roles performed by practitioners that provide maximum opportunity for clients to experience their own effectiveness as they participate in the helping process. Power and control are energizing magnets, drawing the client into the redefinition of his own self-worth, competence, and ability to affect his social and physical worlds. Unfortunately, the very help systems that supposedly assist the poor and the powerless in the search for more rewarding and rewarded lives have earned the reputation of holding power *over* their clients rather than providing them opportunities to exert it; and of encouraging and reinforcing their dependency rather than contributing to their sense of autonomy.

Social workers have been viewed too often as "dirty workers"; i.e., those who impose the restrictive bureaucratic policies aimed at social control rather than at helping. Furthermore, despite the fact that historically, there have been relatively few trained social workers in public welfare departments, the prevailing notion of the setting in which most social workers are found is that of the welfare department. Despite the efforts of professionally trained social workers in family, health, and mental health settings to divorce themselves from the welfare worker stigma, the image prevails. Ironically, it is the welfare setting in which the largest number of black clients could probably be found. Furthermore, the attempt by many professionally trained social workers to impose prestigious models of psychotherapy on clients whose perceptions of need are at an elemental, survival level did not result in the kind of effective resolution of problems that would convince their clients that social workers are truly skillful or that would validate the usefulness of such models for the presentation of problems.

Of course, the helping process in solving social and/or psychological problems is not the exclusive function of any single profession but is engaged in by a variety of professional disciplines with their own particular emphasis and own accompaniment of technicians, supporters, and client-types. Thus psychiatrists place emphasis on their medical background and tend to use the medical model in diagnosis of problems and prescription of "treatment." Their clients are therefore defined as patients and tend to be middle class, Anglo, and introspective. However, the thrust for equality of opportunity in our service delivery system has meant that the psychiatrist's services are offered to some poor and minority persons who are referred by schools, physicians, probation departments, or welfare departments. To insure eligibility, however, it is often necessary to define the locus of the problem in the individual and to impose sanctions for failure to accept the referral (e.g., welfare assistance is withdrawn or probation is rescinded!). It is not surprising that psychiatrists in private practice are conspicuously few in black communities where the marketing principle in operation would mean small incomes to match the small demand from people themselves who have even smaller incomes.

Psychologists have fared little better in black communities although they are more likely to be associated with schools than either psychiatrists or social workers and more identifiable with institutional goals (e.g., school adjustment) or the testing of residents of juvenile hall for court reports. Still, there is no clear-cut evidence that psychologists have been particularly successful in dealing with problems characteristically encountered in black communities or with black client systems. Paraprofessionals and other indigenous persons who have sought to provide helping services have not proved more effective than the professionals despite some instances of success and a great deal of support for the development of "new careerists" from inside black communities. Part of the problem may lie in the tendency for paraprofessionals to use as models the very professionals who had been shown to be ineffective in dealing with black, poor, and other minority clients. Ministers have been accepted in many instances on black communities as legitimate helpers but those who have received training in the behavioral sciences have probably been used to a much more limited extent as counselors than have those ministers whose attraction is based more on charisma and flamboyance.

If it appears that there is no helping discipline that has gained general acceptability in black communities, that is exactly the message. This may be due in large measure to the nature of the professional roles adopted by the practitioners. Because empowerment requires a worker-client relationship in which opportunities for the client to utilize whatever powers are available to him are maximized, it may be useful to look at the opportunities provided clients in the various roles that social workers may perform.

Goldstein has conceptualized a professional role for social workers which incorporates several sub-roles.[1] These include a role of *power and authority* as prescribed by the social worker's status within the unequal and imbalanced relationship; a *socializing* role based on the particular values that energize the problem-solving encounter; and a *teaching* role stemming from the goal of enhanced learning in the problem-solving effort. Goldstein conceives of an integrated set of role behaviors in which the social worker may be expected to perform any or all of these behaviors in any given case situation.

Other theorists have tended to perceive separate sets of role behaviors which are case specific. For example, Middleman and Goldberg have defined four different roles based on different sets of expectations for worker behaviors depending on the client's problem situation: the *advocate* role, which is predicated on the assumption of a conflict situation; the *mediator* role, based on the assumption that the parties apparently in conflict actually have common bonds which can be the basis of mutual self-fulfillment; the *broker* role, in which clients are linked to community resources; and the *conferee* role, in which the worker and client confer together, compare opinions, deliberate, and devise actions to be taken in a problem-solving effort.[2] Whittaker has also suggested four roles: the *treatment agent,* in which the worker utilizes a particular mode of treatment (individual, family, small group) to influence aspects of the client's problem situation; the *advocate-omsbudsman,* which includes almost anything the worker does indirectly on behalf of his client; the *teacher-counselor,* in which problem-solving is defined as a teaching-learning situation; and the *broker of services and resources,* where the worker helps the client to identify where resources are in the community and how the client may secure them.[3]

An analysis of these role classifications, which vary in only minor details, exposes the risks that lie in waiting for the client in desperate need of controlling his own destiny. For example, the *advocacy* role for the social worker begins with an assessment of powerlessness on the part of the client to the extent that the professional must stand in his behalf. The risk of the self-fulfilling prophecy is obvious. In some instances, advocacy for a client may increase powerlessness by reinforcing the client's feelings of his own ineptitude or by generating more repressive repercussions from the opposing system. The *treatment agent* role may suggest or reinforce perceptions of deviance and pathology which are in need of "cure." The unequal power balance in such a relationship, i.e., one based on the medical model, is undeniable. The *broker* role calls for the worker's knowledge of resources being placed at the disposal of the client; however, this linking of client and resources can degenerate into such a paternalistic operation that the client becomes a lowly supplicant to the social worker's Lady Bountiful routine. Even the *teacher* role in our society may have negative valence for those who have had little positive experience with the educational system and for whom the teacher is a representative of oppressive society rather than a means to an end. Given these difficulties for which, black clients, are embedded in the very structure of the role relationships in helping situations, it is suggested here that three possible roles have emerged as appropriate in the pursuit of empowerment.

RESOURCE CONSULTANT
The provision of resources—money, housing, health care, homemaker services—is perhaps the service most desperately sought in poor, black communities. Ironically, the provision of resources may be least helpful in achieving the goal of empowerment if such provision only serves to reinforce a sense of powerlessness and dependency. Dispensing material resources to people puts the practitioner in the primary role of agent of a social agency in particular and society in general; thus, as

pointed out by Pincus and Minahan, clients are bound by legislative and agency mandates, regulations and standards—even when these mandates, regulations and standards serve to increase their sense of powerlessness.[4]

The *resource consultant* role is defined here much more broadly than that of resource dispenser or resource provider; it involves linking clients to resources in a manner that enhances their self-esteem as well as their problem-solving capacities. The consultant's knowledge of the resource systems and expertise in using these systems are placed at the disposal of the client and his participation in the process from identification to location to utilization is intensive. This transcends the limitations inherent in a broker role which may be appropriately implemented without involving the client at all in the process once the resource need has been identified.

The group modality can be particularly effective in providing opportunities for the practitioner to take the consultant role in obtaining resources. Hopkins has described a group work program for black men at the Dr. Martin Luther King Family Center in a black ghetto in Chicago's Near West Side.[5] The group was composed of ten to thirteen fathers who were initially organized as a means of sensitizing the men to their children's developmental needs. However, the fathers soon gave evidence of their greater interest in involving themselves in projects that supported the masculine role—including making money. Hopkins described a benefit party for the agency in which a portion of the profits went to the men themselves. The social worker, as consultant to the project, had accepted as a working principle that each project taken on by the group should have three components: something for the community, something for the group, and *something for each member.* The group was therefore encouraged to make money and distribute the profits equally among its members. This direct approach to obtaining a resource, in this case, financial resources, increases rather than reduces self-esteem while at the same time develops skills that are applicable to other situations.

THE SENSITIZER ROLE

The sensitizer role incorporates all those role behaviors which are designed to assist the client gain the self-knowledge necessary for him to solve his problem or problems. The practitioner is a sensitizing instrument to be used by the client as he explores the determinants of his social functioning and its consequences, particularly as these are related to the problem situation. The particular theoretical approach of the practitioner will bring about the specification of the techniques to be used in this sensitizing effort; however, any technique to be used should provide maximum opportunity for the client to lead the exploration and the practitioner to provide illumination, connections, or direction if indicated. The entire process should be concerned with the client's self-knowledge as a means of identifying those forces operating in the problem situation which can be controlled by the client, i.e., upon which he can exert some form of power.

Self-knowledge as a goal in social work with black clients has often been criticized. However, many problems brought to agencies by black clients cannot be solved by material resources alone. Many of the power deficits they demonstrate are in the area of social and emotional resources which may be much more difficult to provide or even to reach mutual agreement regarding their significance in the problem situation. On the other hand, the key that opens the door to these much less tangible resources is self-knowledge. Yet, for many black clients, to identify self-knowledge as a goal for themselves is tantamount to being defined as "crazy," "sick," or some other indicator that one is flawed or deviant. Other black clients are less concerned with stigma and more concerned with relevance. It is difficult for them to connect self-knowledge with a solution to their problems. Therefore, an attempt on the part of the practitioner to explore aspects of their life situation, past or present, will be perceived as an imposition, although one they may be powerless to avoid. Of course, non-black clients may also have these attitudes. However, their source appears to be the perception of negative valuation of the client and for those clients for whom negative valuations have already produced deep psychic gashes, more of the same can be devastating. Thus it is necessary not only to demonstrate that exploration of psychosocial history in search of self-knowledge is not related to negative valuation of the client but in addition it is necessary to demonstrate that such exploration is in the interest of creating new opportunities for the client to control his life situation.

There are several examples in recent professional literature of cases which point up with chilling clarity the need for practitioners who can move beyond the role of resource dispenser or even resource consultant. These cases demand practitioners who are able to assist clients in gaining the self-knowledge critical for the solution of problems which stem from social and psychological power deficits rather than from material ones. Vera and her mother constitute a case in point:

> Vera, a nine-year-old girl, had frequent abdominal pains, headaches, and other physical ailments, although in-hospital studies revealed no physical basis for the symptoms. The psychiatric opinion was that Vera was developing a neurotic pattern of reaction to the mother's emotional disturbance and past history of mental illness, particularly to the latter's intermittent anxiety states. Vera would then become visibly worried, count the mother's prescribed pills for fear she might take an overdose, and look in on her mother when asleep. The mother had similar psychosomatic symptoms herself, had attempted suicide, and had been in a psychiatric hospital a few years earlier because of a mental breakdown.
>
> In addition to Vera's problems, the mother was beset by the physical problems of her seven-year-old son who had a history of petit mal and grand mal epilepsy. The children were born of a marriage in which she was cruelly treated by her husband and often physically beaten in the presence of the children. Her husband had also been unfaithful to her, and she had obtained a divorce. As a child growing up, Vera's mother had witnessed terrible fighting between her own parents, who separated when she was seven years old. There were other traumatic and tragic episodes in the immediate

family: the mother's sister had been murdered by her husband who, in turn, committed suicide.[6]

Overwhelming environmental and interpersonal conditions are the hard facts of life for many people who live in black communities. The negative valuations from the larger society are expanded and reinforced in the primary relational systems. Self-knowledge under such circumstances is likely to have to begin at a point of such unbearably low self-esteem that only a deep and abiding relationship in which the "other" is willing to experience with the client incredibly painful emotions can free the client to move toward effective self-knowledge. Effective self-knowledge is defined here as understanding the manner in which one's own attitudes, emotions, and behavior patterns influence a problem situation. Armed with such knowledge, Vera's mother could increase the possibilities for controlling the development of negative life events or the implementation of noninstrumental responses to those events such as stomach ailment, suicide attempts, and anxiety states. Certainly, the payoff in terms of Vera and her brother would also be large.

THE TEACHER/TRAINER ROLE
Almost all textbooks on social work practice identify the educational function as an important aspect of that practice. The practitioner engages in a variety of activities that constitute assistance to people and systems in the acquisition of information, knowledge, or skills. Goldstein differentiates between the educational role of the teacher and that of the social worker. The former is concerned with the management of a learning process that has as its goal the acquisition of knowledge related to growth and maturation or the development of special skills. On the other hand, the social worker manages a learning process with much more specific aims, namely, the completion of certain tasks or the resolution of problems related to social living. Furthermore, these problems are generally accompanied

by intense pressures for help or change which imbue the process with a significance often missing from the more routine learning situations, formal or informal, that most people are involved in as part of daily living. The interrelationship between social learning as an ongoing social enterprise and social learning within the professional change experience is easily observable. In fact, it is the failure of the individual to learn the cognitive, interpersonal, and technical skills in the ordinary course of events that increases dramatically the probability that the professional change experience will be necessary. Since negative valuation of blacks has resulted in a severely limited opportunity system for routine learning to take place (including the school as a public mechanism for providing learning opportunities), sometimes the power of individuals and systems to cope with problems can be increased substantially merely by providing the needed information, knowledge, or skills.

The most likely obstacle to the effective implementation of educational strategies with black clients is the fact that so many have experienced only failure, negative valuation, and boredom in the formal educational settings; therefore, any educational strategy fashioned along the lines laid out in these settings will frequently be resisted. Brooks describes how a community mental health center in a black community has dealt with the modification of traditional educational approaches:

> As a vehicle for imparting various child-rearing techniques to the mother and giving an opportunity to discuss other problems of family care, often as the only adult parental figure, a mothers' group was formed to provide a relaxed informal atmosphere for mothers. A prior attempt to offer a course in child-rearing per se had been poorly received by the community. An examination of the mothers in the community revealed that their lack of involvement in a course did not indicate a lack of investment in their children. A structured course threatened many who had limited education and saw the course as pointing out their educational shortcomings, thus reactivating their negative feelings toward schools. Mothers freely gathered on an informal basis to discuss prob-

lems of rearing a family. Various simple techniques were
shared as well as more sophisticated methods presented by
the staff worker.[7]

The informal, nonthreatening group became the vehicle for
an educational strategy, successfully implemented because it
bore little resemblance to the traditional context which had left
such painful memories for some.

THE CLIENT AS SERVICE PROVIDER
One of the most important findings to come out of the studies
of multi-problem families conducted in the St. Paul Family Centered Project was the importance to a client when the opportunity is provided for him to give help as well as to receive it. In
the Family Centered Project the clients' views were sought on
the meaning of service to them. Overton has described the enhancement to the project as a result of client input. "The
clients knew that our bid for their help was not contrived—that
we thought their views important enough to modify our own
practice. . . . In other words we had enough confidence in the
group to *expect* its members to play a giving as well as a taking
role. They in turn were proud of their contributing role and
liked us better for having confidence in their power to assume
it."[8]

Subsequently to this articulation of the value to be derived by
clients who are able to give as well as take, there appeared to
be renewed interest in what Riessman termed the "helper"
therapy principle, i.e., the use of people with a problem to help
other people who have the same problem in more severe form.
Riessman noted that frequently it was the person providing the
assistance who improved rather than the recipient. He then
suggested that "social work's strategy ought to be to devise
ways of creating more helpers! Or, to be more exact, to find
ways to transform *recipients* of help into *dispensers* of help
. . . and to structure the situation so that recipients of help will

be placed in roles requiring the giving of assistance."[9] Unfortunately, however, most of the helper roles that have emerged in help settings are modeled after the "talk" therapies which tend to attract the more middle-class, Anglo-oriented client.

Goldberg and Kane have described a program with a broader conceptualization of the helper role than is usually suggested including an opportunity for clients to provide services-in-kind for others as payment for the services provided to them at the community mental health center.

> In implementing the program we felt that the client's commitment to giving services was a more important therapeutic ingredient than the economic value of the service. Therapist and client therefore discussed the client's vocational skills and experiences, his interests and avocations, as well as areas of service required in the Center or in some instances in the community. Therapist and client came to some agreement about which specific assignment would be taken and approximately how much time would be spent in giving a service. The client was then directed to a staff person, usually a secretary, to receive an orientation for the assignment. Problems the client experienced on the assignment were discussed with the therapist.
>
> In the service-in-kind program are persons who do not earn sufficient income to pay a fee and who might otherwise feel guilty and self-denigrative for getting something for nothing. There are also persons who can afford fees but whom we feel would benefit more from giving of themselves than through paying a fee. When the poor pay fees, they know that their fees are adjusted to their incomes and this reveals quite baldly their economic inferiority. If the client chooses to render services in return for services rendered him, it is likely that he can demonstrate skills and abilities of which he is proud and for which he can be admired. This serves to balance his relationship with those who are assisting him with the problems of which he is less proud.[10]

This program, despite the problems encountered in its implementation, represents an important innovation in the pursuit of enpowerment for powerless people. It provides an opportunity for the client to step out of the supplicant role of one who seeks service into the more favored position of helper or one who provides service. The broader this conceptualization of the client as helper can be interpreted, the greater the probability that clients will be permitted to perform multiple roles. This will provide the mechanism whereby the client with massive needs can at the same time demonstrate strengths and skills which reduce humiliation and crippling self-definitions.

SUMMARY
This chapter has focused on those practitioner roles which hold the most promise for reducing the clients' sense of powerlessness: the resource consultant role, the sensitizer role, and the teacher/trainer role. The resource consultant role was defined more broadly than that of resource dispenser or resource provider; it involves linking clients to resources in a manner that enhances their self-esteem as well as their problem-solving capacities. The sensitizer role incorporates all those role behaviors which are designed to assist the client gain the self-knowledge necessary for him to solve his presenting problem or problems. The teacher/trainer role involves the practitioner as manager of a learning process in which the principal aim is the completion of certain tasks or the resolution of problems related to social living.

Finally, the idea of the client as service provider was briefly considered. This innovation, when broadly conceived, is a potentially effective means of bringing the client into a more egalitarian relationship with the practitioner. Mutuality and complementarity of the two roles act to prevent the reinforcement or extension of the client's feelings of powerlessness.

chapter thirteen

designing service delivery systems

A system of services available to people in a given community would suggest the presence of strong linkages among the organizations or units comprising the system as well as complementarity of their separate programs. One would also expect to discern a relational process for moving clients through and around the system from entry to exit, including a clearly articulated rationale for any branching within the system or rerouting to other systems (e.g., judicial, business, political, etc.) that might occur. However, on the basis of these criteria our system of human services in this country and in almost any region within it can only be described as a nonsystem. Lerner has proposed that our problem stems in large measure from the bureaucratic nature of our service organizations which by definition must "standardize" procedures. This makes them inherently unresponsive to the remarkable amount of variation that characterizes the human condition. Furthermore, this standardization more often than not reflects the main themes in the lives of the dominant group in the ethnosystem, e.g., efficiency, upward mobility, profit, personal responsibility, and the primacy of scientific method for problem-solving. It could also be suggested that the standardization of procedures, policies, and role expectations reflects the negative valuation of minorities, particularly blacks, to the extent that they assume a client population that will be untrustworthy, greedy, insensitive to inconvenience and delay, and rarely intelligent enough to participate in the development of policies regarding the delivery of services to them.

The identification of gaps and deficiencies in the existing delivery systems in the human service arena has become routine and even somewhat ritualistic among helping professionals. There are few today who would suggest that current structures to deal with personal and social distress of any people in the ethnosystem are adequate or even benign. Yet, people in black communities who are experiencing such problems are even more vulnerable than most to ineffective service delivery systems. First of all, the knowledge base necessary to deal effectively with problems that are systemic in origin or that are influenced by systemic variables has been inadequately developed. Intensive efforts to base practice strategies on "knowledge" derived from research studies has been detrimental to the development of effective help systems in black communities. Social scientists have demonstrated a "person-blame" bias which has contaminated this knowledge and reinforced a tendency to hold individuals to blame for their problems, irrespective of other evidence. An examination of the research reports dealing with black Americans indexed in *Psychological Abstracts* during the first six months of 1970 demonstrated this preoccupation with person variables in contrast to system variables.[1] Almost half of these studies attempted to correlate group membership with specific personal characteristics, while another 34 percent identified some personal characteristic which it was concluded either caused or was correlated with a problem characteristic; in contrast, only 19 percent or less than one-fifth of the studies identified a situational or environmental characteristic as a causal factor in regard to a problem characteristic. This means that the knowledge base relating system influences on problem etiology and maintenance is limited. Furthermore, the knowledge we do have tends to be pessimistic in any appraisal of the probability that contemporary service delivery systems can serve as instruments for effective empowerment of people in black communities. Empirical evidence from the field attests to the failure of community-based social action organizations to impact the service delivery system to any significant extent.

Gilbert and Specht have developed a conceptual framework for the analysis of social welfare policy which includes as one of its dimensions "service delivery strategies." [2] These strategies are defined as "the alternative organizational arrangements among distributors and consumers of social welfare benefits in the context of local community systems (neighborhood, city, and county), the level at which the overwhelming majority of distributors and consumers come together." The key question raised by this definition is *who* or *what* determines *which* alternative arrangements will prevail in the distribution of *what kind* of benefits and services? We cannot feel comfortable with the response that the "who" refers to planners, community organizers, or policymakers, since these titles are merely descriptions of functional roles and not of positions in an organization or organizational network. The matter of "which" alternative arrangements, i.e., the matter of choice, is also a thoroughly dependent variable—dependent for the most part on "what kind" of service is to be delivered and to whom. Certainly, a guiding principle for designing service delivery systems in black communities has emerged in the discussions in previous chapters, i.e., *the organizational arrangement for service delivery should maximize the opportunities available for black individuals, groups and communities to reduce feelings of powerlessness and to counteract specific negative valuations of blacks collectively which current organizational arrangements often serve to reinforce.*

The evidence available suggests that organizers and planners in black communities have not appreciated the equal significance of both ends and means in development and implementation of effective service programs. For example, in some cases, means have been emphasized with not enough attention to the viability or value of the projected goal. For the last ten years organizers in black communities have stressed the importance of developing strong community-based organizations as a "power base" which could be used to attract needed social supplies to the community. Warren, however, has demonstrated in his extensive research on black neighborhoods in Detroit that it is not enough to elaborate highly localized neighborhood-oriented groups, since this results in the effective insulation of residents from "the institutional networks and nexuses which serve to perpetuate what is clearly the economic and political inequality between the ghetto and the rest of the urban community." [3] Thus, the proliferation of community-based organizations in black communities attest to the success of the organizing efforts but the organizations created did not bring about the power base anticipated, because of a misreading of their impact on the institutional networks outside the black community.

Other organizers and planners who have sought to improve the quality of life in black communities have placed major emphasis on "ends." Thus, the effectiveness of a program is measured by concrete achievements, like the number of jobs obtained for unemployed residents; the number of housing units rehabilitated; the number of day-care slots made available to working mothers; the dollar amount increase in welfare payments. Yet, the means by which such achievements are realized may in fact render them useless. Thus, power deficits experienced by our clients cannot be reduced by means which reinforce powerlessness. Economic dependency—a form of power deficit—cannot be reduced by welfare programs which are demeaning or arrogantly oppressive. On the contrary, the client is unlikely to develop a sense of his own competence or confidence in his ability to have a positive effect on his environment: rehabilitated housing units that were done without obtaining input from those most likely to live in them, or that become too expensive for residents to rent, obviously may become a negative rather than a positive factor in community life. The ultimate example of this inordinate emphasis on ends without attention to means was given by Lerner, who pointed out that if the only measure of the value of a work therapy program is how many people were put to work, then slavery must have been extremely therapeutic for American blacks!

The remainder of this chapter describes three programs which would appear to have some potential for reducing powerlessness for people In black communities They are not presented as alternatives nor are they viewed as feasible for all black communities. Instead, they represent positive efforts being made by sensitive and committed practitioners and social planners to translate the rhetoric of the past decade into concrete options for people in black communities. Each of these service delivery models can be conceived of as a beginning statement which would need amplification and specification for a given community. Thus they are generic entities which may generate a variety of offspring.

SOCIAL LEARNING CENTERS

An increasing number of behavioral science theoreticians are promoting the concept of the helping person as tutor in problems of living rather than as medical specialist or therapist who is concerned with illness. In effect, all therapeutic schools have placed emphasis on learning as the force which induces behavioral change. Orten and Weiss have identified the educational approaches inherent in four therapeutic approaches which confirm the centrality of theories of learning in dealing with personal and social problems.[4]

In *psychodynamic or analytic* approaches there is an assumption that internal processes mediate between external stimuli and the individual's responses, which explains how problem behavior can be produced by dynamics of which he is not aware, i.e., unconscious conflicts. In order to resolve the conflict, the unconscious must become conscious, for it is only then that the client will be able to make the most appropriate choices for himself and implement them in his behavior. The educational model here is one of learning about self and how functional responses learned in the past may be dysfunctional in the present. This is achieved by a process of uncovering unconscious repressed memories which are relieved of their negative associations.

In contrast to analytic processes, rational processes are based on the assumption that the individual's cognitive processes mediate between internal (emotional) and external stimuli and his responses to them. Man is seen as capable of taking conscious cognitive control of his emotional state as well as of his behavior. *Rational psychotherapy* is based on the assumption that thought and emotion are two entirely different processes, but that they significantly overlap in many respects and therefore disordered emotions can often, though not always, be ameliorated by changing one's thinking. Thus the educational experience provided must emphasize cognitive skills which will be expected to change feelings.

Behavioral modification processes are based on stimulus-response learning theory positing that behavior is determined by one's conditioning history. The learned program that produces problem behavior can be changed, however, by reconditioning or relearning which eliminates undesirable patterns and adds acceptable ones. It is not necessary to know the conditioning history. There is no need to analyze internal processes. The therapist must determine what are: (1) the stimulus conditions that elicit problematic responses, (2) the consequences that serve to reinforce and maintain them, and (3) the additional responses the individual has in his behavioral repertoire that may be reinforced to take the place of problem ones.

Environmental processes focus on the environment as a source of human problems and its change as a means of their relief. The educational aspect involved is learning the sources of environmental stress and strain, the sources of environmental support, and the techniques of bringing about environmental change.

Thus, the concept of education permeates most therapeutic models. However, the delivery systems of therapeutic services emphasize "treatment" rather than education, so that they are offered in clinics, or even when offered by agencies or centers they involve diagnosis, treatment plan, case histories and similar medical concepts. This is unfortunate for all persons seeking help who must place themselves in a sick role to receive it, but it is particularly pernicious in black communities where the negative image held by the larger society is merely accentuated by the stigma associated with receiving services from treatment-oriented centers. The development of educational centers seems a particularly good move, then, from the standpoint of black communities.

Torrey has provided perhaps the most definitive plan for changing existing health and welfare systems into educational systems. He proposes a new umbrella designation of "behavioral scientist" to identify persons who would do all the jobs currently being performed by social workers, psychiatrists, clinical psychologists, applied anthropologists, and a variety of other applied behavioral science disciplines.[5] The work settings would be very broad and might include everything from community retreats to child-care centers to urban institutes. These experts in human behavior would assist individuals, groups, or total communities either in places called Institutes for Human Problems or private offices where people could contract to come and get tutoring. Most importantly, these behavioral scientists would specialize in particular problem areas so that there would be no question as to the nature of his or her competence. Furthermore, groups of behavioral scientists might practice together so that a wide range of problems— marriage problems, sexual problems, alcoholism, drug addiction, depression, etc.—could be handled in a single location. Torrey explains:

> To show how such an expert would differ from the psychiatrists, psychologists, anthropologists, sociologists or social workers who presently exist, let us take sexual problems as an example. A real behavioral scientist in this field would be an expert on such things as how people express sexual feel-

ings and achieve sexual satisfaction, how this is done in other cultures, the effects of pornography, and how sex education should be taught. Included in the person's training would have been the study of research findings on sexual problems and experiences working with individuals with such problems. The result would be a behavioral scientist who was an expert in this field. No such person presently exists for a handful who are self-taught.[6]

Torrey also has ideas about the relationship which should exist between the problem specialists and those parts of society where the problem is likely to surface:

It is estimated that up to 90% of calls for police service do not involve violations of laws but rather problems of living. These calls typically include such things as domestic arguments, runaway children and complaints of bizarre behavior by neighbors. Furthermore, one-half of all arrests are for drunkenness, disorderly conduct, gambling, vagrancy, and minor sexual violations. Many of these calls could be referred to a behavioral scientist when they do not involve a violation of the law. The end result might be a group of behavioral scientists who operate out of a human service center and respond to such calls. They might be likened to meter maids for human problems except that they would not be under the jurisdiction of the police. And law enforcement officials consequently would be freed to respond only to those cases in which a law has been violated.[7]

Torrey does not deal with the basic issues of financing the new system, which perhaps reflects a basic reason why so much social planning fails to meet the needs of black communities. That is, there is a tendency for planners to develop plans without consideration of the basic realities of lives they never encounter, and the majority of whites in this country have little understanding of the exigencies of black existence. Certainly, it is admirable to assume that the market function will permit all who need services to purchase them and those services that are inadequate or ineffective will disappear accordingly through disuse. The idea that blacks possess sufficient income after basic maintenance needs are met to purchase services for which they themselves may perceive no need is untenable. At the same time, the prospect of the availability of educational-type service to deal with specific problems in living is tantalizing enough to consider how such services *might* be financed.

The difficulty in providing services required by most people unable to afford them can be discerned in the operations of three major service systems: the health care system, the employment system, and the educational system. The health care available to the poor is patently of poorer quality (primarily by doctors in training), limited in scope (certain surgical procedures are denied if the patient is unable to pay), and made oppressive and burdensome by myriad bureaucratic procedures designed to assure the taxpaying public that their monies are not going to "undeserving" people. This situation in health care delivery is supported by the American Medical Association, whose representatives have made clear that health care is not a "right" and that those who can afford better care will get better care. The same kind of separate and unequal system exists in employment counseling. State departments charged with assisting the unemployed find jobs are primarily serving low-income and minority clientele. Private employment agencies would perceive any attempt to make services available through the state agency on a basis of ability to pay as an infringement on the private enterprise system; yet there is no question that the stigma attached to not having a job in a society where the work ethic prevails would be considerably lessened when the jobless poor were recipients of the same services provided through the same agency structure as to middle-class engineers, management consultants, and insurance salesmen. Even the educational system, which is supposedly public and equal regardless of whether located in poor or wealthy school districts, in reality operates differentially and to the disadvantage of poor and black students. The possibility then of providing educational services to all persons who need them, regardless of ability to pay and in a manner consistent with the unique life styles that exist in the ethnosystem, seems hardly feasible if experience with the other systems mentioned is an indicator. However, certain factors would suggest that in actuality such a system might indeed by feasible.

There is a crisis in existing systems which makes for a propitious time to introduce change. Almost no one will support the status quo in any of the major service systems—health, education, or welfare—as their deficiencies have become blatant and oppressive even beyond their respective consumer constituencies. Simultaneously, in black communities there is a growing awareness at the grassroots level of citizen power to demand change and a growing expertise among black professionals as to the most effective strategies for achieving that change. What is missing is the organizational commitment to a clearly defined set of goals. It may well be that the transformation of existing social and psychological services in black communities into an educational framework may not only be a reasonable goal but that such a transformation may skip over the boundaries of black communities to take hold in the larger ethnosystem.

In regards to funding such systems, the provision of funds for the purchase of services is not really an adequate beginning. There is a long history of inaccessible, inadequate or ineffective services, so that there is no tradition of hope supporting utilization of helping services in black communities. We have the frustrating paradox that under the present system blacks are constantly being referred for services with sanctions imposed by social control systems (e.g., to conform to requirements of probation, to prevent expulsion of a child from school, or to prevent a child from being removed from the home by welfare authorities), but the services are ineffective and often irrelevant. On the other hand, if the services are thrown into the market place, past experiences may preclude blacks from making use of potentially effective services. It is obvious that what is needed is a network of problem-focused learning centers which provide services to any who request them, on a sliding fee scale according to ability to pay. Referrals may still be made by the social control system, and if individuals or families fall below an income level which permits full payment of fees required to sustain services, the difference can be made up by subsidies in much the same way that government subsidizes housing, mental health services, and educational services.

Reid suggests that a voucher system rather than a subsidy system would be preferable in any effort to reform the service monopolies in the current delivery system.[8] In effect, the purchase of services would be made by the consumers themselves in the open market, even if referred under threat of sanctions by a social control agency. The referring agency would provide vouchers which would then be given to service agencies in return for the problem-solving services. They would not be confined to an agency particularly identified as serving the poor or minority client. They could shop for services wherever available. It stands to reason, however, that services located in black communities would be most likely to have professional practitioners knowledgeable about the life styles and unique pressures experienced by people living in those communities. On the other hand, if agencies outside the community were perceived to have more effective practitioners, there would be no obstacle to seeking them out.

It is clear that there are still problems which need to be anticipated in designing the learning centers where problem-solving is to occur. One could expect, for example, that effective practitioners could command higher fees in wealthy communities and therefore very few would choose to practice in poor communities. Certainly, the absence of psychiatrists in poor communities and their high incidence in affluent communities would appear to attest to this fact. However, it should be realized that psychiatrists have generally been more effective in affluent communities since their interventive strategies were in fact designed with middle- and upper-class persons in mind.

On the other hand, the stranglehold the professions have over the problem-solving enterprise would be reduced by the shift in emphasis from referrals to a psychiatrist, psychologist or social worker to referrals for help with alcoholism, marital problems, or child-parent problems. Thus, the professional identity would have less attraction than a reputation for competence and success. Although the possibility of earning higher fees might determine the locus of some professionals, it is even more likely that professionals who know a given community will experience a higher success rate working in that community which will provide incentive to remain rather than risk a low success rate in a more unfamiliar community setting. Furthermore, it stands to reason that in communities where the incidence of problem behavior is higher, the possibility of stable employment for an adequate practitioner is high.

Of course, if the business and industrial segment of our social system is any model of marketing relationship between producers and consumers, it is a foregone conclusion that the marketing system alone is not sufficient to insure quality services. The recent impetus in the consumer movement has come about exactly because consumers have been seduced into accepting shoddy merchandise, questionable services, and coming back again and again for more. It will certainly be important to develop accountability systems that will serve to assess the extent to which helping practitioners achieve results in their efforts to assist with problems of living. This is not asking that impossible promises to reduce welfare rolls, eliminate delinquency, cure the mentally ill or educate the poor will be required. Newman and Turem have described the parameters of accountability:

> Not all outputs have to be successful nor must all interventions be measured and be statistically and methodologically precise. The concern is with accountability in a political environment in which reasonable men do not require anything resembling perfection. In vocational rehabilitation, for ex-

ample, many cases are closed without attaining success. Yet a preponderance of cases are closed with a claim that clients were rehabilitated since many can be accounted for in addition to those able to meet program objectives. But these are questions of efficiency, which is but one component of accountability. In governmental policy-making it is recognized that reasonable levels of success and a reporting system that retrieves most of what actually occurs are "good enough."[9]

Perhaps the most attractive aspect of this model of service delivery—after its potential for reducing stigma attached to receiving services and the likelihood that services will be both more accessible and more relevant—is that the transformation of existing agencies for delivery of the service model would not be too difficult. Most social agencies would merely have to define more clearly the problems with which their staff is able to deal (e.g., "family agencies" identify the client system but not the target problems), and then reconstitute itself as group practice of essentially autonomous professionals, each of whom is responsible for developing his own reputation for competence. Supportive staff—secretaries, bookkeepers, etc.—would be paid by equal contributions from each practitioner associated with the agency. Less energy would be devoted to the demeaning task of proposal writing to generate funding for ongoing service efforts under the guise of "something special." The fee for service could be set in conjunction with similar agencies and private practitioners as well as the governmental bodies, providing the vouchers to those unable to pay or subsidizing those unable to pay the full amount. The procedure for payment should reduce any possibility that a distinction can be made by consumers or practitioners between those "on voucher" and those paying their own way. The situation that exists with food stamps, in which recipients shop long distances from their neighborhoods to avoid the embarrassment of presenting food stamps in full view of neighbors, should not be duplicated in procedures set up for presenting vouchers for service.

CHURCH-FOCUSED SERVICE SYSTEM
The key to this approach to the delivery of services within black communities lies in the distinction between church-focused and religious or sectarian services. It is a distinction that emerges out of the different experiences of black Americans and white Americans in regard to the significance of religious institutions. It may appear that to call for church-focused services is a regressive leap to the past ascendancy of superstition over logic, of mythology over science. However, the church has since slavery been a far more pervasive influence in black communities encompassing issues beyond salvation and sin all the way to politics and economic development. It is not surprising then that Martin Luther King, Bayard Rustin, Jesse Jackson, and a myriad other black leaders emerged out of religious backgrounds. Despite some erosion in religious commitment when younger generation of blacks is compared with middle-aged and older blacks, the fact remains that the church is the most stable, far-reaching and resourceful organization in black communities.

Catholic, Jewish, and Protestant faiths have developed over the years substantial service organizations of their membership as well as for others in their communities. Catholic, Jewish and Protestant groups have developed schools, hospitals and clinics, family agencies, residential treatment centers for children, adoption services and recreational services. Yet these systems have been no more sensitive to needs in black communities than public agencies or private agencies under secular auspices. Despite substantial proportions of blacks who drift into traditional religious denominations dominated by whites, there is evidence to support the notion that a substantial number of blacks are located in nontraditional religious groups and that some of these groups have access to low-income and black persons to an extent no outsider could achieve.

The establishment of church-related organizations has precedence in black communities, as day-care centers, thrift shops, and even mortuaries are presently sponsored by traditional and nontraditional religious groups. The establishment of one or more practitioners to assist members and non-members of the congregation with problems of living would at first glance appear to threaten the role of the minister, who is viewed by many in the congregation as the fount of all wisdom. However, it is this very strong belief in the minister that will make his sanction of the helping enterprise acceptable to the congregation. Certainly, this can be enhanced by the usual opportunity afforded for "announcements"—written and verbally in Sunday services—in most black churches. Even more in keeping with the cultural style of these churches, as part of the regular church services, would be the utilization of "testimonials" from satisfied service users. Simple expressions of how helpful the human service organization sponsored by the church had been to them in dealing with a specified problem will encourage its use by others. Donations specifically for the organization can be requested from the congregation. However, the major support should come from nominal fees according to ability to pay and the subsidy or voucher system for clients who need it. The support could be further enhanced by the fund-raising activities of traditional church organizations (e.g., missionary societies, choirs, etc.) which might substantially reduce any large amounts of spending necessary to maintain the services. Thus, persons with employment problems, child-parent problems, transportation problems, or housing problems might go more easily to a church-related help system than to a traditional agency designed to meet needs that are not his own. It might also be possible for smaller churches to combine in a consortium arrangement by which all would sponsor the agency and share the costs. We know, of course, that many people in black communities hold no allegiance to any religious organization, but existing agencies would be available to those who preferred a secular sponsored service. The significance of the "Trouble Centers" concept is that it might be able to reach or attract vast numbers of persons who would not be attracted by more traditional approaches. Furthermore, the generic "trouble center" loses its impersonality and alien feeling emanating from most bureaucratic organizational structures, and they will most likely be identified as "True Light Trouble Center," "St. James Trouble Center," or "Southside Trouble Center of the Holiness Church"; thus identifying their auspices and their connection in the life of the community.

The support system provided by money from both church and public would make it economically feasible to render some major modifications in the kind of services provided by Trouble Centers. For example, there might be a telephone "hot line" over which callers could arrange for home visits by counselors if they preferred greater anonymity than that provided by a visit to the Trouble Center; group sessions could be held in homes in the community, to emphasize normality rather than pathology requiring institutional attention. In addition, radio could be used to publicize the centers' programs in much the same way that church services are currently broadcast by churches in black communities. The format, however, would be more effective in a radio talk show in which people could call in for information about problems, and testimonials could again be incorporated.

Despite the fact that considerable attention is given to mass media in black communities—particularly community-directed radio stations, daytime television, confession magazines, etc., very little has been done to utilize these media toward the end of personal and social development in the community. As it now stands there is very little in terms of positive self-image or realistic view of the world to be gained from close attention to these particular forms of mass media. In the 1940s Herzog conducted a classic study of soap opera listeners and discovered that three primary kinds of gratification were received from listening: emotional release, opportunities for wishful thinking, and sources of advice.[10] The advice may even be more important now, as growing complexity and transience in society have reduced the socializing effect of older relatives and stable institutions to an extent that, for many persons in our crowded urban areas, the media is the source of information about what is appropriate behavior for oneself as well as for others. In 1973, Kinzer wrote the following about daytime soap operas which are so popular in black communities:

> . . . the immense popularity of the soaps is a complex affair. While their lusty plots titillate fans' daydreams, their chaos and affliction make the viewer's dull life seem well-ordered and safe by comparison. On *General Hospital,* for example, out of 17 major characters there were four divorces, two premarital pregnancies, four illicit affairs, two male drug addicts, one male alcoholic, one male amnesiac, one male in prison, and one female incarcerated in a mental hospital. Ethnics such as Chicanos, Hungarians, Greeks or Czechs don't appear on the afternoon soaps . . . *Somerset* has two blacks: one is a kind, intelligent lady lawyer, and the other is a gentlemanly crook, now reformed. Both are in the genre of the superblack Sidney Poitier. The soaps do not tackle problems of race prejudice or exclusionary clauses in country clubs; that's for the evening news. Sin is the serious business of the afternoon.[11]

Kilguss perceives soap opera involvement as a depressive, repetitive attempt to master the pain and impulses of life but agrees that this is a personal opinion which can only be corroborated or refuted by future research.[12] However, this does not mean that practitioners must wait to make an effort to use such media forms in a more constructive manner; i.e., in keeping with what we know about healthy interpersonal relationships and effective crisis resolution. Thus, in addition to radio talk shows, it might be possible to develop a daytime serial based on problem situations arising in Trouble Centers which effectively portray the work of the centers with all the rich drama attendant to problems arising out of the human condition. The one-shot documentary or short series would be less expensive to produce and therefore more feasible. At the same time, another media form could be represented in a con-

fession-type magazine based on Trouble Center cases (effectively disguised to assure confidentiality, which could be
published and distributed in beauty parlors, churches,
supermarkets, etc. The important idea would be to use this
method of familiarizing the community with the kind of services
offered, as well as entertainment. It is the latter which is so
foreign to our usual delivery systems—who could call "trouble"
entertainment? Yet it is perfectly apparent from the millions of
persons who view or read about the troubles of others that it is
entertainment in the same way that Shakespeare's *Hamlet,* Ten-
nessee Williams' *A Streetcar Named Desire,* or Cassavetes'
Woman Under the Influence are at the same time huge caul-
drons of trouble yet masterful entertainment.

Clearly, there are some high risks attendant to this type of
delivery system based on problems already existing in the
"home base," i.e., the black church. Although it is the most
ubiquitous organization with a long history of total involvement
in the life of the community, it is also notorious for its authoritarian administration (the minister is in many instances the supreme authority, ruling without constraint), occasional exposés
of corruption in its leadership, internecine warfare among rival
subsystems, and the fact that it often exploits the working and
lower classes, who comprise a majority of the membership, in a
manner that only perpetuates their poverty. Thus, there must
be some built-in mechanisms to avoid insofar as possible the
operation of these negative forces in the development of Trouble Centers. Certainly, the requirement that staff must be
trained in order to qualify for voucher payment could reduce
the likelihood that the Center staff will be made up of the minister's wife and various and sundry other relatives and hangers-
on. Furthermore, the necessary accountability regarding public
monies should also be a constraining force. Newman and
Turem have described the kind of requirements which would
be imposed:

> The system should produce sufficient information to provide
> a record for audit showing that the funds were spent hon-

estly. After that the question of how much one wishes to know to evaluate the program can vary widely. The minimum then is an acceptable fiscal reporting system and a management information system covering program data.[13]

In the long run, however, the most effective way to insure quality service is not through negative sanctions but through positive rewards—particularly to the church leadership, which must cooperate and provide the initiative to develop the Trouble Center network. Possible rewards include frequent publicity, additional membership and therefore additional income to the church, and increased community prestige. These rewards may then be sufficient to compensate for the limited control the church leadership would wield in the board of directors of the Trouble Center and thereby limit its power to direct its operations.

THE COMMUNITY-BASED WELFARE SYSTEM
The two service delivery systems discussed so far have given no attention to any collective assault on major social problems experienced in black communities. An individual or family which turns to a Learning Center or Trouble Center for help may well be victims of larger social institutions, but each presenting problem is worked on as a single entity and not on the basis of its similarity to an entire class of problems produced by oppressive social structures. This does not mean that the practitioner who provides help may not become advocate for the individual or even assist the individual in joining with others, experiencing the same frustration with organizational systems in order to bring about change. Yet there does appear to be a need to deal with the nature of interventions that would go directly to the problem of dysfunctional social institutions.

The programs of the Great Society—particularly the War on Poverty programs—embodied the concept of basic change in the service system to reduce major problems relating to health, poverty, child care, vocational rehabilitation, etc. Moreover, these changes were to occur through the collective involvement of the poor, the minority person, the very people whom the system had alienated and excluded. Yet, after a decade with no dramatic or even modest decrease in most social indicators of distress in inner cities, it was possible for the Nixon administration to declare the War on Poverty a failure and justify devastating reductions in the services generated by that program. In essence, the strategy had been to make funds available to community groups for programs that would be comprehensive enough and involve enough existing organizational systems to make an impact on the problem. Unfortunately, it did not afford community groups enough *power* to do much more than tinker with the status quo—certainly the radical surgery needed to bring about change in intransigent, unresponsive agencies permeated with racist policies and procedures.

The essential system in the current oppressive arrangement is undoubtedly the welfare system. It is the system charged with providing basic maintenance to individuals or families in dire need. Apparently, however, there has been little recognition that the economic system does not provide work for all who want to work, but at the same time there appears to be a subtle message implanted in the operation of the welfare system that those who cannot work are necessarily inferior and their laziness or lack of motivation will only be intensified if the system treats them humanely and with preservation of their dignity and individuality.

Gottschalk has described in great detail an alternative to the welfare system, which is in fact an attempt to deal with problems that have multiple causes, by implementing a multifaceted organizational structure.[14] Even more so, it rejects the notion of an "ideal" welfare system, since in a truly humanistic society with suitable values there should be no need for a formal, bureaucratically designed welfare system. The service delivery model suggested by Gottschalk would be at least superficially compatible with the existing system in order to receive support for the experimentation. However, the goal of the experimentation is actually to create an alternative system in which participants can "gain maximal control of their lives and share in an experience of communal reconstruction." To achieve this, the model seeks to (1) expand the local economy and increase in a multiplier effect economic inputs into the community; (2) create structures that enhance social interaction and mutual aid; (3) promote economic and political integration of the community; (4) build the self-worth of individuals by engaging their energies and talents for the benefits of others. Not emphasized at all is the shopworn cliché of the current system, e.g., assisting individuals to return to self-supporting status. That emphasis is on the individual as an atomized fragment, an adversary of all other individuals in the struggle to survive. Gottschalk's stated objectives emphasize the mutual assistance of people in a common boat, the collective spirit.

The administrative context of Gottschalk's community-based welfare system would be the Community Development Corporation (CDC). The latter part of the 1960s witnessed the emergence of organizations funded in most cases by federal Office of Economic Opportunity (OEO), Model Cities, or Small Business Administration moneys with much smaller contributions from foundations and private industrial concerns. These community development organizations or corporations, once in operation, are concerned with the comprehensive planning for economic improvement in the community. This may mean lending or guaranteeing loans to individual businessmen; purchasing a share of the equity in partnership with individual businessmen; taking the role of landlord by securing land based on their nonprofit, community support status and leasing it to an individual or a small black-owned business; or they may own and operate their own enterprises. Puryear and West suggest that:

> The ability to raise funds gave the (CDC) one of its relative strengths and becomes a prime operating objective. . . .

Through community stock sales they can tap equity money
from local residents who have small savings and the desire to
participate in self-help efforts. They also have the ability to
draw capital from outside sources and convert it into capital
under community control. Because they are broad-based,
have social objectives, and are not usually organizations of a
small number of businessmen who stand to make private
profits [CDCs] become politically legitimate vehicles through
which foundations, government agencies, and private donors
can make contributions of capital.[15]

The heart of Gottschalk's proposal is that a CDC which has
been established in an urban area would in addition operate a
welfare program through an affiliate which would be termed
"Community Corporation," or CIC. Thus, the CDC would
operate the welfare program through this CIC affiliate, which
would be connected to the existing welfare system, at least initially. However, the term "welfare" may be a misnomer, since
Gottschalk's program bears little resemblance to its traditional
namesake:

The CDC would operate the welfare program through its CIC
affiliate, much as it might conduct any other business enterprise, producing services, marketing its products, and paying wages. It would operationally and financially integrate its
social welfare enterprises with its industrial and commercial
enterprises, thus creating a vital link among a multiplicity of
sectors of the local economy. Welfare is thus viewed as an industry which is to be managed as such. Its product is not only
healthy, creative, and happy individuals but also a strong viable community. The CIC would contract with a welfare department for the total support and provision of social services to
about four caseloads or 300 families. Under this contract, a
sum equal to the total assistance service and administrative
costs of four average caseloads would be transferred on a
regular basis to the CIC account. The contract should be for
an extended period of time, i.e. several years, for a fixed sum,
with allowance for the possibility of "cost overruns" resulting
from increases in the cost of living. Individual recipients and
families residing in the CIC area would be invited to enroll on

a voluntary basis. A special effort should be made, however, to get a mixed caseload including all categories of recipients. At least initially and perhaps for the duration, two competitive welfare systems would be operating in the same geographic area. Upon joining, recipients would be invited to become shareholders in the CIC, each entitled to one vote at the annual and special meetings of the corporation. In addition, each would be enrolled as an employee of the corporation and entitled to a guaranteed wage at least equal to his or her former welfare entitlement. By becoming an employee of the CIC, each former recipient contracts with the corporation for the performance of defined, communally beneficial tasks. From the beginning, the principal should be firmly established that child-rearing and caring for the sick and aged are highly valued and important types of work for which wages are paid. Other types of work would include neighborhood cleanup, snow removal, neighborhood park creation, studying or job training, tutoring, block-club organization and so on. Whereas mothers of young children would be paid to care for their own children, they need not be restricted to this type of employment; other types of work would also be available to them. Aged and handicapped persons would be offered duties conforming to their interests and capacities. Some might answer telephones; others might visit the sick. Some might be employed by the community to sit on park benches and smile at passersby, to watch children at play or to help ensure public safety. In sum, all or nearly all participants are employees performing useful and valued work for which they receive a salary. The category of totally disabled and dependent adults would be reduced to a small fraction of the whole if not entirely eliminated.[16]

In addition, the new sponsorship and new status of "employees" rather than "recipients" generate some radical departures from traditional welfare programs for those enrolled. They are now partners in a corporation with important roles to perform. Furthermore, administrative and social service staff hired to enhance the social functioning of "partners," in the same way that accountants or management consultants are hired to promote higher profits for shareholders in a business

enterprise. Gottschalk suggests that former recipients who become staff employees or who engage in work that produces
public goods or services that benefit the general welfare, such
as playground employees, school crossing guards, and teacher
aides would be entitled to "second salaries" to supplement
their guaranteed incomes. However, this still appears to retain
the differentiation of salaries and grants; i.e., charity, with the
expectation that *all* "partners" would make a contribution that
could be classified as "work." Under these circumstances, it
would be preferable to think in terms of a range of jobs available through the corporation—from friendly visiting or child-
watching to secretary or teacher aide.

The major source of the higher level jobs would be not only
within the business enterprises of the Community Development
Corporation but perhaps through job contracts negotiated with
a variety of private commercial and industrial enterprises doing
business in the community. In essence, the former recipient of
traditional public welfare services would elect to move over
into a system which guarantees him or her a job that would
never pay less than a welfare grant but could in fact pay a great
deal more if he has skills or receives training or education to
prepare for higher level jobs. The ability of the Community Development Corporation to generate jobs is enhanced, according to Gottschalk, by the fact that through its CIC affiliate there
will be a steady and reliable flow of income and therefore a
basis for the establishment of a substantial line of credit. Development goes where credit goes, and it would be possible to
use this newly available credit not only in CDC's enterprises but
in providing credit to small, independent businessmen in the
local community and thereby creating additional employment
opportunities.

There is an obvious need for various social programs to provide a support system for the CDC and its entrprises; e.g.,
manpower training programs, day-care programs for children
of working parents, vocational rehabilitation services, etc.
Gottschalk suggests that a maximum adequate salary scale for

members of the CIC be determined; all members would be encouraged to reach the maximum, after which excess earnings would revert to the CIC for such support programs or community programs as described above. Gottschalk admits that some partners might choose to resign from the corporation when their income reaches the maximum adequate level and any additional earnings would have to go into the communal pot:

> This should be their right, though of course it would not be encouraged and the corporation would of course not retain such persons on their payrolls. The success of the system is to be measured primarily in terms of the greater communal and individual satisfaction of its members which is assumed that with time, these satisfactions will be increasingly recognized as being more than material ones.[17]

In moving from utopian planning to pragmatic reality as it relates to CIC as a creation of CDCs, the problems inherent in business enterprises in black communities cannot be overlooked. The highly sophisticated conceptualization involving shareholding, definition of occupational roles, policymaking regarding personnel and hiring practices, etc., suggests the need for highly skilled leadership in this type of complicated, multidimensional organizational design. Yet such leadership has not been found frequently in black communities. It is not a matter of the intelligence or commitment of persons anxious to bring about major social change but it is a matter of knowledge and skills relating to complex business arrangements made even more complex by cultural constraints unique to black communities. For example, a CDC located in a black community in a small Southern city (approx. 100,000 persons) decided to develop a supermarket. This venture was a direct outgrowth of the expressed desires of neighborhood councils which had operated a food cooperative that had been successful in helping poor residents save on food costs. It was therefore assumed that the supermarket would succeed automatically because of the expected community participation. Advertising, promotion, and publicity were all keyed to that strategy. Despite these plans, patronage was slow in developing and some fraction of what community support existed came, not from the low-income black people of the community but from relatively affluent, liberal whites. Much concern was rightly generated over this situation and it was found that to some extent the problems of the supermarket stemmed from preexisting and more widespread attitudes. For example, the following statements from black residents represent powerful feelings: "If it's run by blacks, it can't be as good"; "If it's a low-income supermarket, then the prices should be lower"; "I'm not a low-income person—why should I shop in a store for low-income people?" Pervasive and deeply rooted feelings must be changed if the supermarket is going to succeed, and this will not happen overnight.

As pointed out earlier, a program such as Gottschalk's may not be feasible in every black community. However, Warren has identified some sharply definitive indicators by which feasibility can be judged.[18] He discusses the criticisms which have been made of the CDC approach, centered around the failures of CDCs where implemented to prove themselves a viable solution to economic development problems in black ghettos. Not only has there been confusion of goals from the perspective of these critics but the social and economic goals most often advanced may actually be incompatible—or at least they cannot be achieved simultaneously in the beginning. Warren suggests, however, that the primary determinant of whether the CDC approach is viable for a given black community will depend upon the degree of homogeneity or heterogeneity of that community. Homogeneous black communities hold more real promise for success of a CDC-type approach, due to the similar educational and socioeconomic level of the residents. Most importantly, in homogeneous neighborhoods, existing leaders and their groups appear more effectively interlocked with "the capacity . . . to draw upon outside expertise and yet to retain the credibility of indigenous formal and informal structurees."

SUMMARY

This chapter has challenged the concept of a service delivery "system" in the United States and discussed some of the reasons that the unresponsive and fragmented "nonsystem" of services tends to persist—for example, the bureaucratization of service organizations with a resulting need to "standardize" procedures; the preoccupation with person variables rather than system variables in identifying causal forces in the etiology and maintenance of individual problems; and the failure of organizations in black communities to form a power base from which social action to modify the institutional arrangements of service delivery could be launched.

The remainder of the chapter described three comprehensive programs which have potential for reducing powerlessness of people in black communities: social learning centers; church-focused "Trouble Centers"; and a community-based welfare system. Each of these service delivery models represents a general design which could be modified and specified to meet the needs of a given community.

epilogue

social futurism in black communities

It may appear foolhardy for black communities still trying to get in touch with a past that has been distorted and hidden to place too much emotional and cognitive energy in an effort to capture the future. Yet Toffler, in explaining the significance of *Future Shock,* may have presented the most cogent rationale for looking into the future: "Previously, men studied the past to shed light on the present. I have turned the time-mirror around, convinced that a coherent image of the future can also shower us with valuable insights into today. We shall find it increasingly difficult to understand our personal and public problems without making use of the future as an intellectual tool." [1]

Certainly one of the frustrations for practitioners serving present-day black communities is the lack of connection between the pulsating rhetoric ticking off the relationship between past oppression and present plight and a coherent strategy for substantially ameliorating that plight. The past has not always been pretty, but neither has it been without its victory and transcendence. The capacity of blacks to survive tremendous suffering and hardship is well documented. The fact that they should *have* to endure is intolerable. The overwhelming pressure on the helping practitioner is to help alleviate the pain and hardship and make it unnecessary for black communities to endure it any longer. Yet, their power to achieve this goal appears unalterably weak and ineffectual. In the previous chapters of this book, an attempt has been made to uncover the past, describe the present, and suggest the future in terms of human services in black communities. It may well be that the present weakness of helping professions is due to past inability to anticipate today. The liberals' battles for separate social services after the Civil War (instead of no services at all) made possible a proliferation of separate and unequal service delivery systems that only in the past decade have substantially crumbled; efforts to sensitize the nation to the immense problems of the ghetto—its apathetic people, rampant drug abuse, serious health problems, low educational achievement, etc., have served to justify the fears of white parents to have their children bussed into ghetto schools or ghetto children bussed into their schools. The whole struggle to achieve desegregation of schools failed to anticipate the effect on traditions, community spirit, and sense of identity generated by schools in black communities, and as a result in many instances has led to increased alienation and fragmentation. It is imperative that such mistakes be avoided as we plan today for tomorrow.

There is a tendency to accept the fact that no one—except shamans and astrologers and other varieties of fortunetellers—can pretend to know what the future holds for us. Yet there is even growing evidence that we have sensory capabilities of which we are ignorant and which function in some of us to an extent that is unbelievable to the rest of us. That kind of extrasensory perception is not an issue here. What is at issue is the need for "a new level of competence in the management of change," which involves planners with techniques for developing a sensitive set of indicators that can measure the direction of change under various conditions. These planners would not be in the mold of present-day technocratic planners who are usually remote, undemocratic, unresponsive to local community needs, and slow to respond to evidence of changed conditions. The new breed of planner—more humanistic, more far-sighted and more democratic—must emerge out of what Toffler describes as post-industrial society.

> Every society faces not merely a succession of *probable* futures, but an array of *possible* futures, and a conflict over *preferable* futures. The management of change is the effort to convert certain *possibles* into *probables,* in pursuit of agreed-on preferables. Determining the probable calls for a science of futurism. Delineating the possible calls for an art of futurism. Defining the preferable calls for a politics of futurism.[2]

Determining the probable, delineating the possible, and defining the preferable are important tasks for those practitioners serving black communities. Meinert contends that social work education and practice have given considerable attention to social planning and the knowledge it requires, but they have ignored the methods available for making reasonable conjectures about social future.[3] He describes four forecasting techniques which have potential usefulness for social planning in general and which can easily be adapted to black communities.

Extrapolation involves the analysis of current events, assuming them to be a reasonable model for future events and making forecasts about the future on that basis. This is a risky method of forecasting, depending largely on the extent to which the system's framework has been utilized to insure that interrelated phenomena creating reverberations through multiple systems—political, economic, family, etc.—will be analyzed in terms of these dynamic interrelationships.

The Delphi approach estimates of future conditions are arrived at by polling experts in a systematic way, allowing sequential forecasts as information about group responses are fed back to each expert, who is permitted to change an estimate on the basis of the new evidence. Essentially the final forecast represents an estimate based on expert opinion and intuition and developed out of a collective judgment process.

Simulation refers to a process in which (1) an object or physical model (2) represents an actual system or system part (3) possesses the capability of being manipulated and (4) contains the essence of reality in the manipulation process. Simulations are extremely difficult to design and operate due to the kind of complex variables that make up human systems; but if done, it is possible to compress time and to determine how the system would behave in the future.

Finally, scenario speculation involves making an assumption about some social condition and then logically predict events likely to occur because of it. For example, it could be assumed that a community-based welfare system is actually adopted and then forecasts could be made as to the nature of family life styles, housing patterns, attitudes toward work, child-rearing practices, consumer spending patterns, neighborhood interpersonal relationships, or patterns of voluntary association. Certainly one of the major problems in using scenario speculation as a technique for forecasting the future is determining what reasonable assumptions are possible. However, it has the advantage of expanding one's imagination in considering forecasts. Furthermore, it is appropriately used by an author without access to storehouses of data required for effective extrapolation, or to large numbers of experts who would be difficult to define, or to complex, sophisticated and comprehensive simulations of the American ethnosystem. The following forecasts are primarily scenario speculations whose validity is predicated to a large degree on the reasonableness of the basic assumptions.

THE CONFUSING PRESENT

It is no exaggeration to say that few blacks have clear notions as to whether they do or do not support racial integration, racial separation, community control, the Black Muslins, Rev. Ike, black language patterns, bussing to achieve school integration, the NAACP, the Urban League, black politicians, white politicians, black social workers, white social workers, black businessmen, white businessmen, Afro hair styles, negritude, the inherent superiority of black athletes, the inherent inferiority of all-black schools, the black church, black newspapers, Flip Wilson, Sidney Poitier, Good Times, etc. Of course, some of the lack of certainty can be attributed to the ambivalence created by living a bicultural existence—being simultaneously a member of the black community and a member of the larger ethnosystem. A vote of support or nonsupport for any of these abstractions or even specific individuals depends on a particular set of contingencies. Thus, depending on the context, positions may shift, allegiances change, or preferences wane in strength. Would it be impossible, then, to make predictions on the basis of such unsettled ideas and emotions? The answer, of course, is that you can make fairly accurate predictions, provided you know the context!

The context of change can be defined as the pattern of distribution for blacks on a set of variables which are determined to intervene between race or ethnicity and attitudes or behavior. For example, it is known that middle-income blacks are likely to differ from low-income blacks in a consistent direction in regard to support for community control of major social institutions and probably a ratio of middle- to low-income blacks, given analysis of current economic trends, is also known. It should be possible to use these pieces of knowledge to consider the likelihood of obtaining a given level of support in black communities for programs incorporating elements of community control. You may also be aware that age is another intervening variable, whith younger blacks and older whites more likely to support ideas of community control than older blacks and younger whites. Then, given the distribution of the two racial groups, controlling for age, who are registered voters and active in community power structures, it should be possible to modify projections made on knowledge of race and income level to provide a more accurate prediction of support level for programs of community control. It should be noted that the inputs described so far call for basically quantifiable data; numbers at a given income level, numbers registered to vote, numbers active in political office, serving on critical governmental and civic bodies, etc. However, other nonquantifiable variables may also be intervening to influence levels of support for programs of community control. Level of racial identity of blacks in a given area may be different but impossible to measure directly. Indicators, however, may be present in the level of participation in black-oriented organizations, number of subscribers to black community newspapers and black magazines, etc. Finally, other intervening variables may be even more difficult to measure even indirectly, such as charismatic potential of emerging black leaders, level of distrust by blacks of black enterprises, level of threat experienced by whites as a result of the notion of black control of major institutions serving black communities. Yet, some approximation should also be fed into the final estimate of the support level.

Clearly, even in scenario speculation there needs to be a broad perspective on transacting systems. There are probably also elements of extrapolation and even rudimentary simulation at the mental construct level, and hopefully some empirical monitoring of expert opinions, although nothing so sophisticated or elaborate as required in implementation of the Delphi technique. The challenge is to make an assumption about changing reality which appears to be clearly supportable, and then struggle with the implications of these changes in a dynamic ethnosystem of interrelated and emotionally vested subsystems.

There are assumptions that undergird the forecasts to be made here. These assumptions are to my mind fully warranted by overwhelming evidence in past and present human relationships and social processes; at the same time I recognize the defective mechanisms available to us in knowing the past or present. To quote Toffler again in regard to the use of data in speaking of the future:

> Where "hard data" are available, of course, they ought to be taken into account. But where they are lacking, the responsible writer—even the scientist—has both a right and an obligation to rely on other kinds of evidence, including impres-

sionistic or anecdotal data and the opinions of well-informed people. . . . In dealing with the future . . . it is more important to be imaginative and insightful than to be one hundred percent "right" . . . Even error has its uses. The maps of the world drawn by the medieval cartographers were so hopelessly inaccurate, so filled with factual error, that they elicit condescending smiles today when almost the entire surface of the earth has been charted. Yet the great explorers could never have discovered the New World without them. Nor could the better, more accurate maps of today been drawn until men, working with the limited evidence available to them, set down on paper their bold conceptions of world they had never seen.[4]

In this spirit, the following assumptions are deemed necessary to rationalize the emerging picture of a world—possible but yet to be seen.

THE ASSUMPTIONS
The Afro-American in the United States has a distinct cultural heritage which differentiates him from blacks in Africa or even from blacks in other parts of North and South America. The cultural ties that U.S. blacks have with Africa and all Third World peoples are real and resonant in the challenge to identify the sources of values, emotional styles, and patterns of relating that distinguish blacks from non-blacks. Yet, from the standpoint of the practitioner who must deal with the concrete rather than the abstract, with the everyday extremely personal issues rather than with philosophical and global issues, the relationship between the black ghetto resident and his white landlord, or militant son, or harried welfare worker are the stuff of which relevance is forged. Thus, an assumption on which forecasting the future of black communities in this country must inevitably rest is that it will be determined by what's going on in Harlem and Boston, Savannah and Galveston, Denver and Fresno, and only remotely with the happenings in Nairobi or Port-au-Prince. This is not to de-emphasize the cultural

brotherhood of blacks over the world but to emphasize instead
the pragmatic reality of black Americans as similar in some respects, but very different in many crucial respects, to blacks
anywhere else. The need to assume the special nature of Afro-
Americans in the United States can be discerned in Szwed's
description of Afro-American diversity:

> Peoples of African heritage can also be found in the most
> southern parts of South America, in Colombia and Ecuador,
> on the northern Atlantic coast of South America, in Central
> America and Mexico, in the French Caribbean island of Mar-
> tinique and Guadeloupe, in the "Spanish" islands of Cuba,
> Puerto Rico, and the Dominican Republic, in the black Re-
> public of Haiti, in the Great Plains and maritime provinces of
> Canada, and in all the cities of the New World from Punta
> Arenas, Chile, to St. John's, Newfoundland; they are found
> high in the Andes, on desert slopes, in rain forests, in temper-
> ate farmlands, and in crowded urban areas; they live in mod-
> ern company plantations, mining towns, isolated farmsteads,
> urban ghettos and suburbs, and in closed escaped slave com-
> munities in Jamaica, Mexico, Brazil, and the Guianas; and
> they represent every social and economic level from tribe,
> chiefdom, and peasantry to industrial proletariat, middle
> class, and elite. In short, Afro-Americans constitute an infi-
> nitely varying complex of cultural conditions, all of them re-
> sponsive to separate and differing natural and social environ-
> ments.[5]

Thus, the recognition that black communities are unique entities when compared to other communities in the American ethnosystem does not immediately place them in a category including all other blacks in the hemisphere or in the world. This
is a basic assumption to any forecasting that follows.

*The solution to major social problems currently devastating
black communities lies in the power blacks hold to create of
themselves a true collectivity in which the good of the whole is
the highest value held by the individual.* It is not easy to change
the attitudes welded by generations of black experience in
which mistrust of each other has poisoned myriad attempts to

overcome the hostility of the white man. Yet, for the generation of blacks who grew to maturity in the twenties and thirties it would have been difficult to conceive of the rise of black pride and black power as ideologies with the resulting new value placed on black identity. It would have seemed almost impossible that "bad" hair would become good and "good" hair no longer the requisite of beauty. In like manner, the foods which had been cheap and therefore the mainstay of diets in the ghetto were lifted to prominence and parties featured "chitterlings and champagne"—the dramatic symbolism of bicultural life styles. It may be difficult to conceive now of a time when blacks will not only trust other blacks but will be able to develop collective strength to create collective enterprises. The rhetoric, however, is not the reality, and there is a need to identify the forces in the community which suggest fulfillment of the promise that this mutual trust and togetherness will in fact evolve.

The old adage, "The grass is always greener on the other side of the fence," has been proved disconcertingly true to millions of black Americans who have in recent years been permitted in schools, on jobs, in neighborhoods with white Americans and discovered their own fantasies about the superiority of white culture, life styles or patterns of interpersonal behavior to be exaggerations and distortions of reality. A black teacher who had been caught up in the racist myth of white superiority was assigned to a white middle-class school in the first wave of integration effort and she recalls that the greatest impact on her was made when "middle and upper-class white children gave the *wrong* answer in those pear-shaped tones I had come to associate with everything that's *right* in the world." The reduction in the belief that "white is better" logically leads to a greater willingness to accept the fact that blacks may be equal or even better at a variety of tasks than whites. This is a vital requirement in the establishment of black enterprises requiring the collective action and consistent report of blacks.

Imamu Amiri Baraka (LeRoi Jones) has captured the essence

of the new sense of appreciation for black skills and the thrust for black togetherness in what he terms "a black value system." [6] It is composed of seven objectives—seven being a number of symbolic power: unity, self-determination, collective work and responsibility, cooperative economics, purpose, creativity, and faith. The articulation of these specific objectives represent a milestone in the black movement in the United States since these objectives permit the on-going evaluation of progress based on measures of the extent to which black communities give evidence of having achieved the objectives. In the same vein, *any* program or practices which create disunity, reduce the extent to which persons in black communities determine their own destinies, promote individualism (as opposed to individuality) and a "what's in it for me" attitude, dissipates the strength of purpose which has cultural development as its theme, or stifles creative alternatives to existing conditions can be considered negative, destructive and unacceptable.

Ironically, the blending of ideology and theology, as in the case of the Black Muslims, succeeds in doing the very thing that this value system warns against—the separation of blacks from each other based on the degree of adherence to the formalization of a "Black Nation" defined by a religion. The important thing to remember in regard to these seven objectives is that they are realized by specific *acts,* so that it is not even necessary to define *people* in terms of whether they are or are not *really* black or to exclude whites from the social intercourse in black communities. It is important, however, to define the behaviors of persons—black or white—on the basis of their consequences in regard to these stated objectives for black people so that it will be easy to determine those persons truly committed to the idea that this nation depends for its strength on citizens with strong identities, positive self-images, and active involvement in determining their destiny through the democratic process. No racial or ethnic group can compete effectively with others in the ethnosystem as long as it is regarded as inferior and subjected to discrimination and isolated from the decision-making process.

Thus it is in the best interests of the entire country for blacks to develop a strong cultural identity in order to create the collective strength to overcome racism and dicrimination. The integration that will come after this attainment will not be the cultural suicide of assimilation and loss of identity but the effective biculturalism which comes about only when the cultures are considered of *equal* significance, with no degeneration to the old superior-inferior dichotomy in reverse. Another basic assumption in our scenario of the future will be the existence of a strong cultural force in black communities generating in turn unity, cooperative economics, and the other components of the black value system.

SOME BEGINNING PROGNOSTICATIONS

Given the fact that blacks in the future will achieve a greater collective unity and that the nation, in order to overcome its unemployment problem, will define production in a much broader sense than heretofore, whites will take a new look at their own position in the ethnosystem. It will undoubtedly lead to the rising sense of threat felt by some whites in regard to their own continuing economic and social progress. In such a situation strange bedfellows emerge and the old designations of conservative and liberal, moderates and radicals become even less definitive of attitudes, behavior, and positions on racial and ethnic issues. The tendency toward growing importance of ethnicity among white groups as well blacks and other Third World peoples will continue, since it is in reality a segment of a larger social movement; it can best be defined as an attempt to reduce the effects of overwhelming size and distance which has produced alienation, social isolation, and normlessness to an intolerable extent. The smaller units of social relationships are gaining significance as we recognize the protection they provide against these debilitating social ills. Thus, the neighborhood is coming back "in style" rather than an attempt to identify with the urban megalopolis; and in like manner, it is more comforting to identify with the ethnic group than with the whole human race. Greer is bucking the emotional tide of millions who have gone the route of emphasis on our common humanity and been swept back by the inescapable pressure arising from our differences. Rather than ignore such differences in our desperate search for an unreal ideal, it would be far wiser to meet the reality of difference head-on and learn to manage it so that it works for us—like different instruments in a symphony orchestra—instead of against us.

It can be anticipated that whites will be drawing in from the painful barbs thrown by massive social systems—government and its Watergate, international industrial giants and their manipulations bringing rampant worldwide inflation, huge megastructures in the forms of domes and cylinders and pyramids which increase our sense of insignificance. There will be a struggle to achieve greater privacy, tighter circles on interpersonal relationships, closer linkages to decision-making systems achieved by limiting span of control to that determined to permit maximum access to delegated authorities.

The deliberate narrowing of perspective to more self-contained environments will increase the importance of knowledge about the social and psychological influences of the environment on man. The contemporary scene has witnessed an acceleration of concern about the physical environment and the dangers it holds for all of us from polluted air, polluted water, to the skyscrapers inadequate to withstand earthquakes or fires. However, there is still much to know about the interrelationship of these physical conditions in our environment and the achievement of psychological health or social goals. The depth of our ignorance is probably marked by the controversy over the effects of crowding on human beings. Whereas some research has shown that crowding leads to aggression and biological indicators thought to be indicative of high stress (Hutt and Vaizey, etc.), other researchers have found no such relationship (Draper, etc.), and still others have found aggression higher in *less* crowded situations (Loo, etc.).[7] Clearly, if there is a trend in society for people to have less mobility and greater identification with a given space, it is going to be much more important to understand the effects of a given environment on human behavior. There are indications that there are cultural differences in defining personal space as opposed to social space; that there is a difference in the effects of crowding when the density is in regard to family and friends as opposed to "stranger density." Certainly, in black communities where there has been little to feel positive about in the environment, there is a need for change. Walz, Willenbring and DeMoll propose that social workers develop closer working relationships with environmental designers to enhance social functioning of clients:

> Social workers—recognizing that identity, individuality, self-concept, affection, and self-determination are basic human needs—could begin to develop systemic ideas as to how these needs might be met for their clients through the design of environments. Identity needs, for example, could be met through physical designs that capture and incorporate the symbols, experiences, values, traditions of the subcultural group to be served. *Self-concept* needs could be met through environmental design that makes people feel more positive and more respected within their own society. Needs for *affection* could be met through layouts, spatial arrangements, and materials that encourage companionship and that envelop space in colors and textures eliciting positive emotional responses. *Self-determination* needs could be realized when the cultural symbols of both worker and client dominate the environments in which they live and work.[8]

Urban sociologists such as Gans have criticized the idea that change in physical environment will bring about change in attitudes or behavior and perceive in this notion an elitist bias. From Gans's perspective, a better physical environment will not eliminate poverty but will come about naturally when poverty is

eliminated.[9] Furthermore, people's lives are not significantly influenced by the neighborhoods in which they live, since the important aspects of life are carried on within the context of peer
group, and place of employment. There is much that appears to
be valid in Gans's warning not to overestimate the value of environmental change in changing negative social conditions,
particularly as environmental change has been practiced by
promoting urban renewal. However, a systems perspective
would reveal that these are not variables in a linear relationship
to each other; environment and behavior are mutually interact-
ing and their mutual effects must be included in the network of
interlocking relationships which constitute the causal nexus of
poverty and dysfunctional social behavior. Furthermore, the
even greater containment in a smaller environment that *all* will
be experiencing in the years to come make it imperative that
we understand the significance of environment in that causal
nexus in order to promote more positive outcomes in eliminating social ills and changing dysfunctional behaviors.

The significance of futurism as a strategy for anticipatory
problem-solving has not been lost on black theoreticians. Holden, in a lucid and scholarly analysis of black politics, suggests
the need for a "think tank" for black communities charged with
plotting the alternative designs of the future.[10] More importantly, however, there have been many projections regarding
what the future holds for black communities, most of which are
the extrapolation type of forecasting with some in the direction
of scenario speculation.

Eleanor Norton has described what she perceives as a dramatic shift in the direction of black intellectual thought since
Malcolm X.[11] She concludes that the writings of black intellectuals demonstrate a greater concern in black America for the
personal quest of self-discovery and less emphasis on finding
solutions to the general racial dilemmas confronting the country. Thus blacks are interested in "getting ourselves together"
rather than identifying the white problem and its consequences. The inward-looking mood supports the possibility of

increased black unity as blacks struggle to find consensus or at least an agreement to ignore differences and concentrate on common interests. The phenomenon identified by Norton is in essence a tremendous output of energy and creativity aimed at self-definition and self-determination. The scenario writer might well follow up the implications of this search for a collective identity and pinpoint the consequences in terms of family interaction, participation in the political process, economic progress, and even position on foreign policy. However, the real import of this phenomenon will depend on two conditions; (1) the extent to which an intellectual stance reflects the mood of the masses and (2) whether the emphasis on collective identity results in some tangible or visible improvements in the quality of life for black Americans, e.g., in greater unity and therefore greater political victories or in more positive self-image and greater individual achievement.

Holden has suggested that the next few years are crucial in the development of a critical mass in several interrelated areas to serve as a take-off point for black penetration of the power structure in the United States.[12] These areas can be classified as the exercise of organizational options and development of social programs and have as basic intent the development of the capacity for black political competiton in the ethnosystem.

There are a number of prognosticators who have, for the most part, looked at present trends and predicted what black communities will be like in the not too distant future. Peter Rossi has viewed the various political, economic, and social indicators and concludes that the future will be a continuation—perhaps at an accelerated rate—of the present.[13] He states that the riots which tore apart major urban areas in the North in the sixties will not be repeated, due to growing political organization in black communities. The increased political clout will tend to alleviate the more overt forms of discrimination against the black masses in inner cities. Relations between police and residents will improve, particularly in those instances where police departments are under the direct control of municipal government which will become, of course, increasingly black. Municipal services such as fire, garbage, and transportation are also likely to improve. Since the availability of low-cost housing in urban areas is likely to continue to be extremely limited, housing discrimination will change very slowly for the low-income black; however, middle-class blacks are likely to bid competitively and assertively in the open-housing market. Finally, employment opportunities for blacks should improve somewhat.

Rossi points out that these predictions are based on a number of assumptions which may be problematic: e.g., the assumption that governmental policy at the federal level will continue to make resources available to support a policy of affirmative efforts to advance the cause of black achievement. Another assumption is that no serious depression or recession will occur. Finally and importantly, an assumption is made that racial tensions will not erupt in communal rioting with its escalating properties.

Campbell asserts that "there has been a massive shift in white attitudes away from the traditional beliefs in white superiority and the associated patterns of segregation and discrimination and toward a more equalitarian view of the races and their appropriate relations." [14] This conclusion was based on data accumulated in a study of black and white attitudes in fifteen major cities in 1968 and in a series of sample surveys of the voting age population in the continental United States in 1964, 1968, and 1970. Campbell admits, however, that the shift toward more equalitarian racial views has been uneven, meaning that many whites still retain their prejudices and some areas of the country have moved more than other areas. From the perspective gained by these attitudinal surveys, Campbell predicts that the trend toward racial equality and racial integration will continue.

Gabriel suggests that ethnicity remains a powerful factor in the urban polity because, contrary to general opinion, "ethnic minorities do not appear to be assimilating, i.e., losing a psychological sense of identification with their ethnic group. His research indicates that even among upper-class suburban dwellers, ethnic identification still persists. The point is made that even in the absence of supporting substructural organizations aimed at perpetuating ethnic identification, the internalization by one's early life experiences of some sense of enjoyment and pride in being a member of an ethnic group continues to support ethnic identification. Gabriel concludes:

> It would appear then that ethnic attachments of one sort or another will continue to be a factor in the political behavior of ethnic groups for some time to come. The impact of these identifications will probably be felt with greatest force within the urban political system. As the Negro begins his long trek from ghetto to suburb, ethnic identifications on the part of other groups will probably be revitalized and emerge in more visible form. In such a circumstance, conflict within the urban polity will probably increase substantially. In order to deal with this situation, a premium must be placed upon the development of political instrumentalities which are highly effective in reducing conflict and facilitating compromise. While it is by no means the only requirement, institutional arrangements of local political systems should be made as congruent as possible with the resources and value structure of the electorate. And since the security margins of both the groups already active in the urban political system and those who would gain entrance are low, the urban polity may witness the reemergence of an electorate whose clientele will resemble the clientele served by the old political machine. The results may be that the urban political system of the immediate future may very well come to resemble the older, partronage-oriented, personal political organizations of the past. The paradox is that in an age where progress is hailed as the hallmark of the present, political practitioners may very well have to marshal the lessons of the past in order to ensure an orderly future.[15]

Goodman was asked to address the issue of racial minorities in the delivery of social work services in the 1980s in a special issue of *Social Work* published in 1974.[16] Goodman identifies

several discernible trends which appear to have special significance for black communities. He asserts, for example, that
there will be new conceptualizations of the term "minority"
which will lead to a different formulation of "problem" groups.
This projected expansion of the minority concept to include
women, homosexuals, and other disadvantaged populations
has already begun and by virtue of its very inclusiveness should
force greater precision in the definition of issues, problems,
and problem-solving strategies which affect minority populations differentially. Perhaps most importantly, Goodman views
a continuing and even development of social programs. This
will not only increase competition for scarce resources among
these minorities, but will in the short run serve as an obstacle
to the development of collaborative mechanisms necessary to
resolve the larger issue of their common oppression. However,
this period of collective self-interest on the part of minorities
may be the strengthening factor which will permit true collabo-
ration in the long run.

The problem for practitioners in responding to much of the
theoretical formulation around intergroup relations in the
American ethnosystem is the tendency to react emotionally
rather than cognitively to concepts. For example, the concepts
integration; community control; white power structure; dysfunctional behavior; militant, cultural pluralism; socialization;
or black capitalism tend to take on positive or negative connotations depending upon the context in which they were first encountered. Thus, thereafter when they arise in the course of
our problem-solving efforts, we give an automatic emotional
response which governs our reactions and our interactions.
This fails to take into account the complexity of these abstractions and the tangled threads of contingencies that preclude
simple judgments—positive or negative—as to their relevance,
appropriateness, value, or power in dealing with characteristic
problems of black communities. This is clearly shown in Light's
discussion of the concept "ethnic honor."

Unlike a purely status-based honor, the "sense of ethnic honor is the specific honor of the masses, for it is accessible to anybody who belongs to the subjectively believed community of descent." Hence, the sense of ethnic honor is capable of penetrating even the lowliest home, no member of which joins any voluntary association. Among the "poor white trash" of the American South, the sense of racial honor was a very ugly social characteristic, involving as it did, their interest in the caste subordination of black. Racial honor among Nazis was similarly sordid. . . . Among Chinese and Japanese in the United States, a sense of ethnic honor was joined to the ascriptive basis of social association. As a result individuals, irrespective of social status, were amenable to group controls over their behavior in the interest of maintaining an unsullied ethnic honor. A shared sense of ethnic honor resulted in group standards of everyday conduct which kinship and territorial associations carried into every corner of Oriental society. . . . The extraordinary success of children of Oriental descent in the public schools can be traced to a sense of ethnic honor. Oriental children are enjoined to study hard and achieve scholastic eminence in order to bring credit to their family and their ethnic group. Caste subordination of Negroes involved shared black-white conceptions of the proper place of blacks in a white society. This view did not assign to Negroes a separate ethnic honor but rather deprived them of any valued ethnic identity. So long as these conceptions were shared, there was obviously no room for social conflict between blacks and whites. But this heritage carried with it manifest disadvantages in the urban North. Unlike Orientals, black migrants could not be disciplined by reference to ethnic honor, since Southern-born migrants did not conceive of themselves as having any honor. Especially among the lowest stratum of urban Negroes, peers could rarely induce a fellow to actually refrain from some line of personally advantageous activity lest it discredit or shame blacks in general, nor were there persisting grouplets able to encourage impersonal achievements in the interest of ethnic black honor.[17]

Thus, the concept of ethnic honor may be viewed positively as it relates to the normative force used to enforce functional and individually rewarding behaviors; it may be viewed negatively if these behaviors tend to be destructive or discriminatory in regard to those not included in the ethnic group. Antagonistic consequences in regard to the outgroup are not inevitable; e.g., ethnic honor may demand that all dealing with outsiders be scrupulously honest in order to reflect positively on the group. It is clear, therefore, that to place emphasis on ethnic honor may be positive or negative depending on an entire network of contingent conditions. It requires a cognitive response to the concept to identify these conditions, analyze their multiple effect, and measure the effect by its adherence to nonnegotiable values, priorities and goals. Only then can reasonable judgments of the concept be made.

Practitioners in black communities cannot expect a predictable environment in which they are able to depend on well-defined and accepted practice strategies. On the contrary, one of the few constant factors in that environment will be change, and another factor should be committed helping persons who are steeped in knowledge extracted from all known sources and skilled in the day-to-day struggles to survive and prevail.

A STRATEGY FOR TRANSCENDENCE: A SCENARIO OF THE FUTURE

On the surface, the 1970s appeared to be a decade of retrograde activity in black communities. The nation was feverishly attempting to overcome simultaneously the political infection exposed by Watergate, the traumatic injury to an overheated economy inflicted by Arab oil-producing nations, and the growing conviction in black ghettos that white interests were conspiring to make blacks appear the cause of their own inferior status and thereby insure the favored position of whites in the ethnosystem. However, during the 1970s, the inextricable wedding of the fate of black communities with that of the rest of the nation became crystal clear.

When the economy worsened, blacks were among the

hardest hit. When there was an opening for a dishwasher at Martin Luther King Hospital in Los Angeles during the spring of 1975, the line of applicants stretched around the block as hundreds of unemployed participated in a kind of calculated gamble encouraged by the system. Furthermore, since most employment was outside black communities the process of merely applying at a place where there was rumored to be work involved a seven- to ten-mile trip for ghetto hopefuls. Vietnam and Cambodia were no longer a national priority, only a national embarrassment as they took an irritatingly long time to fashion their own destruction. More importantly, they were symbolic of the immediately preceding decade when guns, bullets, and bombs gained ascendance in the repertoire of problem-solving devices, and into the 1970s, devices that were used frequently and unrestrainedly, particularly in black communities. The national lawlessness had become the local despair. To quote a policeman, speaking of one black community: "The community is behind bars. People can't have their kids in the street because someone will steal their coats or shoot them. If they go to the store they're afraid of being robbed on the way. When they go into the store, they're afraid of getting their purse snatched. When they come out, they're afraid of getting robbed of their groceries and they hope their car's there and when they come home they hope their furniture's in the house."

Black college youth in the 1960s had envisioned a revolution brought about by the mystical combination of their intensity of commitment and the new opportunities available to them to gain the expertise required to succeed in the materialistic society. In the 1970s, however, it was apparent that success in capitalist America—for those not born into the ruling class—is an individual achievement and, despite the fretful tidal restlessness of its masses, there was no mechanism whereby the underclasses would be permitted to rise together. Thus, the young, new middle-class blacks learned the bitter taste of disil-

lusionment and frustration as they recognized the chasm built
of education and income which separated them from the people they had vowed to help.

The apathy and despair of the black masses appeared to be
intractable and potentially explosive as fumblings of possible
new waves of violence were heard with increasing frequency.
This time, however, the message was that now it would not be
Watts or other inner-city areas; it would be Beverly Hills and
Scarsdale and Tanglewood. But the dire predictions were
forestalled by a certain series of events that underscore again
the interdependence of groups in the ethnosystem.

First, there had been the worsening energy situation in which
all efforts to find new sources had ended in disappointment.
That is, until the late 1970s. It was then that a lone inventor successfully developed a solar battery with almost unlimited possibilities for industrial and commercial uses, including a power
source for automobiles. The stock market rocketed upward as
business experts predicted unprecedented growth and pros-
perity. However, there had been sufficient time of scarcity for
ecological interests to gain considerable political power. The
last thing the ecological groups wanted to see was a new rash
of huge automobiles and parking lots and superfreeway systems pockmarking the landscape. So, although there was
power aplenty predicted for an immediate future, the huge automobile industry was shocked as Congress passed legislation
limiting the use of private automobiles. The shock was alle-
viated somewhat by the dramatic expansion of the public transportation system. Detroit was soon working full blast, turning
out sleek little busses that ran on almost invisible magnetized
metal strips embedded in all major thoroughfares in urban
areas so that almost no city dweller was more than two blocks
away from a transit route. In addition there were monorail systems for long trips as well as heliports atop many larger buildings. Best of all, there were no dirty exhaust fumes from the
clean solar-battery-operated engines sensitive enough to sun

rays to make it possible to charge them even on a cloudy winter day.

With an upturn in the economy unprecedented except perhaps at the beginning of the industrial revolution, more money was available. However, scarcity had generated another bit of desiderata—labeled by most as accountability; i.e., programs had to determine whether goals were met. The technology for evaluating the effects of even complicated social programs with abstract goals had been highly developed. Therefore, the expenditure of the new money could be accompanied by clear evidence that it had or had not achieved the goal intended. This new technology changed the face of American politics. The fact of the matter was that politics of compromise could now be substituted by the politics of excellence. If constituents demanded the termination of certain tax shelters for business and industry while another segment of the constituency lobbied vigorously in suppport of such shelter, it was entirely possible for the Congressman to work with his technological advisers to simulate "reality" and determine the alternative consequences for each decision with attendant probabilities. Thus, his decision would be made on the basis of the most probable positive outcome rather than on the principle of the "squeaky wheel." To insure that this would happen, it was necessary to develop a system of computer terminals spotted around urban areas which were linked to the same data banks and computers that the politicians and their advisers used in decision-making activities. It was as predicted by Donald Michael in 1968:

> The extraordinary degree of openness required to operate this way could mean that, over time, the political system, including the citizen, could come to recognize error and failure as natural products of trying to cope with a complex urban environment. No longer would the government have the need to cover up: the degree of ignorance about the feasibility and implications of any program would be evident to the recipi-

ents of the program at the time that it was initiated as well as all along thereafter. Knowing that some error and failure are inevitable, both government and citizens would be able to accept social experiments more easily for what they are, making changes candidly and quickly when needed, without pretending or expecting that the initial plans were more certain to succeed than realistic estimates would suggest.[18]

Perhaps the most important event that made possible the transcendent happenings in black communities all over the country occurred in 1980 when the most unyielding bureaucracy of all—the public school system—was totally reorganized with immediate as well as far-reaching consequences. Essentially, the elementary, junior high, and high school were eliminated as organizing contexts for educational processes. The first three to five years, depending on the individual child, were allotted to education for literacy. The important skill to be taught was reading, with secondary emphasis on arithmetic and writing. Although some attention was given to expanding horizons through exposure to history or geography or science, these subjects were never identified as "units of knowledge" to be mastered during this time but introduced in exercises aimed at helping the student learn to read, write, or manipulate numbers. It was soon discovered that with this kind of specific education goal in the first years, ninety-eight percent of all students, black as well as white, could be taught to read at an eighth-grade level, write a coherent letter or even a short story, and understand number concepts including simple algebra. The next four to six years, again depending on the pace of the child, were devoted to education in the liberal arts. Now that they were literate, the students could begin to use this skill in creating their own literature, music, history (e.g., of their family or neighborhood), art, and in the process learn about how others in human history had done likewise. Finally, the next three to five years were spent in developing "life skills." These involved skills that might be useful in a career; e.g., typing or drafting or newspaper writing, but also skills that are not vocational but related to effective interpersonal relationships such as skill in parenting, dealing with various kinds of personalities, or determining where there are resources for assistance with problems that might arise, like getting a job, finding adequate housing, or obtaining decent medical care. This change in the educational system was welcomed in black communities and made it possible to hold the schools more clearly responsible for the child's level of achievement. Furthermore, it was found to maintain interest and motivation to learn and ability to move into college or university work, to a much greater extent than when forced into a deadly series of "subjects" and learning to pass examinations but forgetting the "content" almost immediately.

Thus, a fortuitous set of events affecting the total society set the stage for dramatic events occurring within black communities. By 1980, there had in fact developed a critical mass of black expertise. However, for real change to occur it was necessary to have in addition a critical balance among expertise, popular leadership or charisma, and financial resources. The probability that all three requirements could be appropriately met had been small before this time. But they all came together in 1980.

A group known as Concerned Athletes for Community Development had been active in implementing a wide variety of projects in various black communities, mostly inner-city areas. It was not until they were contacted by a well-known entertainer that they moved from the minor league into a major league. This entertainer had made a fortune and, unlike many others, had received expert investment advice and now was a millionaire many times over. He had conceived an idea which would require an amount of money even larger than he could manage, and together with some of the Concerned Athletes and some others from the entertainment world they formed the Safari Corporation. Obtaining some of the best available consultation in the country, the idea took shape and with much fanfare in early summer, 1983, Safariland was officially opened on a huge site in the middle of the Nevada desert, within shouting distance of Las Vegas.

It was a startling sight, whether first encountered from the air or from the straight ribbon of highway slicing along its rim. It was made up entirely of circular buildings, some two-story, with what appeared to be thatched roofs and walls of opaque bronze glass. The buildings were all connected by enclosed passageways, also of the same bronze glass, so that once inside a building, no one would have to leave in order to enter any of the other thirty-four! The buildings contained restaurants, hotels, and of course a variety of gambling casinos. The casinos featured new games patterned after traditional African games of chance. There were several buildings, each devoted entirely to a product, like baskets, cloth, pottery, wood carvings, so that the atmosphere was reminiscent of a super-sophisticated African market "under glass." There were camels and evening caravans out into the desert to an "oasis" where, under a huge tent, unveiled dancing girls and big-name entertainers performed. Safariland was a huge success, as growing affluence in the country had created more people with money to spend and looking for something different. Furthermore, the added attraction of gambling fully sanctioned by the state of Nevada was a potent drawing card for those who flew into Safariland's circular, thatch-roofed airport or, if entitled to drive their own car under a business license, made the trip from Los Angeles, San Francisco, Salt Lake City, or Las Vegas.

The founding fathers of Safariland were not ordinary businessmen. In fact, all profits from Safariland were put into the Safari Foundation. Foundation moneys were, particularly in the first few years, used to buy large stock holdings in various American corporations. In addition to Safariland itself, moneys were also earned by means of subsidiary corporations which created most of the souvenirs, T-shirts, comic books, etc., that featured the Safariland emblem and were sold, not only in Safariland but in major department stores, drug stores and souvenir shops in Nevada. With Safariland and its interests stable and prosperous, it was now time to move into the second phase of the Safari Corporation's long-range strategy. Subsidiaries were set up in major cities across the country to operate a network of Safaritown amusement parks. These amusements parks became as ubiquitous as Colonel Sander's Kentucky Fried Chicken or McDonald's Golden Arches had during the 1960s and 1970s. They included elephant and camel rides for children; it had been an ecological happenstance, as a game preserve in Tanganyika had become so overcrowded with animals that hundreds of these animals were given in exchange for the cost of the transportation alone. Each subsidiary had a board of directors made up primarily of community people as well as a director responsible to the board. All directors were selected from among those graduating from the Safari Company's training program. Also, all profits from each local Safaritown would be turned over to the Safari Foundation. Usually more would be returned to the local community for funding of programs aimed at the following:

1. For the development of a community-oriented Cable TV station, including the underwriting of a subsidy program during the first year in order to give an almost free service to the community and thereby introduce and commit them to Cable TV and the community channel.

2. For the building of a community cultural center and assistance in developing local support and an on-going program featuring the performing arts, crafts, art, educational seminars or workshops, etc.

3. For the development of family life training centers in predominantly black neighborhoods to which any parent can apply for assistance in developing skill in family roles, e.g., parent, spouse, child, etc.

4. For the creation and operation of a resource development center in the black community, available for consultation to agencies in any low-income neighborhood regarding the most effective strategies for obtaining support for new as well as existing programs, including assistance with proposal writing; and

5. For the development of a support center for creative edu-

cation projects. This center would finance projects proposed by teachers to enhance motivation, performance, or cultural understanding of children in predominantly black schools where such projects could not be funded by regular public school support.

By 1990, there were Safari subsidiaries operating in over a hundred cities. As a consequence, there was a dramatic increase in the feelings of cohesion and identity in regard to black communities. The physical presence of a cultural center, particularly in those instances where the creative efforts of local community residents were recognized, was an important factor in this cohesion. Improved employment conditions were also a factor, but it was Safari specifically which gave management opportunities (including scholarships in some of the nation's best schools of Business Administration and the support of new schools of Business in predominantly black colleges and universities), to blacks who would not have been able to get the opportunity elsewhere. The employment factor and the increase in community cohesion dramatically reduced the incidence of crime within the community. The success of Safari, Inc., was not only due to the founders' ability to financial resources or ability to recognize and use expertise or commitment in helping black communities but also to the shaping of its socialistic, cooperative spirit to fit within the framework of a capitalist economic system. It was an "if you can't lick 'em, join 'em" strategy, but the joining was on the terms of these communities and not the white bosses. Although its operations were based in black communities, Safari also included any low-income person or non-black person residing in a black community in its offer of services, thus obtaining allies in a struggle against an oppressive system with many poor people as its targets.

Safari, Inc., is not yet, but the critical level of human and material resources is fast approaching if not here already, and what is required is the judicious mixture of mutually supportive dedication into the resource pot in order to move away from the current intolerable status quo in black communities. It should be noted, also, that money and material resources are not enough to make the convoluted mix of business and social enterprise predicted here function effectively; the expertise of a network of helping professionals is crucial. The official atmosphere of the moment notwithstanding, there is an uncertain but intense hope that old assumptions can be reassessed, old inadequacies can be overcome, and out of the vast congested labyrinths of our inner cities, helping practitioners and those who reside within them will be able to construct a mutually acceptable definition of their black community reality.

notes

INTRODUCTION

1. Phillip H. Kramer and Samuel O. Miller, "Eliminating Racial Barriers in Schools of Social Work: A Conceptual Framework," in *Black Perspectives on Social Work Education: Issues Related to Curriculum, Faculty, and Schools* (New York: Council on Social Work Education, 1974), pp. 38–50.

2. Thaddeus P. Mathis, "Educating for Black Social Development: The Politics of Social Organization," *Journal of Education for Social Work* (Winter 1975), pp. 105–12.

3. Thaddeus P. Mathis, "Social Work and Nation Building in the Black Community," in *Diversity: Cohesion or Chaos: Motivation For Survival,* Proceedings of the Fourth Annual Conference of the National Association of Black Social Workers, 1972, Fisk University, Nashville, Tenn., April 4–9.

4. Howard D. Arnold, "American Racism: Implications For Social Work," *Journal of Education for Social Work* (Spring 1970), pp. 7–12.

1. EMPOWERMENT: IN SEARCH OF THE ELUSIVE PARADIGM

1. Robert H. Binstock and Katherine Ely, "The Meaning of Powerlessness," in Binstock and Ely, eds., *The Politics of the Powerless* (Cambridge, Mass.: Winthrop, 1971), pp. 1–2.

2. David Burgest, "Racism in Everyday Speech and Social Work Jargon," *Social Work* (July 1973), pp. 20–25.

3. See particularly, Kenneth Clark, *The Pathos of Power* (New York: Harper and Row, 1974); William Gamson, *Power and Discontent* (Homewood, Ill.: Dorsey Press, 1968); Wally Jacobsen, *Power and Interpersonal Relations* (Belmont, Calif.: Wadsworth, 1972); Si Kahn, *How People Get Power: Organizing Oppresses Communities for Action* (New York: McGraw-Hill, 1970); William J. Wilson, *Power, Racism, and Privilege* (New York: Macmillan, 1973).

4. Barbara Lerner, *Therapy in the Ghetto: Political Impotence and Personal Disintegration* (Baltimore: Johns Hopkins University Press, 1972).

5. Robert Pruger, "The Good Bureaucrat," *Social Work* (July 1973), pp. 26–32.

6. Bertrand Russell, *Power: A New Social Analysis* (New York: Norton, 1938).

7. Clark, *Pathos of Power*, p. 163.

8. Montague Ullman, "A Unifying Concept Linking Therapeutic and Community Process," in William Gray, Frederick Duhl, and Nicholas Rizzo, eds., *General Systems Theory and Psychiatry* (Boston: Little, Brown, 1969), pp. 253–66.

9. Rollo May, *Power and Innocence: A Search for the Sources of Violence* (New York: Norton, 1972); pp. 81–97.

10. Isidor Chien, *The Science of Behavior and the Image of Man* (New York: Basic Books, 1972), p. 10.

11. Chris Argyris, *Intervention Theory and Method: A Behavioral Science View* (Reading, Mass.: Addison-Wesley, 1970).

12. Martin Bloom, *The Paradox of Helping* (New York: Wiley, 1975).

13. Binstock and Ely, "Meaning of Powerlessness," p. 1.

2. BLACK COMMUNITIES: MYTH OR REALITY?

1. Booker T. Washington. "My View of Segregation Laws," *The New Republic*, December 4, 1915, p. 113.

2. Milton Gordon, *Assimilation in American Life: The Role of Race, Religion, and National Origins* (London: Oxford University Press, 1964), pp. 68–71.

3. William M. Dobriner, *Social Structures and Systems: A Sociological Overview* (Pacific Palisades, Calif.: Goodyear, 1969), pp. 252–53.

4. Colin Greer, "Remembering Class: An Interpretation" in Colin Greer, ed., *Divided Society: The Ethnic Experience in America* (New York: Basic Books, 1974), p. 35.

5. Albert Murray, *The Onni-Americans: New Perspectives on Black Experience and American Culture* (New York: Avon Books, 1971), pp. 39–40.

6. Greer, "Remembering Class," p. 27.

7. Michael Novak, *The Rise of the Unmeltable Ethnics* (New York: Macmillan, 1972), p. 8.

8. Greer, "Remembering Class," p. 32.

9. Stokely Carmichael and Charles V. Hamilton, *Black Power: The Politics of Liberation in America* (New York: Vintage Books, 1967).

10. Harold Cruse, "Revolutionary Nationalism and the Afro-American," *Studies of the Left* (February 1962), pp. 76–77.

11. Robert Blauner, *Racial Oppression in America* (New York: Harper and Row, 1972), pp. 82–110.

2. black communities: myth or reality?   415

12. HARYOU, *Youth in the Ghetto: A Study of the Consequences of Power-lessness and a Blueprint For Change* (New York, 1964).

13. Carmichael and Hamilton, *Black Power,* p. 44.

14. Blauner, *Racial Oppression in America,* p. 104.

15. William K. Tabb, *The Political Economy of the Black Ghetto* (New York: Norton 1970), pp. 31–32.

16. Robert Allen, *Black Awakening in Capitalist America* (Garden City, N.Y.. Doubleday, 1969), p. 280.

17. John Sutherland, *A General Systems Philosophy for the Social and Behavioral Sciences* (New York: Braziller, 1973), pp. 37–38.

18. Peter Schrag, *The Decline of the Wasp* (New York: Simon and Schuster, 1970).

19. William J. Wilson, "The Significance of Social and Racial Prisms," in Peter Rose, Stanley Rothman, and William J. Wilson, eds., *Through Different Eyes: Black and White Perspectives on American Race Relations* (London: Oxford University Press, 1973), p. 408.

20. Sutherland, *A General Systems Philosophy,* p. 42.

21. Gunnar Myrdal, *An American Dilemma* (New York: Harper and Row, 1944).

22. Corinne Sherman, "Racial Factors in Desertion," *The Family* (October–December 1923).

23. Melville Herskovitz, *The Myth of the Negro Past* (New York: Knopf, 1941).

24. See Wade Nobles, "African Philosophy: Foundations for Black Psychology," in Reginald Jones, ed., *Black Psychology* (New York: Harper and Row, 1972); also Wade Nobles "African Root and American Fruit: The Black Family," paper presented to the Charles Drew Medical School Conference on the Black Family (November 1972); Alan Lomax, "The Homogeneity of African-Afro—American Musical Style," in Norman E. Whitten, Jr. and John F. Szwed, eds., *Afro-American Anthropology: Contemporary Perspectives* (New York: Free Press, 1970), pp. 181–202.

25. See Murray, *The Omni-Americans;* Myrdal, *An American Dilemma;* and E. Franklin Frazier, Black Bourgeoisie (Glencoe, Ill.: The Free Press, 1957).

26. See Charles Valentine, "Deficit, Difference and Bicultural Models of Afro-American Behavior," in *Challenging the Myths: The Schools, The Blacks, and the Poor* (Cambridge, Mass.: Harvard Educational Review, Reprint Series No. 5, 1971); also Blauner, *Racial Oppression in America.*

27. Blauner, *Racial Oppression in America,* p. 130.

28. Ashley Montagu, *Man's Most Dangerous Myth: The Fallacy of Race* (New York: Macmillan, 1965).

29. Harold Rose, *The Black Ghetto: A Spatial Behavioral Perspective* (New York: McGraw-Hill, 1971), p. 6.

30. Greer, "Remembering Class," p. 19.

31. Gilbert Osofsky, "The Making of a Ghetto," in Richard J. Meister, ed., *The Black Ghetto: Promised Land or Colony* (Lexington, Mass.: Heath, 1972), p. 53.

32. Rose, *Black Ghetto,* p. 21.

33. Anthony Downs, "Alternative Futures for the American Ghetto," *Daedalus* (Fall 1968), p. 1345.

34. Gerald D. Suttles, *The Social Construction of Communities* (Chicago: University of Chicago Press, 1972), pp. 21–43.

35. E. J. Kahn, Jr., *The American People* (New York: Weybright and Talley, 1973), p. 207.

36. Edward Laumann, *Bonds of Pluralism: The Form and Substance of Urban Social Networks* (New York: Wiley, 1973), p. 212.

37. Murray, *The Omni-Americans,* pp. 141–42.

38. Robert Hill, *The Strengths of Black Families* (New York: Emerson Hall, 1972).

39. Lee Rainwater, *Behind Ghetto Walls: Black Family Life in a Federal Slum* (Chicago: Aldine, 1970), pp. 68–69.

40. James Coleman, *Resources for Social Change: Race in the United States* (New York: Wiley, 1971), pp. 18–19.

41. Thomas Meenaghan, "What Means 'Community'," *Social Work* (November 1972), pp. 94–100.

42. Stanley Lieberson, "Stratification and Ethnic Groups," in Edward O. Laumann, ed., *Social Stratification: Research and Theory for the 1970s* (Indianapolis: Bobbs-Merrill, 1970), p. 169.

43. Andrew Billingsley, *Black Families in White America* (Englewood Cliffs, N.J.: Prentice-Hall, 1968), pp. 15–31.

44. *Ibid.*

45. *Ibid.*

46. Kenneth Clark, *Dark Ghetto* (New York: Harper and Row, 1965), p. 171.

47. Richard Hatcher, "Mass Media and the Black Community," *The Black Scholar* (September 1973), pp. 2–10.

48. Carlton Goodlett, "Mass Communication, U.S.A.: Its Feet of Clay," *The Black Scholar* (November 1974), pp. 2–6.

49. Imamu Amiri Baraka (Leroi Jones), "On Control, Communication and Culture: The Ban on Black Music," *Black World* (July 1971), p. 5.

50. Carlton Goodlett, "Mass Communication," pp. 2–6.

51. Robert A. Levine and Donald T. Campbell, *Ethnocentrism: Theories of Conflict: Ethnic Attitudes and Group Behavior* (New York: Wiley, 1972), pp. 81–104.

3. THE HELPING PROFESSIONS IN BLACK COMMUNITIES:
THE SOCIOHISTORICAL PERSPECTIVE

1. Shirley Better, "Introduction," *Directory of Black Community Agencies* (Los Angeles: Association of Black Social Workers, 1972).

2. *Ibid.*

3. *Ibid.*

4. Dorothy Fahs Beck and Mary Ann Jones, *Progress on Family Problems: A Nationwide Study of Clients' and Counselors' Views on Family Agency Services* (New York: Family Service Association of America, 1973), p. 22.

5. Howard N. Rabinovitz, "From Exclusion to Segregation: Health and Welfare Services for Southern Blacks, 1865–1890," *Social Service Review* (September 1974).

6. Frank Watson, *The Charity Organization Movement in the United States: A Study in American Philanthropy* (New York: Macmillan, 1922), pp. 357–58.

7. Howard Goldstein, *Social Work Practice: A Unitary Approach* (Columbia: University of South Carolina Press, 1973), p. 26.

8. Raymond Wolters, *Negroes and the Great Depression* (Westport, Conn.: Greenwood, 1970), pp. 169–87.

9. Gunnar Myrdal, *An American Dilemma* (New York: Harper and Row, 1944); Abram Kardiner and Lionel Ovesey, *The Mark of Oppression: Explorations in the Personality of the American Negro* (New York: World, 1962).

10. Jerome Cohen, "Race as a Factor in Social Work Practice," in Roger Miller, ed., *Race, Research, and Reason* (New York: NASW, 1969), p. 104.

11. Billy J. Tidwell, "The Black Community's Challenge to Social Work," *Journal of Education for Social Work* (Fall 1971), p. 65.

12. James Goodman, "Racial Minorities in the 1980s," *Social Work* (September 1974), p. 583.

13. David A. Hardcastle, "The Indigenous Nonprofessional in the Social Service Bureaucracy: A Critical Examination," *Social Work* (April 1971), pp. 56–63.

14. Benjamin Rush, "Observations," *Transactions of the American Philosophical Society* 4(1799):289–97.

15. Thomas Szasz, *The Myth of Mental Illness* (New York: Harper and Row, 1964).

16. From the *American Journal of Insanity* (1862–63) 19:77, quoted in Ruth Caplan, *Psychiatry and the Community in 19th Century America* (New York: Basic Books, 1969).

17. J. Boudin, *Traite de giographic et de statistique medicalis,* vol. 2 (Paris: Balliere, 1857).

18. Quoted in David J. Rothman, *The Discovery of the Asylum* (Boston: Little, Brown, 1971), p. 112.

19. M. O'Malley, "Psychosis in the Colored Race," *Journal of Insanity* (1914), 71:309–36.

20. W. F. Drewry, "Central State Hospital, Petersburg, Virginia," in H. Hurd, ed., *Institutional Care of the Insane in the U.S. and Canada* 3(77)856:62.

21. E. M. Green, "Psychoses Among Negroes—A Comparative Study," *Journal of Nervous and Mental Disorders* 41(14):697–708.

22. D. C. Wilson and E. M. Lentz, "The Effect of Culture Change on the Negro Race in Virginia as Indicated by a Study of State Hospital Admissions," *American Journal of Psychiatry* (1957), pp. 25–32.

23. Morton Kramer, Beatrice Rosen, and Ernest Willis, "Definitions and Distributions of Mental Disorders in a Racist Society," in Charles V. Willie, Bernard Kramer, and Bertram Brown, eds., *Racism and Mental Health* (Pittsburgh, University of Pittsburgh Press, 1973), pp. 353–462.

24. Kilton Stewart, "Dream Exploration Among the Senoi," reprinted in Theodore Roszak, ed., *Sources* (New York: Harper and Row, 1972), pp. 20–38.

25. Erik Erikson, *Identity, Youth, and Crisis* (New York: Norton, 1968).

26. Charles Pinderhughes, "Racism and Psychotherapy," in Willie, Kramer, and Brown, *Racism and Mental Health*.

27. Joel Kovel, *White Racism: A Psychohistory* (New York: Vintage Books, 1970); J. Dollard and N. Miller, *Personality and Psychotherapy* (New York: McGraw-Hill, 1950); James Comer, "White Racism: Its Past, Form, and Function," *American Journal of Psychiatry* (December 1969).

28. Alexander Thomas and Samuel Sillen, *Racism and Psychiatry* (New York: Brunner/Mazel, 1972).

29. Martin H. Jones and Martin C. Jones, "The Neglected Client," *The Black Scholar* (March 1970), pp. 35–42.

30. "Black Psychiatrist Uses Racial Myths to Speed Therapy," Roche Laboratories newsletter, undated.

31. Edwin J. Thomas, "Behavioral Modification and Casework," in Robert Roberts and Robert Nee, eds., *Theories of Social Casework* (Chicago: University of Chicago Press, 1970), p. 190.

32. Albert Bandura, "Psychotherapy as a Learning Process," in *Psychological Bulletin* (1961), pp. 143–57.

33. William Hayes, "Radical Black Behaviorism," in Reginald Jones, ed., *Black Psychology* (New York: Harper and Row, 1972), pp. 51–60.

34. See Carl Rogers, "Client-Centered Therapy," in C. H. Patterson, ed., *Theories of Counseling and Psychotherapy* (New York: Harper and Row, 1966).

35. Abraham Maslow, *Motivation and Personality* (New York: Harper and Row, 1970).

36. Sterling Plumpp, *Black Rituals* (Chicago: Third World Press, 1972).

37. *Ibid.*

38. Prentiss Taylor, "Research for Liberation: Shaping a New Black Identity in America," *Black World* (May 1973), pp. 65–67.

39. Robert Hill, *Strength of Black Families* (New York: Emerson Hall, 1972).

40. Gary Marx, "Religion: Opiate or Inspiration of Civil Rights Militancy Among Negroes," in Russell Endo and William Strawbridge, eds., *Perspectives on Black America* (Englewood Cliffs, N.J.: Prentice-Hall, 1970).

41. Scott Briar and Henry Miller, *Problems and Issues in Social Casework* (New York: Columbia University Press, 1971), p. 80.

42. Joseph Ben-David, "How to Organize Research in the Social Sciences," *Daedalus* (Spring 1973), pp. 39–51.

43. Harry R. Targ, "Social Science and a New Social Order," *Journal of Peace Research* (1971), no. 3–4, pp. 207–20.

4. THE MYSTIQUE OF SCIENCE-BASED PRACTICE

1. Melville Herskovitz, *The New World Negro* (Bloomington: Indiana University Press, 1966), pp. 78–81.

2. Gwynn Nettler, *Explanations* (New York: McGraw-Hill, 1970).

3. See an analysis of this theme in the sociological literature in T. Abel, "The Operation Called Verstehen," *American Journal of Sociology* (November 1948), pp. 211–18.

4. Nettler, *Explanations,* p. 177.

5. Theodore Roszak, *The Making of a Counterculture* (Garden City, N.Y.: Doubleday, 1969).

6. William Hedgepeth, *The Alternative: Community Life in New America* (New York: Macmillan, 1970), p. 184.

7. Clifford Adelman, *Generations: A College in Youthcult* (New York: Praeger, 1972), pp. 8–9.

8. Roszak, *The Making of a Counterculture,* p. xii.

9. Arthur Vener, Mary Margaret Zeenglein, and Cyrus S. Stewart, "Religion, Authoritarianism and Adolescent Deviance," a paper presented to the American Sociological Association, New York, August 29, 1973.

10. James R. Killian, "Toward a Research-Reliant Society: Some Observations in Government and Science," in Harry Woolf, ed., *Science as A Cultural Force* (Baltimore, Md.: Johns Hopkins Press, 1964).

11. Catherine Roberts, *The Scientific Conscience: Reflections on the Modern Biologist and Humanism* (New York: Braziller, 1967).

12. Michael Polyani, *Personal Knowledge: Toward a Post-Critical Philosophy* (Chicago: University of Chicago Press, 1958).

13. Dennis Forsythe, "Radical Sociology and Blacks," in Joyce Ladner, ed., *The Death of White Sociology* (New York: Random House, 1973), pp. 213–33.

14. Karl Marx and Friedrich Engels, *The Communist Manifesto,* 1848.

15. Irvin Child, *Humanistic Psychology and the Research Tradition: Their Several Virtues* (New York: Wiley, 1973).

16. Abraham Maslow, *The Psychology of Science* (New York: Harper and Row, 1966), p. 72.

17. Forsythe, "Radical Sociology and Blacks," p. 222.

18. Peter Rose, Stanley Rothman, and William J. Wilson, eds., *Through Differnt Eyes: Black and White Perspectives on American Race Relations* (New York: Oxford University Press, 1973), p. xv.

19. James Tillman and Mary Tillman, "Black Intellectuals, White Liberals and Race Relations: An Analytic Overview," *Phylon* (Spring 1972), pp. 54–66.

20. Nathan Hare, "The Sociological Study of Racial Conflict," *Phylon* (Spring 1972).

21. Robert Williams, "Scientific Racism and IQ: The Silent Mugging of the Black Community," *Psychology Today* (May 1974), pp. 32–42.

22. Derek Phillips, *Abandoning Method* (San Francisco, California: Jossey-Bass, 1973).

23. See particularly, Wade Nobles, "Psychological Research and Black Self-Concept: A Critical Review," *Journal of Social Issues* (1973), 29(1); Gloria Johnson Powell, "Self-Concept in White and Black Children," in Charles Willie, Bernard Kramer, and Bertram Brown, eds., *Racism and Mental* Health (Pittsburgh: University of Pittsburgh Press, 1973), pp. 299–318.

24. Abram Kardiner and Lionel Ovesey, *Mark of Oppression* (New York: Norton, 1951); William Grier and Price Cobbs, *Black Rage* (New York: Basic Books, 1968).

25. E. Earl Baughman, *Black Americans* (New York: Academic Press, 1971), pp. 37–50.

26. Daniel P. Moynihan, *The Negro Family: The Case For National Action* (Washington, D.C.: U.S. Dept. of Labor, Office of Policy Planning and Research, March 1965).

27. Phillips, *Abandoning Method,* p. 88.

28. Gunnar Myrdal, *An American Dilemma* (New York, Harper and Row, 1944).

29. Arthur Jensen, "How Much Can We Boost IQ and Scholastic Achievement?" *Harvard Educational Review* (Winter 1969).

30. Nielson Smith, "Who Should Do Minority Research," *Social Casework* (July 1973), pp. 393–97.

31. Joan Moore, "Social Constraints on Sociological Knowledge: Academics and Research Concerning Minorities," *Social Problems* (1973), 21(1):65–77.

32. Charles DeBono, *Lateral Thinking for Management: A Handbook of Creativity* (New York: American Management Association, 1971).

5. . . . IN GENETIC FICTION
1. Jerry Hirsch, "Behavior-Genetic Analysis and Its Biosocial Consequences," in Kent S. Miller and Ralph Mason Dreger, eds., *Comparative Studies of Blacks and Whites in the United States* (New York: Seminar Press, 1973), pp. 34–53.

2. Karl Pearson, "The Problem of Alien Immigration into Great Britain, Illustrated by an Examination of Russian and Polish Jewish Children," *Annals of Eugenics* (1925), 1(5):127.

3. Joseph Arthur de Gobineau, *Essay on the Inequality of the Human Races* (Paris: P. Belfond, 1967).

4. See the entire edition of Joyce Ladner, ed., *The Death of White Sociology* (New York: Random House, 1970).

5. Richard Goldsby, *Race and Races* (New York: Macmillan, 1970), p. 23.

6. *Ibid.*

7. *Ibid.*, p. 55.

8. Jacques Maquet, *Africanity: The Cultural Unity of Black Africa,* trans. by Joan R. Reyfield (New York: Oxford University Press, 1972), p. 13.

9. T. E. Reed, "Caucasian Genes in American Negroes," *Science* (1969), 165:762.

10. Arthur Jensen, "How Much Can We Boost IQ and Scholastic Achievement," *Harvard Educational Review* (Winter 1969).

11. Richard Hernstein, *IQ in the Meritocracy* (Boston: Atlantic-Little, Brown, 1973).

12. As quoted in Godfrey Hodgson, "Do Schools Make a Difference?" *Atlantic Monthly* (March 1973), pp. 35–46.

13. Peter Watson, "Toward a New Gauge of Intelligence," *Illustrated London News and Sketch* (March 1972).

14. An excellent account of the history of scientific study of Negroes in the United States is given in John Heller's *Outcasts from Evolution: Scientific Attitudes of Racial Inferiority, 1859–1900* (Chicago: University of Chicago Press, 1971). It contains a bibliographical essay with references to literature from the time period covered in the text to the 1960s.

15. Lee Rainwater, "Neutralizing the Disinherited: Some Psychological Aspects of Understanding the Poor," in Vernon L. Allen, ed., *Psychological Factors in Poverty* (Chicago: Markham, 1970), p. 20.

16. Jack Slater, "The Rise of Cancer in Black Men," *Ebony* (July 1974), pp. 92–100.

17. Hamilton Bims, "Why Black Men Die Younger," *Ebony* (December 1974).

18. K. E. Moyer, "The Physiology of Violence," *Psychology Today* (July 1973), pp. 35–39.

19. Harry Edwards, "The Sources of the Black Athlete's Superiority," *The Black Scholar* (November 1971), p. 35.

20. *Ibid.*

21. Robert Chrisman, "The Athlete as Cultural Hero," *Los Angeles Times,* January 12, 1975, Part VII, pp. 1, 4.

22. Frances Cress Welsing, "The Cress Theory of Color Confrontation and Racism," *The Black Scholar* (May 1974), pp. 32–40.

23. Goldsby, *Race and Races,* p. 22.

24. Tabitha Powledge, "The New Ghetto Hustle," *Saturday Review of the Sciences,* January 27, 1973.

25. Charles Benedict Davenport, *Heredity in Relation to Eugenices, Medicine, and Society,* (New York: Arno Press, and *New York Times*), 1972.

26. Amitai Etzioni, *Genetic Fix* (New York: Macmillan, 1973), p. 22.

6. . . . IN BLACK FAMILIES

1. "Conversation with Frances Welsing," *Essence* (October 1973), p. 51.

2. Daniel P. Moynihan. *The Negro Family: The Case for National Action* (Washington, D.C.: U.S. Dept. of Labor, Office of Policy Planning and Research, March 1965).

3. Robert Hill, *The Strength of Black Families* (New York: Emerson-Hall, 1972).

4. Lee Rainwater, "Neutralizing the Disinherited: Some Psychological Aspects of Understanding the Poor," in Vernon L. Allen, ed., *Psychological Factors in Poverty* (Chicago: Markham, 1970), p. 21.

5. Andrew Billingsley, *Black Families in White America* (Englewood Cliffs, N.J.: Prentice-Hall, 1968), pp. 15–22.

6. *Ibid.*

7. Robert Staples, "Towards a Sociology of the Black Family: A Theoretical and Methodological Assessment," *Journal of Marriage and the Family* (February 1971).

8. Carol Stack, "The Kindred of Viola Jackson: Residence and Family Organization of an Urban Black American Family," in Norman E. Whitten, Jr., and John F. Szwed, eds., *Afro-American Anthropology: Contemporary Perspectives* (New York: Free Press, 1970), p. 311.

9. Jacquelyne Jackson, "Black Women in a Racist Society," Charles Willie, Bernard Kramer, and Bertram Brown, eds., *Racism and Mental Health* (Pittsburgh: University of Pittsburgh Press, 1973), p. 211.

10. Pauli Murray, "The Negro Woman in Search of Equality," paper presented at Leadership Conference, National Council of Negro Women, in Washington D.C., November 1963, pp. 11–12; 12–13.

11. Joyce Ladner, *Tomorrow's Tomorrow: The Black Woman* (Garden City, N.Y.: Doubleday, 1972), p. 276.

12. Wade Nobles, "African Root and American Fruit: The Black Family," *Journal of Social and Behavioral Sciences* (Spring 1974).

13. Robert Staples, "Research on Black Sexuality: Its Implications for Family Life, Education, and Public Policy," *Family Co-ordinator* (April 1972), pp. 183–88.

14. Jessie Bernard, *Marriage and Family Among Negroes,* p. 28.

15. Hyman Rodman, "The Lower-Class Value Stretch," *Social Forces* (December 1963), pp. 205–15.

16. Alexander Thomas and Samuel Sillen, *Racism in Psychiatry* (New York: Brunner/Mazel, 1972), p. 83.

17. Jeanne Spurlock, "Some Consequences of Racism for Children," in Charles Willie, Bernard Kramer, and Bertram Brown, eds., *Racism and Mental Health,* p. 151.

18. *Ibid.,* p. 153.

19. Wade Nobles, "Psychological Research and Black Self-Concept: A Critical Review," *Journal of Social Issues* (1973), 29(1).

20. Alvin Pouissant and Carolyn Atkinson, "Black Youth and Motivation," in Reginald Jones, ed., *Black Psychology* (New York: Harper and Row, 1972), pp. 113–23.

21. Susan Houston, "Syntactic Complexity and Information Transmission in First Graders: A Cross Cultural Study," *Journal of Psycholinguistic Research* (April 1973), pp. 99–114; also "Black English," *Psychology Today* (March 1973), pp. 45–48.

22. Leon Chestang, "Character Development in a Hostile Environment" (Chicago: University of Chicago School of Social Service Administration, Occasional Paper Number 3, November 1972), pp. 7–8.

23. *Ibid.,* pp. 10–11.

24. Alvin Pouissant, "Blaxploitation Movies—Cheap Thrills that Degrade Blacks," *Psychology Today* (February 1974).

25. Alvin Ramsey, "The Rape of Miss Jane Pittman," *Black World* (August 1974).

7. . . . IN PEER GROUPS

1. Group for Advancement of Psychiatry, *Normal Adolescence: Its Dynamic and Impact* (New York: Scribner, 1968), pp. 68–69.

2. Margaret Hartford, *Groups in Social Work* (New York: Columbia University Press, 1971), pp. 29–62.

3. Robert E. Clark, *Reference Group Theory and Delinquency* (New York: Behavioral Publications, 1972).

4. Group for Advancement of Psychiatry, *Normal Adolescence,* pp. 69–70.

5. James F. Short, Jr., and Fred L. Strodtbeck, *Group Process and Gang Delinquency* (Chicago: University of Chicago Press, 1965), p. 236.

6. *Ibid.*

7. Joyce Ladner, *Tomorrow's Tomorrow: The Black Woman* (New York: Doubleday, 1971).

8. Dana B. Stebbins, "'Playing It by Ear,' in Answering the Needs of a Group of Black Teen-Agers," in Irving H. Berkovitz, ed., *Adolescents Grow in Groups: Experiences in Adolescent Group Psychotherapy* (New York: Brunner/Mazel, 1972), pp. 129–30.

9. Gerald Suttles, *The Social Construction of Communities* (Chicago: University of Chicago Press, 1972), p. 206

10. *Ibid.*

11. *Ibid.*

12. *Ibid.*

13. Nicholas Babchuk and Ralph V. Thompson, "Voluntary Associations of Negroes," *American Sociological Review* (1962), 27:647–55.

14. Charles R. Wright and Herbert H. Hyman, "Voluntary Association Memberships of American Adults: Evidence from National Samples," *American Sociological Review* (1958), 23:290.

15. Jack C. Ross and Raymond H. Wheeler, *Black Belonging: A Study of the Social Correlates of Work Relations Among Negroes* (Westport, Conn.: Greenwood, 1971).

16. Donald Warren, *Black Neighborhoods: An Assessment of Community Power* (Ann Arbor: University of Michigan Press, 1975), pp. 137–41.

8. . . . IN SCHOOLS
1. John A. Clausen, "Perspectives on Childhood Socialization," in John Clausen, ed., *Socialization and Society* (Boston: Little, Brown, 1968), p. 153.

2. Colin Greer, *Divided Society: The Ethnic Experience in America* (New York: Basic Books, 1974), pp. 9–23.

3. James S. Coleman et al., *Equality of Educational Opportunity* (Washington, D.C.: U.S. Government Printing Office, 1966).

4. Godfrey Hodgson, "Do Schools Make a Difference?" *The Atlantic* (March 1973), pp. 35–46.

5. Christopher Jencks, *Inequality: A Reassessment of the Effect of Family and Schooling in America* (New York: Basic Books, 1972).

6. Kenneth Clark, "Social Policy, Power, and Social Science Research," *Perspectives on Inequality* (Cambridge: Harvard Educational Review, 1973), p. 83.

7. Daniel P. Moynihan, "Equalizing Education: In Whose Behalf?" *The Public Interest* (Fall 1972).

8. Neil Postman and Charles Weingartner, *Teaching as a Subversive Activity* (New York: Delacorte, 1969).

9. Susan Stodolsky and Gerald Lesser, "Learning Patterns in the Disadvantaged," *Harvard Educational Review* 37:546–93.

10. *Ibid.*, p. 586.

11. Ray Rist, "Student Social Class and Teacher Expectations: The Self-Fulfilling Prophecy in Ghetto Education," *Harvard Educational Review* (August 1970) 40:411–51.

12. *Ibid.*, p. 444.

13. R. Rosenthal and Lenore Jacobson, *Pygmalion in the Classroom* (New York: Holt, Rinehart and Winston, 1968).

14. David Armor, "The Evidence on Busing," *The Public Interest* (Summer 1972).

15. James Coleman et al., *Equality of Educational Opportunity*, p. 21.

16. Kenneth Carlson, "Equalizing Educational Opportunity," in LaMar P. Miller and Edmund Gordon, eds., *Equality of Educational Opportunity: A Handbook for Research* (New York: AMSCO, 1974), p. 125.

17. Charles Silberman, *Crisis in the Classroom* (New York: Random House, 1970).

18. Kenneth Carlson, "Equalizing Educational Opportunity," pp. 125–26.

19. Thomas Powers, *Diana: The Making of a Terrorist* (Boston: Houghton Mifflin, 1971), p. 71.

20. Jonathan Kozol, "Politics, Rage, and Motivation in the Free Schools," *Harvard Educational Review* (August 1972), p. 414.

21. Alvin Toffler, *Future Schock* (New York: Random House: 1970), p. 403.

9. . . . IN ORGANIZATIONS

1. Jerald Hage and Michael Aiken, *Social Change in Complex Organizations* (New York: Random House, 1970), p. 5.

2. Walter Stafford, "Issues and Crosscurrents in the Study of Organization and the Black Communities," in Joyce Ladner, ed., *The Death of White Sociology* (New York: Random House, 1970), pp. 344–60.

3. Lee Rainwater, "Neighborhood Action and Lower-Class Life-Styles," in John Turner, ed., *Neighborhood Organization for Community Action* (New York: NASW, 1968), p. 31.

4. *Ibid.*

5. Alvin Toffler, *Future Shock* (New York: Random House, 1970).

6. Joseph H. Kahle, "Structuring and Administering a Modern Voluntary Agency," *Social Work* (October 1969), pp. 21–28.

7. Rory O'Day, "Intimidation Rituals: Reactions to Reform," *Journal of Applied Behavioral Science* (July–September 1974), 10(3):373–86.

8. *Ibid.,* p. 383.

9. Peter M. Blau, *Exchange and Power in Social Life* (New York: Wiley, 1964).

10. Peter Blau and W. Scott, *Formal Organizations* (San Francisco: Chandler, 1962).

11. Dwight Harshbarger, "The Human Service Organization," in Harold W. Demone, Jr. and Dwight Harshbarger, eds., *A Handbook of Human Service Organizations* (New York: Behavioral Publications, 1974), pp. 22–36.

12. Francis P. Purcell and Harold Specht, "The House on Sixth Street," *Social Work* (October 1965), pp. 69–76.

13. *Ibid.,* p. 72.

14. William B. Gould, "Labor Relations and Race Relations," in Sam Zagoria, *Public Workers and Public Unions* (Englewood Cliffs, N.J.: Prentice-Hall, 1973), p. 149.

15. Harold Rose, *The Black Ghetto: A Spatial Behavioral Perspective* (New York: McGraw-Hill, 1971), p. 133.

16. Lawrence Rosen, "The Policemen," in Peter Rose, Stanley Rothman, and William J. Wilson, eds., *Through Different Eyes: Black and White Perspectives on American Race Relations* (New York: Oxford University Press, 1973), p. 286.

17. James Q. Wilson, *Varieties of Police Behavior* (Cambridge, Mass.: Harvard University Press, 1968), pp. 286–93.

18. Alan Altshuler, *Community Control: The Black Demand for Participation in Large American Cities* (New York: Pegasus, 1970), p. 44.

19. Robert Fogelson, "Violence as Protest" in Robert H. Connery, ed., *Urban Riots: Violence and Social Change* (New York: Vintage, 1969), p. 34.

20. Edward Jones, *Blacks in Business* (New York: Grosset, 1971).

21. Abram Harris, *The Negro as Capitalist* (Philadelphia: American Academy of Political and Social Science, 1936).

22. John Seder and Berkeley Burrell, *Getting It Together: Black Business in America* (New York: Harcourt, Brace, and Jovanovich, 1971), p. 210.

23. Ivan Light, *Ethnic Enterprise in America: Business and Welfare Among Chinese, Japanese and Blacks* (Berkeley: University of California Press, 1972).

24. *Ibid.*, p. 36.

25. Edward Jones, *Blacks in Business,* p. 118.

26. Eugene Genovese, *Roll, Jordan, Roll: The World the Slaves Made* (New York: Pantheon Books, 1974).

27. James Coleman, *Resources for Social Change: Race in the United States* (New York: Wiley, 1971), pp. 38–42.

28. Detailed accounts of Father Divine and his movement can be found in Ivan Light, *Ethnic Enterprise in America;* Roi Ottley, New World A-Coming (New York: Houghton, 1943); Robert Allerton Parker, *The Incredible Messiah* (Boston: Little, Brown, 1937); Sara Harris, with the assistance of Harriett Crittenden, *Father Divine: Holy Husband* (Garden City, N.Y.: Doubleday, 1953); Marcus Bach, *Strange Sects and Curious Cults* (New York: Dodd, Mead, 1961).

29. Light, *Ethnic Enterprise in America,* pp. 144–45.

30. James L. Sundquist, "Jobs, Training, and Welfare for the Underclass," in Kermit Gordon, ed., *Agenda for the Nation* (Washington, D.C.: Brookings Institution, 1968), p. 58.

31. Sylvia K. Selekman and Benjamin M. Selekman, *Power and Morality in a Business Society* (New York: McGraw-Hill, 1956), p. 55.

32. Franklin A. Zweig, "Welfare Workers," in Rose, Rothman, and Wilson, eds., *Through Different Eyes,* pp. 237–56.

33. *Ibid.*, p. 246.

34. Phillip Kotler, "The Elements of Social Action," *American Behavioral Scientist* (May/June 1971), pp. 691–718.

35. *Ibid.*

36. Charles Grosser, *Helping Youth: A Study of Six Community Organization Programs* (Washington, D.C.: Office of Juvenile Delinquency and Youth Development, Social and Rehabilitation Service, U.S. Department of Health, Education and Welfare, 1968).

37. Franklin Fogelson and Harold W. Demone, Jr., "Program Change Through Mental Health Planning," in Harold W. Demone and Dwight Harshbarger, eds., *A Handbook of Human Service Organizations* (New York: Behavioral Publications, 1974), p. 337.

10. CHARACTERISTICS OF THE NONRACIST PRACTITIONER

1. Florence Hollis, "The Psychosocial Approach to the Practice of Casework," in Robert Roberts and Robert Nee, eds., *Theories of Social Casework* (Chicago: University of Chicago Press, 1970), p. 42.

2. Edwin Thomas, "Behavioral Modification and Casework," in Roberts and Nee, *Theories of Social Casework,* p. 199.

3. Charles B. Truax and Kevin M. Mitchell, "Research on Certain Therapist Interpersonal Skills in Relation to Process and Outcome," in Allen E. Bergin and Sol L. Garfield, eds., *Handbook of Psychotherapy and Behavior Change: An Empirical Analysis* (New York: Wiley, 1971), pp. 299–344.

4. T. R. Sarbin, R. Taft, and D. E. Bailey, *Clinical Inference and Cognitive Theory* (New York: Holt, Rinehart, and Winston, 1960).

5. Martin Bloom, *The Paradox of Helping* (New York: Wiley, 1975), p. 121.

6. *Ibid.,* pp. 127–37.

7. Jack Rothman, "Three Models of Community Organization Practice," in *Social Work Practice, 1968* (New York: Columbia University Press, 1968), pp. 16–47.

11. ENGAGING BLACK CLIENT SYSTEMS

1. Clemmont E. Vontress, "Racial Differences: Impediments to Rapport," *Journal of Counseling Psychology* (1971) 18:7.

2. Charles O'Shea, "Two Gray Cats Learn How It Is in a Group of Black Teen-Agers," in Irving Berkovitz, ed., *Adolescents Grow in Groups: Experiences in Adolescent Group Psychotherapy* (New York: Brunner/Mazel, 1972), pp. 138–39.

3. *Ibid.*

4. Claudia Mitchell-Kernan, "Signifying, Loud-Talking, and Marking," in Thomas Kochman, ed., *Rappin' and Stylin' Out: Communication in Urban Black America* (Urbana: University of Illinois Press, 1972), pp. 323–24.

5. Si Kahn, *How People Get Power* (New York: McGraw-Hill, 1970), p. 9.

6. Barbara Lerner, *Therapy in the Ghetto: Political Impotence and Personal Disintegration* (Baltimore: Johns Hopkins University Press, 1972).

7. Stewart E. Perry, "National Policy and the Community Development Corporation," *Law and Contemporary Problems* (Winter 1971), 36:298.

8. Thomas M. French, *The Integration of Behavior: Basic Postulates* (Chicago: University of Chicago Press, 1952), pp. 50–53.

9. Susan Edelson et al., "A Follow-Up Study of Pre-Marital Counseling Program in a County Public Health Department," University of Southern California, unpublished master's thesis, 1970.

10. Lillian Ripple, Ernestine Alexander, and Bernice Polemis, *Motivation, Capacity, and Opportunity: Studies in Casework Theory and Practice,* Social Service Monographs, 2d ser., No. 3 (Chicago: School of Social Service Administration, University of Chicago, 1964).

11. Lerner, *Therapy in the Ghetto,* pp. 159–61.

12. William Grier and Price Cobbs, *Black Rage* (New York: Basic Books, 1968), pp. 149–50.

13. Leon Chestang, *Character Development in a Hostile Environment,* Occasional Paper No. 3 (Chicago: School of Social Service Administration, University of Chicago, 1972).

14. Charles Pinderhughes, "Racism and Psychotherapy," in Charles V. Willie, Bernard Kramer, and Bertram Brown, eds., *Racism and Mental Health* (Pittsburgh: University of Pittsburgh Press, 1973), p. 69.

15. Alexander Thomas and Samuel Sillen, *Racism and Psychiatry* (New York: Brunner/Mazel, 1972), p. 139.

16. Robert Carkhuff and Bernard Berenson, *Beyond Counseling and Therapy* (New York: Holt, Rinehart, and Winston, 1967), p. 75.

12. EMPOWERMENT AND THE ROLE OF THE PRACTITIONER

1. Howard Goldstein, *Social Work Practice: A Unitary Approach* (Columbia: University of South Carolina Press, 1973), pp. 83–103.

2. Ruth R. Middleman and Gale Goldberg, eds., *Social Service Delivery: A Structural Approach to Social Work Practice* (New York: Columbia University Press, 1974), pp. 54–80.

3. James E. Whittaker, *Social Treatment: An Approach to Interpersonal Helping* (Chicago: Aldine, 1974), pp. 56–61.

4. Allen Pincus and Anne Minahan, *Social Work Practice: Model and Method* (Itasca, Ill.: F. G. Peacock, 1973), p. 31.

5. Thomas Hopkins, "The Role of the Agency in Supporting Black Manhood," *Social Work* (January 1973), pp. 53–59.

6. David Hallowitz, "Counseling and Treatment of the Poor Black Family," *Social Casework* (October 1975), p. 458.

7. Carol Brooks, "New Mental Health Perspectives in the Black Community," *Social Casework* (October 1974), p. 494.

8. Alice Overton, "Taking Help from Our Clients," *Social Work* (April 1960), pp. 42–50.

9. Frank Reissman, "The 'Helper' Therapy Principle," *Social Work* (April 1965), p. 28.

10. Carl Goldberg and Joyce Kane, "A Missing Component in Mental Health Services to the Urban Poor: Services In-Kind to Others," in Dorothy Evans and William Claiborne, eds., *Mental Health Issues and the Urban Poor* (New York: Pergamon Press, 1974), p. 102.

13. DESIGNING SERVICE DELIVERY SYSTEMS

1. Nathan Caplan and Stephen Nelson, "Who's To Blame?" *Psychology Today* (November 1974).

2. Neil Gilbert and Harry Specht, *Dimensions of Social Welfare Policy* (Englewood Cliffs, N.J.: Prentice-Hall, 1974), pp. 32.

3. Donald Warren, *Black Neighborhoods: An Assessment of Community Power* (Ann Arbor: University of Michigan Press, 1975), p. 133.

4. James D. Orten and Diane P. Weiss, "Strategies and Techniques for Therapeutic Change," *Social Service Review* (September 1974), pp. 355–56.

5. E. Fuller Torrey, *The Death of Psychiatry* (Philadelphia: Chilton, 1974), pp. 187–200.

6. *Ibid.*, p. 188.

7. *Ibid.*, p. 190.

8. P. Nelson Reid, "Reforming the Social Service Monopoly," *Social Work* (November 1972), pp. 44–54.

9. Edward Newman and Jerry Turem, "The Crisis of Accountability," *Social Work* (January 1974), p. 13.

10. Herta Herzog, "Psychological Gratifications in Daytime Radio Listening," in Theodore Newcomb and Eugene Hartley, eds., *Readings in Social Psychology* (New York: Holt, 1947).

11. Nora Scott Kinzer, "Soapy Sin in the Afternoon," *Psychology Today* (August 1973), p. 46.

12. Anne F. Kilguss, "Using Soap Operas as a Therapeutic Tool," *Social Casework* (November 1974), pp. 525–30.

13. Newman and Turem, "Crisis of Accountability," pp. 14–15.

14. Shimon S. Gottschalk, "The Community-Based Welfare System: An Alternative to Public Welfare," *Journal of Applied Behavioral Science* (March–June 1973), pp. 233–42.

15. Alvin Puryear and Charles A. West, *Black Enterprise, Inc.* (Garden City, N.J.: Anchor/Doubleday, 1973).

16. Gottschalk, "Community-Based Welfare System," pp. 236–37.

17. *Ibid.*, p. 240.

18. Warren, *Black Neighborhoods*, pp. 130–49.

EPILOGUE: SOCIAL FUTURISM IN BLACK COMMUNITIES

1. Alvin Toffler, *Future Shock* (New York: Random House, 1970), p. 4.

2. *Ibid.*, p. 460.

3. Roland G. Meinert, "Futures Forecasting," *Social Work* (November 1973), pp. 48–52.

4. Toffler, *Future Shock,* p. 476.

5. John Szwed, "Discovering Afro-America," in John Szwed, ed., *Black America* (New York: Basic Books, 1970), pp. 291–92.

6. Imamu Amiri Baraka (Leroi Jones), "A Black Value System," in *Contemporary Black Thought: The Best From the Black Scholar* (Indianapolis: Bobbs-Morrill, 1973), pp. 71–79.

7. Corinne Hutt and M. Jane Vaizey, "Differential Effects of Group Density on Social Behavior," *Nature* (1966) 209:1371–72; Patricia Draper, "Crowding Among Hunter Gatherers: The Kung Bushmen," *Science* (October 1973), pp. 301–3; and Chalsa Loo, "The Effects of Spatial Density on the Social Behavior of Children," *Journal of Applied Social Psychology* (1972) 2:372–81.

8. Thomas Walz, Georgiana Willenbring, and Lane De Moll, "Environmental Design," *Social Work* (January 1974), pp. 40–41.

9. Herbert Gans, "Social and Physical Planning for the Elimination of Urban Poverty," in Bernard Rosenberg et al., *Mass Society in Crisis* (New York: Macmillan, 1964), pp. 629–45.

10. Matthew Holden, Jr., *The Politics of the Black "Nation"* (New York: Chandler, 1974), pp. 179–83.

11. Eleanor Norton, "Future Trends: New Black Directions—A Reappraisal," in Melvin Steinfield, ed., *Cracks in the Melting Pot: Racism and Discrimination* (Beverly Hills, Calif.: Glencoe Press, 1970), p. 341.

12. Holden, *Politics of the Black "Nation,"* pp. 187–212.

13. Peter H. Rossi, "Urban Revolts and the Future of American Cities," in David Boesel and Peter H. Rossi, eds., *Cities Under Siege: An Anatomy of the Ghetto Riots, 1964–68* (New York: Basic Books, 1971).

14. Angus Campbell, *White Attitudes Toward Black People* (Ann Arbor, Mich.: Institute for Social Research, 1971), p. 159.

15. Richard A. Gabriel, *The Ethnic Factor in the Urban Polity,* Bureau of Government Research of the University of Rhode Island (Summer 1973), pp. 147–48.

16. James A. Goodman, "Racial Minorities in the 1980s," *Social Work* (September 1974), pp. 580–84.

17. Ivan Light, *Ethnic Enterprise in America: Business and Welfare Among Chinese, Japanese and Blacks* (Berkeley: University of California Press, 1972), pp. 187–88.

18. Donald Michael, "On Coping With Complexity: Urban Planning and Politics in 1976," in Franklin Tugwell, ed., *Search for Alternatives: Public Policy and the Study of the Future* (Cambridge, Mass.: Winthrop, 1973), reprinted from "The Conscience of the City," *Daedalus* (Fall 1968).

index